Media Diversity

Economics, Ownership, and the FCC

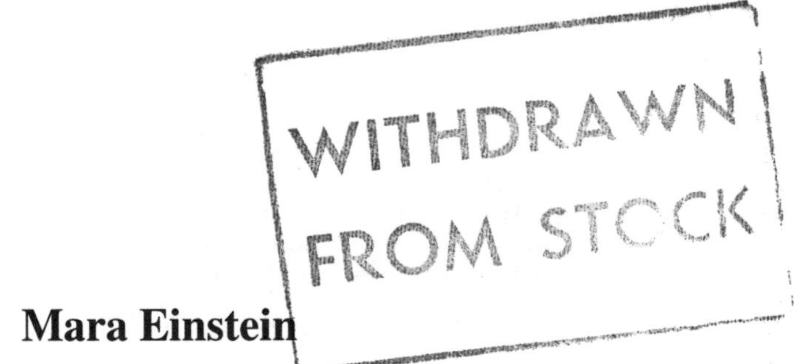

Mara Einstein

LAWRENCE ERLBAUM ASSOCIATES, PUBLISHERS
2004 Mahwah, New Jersey London

Lawrence Erlbaum Associates, Inc., Publishers
10 Industrial Avenue
Mahwah, New Jersey 07430

Cover design by Sean Trane Sciarrone

Library of Congress Cataloging-in-Publication Data

Einstein, Mara.
Media diversity : economics, ownership, and the FCC / Mara Einstein.
p. cm.
Includes bibliographical references and index.
ISBN 0-8058-4241-1 (alk. paper)
ISBN 0-8058-5403-7 (pbk. : alk. paper)
1. Television—United States—Mergers. 2. Television and politics—United States. 3. Television programs—Syndication—United States. 4. Monopolies—United States. 5. United States. Federal Communications Commission.
I. Title.
HE8700.8 .E37 2002
384.55'1'0973—dc21 20021925455
CIP

Books published by Lawrence Erlbaum Associates are printed on acid-free paper, and their bindings are chosen for strength and durability.

Printed in the United States of America
10 9 8 7 6 5 4 3 2

Contents

Preface

Consolidation of the media industry has been the focus of scholars and regulators for decades. The prevailing wisdom is that the more concentrated the media industry, the less diverse the communications landscape. Intuitively, this seems to make sense. Fewer voices should mean fewer opinions; fewer opinions mean less diversity.

When you look at the data across a variety of media, however, that is just not the case. In study after study, scholars have determined that there is no proven causality between media ownership and programming content. This book adds to that body of knowledge by examining diversity within the television marketplace. It also takes scholarship further answering the question: If consolidation is not the culprit in affecting diversity, specifically television diversity, then what is?

I suggest television's reliance on advertising as its primary source of revenue is the reason we have so few program choices. This economic structure inherently puts limits on program content that far outweigh anything that occurs due to media consolidation. These limits include time length for program, a "lowest common denominator" mentality because advertising perforce requires that programmers generate large audiences, and finally, programming cannot be too controversial or denigrate consumer products or their producers because they are footing the bill.

My interest in researching diversity came about when I encountered the financial interest and syndication rules, or fin-syn, when I was doing television research in business school in the 1980s. These rules, which forbid the broadcast networks from owning the programming that appeared on their air, were established in 1970 and were the source of much controversy throughout the 1980s. When the rules were repealed in the 1990s, I was working at NBC and began to see the impact of the rules' repeal, both in the changing structure of the industry and in the changing make up of companies into vertically integrated corporations. I became interested in network favoritism toward their own programming—would the networks keep shows in which they had an equity stake on air longer, give them preference over nonowned programs, give them preferred slots on the prime time schedule? We now know all of those things happen, and in the years since the rules' repeal, this has become the standard way of doing business. The question then became one of diversity. Are these business practices affecting the kinds of programs that appear on the air?

These questions arose because in writing about fin-syn, I could not help but be confronted with the issue of diversity. The largest hurdle in dealing with diversity is trying to figure out what it is. Is diversity measured by the number of producers, the type of producers, the number of outlets, the type of programming, or some combination of all of these? While I, and the courts, have concluded that program diversity is the underlying issue, the Federal Communications Commission (FCC) has always run head on into the First Amendment. How does the Commission regulate content without being able to regulate content? As a fallback position, the FCC has depended on structural regulation, that is, regulating the structure of the industry in hopes of achieving content diversity. The results have been disappointing. My conclusion is that diversity as a policy goal needs to be reevaluated. Without an agreed upon definition, it is a worthless goal and one doomed to fail. Moreover, quality—not diversity—seems to have been the real goal all along.

This book will appeal to anyone interested in the media consolidation debate. While those opposed to media concentration have been very successful in getting their voices heard, scholarly disagreement with this theory has been decidedly silent. In part, I believe this has had to do with the thought that the media can defend themselves—and they can. This work weighs in as an unbiased look at consolidation by examining the entertainment area of programming. Beyond its use in academic settings such as communication policy courses, the book will interest a significant number of broadcast professionals, media policymakers, communication lawyers, and academics. It is certainly a must-read for those interested in the other side of the media monopoly argument.

Media Diversity travels the path of diversity and uses the financial interest and syndication rules as a case study for this process. The first chapter reviews the market versus regulatory approach to creating diversity in the television marketplace. Key regulations that attempted to create diversity are reviewed and major studies of media diversity are analyzed.

Chapters 2 and 3 are histories of the financial interest and syndication rules. Chapter 2 covers the early years when the rules were established and the political climate in which they were created. Chapter 3 begins in the early 1980s when the rules were first under consideration for repeal and continues until 1995 when the rules were finally eliminated.

Chapter 4 gives a history of the structure of the television industry that parallels the time of fin-syn. During the 1970s, the three major broadcast networks dominated the television landscape. By the 1980s, cable had begun to make its mark, and Fox was the first new broadcast network in 50 years. With the repeal of the rules in the 1990s, two more new networks came into existence—UPN and The WB—and independent production had virtually disappeared due to the vertical integration of the television industry. These structural changes are examined in light of their implications for diversity.

Chapter 5 provides a quantitative analysis of the diversity of network television programming. Prime-time television programming is assessed in the years surrounding the creation of fin-syn and the years of its repeal. Diversity of programming is analyzed against the consolidation of the television industry. As the industry became more concentrated, programming became more diverse. The reasons for this are discussed.

Chapter 6 examines the prime-time programming selection process through in-depth interviews with industry executives and program producers. These executives discuss how regulation, and its accompanying change in economics, has affected how they choose programming for the television schedule.

In the final chapter, I make suggestions for how to overcome the diversity definition hurdle. I also provide a case study of how diversity can be achieved using the children's television marketplace as a model.

No book gets written alone, so there are many people I would like to thank. The beginnings of this work came out of my dissertation and, therefore, I would like to thank my committee, Ted Magder, Yochai Benkler, and my chair, Todd Gitlin. While at Queens College, I received support from the City University of New York Publishing Programming. I would like to thank our fearless leader, Nora Eisenberg, as well as my fellow writers Gila Acker, Arthur Costigan, Trudy Milburn, Premilla Nadasen, Joon-Hwan Oh, and Susan Will. Many very busy Hollywood executives gave freely of their time including Warren Littlefield, Ted Harbert, Flody Suarez, Stephen McPherson, Matt Williams, Rob Burnett, and Paul Haggis. To all, my heartfelt thanks for your generosity of time and spirit. I would also like to thank their assistants who were so gracious in accepting my calls and allowed me to harangue them for information, in particular Patty Mann and Gian Sardar, who were always helpful and encouraging.

I am very grateful to Linda Bathgate, my editor at LEA, for her support, advice, and patience. She is the definition of mensch. I would also like to thank Karin Bates for holding my hand through this process and answering my many questions.

I am blessed with a very understanding husband who has given his unwavering support and love throughout the writing of this book. To Jeff, I offer my sincerest love and gratitude. While not as supportive, I want to thank my 3-year-old daughter, Cayla, for being as helpful as she could be. Having the two of you to come home to is life's greatest blessing. I also wish to thank my mother, Barbara Schwartz, who as an educator instilled in me at a very early age the joy of learning.

In conclusion, this book is dedicated to the memory of the man who taught me the most about life, about hard work and about achieving your goals—my father, Jerry M. Schwartz. My dad passed away in May 2002 before he had a chance to see this work published. My dad was forever proud of his daughter, "The Professor." I hope you're still proud. I miss you.

—*Mara Einstein*
Queens College
August 2002

1

Diversity and the FCC

BACKGROUND

Based on the Communications Act of 1934, holders of broadcast licenses are required to serve the "public interest, convenience and necessity." Since that line was written almost 70 years ago, the courts, the Congress, and the Federal Communications Commission (FCC) have been negotiating the meaning of this passage. One concept that has been tied intrinsically to the "public interest" is diversity, specifically diversity of opinion.

The quest for diversity stems from two principles of the American capitalist society—the First Amendment, which states that "Congress shall make no law abridging the freedom of the press," and the "marketplace of ideas" metaphor, which stems from this Amendment. As the Supreme Court has stated:

> At the heart of the First Amendment lies the principle that each person should decide for him or herself the ideas and beliefs deserving of expression, consideration, and adherence. Our political system and cultural life rest upon this ideal. Government action that stifles speech on account of its message, or that requires the utterance of a particular message favored by the Government, contravenes this essential right. Laws of this sort pose the inherent risk that the Government seeks not to advance a legitimate regulatory goal, but to suppress unpopular ideas or information or manipulate the public debate through coercion rather than persuasion. (*Turner Broadcasting System, Inc. v. FCC*, 1994)

As this suggests, under the First Amendment, it is anathema for government regulators to impose restrictions on society in terms of what types of information should be made available to citizens and who should present that information. Rather, the hope is that a free and open communication marketplace will create a multitude of voices and opinions that will allow for robust debate on the part of the citizenry so that they may become well informed and full participants in a democratic society. The First

Amendment, however, is not absolute, and market forces alone have not, to date, achieved this idealized marketplace of ideas. Therefore, policymakers have regulated the media in one way or another in an attempt to achieve a multitude of opinions.

These two methodologies—open market and regulation—represent the two schools of thought about how best to create diversity. Market proponents believe in the efficiency of market forces to create the breadth of diverse voices in society. According to this school of thought, let communications companies freely compete, and they will create as much programming as the market will bear. Social scientists, on the other hand, believe regulation is needed for diversity and other social needs to be met. These needs include, among others, creating informed citizens (through the presentation of public affairs programming) and teaching children (through educational and informational programming). Social scientists and media critics believe this pro-social programming will not be created without regulation and that diversity will be threatened by the pursuit of profit over public interest.

Market proponents assert that media policy's effectiveness should be analyzed from an economic point of view. If the communications marketplace is efficient economically, it will by definition (or default) create a diversity of choices. For the market to work efficiently, it must not be "hampered" by government regulation. In this open-market system, society is better off overall from two perspectives: First, there is an efficient and thriving market of communications goods that provides jobs and capital, and second, those producers will create a plethora of programming to suit the available markets for its goods.

To create these jobs and content, media producers have become large multinational corporations. The structure of these media companies is increasingly one of vertically integrated organizations, that is, an organization that integrates processes from production through distribution. From an economic perspective, this is more efficient than producing products in separate institutions. Integrated corporations achieve economies derived from one company producing multiple products that are similar. Scale economies are achieved because costs can be amortized over many products rather than a single product. For instance, if a television production company is producing only one show, that company has to apply all costs to that single production. However, if the company is producing several shows, they can spread costs, particularly general and administrative costs, over many programs. Similarly, economies of scope are achieved when a company produces multiple products that are in some way compatible, for instance, McDonald's selling hamburgers and french fries. Likewise, media companies can produce all types of complementary entertainment including television programs, movies, DVDs, books, and CD-ROMs all of which have similar content. For example, Viacom might produce a *Bob the Builder* television show as well as a *Bob the Builder* book, CD-ROM, and video. By producing similar content over many forms, the company can more efficiently produce a profit.

It has been argued that this vertically integrated structure has become a significant barrier to entry into the media business, ultimately causing concentration of the industry in the hands of a limited number of global organizations. This is because "new competitors must enter multiple stages to avoid dependence on rivals for supplies or access. Multiple stage entry is always more costly, difficult, and risky than single stage entry" (Litman, 1998, p. 229; see also Owen & Wildman, 1992, and Vogel, 2001). This vertical integration has led to market dominance by a handful of corporations, so-called media monopolies, further restricting marketplace diversity (Bagdikian, 1992; McChesney, 1997; Miller, 1996).

Several theorists, notably Steiner (1952), hypothesized that media monopolies are actually more likely to produce diversity than a multitude of players. Under his scenario, if there are three radio channels and three producers, the three producers are all going to compete to attract the largest audience. If most people like situation comedies, for instance, at least two of the channels are going to be programmed with situation comedies to attract the largest audience. This will happen, because no station is going to let its competitor grab the largest market share, and, therefore, the largest advertising revenue. If, however, there is only one monopoly exhibitor in the market, he or she is likely to program two channels with different types of shows to achieve the largest audience overall.

Other scholars have built on this theory. For example, Shooshan and Sloan (1982) suggested that limiting radio ownership was detrimental to diversity, because while a single entity can own an AM and an FM station, that same entity could not own two FM stations. The AM/FM combination would have an unfair advantage in the market over the single station owner. The same situation would translate into the television market, where broadcasters are limited in the number of outlets they can present, while cable operators can offer hundreds of options to viewers. The courts have recently come to this conclusion as well as have repealed, or at least remanded, many ownership rules back to the Federal Communications Commission for reevaluation. Steiner's theory, in combination with economies achieved through larger institutions, helps explain why market supporters are not as concerned with media consolidation, and its supposed accompanying detrimental effect on diversity, as are many media critics.

Free market detractors claim that the school "promotes cultural uniformity and excludes minority social interests from expressing their views" (Iosifides, 1999, p. 153). Left to their own devices, communications companies will produce what is likely to make them the most profit. Because our broadcast system is based on advertising and advertising is based on the size of the audience, producers are going to create programming that will produce the largest audiences. To produce the largest audiences, programming must appeal to a broad spectrum of people, not minority tastes.

> If most viewers want the same types of programs and television is supported by advertiser payments, competing broadcasters are likely to offer highly similar programs targeted to this mass audience. From the perspective of social welfare, the number of programs designed to satisfy majority tastes will be excessive because competing channels will find it most profitable to carve up the majority-taste audience with close substitutes that do little to increase overall viewer satisfaction. (Owen & Wildman, 1992, p. 99)

This means that *when audiences have similar preferences*, then programming will be similar. This so-called common denominator programming is not going to serve the needs of all audiences, particularly audiences that are not attractive to advertisers, specifically older, poorer, and minority audiences. Minority interests will be served only when the number of channels is large enough to attract an audience large enough to attract advertisers. There are, however, biases in television "against programs that cater to minority-interest tastes, against expensive programs, and in favor of programs that produce large audiences" (p. 148). These inherent biases are the reason that the social school calls for regulation to insure that these audiences are served.

Television's dependence on advertising for its financial support is what leads to limited diversity. As Owen, Beebe, and Manning (1974) explain "competition under advertiser support tends to produce less diversity and more 'wasteful duplication' than is socially optimal .... Duplication occurs because there is a tendency for a decentralized system of broadcasting, with limited channel capacity, to produce rivalry for large blocks of the audience with programs that are, if not identical, at least close substitutes" (p. 101). Thus, advertising-supported programming contributes to the lack of diversity. But this passage was written before cable was widely distributed, and it would seem logical that increasing the number of channels would increase diversity. Depending on your definition of diversity—a major stumbling block in this debate that will be discussed in the next section—this may or may not have happened. On the one hand, programming fills all kinds of viewer niches from music to women's programming to Spanish-language channels to programming for golf enthusiasts. However, the same producers who create programming for the broadcast networks produce programming for the majority of large scale cable networks, or alternatively, cable channels air network reruns that do not contribute to diversity. Many cable networks are also owned by the same companies that distribute broadcast networks (e.g., Disney owns ABC and ESPN) or are owned by companies that distribute a number of cable networks (e.g., AOL Time Warner owns TBS, TNT, CNN, TCM, CNNfn, etc.). These companies rationalize their businesses along economic lines, for example cable networks need to pursue advertising dollars the same way that broadcast networks do. Even if programming is geared toward a niche market, that market has to be large enough to attract advertisers.

Youn (1994) has demonstrated that there is some increased level of diversity, but this may not necessarily be a good thing:

> That viewers can freely choose what they prefer to watch is a big advancement. However, we cannot ignore a negative implication in this finding. The same results may imply that TV viewing tends to become an unbalanced diet of very limited types of programs. (p. 472)

Diversity may have been achieved, but what is also created is a fragmented audience that limits itself to watching only the kinds of programs that it likes—not necessarily what would serve a democracy. Because providing additional outlets does not necessarily mean more diversity nor does it mean more "prosocial" content, the social school would again suggest a need for government intervention.

Beyond diversity, at issue is the fact that certain messages are transmitted through the television medium and others are not. Viewers do not decide the messages available to them. The producers and the distributors of the programming determine those messages. These distributors and producers work within a framework that guides their program choices.

Critics of the media, and in particular television, claim this framework is based on the political, economic, and social structure within which television is situated. They denounce the hegemony of the media and the ever-increasing power of the consolidated media conglomerates. These criticisms stem from the idea that whoever owns the media, sets the agenda for what will be communicated by that medium. In the United States, these media owners are multinational corporations who in turn are dependent on other multinational corporations (advertisers) for their profits. These media corporations control the pipeline and, therefore, control the messages the medium transmits. Because of this, the majority of messages on television support the ideas of progress, materialism, and increasing consumption—ideas good for the economy, good for the American consumer, and of course, ultimately good for television's profits (see Andersen, 1995).

Even while these two schools—open market or regulation—disagree sharply as to the best means of getting to diversity, they both believe in the marketplace of ideas (Entman & Wildman, 1992). Neither school has been successful in demonstrating their superiority over the other, though the FCC has tended to lean toward the economic school over the social scientists, particularly over the past 20 years. This market philosophy has led to massive deregulation, which in turn has led to significant changes in the structure of the television industry, specifically increased consolidation of media ownership. Concentration of ownership in a limited number of hands, and the assumed corresponding lack of diversity, is a major concern for the proponents of the social school.

Scholars have begun to believe that the inability of the market to create more diversity is due in part to the marketplace of ideas metaphor being out of date and in fact stifling diversity rather than promoting it. Le Duc (1982) attributes the lack of diversity to the FCC relying on channels (outlets) as the nexus of competition rather than the content itself. Relying on technology is inappropriate as the means to create diversity. He calls for "a reformulation of the meaning of 'marketplace' in this era of modern mass media" (p. 177), suggesting that media producers be held accountable for the cultural environment in the same way companies need to be regulated in terms of the natural environment. Entman and Wildman (1992) suggest that the two schools are blinded by their own rhetoric. The market school is too focused on economic efficiency to notice things they cannot quantify "such as the value of citizen participation in the political process" (p. 17). Similarly, the social school fails to take into account that there are limits on human ability to consume information and that certain economic considerations are unavoidable. And so, these researchers suggest a possible new metaphor—that of a Macintosh computer. "This metaphorical Macintosh suggests that it may be useful for communications policy to stress easy, speedy, yet playful access to a wealth of information and intellectual tools, rather than to a mere diversity of ideas" (p. 17).

One major issue that did not exist for our forefathers is an overabundance of information. Within this overwhelming overload of communication, there is diversity. The issue has become (a) how to find it and (b) how much can you process when you do. The big corporations have a key advantage in being able to promote and market their messages louder than others, therefore, finding alternative voices becomes more difficult—though not impossible. As for retention, the human brain cannot process any more information now than it did 200 years ago. "There is controversy as to whether the limitations of the short-term memory capacity is 5–9 portions of information or 3–5, but [there is] agreement that the capacity is limited and varies across individuals" (Heeter, 1985, p. 131). This concept also holds true for the number of television channels. While working at VH1, our research found that individuals tended to watch approximately seven channels on a regular basis with another four channels that they would check out on a regular basis. Past 11 channels, people cannot be aware of what is available to them. In fact scholars have found that "viewers may systematically avoid large numbers of channels and by default become relatively heavy users of those in their repertoires. In the aggregate, then, new media audiences could move to the extremes of use and non-use, or polarize" (Webster, 1986, p. 84). What this suggests is that as you put more choices in front of viewers, they will coalesce around a handful of channels. Therefore, diversity and the marketplace of ideas are interesting in theory but in practice have serious limitations.

The marketplace of ideas being outdated is only part of the problem. The lack of an agreed upon definition of diversity, the lack of evidence supporting a link between structural regulation and content diversity, and the continuing dependence on advertising as the predominant means of programming support all contribute to a narrowly defined informational marketplace.

DIFFICULTIES WITH DEFINING DIVERSITY

So far, no one has been able to develop a working definition of diversity—not the content providers, not the policymakers, not the scholars, and not the courts. Not only is diversity difficult to define, it is equally difficult to measure (Owen, 1977, 1978; Entman & Wildman, 1992). This has made diversity as a policy goal very difficult, if not impossible, to achieve. A major reason for the lack of definition is that regulating content comes into direct conflict with the First Amendment. The federal courts are likely to shoot down any attempt to regulate specific programming. Rather, policymakers use structural diversity, that is diversity of media ownership or diversity of producers, as a proxy for content diversity. As this suggests, the FCC has made assumptions about the interrelationship between media sources and media content. Specifically, if you regulate who makes television programming or how many people make television programming, you will affect the different types of programming that appear on the air. Under this assumption, for instance, the Commission has adopted "reasonable expectation" as their standard for evaluating minority ownership (Kleiman, 1991, p. 413). Instead of minorities having to prove they would better serve a minority audience, the simple fact that the owner is a minority is enough. Similarly, the FCC and the courts have demonstrated that they use ownership diversity as a substitute for content diversity in numerous decisions from ownership caps to the financial interest and syndication rules to retransmission consent. Research, however, has not been borne out this interconnectedness. While this will be examined more thoroughly below, it is important to note at this point that the connection between ownership and content and larger numbers of producers and content has only been established on a very limited basis.

> The research on the determinants of program-type diversity suggests a *possible* relationship between source diversity and program diversity. However, the evidence at this point is qualified, to say the least, and even contradictory to a certain degree. Research in this area has thus not yet definitively answered the causality question. (Napoli, 1999, p. 21; italics added)

Beyond issues with the First Amendment, the FCC has avoided defining content diversity simply because it is a difficult concept to define. As Ronald Cass (1981) suggests in *Revolution in the Wasteland*:

> Diversity is by no means a self-defining term. Even if agreement can be reached that diversity in programming means that many different program types are available for consumption, that definition is not helpful without consensus on how programs will be divided among different types .... Before we can identify the different categories that should be represented, we need some understanding of the reason for desiring diversity. One possible reason is that diversity has value—*i.e.,* a range of program choices that encompasses many different types of programs is more valuable than one that does not. (p. 59)

Therefore, a major problem with defining diversity is in determining what it is and how much is enough. While critics of television expect diverse programs to be very unlike each other, the viewing audience may not wish to have vastly different viewing choices. As Cass so straightforwardly puts it, "What is clear *a priori* is that nearly everyone would value having more choices over having fewer choices and also that everyone would value having many choices that are attractive to him over an equal number of choices not all of which are of interest" (p. 60).

Cass (1981) suggests an array of programming, with varying degrees of diversity, would be best to serve the public interest. This scheme would consist of a broad palette of programming that is narrowly or broadly targeted to suit individual needs for programming, when the audience wants it:

> Ideally, then, what would be in the public interest is presentation of all the programs that could command payments in excess of their costs of production and distribution, regardless of the similarity or dissimilarity of the programs and the size or composition of the audience. (p. 61)

Greenberg and Barnett (1971) agree with Cass's assessment that broad diversity may not be what the viewing public is looking for. "As evidenced by the rapid expansion in CATV [cable television] subscriptions …, the public values additional choices even within the customary range of television fare. It is willing to pay fairly substantial amounts to receive additional programming of the same 'general type' as those already being received without charge" (p. 93). The problem with these suggestions is that they do not take into account those underserved by the current broadcast system, that is, audiences that advertisers undervalue or ignore. Given the economics of our broadcast system, it may not be possible to serve every public interest, however. Again, making it difficult to define how much diversity is enough.

The FCC's thinking has been similar to that of Cass, Greenberg, and Barnett, because of their focus on structural regulation. If the number of outlets could be increased through the expansion of new technologies or the number of producers because of new opportunities to present their point of view, the public interest would be better served. Intuitively, this seems true because there would be more choices for the viewing audience and more of an opportunity to provide that audience with some type of programming they would like at any given time. Audience viewing patterns and the content provided by the expanded options do not, however, always mean new and diverse voices, as presented earlier.

Within the scholarly community, there is no agreement about diversity either. Some scholars speak of product, idea, and access diversity (Entman & Wildman, 1992). Others speak of outlet, source, and exposure diversity (Napoli, 1999), still others diversity of ideas, products, issues, content, person, and geography (Iosifides, 1999). Policymakers have coalesced around source diversity, outlet diversity, and content diversity. Source diversity has two components—diversity in terms of the actual number of people creating programming and diversity in the types of people who produce that programming. Outlet diversity is about increasing the number of channels through which information is distributed to the public. Content diversity, increasing the variety of programming and points of view, is the ultimate goal though this is rarely regulated because of First Amendment issues.[1] The assumption on the part of policymakers is that there is an inherent link between these types of diversity, that is, that increasing source diversity or outlet diversity will lead to increased content diversity.

REGULATING BROADCAST DIVERSITY

Diversity as a media policy can be traced back to the 1879 Postal Act. Reduced postal rates for magazines through the use of second-class mailing permits allowed for a more widely disseminated print product. Today, the "public interest" clause of the Communications Act of 1934 is the basis for much of the broadcast diversity

[1]The major exception to this is children's programming. Under the Children's Television Act, broadcasters are required to present three hours per week of programming targeting those under 16 years of age.

policy that exists. The "public interest" clause and the rights of the audience over that of the broadcaster, which the Supreme Court has supported, were central to the emergence of diversity as an FCC policy issue. Part of serving the public interest has meant providing a diversity of viewpoints through the broadcast spectrum (Kleinman, 1991). Finding an effective way to regulate that diversity, however, has been elusive.

The following outlines some of the major examples of how policymakers have regulated source diversity and outlet diversity. These examples provide an overview of how regulating structure is ineffective in providing content diversity.

Outlet Diversity

Regulating the Radio Spectrum. The regulation of outlet diversity has a long history stemming from broadcasting's nascent stage. The first major legislation affecting broadcasting was The Radio Act of 1912. Prior to the enactment of this legislation, anyone could send information across the airwaves. When the airwaves became so crowded that it was becoming difficult for military and government messages to be transmitted, the government found it necessary to take control of the airwaves. In *Tube of Plenty*, Barnouw (1990) gives a picturesque description of the mayhem that existed prior to the creation of the 1912 Act:

> On the Eve of World War I, the air was a chaos of crackling codes, voices and music ... Much of the transmission was army and navy communication, relating to training and maneuvers. Another large part was contributed by the irrepressible amateurs, already numbering thousands, who were anathema to the military; their chatter was said to interfere with military communication. Another part of the transmission was related to technical experimentation by individual inventors, universities, government agencies, corporations. (p. 17)

Without government regulation, the radio waves were filled with a diversity of voices. Government, amateurs, universities, and corporations had equal access to the airwaves and to audiences. This abundance of information, however, came into conflict with the existing technology. Too many voices meant no one was getting heard, and the government began to regulate the industry.

The Radio Act of 1912 had three main components. First, the act established government control of the airwaves through the issuing of licenses. Second, the spectrum was allocated based on what the government considered priority of uses. Third, individual communications, such as distress calls, were given priority over amateur communications (Krattenmaker & Powe, 1994).

A fundamental failure of the 1912 Act, as with the Communications Act that followed it, was that it did not anticipate advances in technology or the methods by which existing technology would be used. Regulations were based on spectrum allocation, that is issuing licenses to broadcasters allowing them to use a segment of the radio spectrum on which they can send their signal through the air. Underlying the need to mete out this resource is the concept of "spectrum scarcity." Spectrum scarcity, a lack of spectrum on which to transmit a signal, was a myth almost from the time of its inception. As early as the mid-1920s, technology existed that would overcome the perceived shortage in spectrum. Seventy years later, technology had increased so that only a limited part of the spectrum was allocated to broadcasting. In 1983, Pool explained that "only about 2 percent of that spectrum is now devoted to broadcasting for both radio and television, but of the frequencies that policy makers considered in the 1920s, as much as half was dedicated to radio broadcasting" (p. 115).

Thus the need to have a license to broadcast and the belief in spectrum scarcity was a government choice—a choice to ensure management of the ether by the government, and not by private interests (Krattenmaker, 1998, p. 11). Spectrum allocation proved to be a boon for the major broadcast networks. Because of the "limited" spectrum and the need to avoid interference among stations, there could only be three networks, thus restraining competition and diversity in this market. Therefore, this choice to grant licenses and allocate spectrum established the character of the broadcast industry for the next 80 years: A system of a few broadcasting to many, dominated by large corporations as the source of the transmissions.

The second significant piece of broadcast legislation was The Radio Act of 1927, which was the first act to declare that the airwaves were a public resource. Though the 1912 Act had issued licenses, it did not specifically declare that ownership of the spectrum belonged to the government. This act filled that gap. Additionally, the government, through the Federal Radio Commission (FRC), would determine who would be granted licenses free of charge:

> The FRC reclassified and reordered broadcast stations while refusing to expand the broadcast band. The outcome continued [Secretary of Commerce] Hoover's policy of favoring larger, established commercial broadcasters. The second step was acknowledging that programming counted and weeding out those stations that aired the less favored types. The first step slew the weak; the second destroyed the different. (Krattenmaker, 1998, p. 15)

The implementation of the regulation by the FRC helped establish the broadcasting industry as it now exists. It gave licenses to the broadcast establishment over marginal stations. The regulation built on the broadcast model of a few to many over a diversity of points of view, and it solidified the concept of national networks and the feasibility of advertising as financial support for the medium.

The 1927 Act was followed by the Communications Act of 1934, which is still the basis for much broadcast regulation. Similar to its predecessor, the 1934 Act had additional provisions. The act changed the FRC to the FCC—the Federal Communications Commission—and outlined the general powers of this independent agency. The Commission's primary power lay in the ability to grant broadcast licenses with specific reasons for renewal and fines to be assessed for noncompliance. To retain their licenses, the 1934 Act specified that broadcasters are required to serve the "the public interest, convenience or necessity."

The Communications Act of 1934 cemented the structure of broadcast television, which had been developed during the time of the previous acts. That business structure was one of a few broadcasting to many, with those limited few dependent on advertising for revenue. In terms of diversity, this structure was limiting—a handful of voices instead of many and a propensity to select programming that is going to generate revenues rather than serve the public interest. Broadcast licensees, first in radio and then in television, primarily pursued affiliation agreements with one of the networks. "Broadcasters applied for television licenses only in those communities where market size and limited competing assignments made affiliation with one of the three television networks certain; they refused to apply for licenses in any community where such affiliation might not be possible" (Le Duc, 1982, p. 167). So, right from the beginning, the interests of broadcast stations were more national than local in scope. This structure quashed any diversity from a multitude of outlets. This structure also hampered programming diversity. As Cantor and Cantor (1992) so aptly put it, "Content in an advertiser-supported system that is not otherwise held to specific criteria serves primarily as a vehicle for advertising. This affects topics, their treatment, and the organization of that treatment" (p. 8). Reliance on advertising rather than government funding determined that programming would be based on popularity, because a mass audience was the product being sold to advertisers. "The initial decisions, as exemplified in the 1934 statute, made radio and later television a business first and a public service second" stated Comstock (1991, p. 5). The Communications Act established the business model and then attempted to find a means by which to have it serve the public interest. This retrofitting of priorities is a fundamental issue that would affect American program diversity even to the current day.

Cable Television Acts. Broadcast and cable television have been regulated differently over the years. This situation has primarily occurred for diversity reasons. Because broadcasting is free over-the-air television, the FCC has often taken steps to protect this segment of the television industry. Even today, more than 30% of television viewers do not get their programming from cable. These viewers are entitled to free programming because the spectrum is a public good, that is, broadcasters are trustees of the airwaves for the public. It is up to the FCC to ensure broadcasters can continue to serve this purpose, which means keeping them economically viable. Therefore, when cable television threatened broadcasting's livelihood because of competition for advertisers, the Commission stepped in to protect broadcasters. Similarly, when cable threatened not to carry broadcast stations on their systems, Congress and the FCC forced their carriage. Though broadcasting was regulated by the FCC from its inception in the 1930s because of spectrum scarcity, cable did not come under FCC jurisdiction until the 1984 Cable Act. That was only the first step. Since that time, the Cable Act of 1992 and the Telecommunications Act of 1996 have put additional restrictions on the industry.

The Cable Communications Policy Act of 1984 (the 1984 Cable Act) changed cable law in three ways. First, local authorities could not regulate cable rates in areas where the franchise faced "effective competition." This part of the rule proved ineffective because the FCC defined "effective competition" as an area that received three broadcast signals, thus eliminating rate regulation for the majority of cable systems. Second, the act "regularized the franchise renewal process" (Krattenmaker, 1998, p. 533). This meant that incumbent cable systems had "renewal expectancy" and added protection before a franchise could be terminated. Third, cable operators were required to provide lease access to commercial programmers. This provision turned out to be ineffectual because it did not provide standards for determining if operators charged unreasonable rates for this service.

Some additional provisions of the 1984 Cable Act apply to diversity. Cable operators are allowed to carry broadcast signals from other communities—something started in the early years of the industry. However, the FCC restricts importing programming that duplicates local transmissions. Cable operators can be prohibited from importing a network affiliate from a distant market, because that would duplicate programming on the local affiliate. In the case of syndicated and sports programming, blackout provisions exist to protect the local station. Exclusivity agreements exist between the station and the syndicator or sports franchise and help to maintain ratings, and thereby not dilute the advertising rates. Any imported programming must be blacked out. These are the so-called syndex rules, for syndication exclusivity. This does nothing for diversity in that the imported channels are blacked out and no alternative programming replaces it.

Another provision of this act entitled cable program service providers (networks) to scramble their programming to deter theft of their programming by satellite users. Scrambled programming meant satellite users would have to pay to see something with their backyard dish, either by purchasing a decoder box or by subscription. Also, individual satellite ownership became legal. The FCC expected this to turn Direct Broadcast Satellite (DBS), or Direct to Home (DTH) as it was known at the time, into a legitimate business competitor. However, when the cable networks began to scramble their programming, DBS sales plummeted from 735,000 systems in 1985 to 225,000 units in 1986, while an estimated 60 percent of retailers left the industry (Orbit Communication, n.d.). While DBS had become legal, without free programming, consumers lost interest. Instead of creating a viable competitor for cable, it virtually killed the industry for almost 10 years.

Constituents' concern over cable rates and complaints to their senators and congressmen lead to the "Cable Television Consumer Protection and Competition Act of 1992." Also known as the Cable Act of 1992, this legislation radically changed cable regulation from the preceding act. Rate regulations were instituted in response to consumer pressure. Restrictions on programming, particularly as they relate to broadcasters, were created to respond to the belief that cable was becoming a dominating force in the television arena and, therefore, stifling diversity. Provisions put limitations on vertical and horizontal integration, which policymakers were concerned might lead to independent voices not being heard. If cable operators became too large (serving a majority of subscribers), they might exercise monopsony power, that is purchase power, over program suppliers. If cable operators began to own too many cable networks as well, they might only program those networks in which they had an equity stake. (A parallel situation to that of the networks when the FCC created fin-syn.) Leased access was an additional, though not very effective, way to provide independent programmers with access to cable audiences.

The 1992 Cable Act covered three areas of cable regulation. First, Congress created rate regulations, over the objections of the FCC. The pricing structure was done as a tiered process, working as follows: Cable operators were required to create a "basic tier" of services, which was to be priced separately from other programming options and had to be purchased as a prerequisite to subscribing to other services. A basic tier consists of local broadcast stations and PEG channels—public, educational and governmental channels—and the operator can add other satellite services. This structure would allow someone who only wanted cable to improve reception, for instance, to not have to pay for additional programming they did not want. The cable operators could then create premium tiers, for which they could charge additional fees. Under this rule, the cable operators could create packages of programming and only the most minimal package, the basic tier, would be FCC regulated. Increased channel capacity and improved technology would enable cable to overcome some of the rate restrictions these rules created.

The second area the 1992 Act covered was a set of provisions meant to foster competition within the industry and among other multiple video program distributors, such as DBS. One method policymakers used to create competition was by limiting the number of cable subscribers any one multiple-system operator could serve. From a local perspective, this is a seemingly useless provision because cable systems are local monopolies. However, the FCC was concerned that the operators would gain undue power in their ability to purchase programming. In the same way that broadcasting has ownership caps, so too the Commission put an upper limit on cable ownership. This number was 30% of U.S. television households. In March 2001, a federal court struck down the cap on cable systems, claiming that it violated the First Amendment. The Commission began reviewing cable ownership rules in September of that year and the issue is still under review (Krasnow & Berg, 2002, p. 39).

A more effective policy, at least in terms of source diversity, put restrictions on the number of services that a cable operator could put on their system in which they had an equity stake. A major issue with cable is its function as a gatekeeper of information. Cable operators decide which networks will be on a cable system and which will not. Many cable operators have an equity stake in cable networks. For instance, AOL Time Warner owns cable systems as well as CNN, HBO, and TNT among others. The FCC was concerned that companies such as AOL would program all of its own networks without giving "shelf space" to other networks in which they did not have an equity stake. Therefore, the FCC extensively regulated the contracts between cable operators and networks with similar ownership. This rule, however, was vacated by the D.C. Circuit at the same time as the cable ownership caps. The existing rule limited operator-affiliated programming to 40% of the system's programming; based on constitutional grounds, the court determined the rule was not justified (Krasnow & Berg, 2002, p. 39). The last competitive provision was the program access rules. These rules prohibited cable operators, specifically those that are vertically integrated, from engaging in competitive practices that hinder other multi-channel programming distributors, that is, DBS operators from providing programming to customers. In particular, the FCC was concerned about price discrimination and exclusivity, thereby keeping cable networks from providing their services to DBS distributors. These rules have been extended through 2007.

In the third area covered by the act, Congress attempted to create a more equitable system between cable networks and broadcast networks. This led to the must-carry rules and retransmission consent. Must-carry rules require that a cable system "must carry" the broadcast networks in its area. If the cable system has more than 12 channels, one third of their channels need to be devoted to broadcast stations. In systems with less than 12 channels, three channels must be devoted to broadcasters. All public television stations are automatically included in the program lineup. Separately, under retransmission consent, cable operators are required to pay broadcasters for their programming, which is standard practice with cable networks. For example, an AOL Time Warner cable system might pay 50 cents per subscriber per month to have MTV on one of its cable systems. While MTV was getting this guaranteed monthly revenue, broadcasters were getting nothing from cable operators even though they delivered the largest audiences on the system. When the must carry and retransmission consent rules were created, there was much confusion over what they meant because they were inextricably linked. The language in the *FCC Report and Order* regarding these rules exemplifies this confusion:

> While each of the provisions [must carry and retransmission consent] is distinct and functions in a separate fashion, they are related in that, with respect to local cable carriage, for example, television broadcasters on a system-by-system basis must make a choice once every three years whether to proceed under the mandatory carriage rules or to govern their relationship with cable operators by the retransmission consent requirement. (Broadcast Signal Carriage Issues, 1993, at 2)

Local stations can choose retransmission consent with must carry, meaning the operator must air the station and gets to do so for free. Alternatively, the station can forego must carry and negotiate retransmission consent. What this meant in reality was the smaller stations that were likely to be dropped from the system opted for a straight must carry to ensure they would be carried on the system. The major networks, which were virtually guaranteed carriage (because what cable system will not offer CBS?), opted for retransmission consent, that is payment. However, rather than a per-subscriber fee, the broadcast networks negotiated carriage for their fledgling cable networks because there was no other way to guarantee shelf space. ABC, for instance, got carriage for its ESPN2 network; NBC did the same for its news channels.

After the approval of the 1992 bill, cable operators opposed the must-carry rules based on First Amendment considerations. After all, the FCC was telling cable operators what content to put on their systems by requiring that they carry the broadcast networks. Similarly, by putting broadcast stations on the system, they were eliminating cable networks—smaller, more niche programming—from having access to audiences. After reviewing the case twice (in *Turner I* [1994] and *Turner II* [1997]), the Supreme Court determined that the rules were not in violation of the First Amendment because the rules were content neutral. As the court stated in *Turner I*, "Although the provisions interfere with cable operators' editorial discretion by compelling them to offer carriage to a certain minimum number of broadcast stations, the extent of the interference does not depend upon the content of the cable operators' programming" (*Turner Broadcasting System, Inc. v. FCC* [Turner I]). The court was not trying to present one point of view over another but rather to "preserve free programming for ... American[s] without cable." As part of that goal, the Court determined that there was a need to assist smaller broadcasters in remaining viable over the interests of new cable networks. Giving these outlets assistance was important in preserving the diversity that Congress was attempting to create through this act. Specifically, "(1) preserving the benefits of free, over-the-air broadcast television, (2) promoting the widespread dissemination of information from a multiplicity of sources, and (3) promoting fair competition in the market for television programming" (*Turner I*). The Court was specifically concerned about the economic viability of broadcasting because of stations not being carried by cable systems. There was evidence before Congress and the Court that cable operators would drop broadcast stations to benefit cable networks. This was particularly prevalent because cable operators were becoming increasingly more integrated companies owning networks as well as systems. These operators had an economic incentive to put programming in which they had a financial interest on their systems rather than broadcast channels. Must carry remains on the books today.

Though not exclusively a cable act, the Telecommunications Act of 1996 (Telecomm Act) had a major impact on the cable industry. First, it deregulated cable rates on expanded tiers. The basic tier, however, remains regulated. Second, to increase competition in the multichannel video market, the act allowed telephone companies to provide video programming and cable operators to provide phone service.

There was one other interesting and not necessarily expected consequence of the 1996 Telecomm Act. Under this legislation, broadcasters were put on a timetable by which to transition from analog to digital technology. While they are making this transition, broadcasters want cable operators to carry both their analog and digital signal. This is called dual or digital must carry. Cable operators, not surprisingly, oppose this suggestion because a large percentage of their capacity would be taken up with broadcast channels, much of which will be duplicative while the transition is occurring. In addition, though broadcasters are required to return to the government the analog spectrum by 2006, many in the industry do not believe that will happen. If broadcasters retain the full 12 MHz of spectrum—both analog and digital—and they are already on the cable systems, it will be difficult—if not impossible—for cable operators to kick them off at a later date. As of January of 2001, the FCC determined that "based on the existing record evidence, a dual carriage requirement appears to burden cable operators' First Amendment interest substantially more than is necessary to further the government's substantial interests" (Amendment of Part 76, 2001). Currently, cable operators are required to carry the broadcaster's "primary video signal." This rule continues to be in effect.

Over the last almost 20 years, the cable industry has been up and down in terms of regulation. While more heavily regulated in the early 1990s due to consumer complaints, the industry has been significantly deregulated since that time. The regulations that remain are meant to promote diversity. However, as we have seen, the effectiveness of these rules is mixed at best. For instance, must carry and retransmission consent did ensure carriage for smaller broadcasters on the one hand. On the other hand, however, they actually reduced diversity by giving additional cable space to already powerful program distributors such as Disney and NBC. Regulation of DBS virtually eliminated the business for a decade. Probably the biggest failure in creating competition was the 1996 Telecomm Act. By letting cable operators and phone companies compete head-to-head the expectation was that cable systems would no longer be natural monopolies. Six years later, there is still no widespread competition from phone companies.

Broadcast Ownership Rules. The FCC has been regulating limits on broadcast station ownership since 1938. These limitations have been a part of the FCC's goal "to maximize diversification of program and service viewpoints as well as to prevent any undue economic concentration contrary to the public interest" (FCC 1983 Notice of Proposed Rulemaking, quoted in Besen & Johnson, 1984, p. 5). Later in this document the Commission emphasizes that these rules are not for "the enhancement of economic competition, but rather, the advancement of diversity in sources of information in order to further First Amendment values" (at 41). Therefore, limitations are in the interest of diversity first and foremost, while competition is a secondary goal.

In limiting the ownership of stations, the FCC takes into consideration the number and type of station (AM versus FM versus television), as well as the size of the station and the market. Additionally, the FCC seeks to balance multiple tasks including maintaining the health of the industry, monitoring concentration and the level of competition, and evaluating the extent of minority ownership, among others (Krattenmaker, 1998, p. 308).

These regulations cover two broad areas. One area that has received a lot of attention is that of ownership "caps." These are limitations that the FCC puts on the number of radio and/or television stations that can be owned by a single entity, whether on a national or local basis. Another broad area is limitations on cross ownership, including ownership of a broadcast television station and a cable system, or a broadcast station and a newspaper within the same market. Underlying these policies is the idea that outlets owned by a multitude of companies will achieve greater diversity than will more concentrated ownership.

In 1954, the FCC in amending its multiple ownership rules prohibited a group owner from having more than seven AM radio stations, seven FM radio stations, and seven television stations, colloquially known as the "Seven Station Rule," or the group ownership rule. Over the next 20 years, the Commission would add other ownership limitations affecting the number of stations in the same region, limiting ownership of service in a market to one station (the duopoly rule—will be covered separately herein); cross-ownership rules that prohibited broadcast and cable ownership and broadcast and newspaper in a single market, and limiting the number of television stations owned by one company in the major broadcast markets—the top 50 policy (Besen & Johnson, 1984, p.1). By 1979, the top 50 rule was repealed. The regional concentration rule was repealed in 1984. The Seven Station Rule was revised in 1984 to allow a single owner to have 12 stations of each type. Under consideration, the Commission added an additional stipulation that a single owner could not have more than 25% coverage of U.S. television households (Review of the Commission's Broadcast Ownership Rules, 2000).

When the Commission reduced the limits on radio and television ownership in the 1980s, it was because of "the explosion of media outlets since the advent of the ownership rules, the extremely fragmented structure of the broadcasting industry and the fact that viewpoint diversity is primarily a function of local, and not national alternatives" (Revision of Radio Rules and Policies, 1992). The exponential growth of media outlets, particularly the growth of cable, was putting economic stress on other media players because they compete for the same audience and advertisers. Cable networks such as MTV and VH1 were pulling audiences away from radio in a way that had not happened previously. The availability of alternatives to radio forced the medium to expand its uses and did so by becoming fragmented in its programming options. Because specialized programming led to fragmented audiences, economic considerations for the industry changed. That is, specialized audiences meant smaller audiences, which translated into reduced advertising dollars. At the same time, radio is a local medium and competes with other local media for advertiser dollars. Throughout the 1980s and into the 1990s, radio lost successively more money to cable and saw its own profits virtually disappear. Additionally, most radio stations are small operations. The FCC wanted to insure their viability and, therefore, diversity. The only way to do that was to improve the economics in some way which meant allowing them to join with other stations so as to be able to share back-room operations such as sales, administration, and marketing. The belief was also that increased profits would lead to increased investments in programming. Broadcast television's situation paralleled that of radio. Cable television was not growing the overall advertising money but rather stealing it from older, more traditional media. Because since broadcasters are dependent on advertising as their primary source of revenue, the only way to remain profitable when revenues are shrinking is to reduce costs. Multiple station ownership allow for economies of scale that significantly reduce overhead.

By the 1990s, the trends begun in the 1980s had become more entrenched. This led to the FCC making recommendations to further reduce limits on radio ownership both in terms of national caps and in individual markets. The Commission initially recommended that station groups could own up to 30 AM and 30 FM stations nationally and up to three AM and three FM stations in a single market with additional restrictions in terms of overall percentage of ownership. This cap was determined to allow an acceptable level of concentration. Also the Commission had evidence that local diversity would not be compromised because local news reporting was done autonomously. The existing rules had prohibited two AM and two FM stations in the same market, though an AM/FM ownership was permitted. The FCC believed the existing rules actually hampered diversity by making it more difficult for owners to amortize their costs over multiple stations in a market. The recommended 30/30 and 3/3 limits were revised under pressure from Congress to 18 and 18 on a national basis and two AM and two FM station in one market where there are at least 15 stations in the market. Part of Congress' objection was that the numbers seemed to be arbitrary.

All of this became moot with the Telecommunications Act of 1996. The objective of the 1996 Act includes "stimulating private investment, promoting competition, and protecting diversity of voices regarding broadcast ownership, licensing, and allocation of the broadcast spectrum" (Fortunato & Martin, 1999). The act attempts to achieve these objectives in a number of ways. First, limits on station ownership were reduced or eliminated. National limits on radio ownership were completely eliminated. As for local limits, in the largest markets of more than 45 stations, a single owner can have eight radio stations, with only five being in a single band (either AM or FM). This number is prorated downward for smaller radio markets. Television limits were significantly reduced. Prior to the act, companies could only own up to 12 stations reaching no more than 25% of U.S. households. Now, companies can own an unlimited number of television stations covering up to 35% of the country—these are the so-called ownership caps that are currently being hotly contested in the courts. The 35% cap may, in fact, disappear in light of recent court rulings.

Another way to open competition was to revise other ownership rules. Local market ownership came under review in the 1996 Act. While a decision was not made at that time, the FCC was required to hold a rulemaking proceeding to evaluate the rules that did not allow ownership of stations within 50 to 70 miles of one another, the Grade B contour of the station's signal. The rule was changed in 1999, allowing a single company to own more than one station within the same Designate Market Area (DMA), Nielsen's definition for a local market. At the same time, the FCC relaxed the one-to-a-market rules, which had prohibited television and radio cross ownership.[2] Finally, the act prohibited any of the four major net-

[2]As well, a television station owner may soon be able to own a cable franchise. Ownership of a television station and a newspaper in the same market is still prohibited, but this too is under debate in the court system.

works—ABC, CBS, NBC and FOX—to merge with one of the new networks that were emerging at that time—The WB and UPN. This was to promote diversity within the broadcast sphere. The FCC has since waived that provision for Viacom, which owned UPN and gained ownership of CBS with the purchase of that company in 2001.[3] By allowing networks to own more stations and have control of more bandwidth, the government has given broadcasters a means to respond to increasing competition. Whether they have increased diversity is another issue.

The ownership caps and the cross-ownership rules are still being heavily contested by policymakers and the courts and so a little more detail is needed here. Early in 2001, the Washington DC Circuit Court struck down the 30% ownership cap on cable systems. Because the court believed that the FCC could provide no justification for a limitation on the number of subscribers, the same argument could be made about caps on broadcast ownership. In February 2002, the same court asked the Commission to reconsider broadcast ownership caps and overturned rules prohibiting television and cable ownership in the same market. Though not being pressured to do so, the FCC is also considering revising or eliminating its television and newspaper cross-ownership regulations. Together with the duopoly rule, which will be discussed later, these decisions all but eliminate any kind of restriction on broadcast ownership—even if they are not overturned on appeal.

The National Television Station Ownership Rule, which limits the number of stations any one entity can own, was created to promote the power of the local affiliate and thus promote diversity. In addition, the rule was meant to prevent concentration of economic power within the industry. The rules were successful in creating diversity; however, they severely impeded the ability of broadcasters to be economically viable. So, as we saw, over the years this rule was relaxed. With the possible elimination of the rule, local broadcasters—particularly network affiliates—fear that undue power will be put into the hands of the broadcast networks. The issue, however, is not one of David versus Goliath but rather one giant against another. Most local broadcasters are not singly owned stations but rather are part of large station groups, like Tribune, which owns 23 stations reaching close to 29% of U.S. households (Trigoboff, 2002, p. 46). The networks are also major owners of television stations through their owned and operated stations, which are simply affiliates owned by a network. In fact, Viacom, Fox, NBC, and ABC are all within the top six largest television station groups. Therefore, in terms of size, many station groups are formidable opponents for the networks, and while they may not own a broadcast network, many own newspapers and other media in addition to their television holdings.

The real issue is how far the balance of power in the relationship might swing in favor of the networks. As it is, the networks are vertically integrated companies producing their own programming, distributing it through the network, and then exhibiting it on their owned and operated stations, most of which are in major television markets. Because the networks can only own slightly more than a third of their affil-

[3]Other provisions within the act include the rollout of digital transmission, introduction of the "V-chip" and the permission for cable operators to provide phone service and vice versa.

iates, stations not owned by the network have say in issues such as programming and affiliate compensation, monies paid by the network to affiliates to air their programming. If the networks come to own the majority of their affiliates, they have no reason to answer to anyone but themselves.[4]

There is every reason to think that the networks intend to purchase as many stations as they can. While NBC and ABC own stations reaching 30.4 and 23.8% respectively, Viacom (owner of CBS and UPN) and News Corporation (owner of Fox) are already over the 35% limit. When Viacom bought CBS, it already owned 19 television stations, and the purchase put them over the limit (Wired, 1999). Recently, the FCC gave the company a waiver in light of the fact that the rules are expected to change (McClintock, 2002c, p. 1). Similarly, News Corporation bought a group of stations from Chris-Craft, which also put its ownership statistics over the cap. They too have been given a waiver. In April 2002, the FCC gave final approval for NBC to merge with Telemundo, a Spanish-language broadcaster. It is not likely NBC's interest in serving the Spanish community that prompted this purchase so much as the valuable broadcast properties Telemundo owned.[5] This purchase will put NBC over the 35% cap as well.

In terms of cross-ownership rules, two things are at issue—television and cable ownership and television and newspaper ownership. In the same decision in which the circuit court remanded the 35% cap, it voided the rule for television and cable ownership. Again the court said the FCC failed to prove that the broadcast-cable ban was necessary to protect competition. When the rules were enacted in 1970, there were few stations and little cable distribution. Now, with a multitude of channels and the growth of direct broadcast satellite, the court did not see that the Commission could justify the rules. In fact, Congress had eliminated the statutory prohibition against this cross ownership in the 1996 Telecomm Act, though they did not force the FCC to eliminate its rule, so policymakers have been moving in this direction for a number of years. Because the change in this rule is so recent, there are yet to be effects in the marketplace. However, "Everything's in play" as the title of a *Broadcasting & Cable* article suggests (Higgins & McClellan, 2002, p. 18). Expectations are that large media companies may merge, including possibly AOL and NBC, though this is speculation at this point. With the repeal of this television/cable rule, the Commission is also likely to repeal the television-newspaper cross-ownership rule. The rule banning cross ownership of newspapers and television stations was created in 1970. Four years later, the Commission came out with their final rules. There was one major flaw with these rules as Shooshan and Sloan (1982) explain, "The broadcast/newspaper cross-ownership rules are aimed at increasing diversity and concentration of control; yet, by grandfathering existing combinations, the rules diminish diversity by creating artificial barriers to entry" (p. 162). Because

[4]There are also syndication issues. Because the networks own stations in major markets, they can make or break the success of a syndicated program. This is covered more fully in chapter 4.

[5]NBC also has partially ownership of Pax Communications, the seventh network and the third largest television station group.

some companies could have this dual ownership and others could not, there was an unfair advantage in the marketplace. The rules also seemed to work against diversity because economically it would make sense to combine operations with a television station and a newspaper, if it would help save the newspaper. After all, newspaper-newspaper combinations are allowed for the same purpose. Elimination of these rules will allow for more of these combinations, but it may be too late as many newspapers have folded due to increasing economic competition.

Duopoly Rule. The duopoly rules are a subset of the ownership rules. Much of the history of these rules were covered in the preceding section, but some highlights will be added here. The FCC first adopted duopoly rules between 1941 and 1943. These rules barred ownership of two broadcast stations in the same market. The Commission amended these rules in 1953, specifying the number of television and radio stations (AM and FM) that a single entity could own (Geller, 1982, p. 150). In 1991, the FCC began investigating whether to loosen restrictions on the television industry. In 1995, after further analysis, the Commission began to consider a new way in which to assess economic and diversity issues. In particular, they were looking for a threshold number for determining a minimum number of voices by which to maintain diversity within a market, taking into consideration that cable and DBS, though alternatives to broadcast television, are not free. While working on this, the Telecomm Act removed radio limits, introduced the 35% cap, and left local regulation to the FCC.[6] In 1999, the duopoly rules were changed so that station groups are now allowed to own two television stations in a market. As discussed earlier, this had been strictly prohibited through most of radio and television history. The duopoly rule—for two stations in a market—allows for ownership of two stations in a market only if there are seven or more other broadcast owners in the market. This came to be known as the "eight-voices rule."

Because of the eight voice restriction, duopoly has been limited to only a few dozen major markets. In New York, for example, there are at least 15 stations and thus far only one duopoly with News Corp., parent of Fox broadcasting, owning Channel 5, the Fox affiliate, and Channel 9, the UPN affiliate. Since 1999, there have only been 70 duopolies created in approximately 40 markets (Schiesel, 2002).

In its biennial review, the FCC recommended retention of these rules. In February 2002, Sinclair Broadcasting Group, a large broadcast station owner, petitioned the DC circuit (Krasnow & Berg, 2002, p. 45). In April 2002, the circuit court in Washington ordered the FCC to reassess the duopoly rules that prohibit station groups from owning more than one station in small to medium-size markets (McClintock, 2002b, p. 1). In making this decision, the court stated that the Commission had not fully explained why other media, such as newspapers and cable,

[6]The Telecomm Act also required the FCC to review the television rules every 2 years to determine whether they were still necessary. The Commission's inability to adequately justify these rules on a biannual basis is what some have claimed have led to the circuit court vacating the rules.

were not included within the eight voices. This decision opens the possibility for duopolies to exist outside the major urban markets.

Eliminating the duopoly rules will also lead to added consolidation of the industry. When the rules were originally changed in August 1999, CBS approached Viacom about a merger that was announced a month later (Higgins & McClellan, 2002, p. 18). Viacom, now owner of CBS as well as UPN and the country's largest station group, has duopolies with an affiliate corresponding with each of its two networks in Los Angeles, Philadelphia, San Francisco, Boston, Dallas, Detroit, Miami, and Pittsburgh. The only reason Viacom is not larger, with more duopolies in the top 10 markets, is because News Corporation bought a station group from Chris-Craft, former partner with Viacom on UPN and former owner of many of its affiliate stations. These UPN affiliates are now part of Fox's station group. In 2002, Fox also bought a Chicago television station, WPWR, giving the company duopolies in the top three markets and nine overall (McClellan, 2002a, p. 8). NBC also has a number of duopolies due to mergers. Shortly after the ruling, NBC purchased a 32% stake in Pax Communications, a company with a plethora of stations. In April 2002, however, NBC merged with Telemundo, creating duopolies in six major markets including New York, Chicago, and Miami. While Pax initially opposed the Telemundo deal because their deal with NBC was under the assumption that NBC would eventually purchase the remainder of the company, Paxson is now trying to get NBC to let them out of their deal so someone else can buy them. Networks are not the only companies with duopolies. Most large station owners have duopolies in most major television markets such as New York, Los Angeles, and Chicago.

The expectation is that duopolies will spread to medium and smaller markets, and the networks will continue to buy up as many stations as the law will allow. This means more consolidation both vertically and horizontally because large station groups will get larger and networks will have more control over the distribution aspect of their business.

Source Diversity

Fairness Doctrine. The Fairness Doctrine was an FCC regulation that was in effect from 1949 until 1987. It required broadcasters to present controversial issues facing their community in a balanced manner as a condition for obtaining a broadcast license. This was not an equal time requirement but rather a means for preventing a broadcaster from only presenting one side of an issue. The landmark decision that upheld the constitutionality of the doctrine was the *Red Lion* case.

By the mid-1960s, television had come out of its nascent stage. Television was in 53.8 million homes or 95% of the United States (Media Dynamics, 1998, p. 18). Issues of a technological nature that faced Congress and the FCC, such as how to divide up the spectrum, were replaced by issues of content and access. Who has the right to say what to whom? Who has the right to determine what was on television? Should it be the license holders? Should it be the federal government and if so would there be serious First Amendment implications? These issues came to a head in June 1969 with the *Red Lion* case.

The Red Lion Broadcasting Company owned station WGCB in Pennsylvania. During a "Christian Crusade" program, Reverend Billy James Hargis discussed a book called *Goldwater—Extremist on the Right* by Fred J. Cook. Hargis claimed "that Cook had been fired by a newspaper for making false charges against city officials; that Cook had then worked for a Communist-affiliated publication; that he had defended Alger Hiss and attacked J. Edgar Hoover and the Central Intelligence Agency; and that he had now written a 'book to smear and destroy Barry Goldwater'" (*Red Lion Broadcasting Co. v. FCC*, 1969). Cook learned of the broadcast and demanded equal time to respond because he had been personally attacked. WGCB refused. Cook took his case to the FCC, which affirmed that the broadcast was a personal attack and required the station to provide airtime for Cook to respond. The judgment was appealed to the Supreme Court, which found that

> in view of the scarcity of broadcast frequencies, the Government's role in allocating those frequencies, and the legitimate claims of those unable without governmental assistance to gain access to those frequencies for expression of their views, we hold the regulations and ruling at issue here are both authorized by statute and constitutional. (*Red Lion Broadcasting Co. v. FCC*, 1969)

Access to the airwaves was justified in *Red Lion* due to spectrum scarcity. Unlike in print, where "anyone" could produce a pamphlet or write a letter to the editor, not everyone could own a television station, and people who opposed the views of the license holder deserved to be heard.

While *Red Lion* differentiated regulation of broadcast from print because of spectrum limitations and upheld the audience's right over the broadcaster's, it did not stand as the final say on the Fairness Doctrine. Five years after this decision, the Court determined that under the doctrine "political and electoral coverage would be blunted or reduced" in *Miami Herald Publishing Co. v. Tornillo* (1974). Rather than presenting both sides of a controversial issue, broadcasters were editorializing on issues that would not create controversy, or they were not editorializing at all. By 1984, the Court again reviewed the doctrine in *FCC v. League of Women Voters* (1984). Here the Court determined that not only was the doctrine limiting debate, that is diversity, it was also based on a flawed theory—that of spectrum scarcity.

This decision would lead to the FCC repealing the doctrine. In their statement, the Commission said:

> We no longer believe that the Fairness Doctrine, as a matter of policy, serves the public interests. In making this determination, we do not question the interest of the listening and viewing public in obtaining access to diverse and antagonistic sources of information. Rather, we conclude that the Fairness Doctrine is no longer a necessary or appropriate means by which to effectuate this interest. We believe that the interest of the public in viewpoint diversity is fully served by the multiplicity of voices in the marketplace today and that the intrusion by government into the content of programming oc-

> casioned by the enforcement of the doctrine unnecessarily restricts the journalistic freedom of broadcasters. Furthermore, we find that the Fairness Doctrine, in operation actually inhibits the presentation of controversial issues of public importance to the detriment of the public and in degradation of the editorial prerogative of broadcast journalists. (The Wisdom Fund, 1997)

In this case, the FCC eliminated a rule that was meant to increase content diversity, because of an increase in outlet diversity. By the 1980s, there were significantly more sources of television than in the 1960s, due to expanded availability of cable, an increase in the number of independent broadcast stations, as well as the introduction of a new broadcast network, Fox. Either way, the Fairness Doctrine appears to have done more to squelch diversity than it did to promote it.

Minority Licensing Policies. In the 1960s, the FCC and the courts began to include minority ownership and hiring practices within their concept of diversity. This was driven by changing societal interests, particularly the Civil Rights movement, and in this case the National Advisory Commission on Civil Disorders also known as the Kerner Commission (Mason, Bachen & Craft, 2001, p. 38). The Kerner Commission criticized the media for presenting a white, male-dominated point of view and blamed the media for being instrumental in racial riots that occurred at that time.

This criticism was coming at the same time as the landmark *Red Lion* decision. Because under that decision the Supreme Court had determined that the broadcast spectrum was a scarce resource, the FCC was able to put restrictions on broadcasters as public trustees of that resource. Part of those restrictions included regulations in terms of equal opportunity hiring practices. In this initial stage, FCC policy did not consider including minority ownership as a consideration for granting or renewing a broadcast license, because they did not accept that there was de facto a causal relationship between minority ownership and minority programming. Rather, they decided "black ownership cannot and should not be an independent comparative factor ... rather, such ownership must be shown on the record to result in some public interest benefit" (*TV9 v. FCC,* 1973).

That position changed in 1973 when the Court of Appeals for the District of Columbia considered a petition for a Florida television license that had been rejected. The petitioners were African American. The court stated that "'minority ownership is likely to increase diversity of content' and that providing a comparative advantage to minority applicants was 'integral to the FCC's responsibility to promote the public interest'" (Mason et al., 2001, p. 39). Now, minorities would not have to demonstrate that they would produce minority programming. Instead, the FCC would assume that there was a "reasonable expectation" that this would occur. By 1978, the FCC developed a policy statement on minority broadcasting.

> The views of racial minorities continue to be inadequately represented in the broadcast media. This situation is detrimental to not only the minority audience but to all of the viewing and listening public. Adequate representation of minority viewpoints in

> programming serves not only the needs and interests of the minority community but also enriches and educates the non-minority audience. It enhances the diversified programming which is a key objective not only of the Communications Act of 1934 but also the First Amendment. (Statement of Policy on Minority Ownership of Broadcasting Facilities, 1978)

Based on this policy, which in large part was driven by Congress, the FCC took additional steps to further minority ownership. First, the FCC considered minority status in comparative license applications. Second, the Commission created the "distress sale" program. This program would allow a license holder who was facing having their license revoked to transfer that license to a minority through a distress sale. This would give minorities privileged access to licenses that became available.

During the mid-1980s when much of the broadcast industry was deregulated, the FCC claimed it would abandon minority-related policies. This change was instigated after a case regarding female representation in broadcasting was rejected by the DC Circuit (*Steele v. FCC*, 1985). In this case, the FCC gave preference to a woman on a license decision. On appeal, the losing party (a man) claimed sexual discrimination and the court agreed. After this decision, the FCC determined that gender and race classifications were invalid:

> The FCC concluded that neither itself, Congress, nor the courts had developed a record indicating the existence of a nexus between ownership and viewpoint diversity or the need for minority or gender preferences to achieve content diversity. (Kleiman, 1991, p. 417)

It was no wonder that the Commission wanted to vacate these rules. However, while the FCC was ready to walk away from these policies, Congress was not. In 1987, Congress specified in its budget allocation for the FCC that funds were not to be used to change or repeal gender or minority policies. So, through the 1990s, FCC policies continued to reflect an interest in promoting minorities within the broadcast industry through hiring standards and ownership policies with regards to licensing. These policies were another means for the Commission to allow for a diversity of voices. To that end, media policies have favored minority ownership assuming a correlation between minority ownership and minority programming.

Majority broadcasters challenged these policy decisions, however, and were given hearing in front of the Supreme Court. In *Metro Broadcasting Inc. v. Federal Communications Commission* (1990), the Court upheld minority ownership practices. *Metro* affirmed minority ownership "as a means of achieving greater programming diversity." This decision confirmed that minority owners broadcast different content than the majority, that is, there is a correlation between minority ownership and minority programming. "This judgment—and the conclusion that there is a nexus between minority ownership and broadcasting diversity—is corroborated by a host of empirical evidence." Much of this evidence demonstrated that minority broadcasters present more news topics of interest to minorities, avoid racial and ethnic stereotyping, and there is a tendency for minority owners to hire more minorities.

Through much of the 1990s, FCC policies continued to reflect an interest in promoting minorities within the broadcast industry through hiring standards and ownership policies with regards to licensing.[7] In 1995, the Court overturned *Metro* (*Adarand Constructors, Inc., v. Pena*, 1995). The decision was overturned "only to the extent that it used intermediate scrutiny to review a federal program employing ethnic or racial classifications .... Intermediate review requires only that the asserted government interest be 'substantial' or 'important' as opposed to 'compelling.'" Rather what the Court was requiring was "strict scrutiny," a standard that states that racial classifications are constitutional if they are narrowly focused and further "compelling governmental interests" (court decision). This meant that stricter standards were being applied to minority practices. While the Court had found that broadcast diversity was an important issue, it was not compelling—the stricter standard—and to that extent *Metro* was overruled, making it more difficult for the FCC to implement race-specific policies.

By 1998, the Court of Appeals for the District of Columbia rejected the FCC's hiring regulations based on race. In *Lutheran Church-Mission Synod v. Federal Communications Commission* (1998), the connection between the diversity of the workforce and content was put to the test. The Lutheran Church had two radio stations in Clayton, Missouri. One was a commercial station and one was not. The noncommercial station featured religious programming, and the license holder claimed that they needed to hire people with expertise in this area to run the network. The FCC said that nonprogramming-related personnel did not have to meet this requirement. This argument, in the end, worked against the FCC because it contradicted the need for specialized EEO policies. Specifically, if someone does not have to be Lutheran to produce Lutheran content, then racial and ethnic personnel are not necessary to produce more diverse programming.

The *Lutheran Church* decision changed the tide of minority practices by suggesting that the government should not specifically encourage content that framed issues in terms of race. This would be equating "thoughts with behavior."

> We do not mean to suggest that race has no correlation with a person's tastes or opinions .... We doubt, however, that the Constitution permits the government to take account of racially based differences, much less encourage them. (*Lutheran Church-Mission Synod v. FCC*, 1998)

One of the court's issues with framing the diversity discussion in terms of race is that there is limited empirical evidence that minority ownership leads to more di-

---

[7]It should be noted here that minority status did not extend to women. The courts did not uphold the connection between gender ownership and content (*Lamprecht v. Federal Communications Commission,* 1992). This was knocked down by the Court based on First Amendment grounds, because no empirical evidence could provide a connection between ownership and content.

verse programming, the assumption underlying these policies and which was in complete opposition to the decision in *Metro*. The Commission was hamstrung by the *Adarand v. Pena* decision, which required stricter standards to show preference for one group over another. What has hampered minority ownership as much as anything else has been the consolidation of the media industry. Dominance by large multinational corporations makes it nearly impossible for smaller, usually minority, business owners to enter the industry.

Fin/syn and Prime Time Access Rule. While the remainder of the book will evaluate the financial interest and syndication rules in detail, a discussion of source diversity regulation would not be complete without some mention here. Because the Prime Time Access Rules were instituted at the same time and because they attempt to achieve some of the same goals, they will be discussed in tandem.

The networks were an oligopoly and therefore had unlimited control over the national airwaves. Three entities—ABC, CBS, and NBC—determined which programs Americans could watch. The FCC found that "the networks have gradually—since about 1957—increased their economic and creative control of the entire television program process. Between 1957 and 1968 the share of network evening program hours (entertainment and other) either produced or directly controlled by networks rose from 67.2 to 96.7 percent" (Herskovitz, 1997, p. 178). Not only did they control the programming, but according to Cantor and Cantor (1992), "the networks had accepted virtually no entertainment programs for network exhibition unless they were given a financial interest in those same programs" (p. 45). This was a particular issue in the 1960s because the three broadcast networks were the only national means of program distribution.

By 1970, the networks' control over programming began to concern the Justice Department. An antitrust lawsuit was launched against the networks, and consent decrees were signed (not until late in the decade) that prevented the networks from owning their prime-time programming. Any programs that the networks produced had to be sold to a syndicator for a one-time payment, thus eliminating their financial interest in the program after its initial network airing. These consent decrees made the television networks distribution mechanisms for entertainment programming and removed them from the production business except on a limited basis.

These consent decrees were initiated at the same time that the FCC adopted the financial interest and syndication rules (fin-syn) and the Prime Time Access Rules (PTAR). Fin-syn limited the networks' ownership of programming with the objective of increasing diversity in the marketplace. This piece of legislation was enacted specifically to control the power of these television networks by limiting ownership in programming that they broadcast during the prime-time hours of 8 p.m. to 11 p.m. The rules separated ownership of production from ownership of distribution and significantly hampered the networks' ability to be vertically integrated. The rules were also meant to increase the number of companies producing programming for the prime-time hours. Their objective: to create a more competitive marketplace—increase source diversity—and to increase diversity in content.

These rules meant that the networks could not ask producers for a financial interest in their programming to put the show on the prime-time schedule, which at the time was common practice. The networks could only purchase a licensing agreement for programming they did not produce. As well, the networks could not syndicate programming in the United States. This affected the networks in two ways. First, syndication of programming is a lucrative revenue stream that would no longer be available to the networks. Second, the networks could no longer keep off the market those programs they did not want their competitors to have, a practice known as warehousing.

PTAR was introduced to limit the number of hours in prime time that were programmed by the network. The PTAR specifically limited the amount of network programming for network-affiliated stations in the top 50 markets. During prime-time hours (7–11 p.m. on the East Coast, Monday–Saturday) only 3 hours per night could be network programming.[8] By limiting the number of hours that the networks could broadcast, the FCC was hoping this rule too would increase diversity in programming as well as encourage new producers and increase locally produced programming. One other provision of the PTAR was that it prohibited scheduling off-network syndicated programming into this time period since a main goal of the rules was to encourage independent television production. While it was hoped the rule would foster local programming, this did not happen. Instead, this hour became filled with shows that were inexpensive to produce, primarily game shows.

Within the context of the financial interest and syndication rules, the FCC did not define diversity even though this was one of the key goals of this regulation. What the Commission did say was that they wanted to increase the number of producers of television programming, so that network affiliates would have more choice in putting together their program schedule:

> Our objective is to provide opportunity—now lacking in television—for the competitive development of alternative sources of television programs so that television licensees can exercise something more than a nominal choice in selecting the programs which they present to the television audiences in their communities .... (Amendment of Part 73, 1970, p. 397)

Additionally, more program choice would improve programming available to independent stations as well, making them more viable competitors with the networks. It was hoped that this increase in providers and outlets would of itself create content diversity. The FCC, in fact, stated that they did not want to be in the quality business, which is why they focused on these two other forms of diversity:

> We emphasize again that it is not our objective or intention to ... promote the production of any particular type of program—whether or not it be included within the pres-

[8]The time period from 7 to 8 p.m. came to be known as prime access. It is also known as early fringe.

> ent category of quality high cost programs. The types and cost levels of programs which will develop … must be the result of the competition which will develop among present and potential producers seeking to sell programs to television broadcasters and advertisers. (Amendment of Part 73, 1970, p. 397)

After a contentious 20-year battle between the broadcast networks and Hollywood studios, the financial interest and syndication rules were repealed in 1995 and the Prime Time Access Rules a year later. As we have seen with other forms of source diversity, no connection exists between who and how many people produce programming and the diversity of content. Yes, there were more independent television stations, but that was more likely attributable to the expansion of cable. Yes, there were more producers, but the content they developed was no different after the rules were repealed.

Outlet/Source Diversity Conclusion. As all of these examples have shown, outlet diversity and source diversity are poor proxies for content diversity. Le Duc (1982) provides an explanation as to why outlet diversity has failed:

> We have looked upon each individual broadcast station as a source of programming diversity, when in fact the station has functioned much as a motion picture theater or record shop. No one would suggest that building more motion picture theaters would create more feature films, and yet this is exactly the hope the FCC has followed in the field of broadcasting. (p. 171)

It is not the number of outlets that is the issue. Just as creating more theaters provides more places to see the same content, the same is true for television. In terms of source diversity, though there are many producers, their work must all be funneled through broadcast or cable networks that a handful of companies own. This structure is not one that can easily change given the economics of the industry. It simply costs millions of dollars to produce a television show, and not many companies can afford to do that. Once the show is produced, it must be marketed to viewers in an extremely cluttered communication environment, an expertise that is also limited. Finally, the show must generate significant advertising revenue that needs to be managed. Even if there were thousands of producers, nothing suggests that they would produce programming that is any different than what is already available, particularly given the economic constraints.

The FCC has not demonstrated that regulation has done anything to improve content diversity. In fact, scholars have suggested that it has done just the opposite. "The FCC's broadcast ownership rules have not met this goal [content diversity]. Rather, they have preserved pre-existing ownership arrangements; banned new entrants from competing effectively, and actually served to deny viewers and listeners a broader range of program choice" (Shooshan & Sloan, 1982, p. 158). The exception to this is the Children's Television Act, the only regulation to require a specific type of program content.

Children's Television Act. On October 18, 1990, Congress enacted the Children's Television Act (CTA). The purpose of this act was to improve the number, or diversity, of broadcast television programming for children that is both educational and informational. In this act, the FCC was required to evaluate how a broadcaster had served the needs of children in the application renewal process. The rules the FCC drafted were initially vague in stating how the broadcaster should comply—saying merely that broadcasters had to air "some" children's programming. In response to children's interest groups and its own research, the FCC recrafted the rules of the act. These revised rules required broadcasters to air 3 hours of children's programming per week, specified what the programming should be, and stated that the show needed to be identified with a label to assist parents in finding this programming for their children.

Congress enacted the Children's Television Act for two main reasons. First, ample evidence shows that children, particularly from lower- and middle-income families, benefit from exposure to educational programming. Studies demonstrated that children watch on average 3 hours of television per day. Much of that programming was found, according to surveys with children, to promote negative or inappropriate behavior. Second, Congress determined that the market alone would not create educational programming such as *Sesame Street* or other public television fare.

There is good economic reason for this. Broadcasters depend on advertising for their revenues, and children's programming provides a plethora of disincentives. Revenues are derived from the size of the audience and the value of the audience to advertisers. Though children are of value to some advertisers, they are less lucrative than many other demographic groups. First, as a group they are smaller than adult populations. Educational programming cannot be created for the full spectrum of children 2 to 17 years of age. Rather, this group is segmented further into three subsegments based on developmental ages. Entertainment programming, as opposed to educational programming, is more likely to appeal across these young segments. Because from a revenue perspective children generate less advertising dollars than other demographic segments, broadcasters aired children's programming before 7 a.m., so as not to lose money during valuable daytime hours. All in all, broadcasters have little incentive to present children's programming.

The Commission took steps to specify the requirements of the Children's Television Act in 1996. The vagaries of the initial rules led to varying levels of compliance by broadcasters. Two main issues that needed to be clarified were the definition of what constitutes children's programming and how much of that educational and information programming for children would constitute compliance. Programming for children, what the FCC called "core programming," was defined as "a show [that] must have serving the educational and informational needs of children as a significant purpose" (Policies and Rules Concerning Children's Television Programming, 1996). Additionally, these shows must be regularly scheduled programs of at least 30 minutes in length and air between 7 a.m. and 10 p.m. In terms of how much programming, the FCC required broadcasters to air 3 hours per week of "core" programming. If the broadcasters did not air 3 hours per week of core programs, they would need to demonstrate a commitment to children's programming that was equivalent to this amount. By doing so, the broadcaster's application would receive staff approval, rather than review by the full Commission.

Not surprising, First Amendment red flags went up. The Commission was, after all, telling broadcasters to air specific content. Opponents of the CTA raised two arguments. First, they said the regulation was unconstitutional and second, opponents objected to the quantification of the requirements. The first of these obviously has broader diversity implications. Congress, however, had addressed constitutionality in the act itself by saying "it is well within the First Amendment strictures to require the FCC to consider, during the license renewal process, whether a television licensee has provided information specifically designed to serve the educational and informational needs of children in the context of its overall programming" (Senate Report, quoted in Krattenmaker, 1998, p. 225). As users of the radio spectrum, broadcasters have free access to a public domain. As such, they are "public trustees," and certain requirements accrue to that trust, including serving the needs of children. In *Turner Broadcasting v. FCC* (1994), the Court made a distinction that the FCC can ask broadcasters what they have done to serve the needs of their communities, but the Commission cannot impose what topics those should be. Specifically, the *Turner* Court stated that "broadcast programming, unlike cable programming, is subject to certain limited content restraints imposed by statute and FCC regulation." These content requirements are "viewpoint neutral" and are imposed as part of the requirement of the broadcaster to serve the public interest.

Of all the regulations reviewed, this is the only one that has had a direct impact on diversity. There was limited children's programming, and then due to specific content regulations, there was more. This is the key. Instead of using outlet and source diversity as proxies, the issue was addressed as it should be—from the point of the content itself. Though this has obvious First Amendment implications, it is true that the court makes exceptions when it comes to children. This act may not be the prototype of what can be done for all programming, but it does demonstrate that specific content requirements are most successful in achieving diversity.

MEDIA DIVERSITY STUDIES

There have been a significant number of studies about diversity of content in the media. Whether through regulating ownership, producers or outlets, there is no consensus that regulating any of these things will lead to an increase in content diversity.

Television Studies

There was some initial support for the hypothesis that more outlets create more diversity. Levin (1971) found that an increase in the number of commercial stations increased diversity (an increase of from one to six stations increased diversity 20%, based on the Diversity Index, a weighted ranking of program categories in a market). But, as the number of viewing options rises, the rate of increase in options declines (pp. 84–85). Thus, increasing outlets only works to a certain point. In terms of programming, this suggests that more is better, but too much more doesn't make much difference.[9]

Given that more is better, at least up to a point, how do you measure diversity? Several researchers (Dominick & Pearce, 1976; Long, 1979) have developed different types of diversity indices over the years. These indexes had some variation on counting program types and then dividing by the number of hours of programming. More recently, researchers (Litman, 1979; Lin, 1995) have turned to economic theory for developing means to evaluate concentration of program types.

Dominick and Pearce (1976) assessed diversity in the prime-time schedule from 1953 to 1974. These researchers used an index that summed the percentage of the top three categories per season and divided by 100.[10] This method evaluated the extent to which a limited number of categories dominate the prime-time schedule. Using this method, they found that except for two minor periods, diversity had been steadily dropping over these two decades. So much so that by 1974 only three program types, action/adventure, movies, and general drama, made up 81% of the prime-time schedule. This is versus less than 40% in 1953 and 60% in 1963 (pp. 76–77). These researchers also found that there was a correlation between diversity and profits. "As profits increased, diversity went down ... in other words, as profits went up, more and more programs appeared in fewer and fewer categories" (p. 79).

Long (1979) had come to the same conclusion when he evaluated network program diversity during the early years of television (1946–1956). For his study, Long looked at a private and a public component of the broadcasters. The private component was a measure of profitability. The public component was a measure of money spent on programming and the diversity of that television programming. Long wanted to determine historically whether there was a correlation between improved economic (private) performance for the broadcasters and deteriorating programming for the viewers (public). "[The study] found that while network program expenditures may have positively affected programming quality, network program schedules negatively affected programming diversity" (p. ii).

Long's index evaluated the networks on a weekly basis. Using this method, Long found that both overall diversity as well as diversity of specialized appeal programming is affected. Specialized appeal programming steadily declined over the time period studied, while overall diversity increased until 1953, then dropped precipitously after 1954. Long attributed this lack of program diversity to the structure of the industry, which is one of an oligopoly. As the networks became more powerful, their attention turned to private interests rather than public.

Other researchers (Lin, 1995; Litman, 1979) have used indices to evaluate diversity on a network individually or across networks during a particular half-hour time

[9]Seems to coincide with people's ability to retain information.

[10]Dominick and Pearce's categories were: newscasts, documentary/public affairs, quiz/game, interview/talk/demonstration, sports, movies, situation comedy, comedy, variety, musical variety, general variety, dramatic anthology, action/adventure, general drama, and miscellaneous.

period. Evaluating program diversity within a single network schedule is known as vertical diversity. (Vertical diversity has also been used to evaluate the entire prime-time schedule.) A drawback with assessing the television landscape this way is that it does not reflect the viewing options available to an audience at any given time. Litman (1979) provides an excellent example of the flaw in using vertical diversity analysis:

> Assume each of the networks decides to offer a new documentary program in its schedule. This would increase the vertical diversity in each network's schedule; however, if these new documentaries are broadcast opposite each other, then the viewer has no choice at that point in time. Hence, changes in vertical network diversity may not fully translate into increased viewer options. (p. 403)

Baxter (1974), in addition to Litman, has pointed out the FCC uses the vertical approach to assess whether there is balance in the network schedule. There was traditionally a balance because of the limited spectrum—with only a restricted number of stations on the air, each station needed to be diverse to produce an aggregate balance.

To provide a better view of program options, measuring horizontal diversity makes more sense. Greenberg and Barnett (1971) support this idea stating "the number of different television offerings available during a given time period is a most important measure of diversity and choice" (p. 93). Horizontal diversity is assessed by evaluating the viewing options available during each half-hour period of programming.

Litman used empirical tests to assess diversity both horizontally and vertically. Vertically, he used the Herfindahl index. This index is a measure of concentration. The greater the Herfindahl index, the higher the concentration of just a few types of programming (less diversity). Litman found that when the networks were more "rivalrous," that is, when they were more competitive, the concentration of program types decreased (more diversity). Horizontal diversity is measured by counting the types of programming across a half-hour period. At the time, because there were only three networks, the index was assessed in the following way: one represented perfect imitation (no diversity) and three represented perfect diversity. Again, Litman found increased diversity after there had been a shake up in the industry, which caused the networks to be more contentious.

More recently, Lin (1995) used the Herfindahl index to examine diversity throughout the 1980s. She found that diversity had declined during the 1980s. Competition from media other than television, that is videos, did not impact diversity in the way that competition among the networks would. This was a study of the 1980s, however, and the full impact of these media had not yet reached their full penetration. Lin suggests that this is the reason the new media had not triggered a change in network programming. The two formats that saw the largest growth during the decade were newsmagazines and reality programs, the cheapest types of prime-time programming to produce. Networks were "seeking a more efficient ratings yield for their programming dollar" (Lin, 1995, p. 25).

Other more recent diversity studies have expanded beyond broadcasting. Napoli (1997) provides the following review of the literature:

> Wildman and Lee (1989) computed diversity indices for the broadcast networks, superstations, basic cable, and pay cable channels, finding a negative relation between program repetition and content diversity. De Jong and Bates (1991) focused exclusively on cable television, finding not only an increase in channel diversity over time but an increase in the rate at which diversity has been increasing. Litman, Hasegawa, Shirkhande, and Barbatsis (1994) measured program type diversity for a week of programming in 1992 for the four main television networks, basic cable channels, premium cable channels, and PBS. The results indicated a moderate degree of program type concentration across all four categories of programmers. Grant (1994) also cast a wide net, looking at diversity across 41 U.S. broadcast and cable networks .... His results indicated that increasing the number of channels of a particular type did not lead to increased diversity of program types .... (pp. 61–62)

Napoli (1996) himself focused on broadcast syndication and found that this type of programming had both program-type (content) and source diversity, creating more diversity than broadcast networks, pay cable, public television, or pay-per-view. What all this research suggests is that even beyond broadcast television, there is no agreement as to whether diversity is increasing. Some researchers suggest that with added cable outlets there is more diversity, while others say this is not so because the programming that is provided is off-network syndication—certainly not new and diverse content.

Program-type diversity studies, research that quantifies diversity through analyzing changes in the number of program genres, have their critics. Owen (1978) has argued that program-type diversity does not take into account the variety of programming within a genre: "Not all public affairs shows are alike, just as all westerns are not alike. There may be as much 'diversity' *within* traditional program types as *among* types" (Owen, 1978, p. 44). De Jong and Bates (1991), might argue, however, that measuring diversity from within the program level is no more effective because at what point do you determine that the diversity is significant. "One could argue that any two programs, or even any two episodes of the same program, are different, and thus contribute to diversity. On the other extreme, it can be, and indeed has been, argued that there is not real difference among any of the programs provided by American commercial television" (p. 160). Another concern that Owen has with these types of research is that they do not connect the producer with diversity of programming (p. 46), which he argues is a more fundamental First Amendment issue. Other researchers argue that media outlets are more important in creating diversity (Besen, Krattenmaker, Metzger, & Woodbury, 1984, p. 26).

The value in program-type diversity studies is that they can evaluate changes in program diversity in relationship to changes in economic factors. The current study adds to this body of work by linking the changes in diversity to a specific regulatory change. It also specifically links program-type diversity to the source of the program, a major criticism of previous works. While not taking into account outlet diversity, there is little evidence that more outlets will translate into more diversity though this is a popular idea.

> The belief is that more media outlets have produced more diversity and choice. But what this increasingly fashionable argument ignores is that prevailing market structures determine and impose limits on the 'diversity' generated by expansion .... In a contemporary context, this means a class filter imposed through the high costs of market entry; an unequal relationship between large and small competitors; often oligopolistic market domination; and the constraints imposed by catering for the mass market. (Curran, 1991, p. 94)

Similarly De Jong and Bates (1991) explain that "the mere number of services and/or signals is not the same thing as diversity: Many services appear to offer essentially the same type of programming, and therefore may not contribute to increased diversity" (p. 160). This, and other research cited above, supports the argument of outlet diversity being an ineffective proxy for content diversity as discussed in the previous section.

Audience behavior research also suggests that increasing the number of outlets may not be the means to increasing the diversity of messages for viewers. As viewers are exposed to more and more choices, they do not necessarily opt to watch the choices available to them (Webster & Phalen, 1994; Wober, 1989). Within the television industry, the rule of thumb is that people watch seven channels on a regular basis and an additional four that they periodically will turn to if nothing they like is on their main networks of choice. So, as Levin suggested more than 30 years ago, providing viewers with more choices than six has diminishing returns for diversity.

Minority and Diversity

Policymakers initially used "reasonable expectation" as the standard for minority policy, but 30 years later this standard came into question. The Supreme Court became concerned with equating "thoughts with behavior," a dangerous assumption. In particular, the Court has an issue with framing the diversity discussion in terms of race, because there is limited empirical evidence that minority ownership leads to more diverse programming, the assumption underlying these policies.

Mason et al. (2001) review the literature in this area and determine that "social science research addressing the relationship between ownership and programming is neither voluminous nor consistent" (p. 44). Two studies, one of African-American radio stations and one of Spanish-language stations, showed no connection between minority ownership and increased public affairs programming for these audiences. Another study by Jeter found that while the music play list was more diverse on a minority owned station, there was no significant difference in public affairs programming. The researchers also review three studies by Marilyn Fife. Her television studies found that "minority-owned stations tend to devote more news time to topics of minority interest and to avoid racial and ethnic stereotypes in portraying minorities" (p. 46).

In their own study, Mason et al. (2001) interviewed close to 100 news directors at minority owned stations; personnel at majority-owned stations were also interviewed to provide comparison data. Both radio and television stations were part of the sample. Their own findings demonstrate there is some correlation between minority ownership and content in radio but not in television:

> [Radio stations] report delivering a wider variety of news and public affairs programming and more ethnic and racial diversity in on-air talent and identify their intended audience more in terms of racial and ethnic characteristics ... the minority radio station owners appear to be more integrated in their stations, more actively involved in decision-making regarding news and public affairs. Television owners are, for the most part, not involved in the stations' day-to-day programming decisions .... The question that directed this study was whether the race and ethnicity of a broadcast station's owner has a measureable and meaningful influence on the diversity of programming aired in markets in which the station operates. The results offer a number of indications that such a relationship exists particularly for radio stations .... For television, however, the ownership differences that emerge quite strongly and consistently for radio stations are mostly absent. (pp. 62–63, 67–68)

The difference in diversity between radio and television in this study can be, in part, attributed to the difference in the functions of the media themselves. Radio is a very targeted medium, programmed to appeal to specific audiences for specific advertisers. Television, on the other hand, is a broadcast medium. It is meant to appeal to broader interests and, therefore, is programmed to serve a larger audience. As well, almost all of the stations researched were group owned, meaning that many programming decisions were made nationally rather than at the local level. Thus, economics has as much if not more to do with how stations are programmed, particularly television, as does who owns the station. This calls into question using minority ownership as a basis for promoting diversity.

Media Concentration and Diversity

Much of the brouhaha surrounding diversity today coagulates around media consolidation, or media monopolies, which Ben Bagdikian wrote about in the 1980s. Coming out of his seminal work, *Media Monopolies*, Bagdikian developed the homogenization hypothesis. Under this hypothesis, the concentration of the industry into the hands of a few vertically and horizontally integrated multinational corporations would lead to homogeneous media content that serves only the interests of this handful of owners. Without competition, these large corporations can produce what they want in a way that is most beneficial to their bottom line. While this would seem intuitively to make sense, the empirical research to date is inconsistent in supporting this assumption. While to this point, we have examined the television industry, it is instructive to see that the theory does not hold in other media as well.

Entman (1985) evaluated the relationship between local newspaper monopoly ownership and diversity of content. He wanted to test the assumption that local newspaper monopolies are by definition less diverse. As with researchers in television, Entman analyzed diversity both vertically, the level of disagreement within a single newspaper, and horizontally, variance in content across newspapers. Entman analyzed traditional monopoly, single paper towns, as well as what he calls "quasi-monopoly," joint ownership agreements where a single company owns two papers or two companies own two papers and have joined operations. Under this analysis, then, local newspaper monopolies will have less vertical diversity and quasi-monopolies will have less horizontal diversity than in a competitive newspaper market. Entman's analysis found no consistent relationship between competition and news diversity when measured either horizontally or vertically. If fact, he suggests similarly to Steiner, that a monopoly or quasi-monoply scenario is better suited to provide a diverse news product.

Social scientists have also tried to determine a connection between diversity and concentration in the music industry. In this instance, as we saw with other diversity studies, the findings are inconclusive. Peterson and Berger (1975) found that "periods of market concentration are found to correspond to periods of homogeneity, periods of competition to periods of diversity" (p. 158). On the other hand, Lopes (1992) did not find that concentration had a negative effect on diversity, even though he was studying an even more concentrated industry than that examined by Peterson and Berger.

Peterson and Berger (1973) measured diversity in two ways. First, they counted the number of different songs that appeared on *Billboard's* top-10 list each year. They argued that this simple number will show diversity. They also analyzed new versus established artists who made the list and found a correlation between diversity and competition in that when competition increased, diversity increased.

Peterson and Berger (1975) concluded that during the early time period of their study—the 1940s and early 1950s, there was significant concentration within the music industry that led to a decided lack of diversity. The similarity in music was attributed to vertically integrated corporations controlling not only the types of music produced but also the methods for marketing and distributing their products. By the mid-1950s, diversity increased significantly with the advent of rock and roll. Radio had become a major marketing tool for records, and independent labels were able to use this medium as effectively as their large competitors. A cycle of concentration and diversity continues to repeat throughout the 1960s and into the early 1970s. The authors suggest that diversity is highest when there is less concentration in the industry and when vertically integrated corporations allow their various divisions to compete like individual companies.

Lopes (1992) performed a similar analysis on a much more dynamic industry. The music industry became more consolidated by the 1990s as Peterson and Berger (1975) had predicted. However, diversity fluctuated throughout the 1970s and 1980s; in fact, diversity was at the same level at the beginning of the period studied (1969) as it was the end (1990). So, while the industry became more concentrated, diversity was not affected by it.

Lopes used the idea of an "open" versus "closed" system to explain the changes in music production. The 1940s and 1950s was dominated by a closed system according to Peterson and Berger (1975). The music charts were dominated by records from a limited number of producers. Under the open system that music companies now use, though they control production and distribution, the companies are made up of multiple record labels rather than one or two. Also, they have agreements with independent labels as well. The open system is beneficial to the health and viability of the music business, because to stay relevant to the consumer it must constantly be finding new artists and genres. This systems works like the movie industry—independent producers create the films, and then they are distributed by the major labels.

Media concentration studies that test the homogenization hypothesis are inconsistent in their findings. As with all the diversity studies evaluated, there is no conclusive evidence that there is a correlation between the variable being studied, in this case media concentration, and changing levels in diversity. While intellectually this would seem to make sense, there is just no empirical support for it.

CONCLUSION

Diversity as a regulative policy is fraught with problems. Key among them is that the type of diversity policymakers want to achieve—content diversity—cannot under ordinary conditions be regulated because of the First Amendment. To compensate for this, the FCC has used outlet diversity and source diversity as proxies. Even the Commission understands that is this less than optimum as is demonstrated by this quote from a speech by Reed Hundt (1996), former FCC chair, "Structural rules promoting outlet and source diversity, however, do not necessarily give us ... program diversity" and "program diversity is more complicated, but perhaps most important." The FCC's inability to successfully create content diversity has led to rampant deregulation of the media industry.

It is not just the inability to regulate diversity that is the problem. Diversity, itself, has issues—primarily that no one can agree on what it is. While we use the term *diversity,* what we really mean is the ability to speak freely. "Diversity of programming has nothing to do with freedom of expression. Diversity in either the *sources* of programming or the *control* of access to the media does have clear relationship to freedom, but this is not what is commonly meant by program diversity" (Le Duc, 1982, p. 46). What we really want when we say diversity is quality programming, whether it is public affairs programs, children's programming, or yes, even entertainment programming. Instead, what regulation has done is support broadcasters over new media options, forced programmers to come up with new economic models to compete in an overly crowded media environment, and perpetuated an economic system of 24-hour-per-day program service based on advertising support, which perforce creates redundancy and inexpensive programming.

The remainder of this book is an in-depth analysis of the financial interest and syndication rules and their impact on the structure and diversity of the television landscape. It attempts to answer the following questions by evaluating diversity in terms of production, distribution, and programming. For instance, does it matter who produces television programming? Does it matter if the networks are producing the programming instead of, or in addition to, the Hollywood studios? Does it matter if there are 3 broadcast networks or 100 cable channels? Does that increase diversity? Does it make any difference who finances the programming, because it is likely that this will have an impact on the creative? Finally, does it matter who owns the alternative program outlets, that is the newer broadcast networks as well as the cable networks? Do these factors affect diversity or is the programming landscape a fait accompli based on the economic and technological makeup of the medium?

2

The Financial Interest and Syndication Rules (1960–1976)

INTRODUCTION TO THE FINANCIAL INTEREST AND SYNDICATION RULES

The financial interest and syndication (fin-syn) rules were a significant piece of television regulation that had a major economic and social impact on the television industry. Instituted in 1970, these regulations were enacted to control the power of the television networks by limiting ownership in programming that they broadcast. Over the years, the rules would be subject to renegotiation and modification until they were finally repealed in 1995. This chapter reviews the history of the creation of the rules. The following chapter outlines the history of the rules' repeal.

Initially, the rules applied to the entire broadcast day but were ultimately limited to programming that aired during the prime-time hours of 8 p.m. to 11 p.m. The rules significantly hampered the networks' ability to be vertically integrated and separated ownership of production from ownership of distribution. This was not the goal of the FCC in implementing these rules. Rather, they were meant to increase the number of companies producing programming for the prime-time hours, thus creating a more competitive marketplace and ultimately leading to an increase in diversity of programming content.

A battle raged for more than a decade between those who opposed the rules (the networks affected by them—ABC, CBS, and NBC), and those who wanted the rules to remain in place (production companies, the Motion Picture Association of America [MPAA] and during the 1980s, even the president of the United States). The television networks ultimately won the battle to own and syndicate the programming they broadcast. They did this by claiming that since the laws had been enacted, there existed increased competition from Fox (which was never subject to these laws) and independent stations, as well as cable and direct broadcast satellite. The networks claimed that these competitors had changed the marketplace and that this diversity of programming outlets meant there was no longer a need to regulate program production on the networks because producers could distribute their programming through a larger number of outlets. Their argument hinged on the idea that increased program channels (outlet diversity) would create more opportunities for producers (source diversity) and, therefore, more choices for viewers (content diversity). What we will see is that the networks were in fact correct in their contention that they should not be regulated to increase diversity. However, it was because structural regulation does not affect program content, not because increased outlets would lead to increased content diversity.

REGULATING BROADCAST TELEVISION—WHY FIN-SYN WAS CREATED

The FCC has no direct jurisdiction over the broadcast networks. They license the individual stations, not the networks. This makes the financial interest and syndication rules particularly interesting. The goals of the rules—diversity and increased competition in television programming—were proposed because there was undue concentration in the industry centralized in the hands of the broadcast networks. The rules specifically limited the networks' ability to own and syndicate programming, something technically the FCC should not be allowed to do. The reasoning behind the rules, however, was to create more and diverse programming on local stations, both those affiliated with a network as well as independent stations, which allowed the FCC to circumvent this issue. The rules were an attempt by the Commission to compensate for the economic advantage the networks had as beneficiaries of spectrum allocation.

The 1960s were a time when the FCC was no longer simply faced with technological issues but with ones of content and access. Access was controlled by the FCC's allocation of the spectrum, which had given preference to broadcasters over others seeking access. New at this time was the *Red Lion* case (discussed in the previous chapter). This landmark case would be instrumental in guiding television policy because it affirmed the idea of spectrum scarcity and supported the Fairness Doctrine, which allowed opposing points of view to be heard over the nation's airwaves.

One group in particular that was trying to be heard throughout the late 1960s and early 1970s was the Democratic Party. As the party out of power, the Democrats had less access to the airwaves than the Republicans did. The president has the right to ask for time from the networks. Other politicians do not. During his presidency, Nixon regularly requested time from the networks for prime-time addresses, particularly to explain his policies about Vietnam. Because 90% of TV audiences would hear an address like that, it was virtually impossible for the Democrats to get out an opposing message without the same kind of access. At first, the Democrats attempted to buy time to respond to Nixon's policies, but CBS turned them down. Because of this rejection, the "FCC consider[ed] a request for a declaratory ruling that would limit the broadcasters' right to deny use of their facility to those seeking access to them, whether by purchase or by requests for free time" ("Freer Public Access," 1970, p. 28). This type of access is similar to that expressed by the Fairness Doctrine. The networks, however, were able to thwart any additional regulation by claiming that additional requirements of the Fairness Doctrine should not include requiring the networks "to sell time to partisans" (p. 29).

CBS was not unsympathetic to the Democrats' plight. Frank Stanton, president of CBS, was aware of Nixon's abundant use of the airwaves and decided to create a show called *The Loyal Opposition*, which would provide the party out of power with access to the national airwaves. In this case, it meant the Democratic Party. The Nixon Administration was vehemently opposed to providing free airtime to the Democratic National Committee (DNC), which would represent the party on air. Nonetheless, the Chairman of the DNC appeared on CBS free of charge:

> The White House promptly had the Republican National Committee (RNC) file a complaint with the FCC demanding Equal Time or the equivalent under the Fairness Doctrine .... The FCC decided that since the DNC had been given free time by the CBS network, the RNC had to be given an equal chance to respond to the DNC .... An appellate court ultimately reversed the FCC's decision granting reply time to the RNC for *The Loyal Opposition* with a condemnation sharply critical of the FCC's reasoning. (Dunham, 1997, pp. 103–105)

The FCC opposed CBS's broadcast because they believed it to be party oriented rather than issue oriented. Even so, the Commission did admit that the president's use of prime time to present his views was unbalanced and noted that "spokesmen for the other side must also be given a reasonable opportunity for expression of their views" (FCC, 1971, p. 32). These issues surrounding access and the Fairness Doctrine demonstrate how difficult this idea of balance is and equally how difficult it was to achieve given the limitations of the medium.

Nixon was also vehemently opposed to the networks in general for what he considered to be their biased reporting of his administration, among other things. During his administration, rules that limited the power of the broadcast networks were created. This was another method for providing access to the airwaves. By limiting the power of the broadcast networks, you thereby give access to others and so increase the diversity of voices on the airwaves. Adopted by the FCC on May 4, 1970 (Amendent of Part 73, 1970, p. 382) and taking effect October 1971, a new regulation called the Prime Time Access Rule (PTAR) was introduced to limit the control of the three networks by lessening the number of hours in prime time that are programmed by the networks. This rule was part of the same set of regulations as the financial interest and syndication rules. It was initiated in part by a request from Westinghouse Broadcasting Company for the FCC to curtail the power of the broadcast networks. Westinghouse, as a station group owner, felt that its ability to program its stations was being limited by the programming the networks provided. They recommended a plan for opening the airwaves for affiliates, which in time became the Prime-Time Access Rule. The rule was this: one hour (7-8 p.m.) was given back to the affiliates in hopes of increasing local programming and giving more power to independent producers.

This would apply only to network-affiliated stations in the top 50 markets. During the prime-time hours (7-11 p.m. on the East Coast) Monday through Saturday, only 3 hours per night could be network programming.[1] By limiting the number of hours that the networks could broadcast, the FCC was hoping this rule would increase diversity in programming by encouraging new producers to enter the marketplace and by increasing locally produced programming.

> Our objective is to provide opportunity—now lacking in television—for the competitive development of alternate sources of television programs so that television licensees can exercise something more than a nominal choice in selecting the programs which they present to the television audiences in their communities.
>
> We believe that substantial benefit to the public interest in television broadcast service will flow from opening up evening time so that producers may have the opportunity to develop their full economic and creative potential under better competitive conditions than are now available to them .... A principal purpose of our prime time access rule is to make available an hour of top-rated evening time for competition among present and potential nonnetwork program sources seeking the custom and favor of broadcasters and advertisers so that the public interest in diverse broadcast service may be served. (Amendment of Part 73, 1970, p. 397)

Thus, while the FCC did not define diversity specifically, it implied that by increasing the number of producers in the market, programming would become more diversified. One other provision of the PTAR prohibited scheduling off-network syndicated programming in this prime-time access period, because a main goal of the rules was to encourage independent television production.

Certain marketplace conditions led to the need for these rules at this time. In the top 50 markets, 153 out of 224 stations, or 68%, were network affiliates. Of all the television stations in the United States at that time, 499 out of 621 were network affiliates; 80% of local stations carried network programming. This highlights the advantages of the networks due to spectrum allocation and demonstrates just how little competition there was to network programming. In fact, there was an independent competitor in only 14 of the top 50 markets. Therefore, the three major broadcast networks among them virtually controlled what the television viewer could watch. The issue of network control of programming becomes most acute when examining the prime-time hours. The FCC found that:

> network affiliates in 1968 carried an average of between 3.3 and 4.7 (depending upon size of market) hours a week of nonnetwork programming between the hours of 7 to 11 p.m. out of the total of 28 hours. Between the hours of 7:30 and 10:30 p.m. the figure is from 1.2 to 1.6 hours ... nonnetwork programming [time periods not programmed by the network] is increasingly composed of off-network programs. A concomitant to this control of access has been the virtual disappearance of high cost, prime time, syndicated programming, the type of programming (other than feature

[1]The time period from 7–8 p.m. came to be known as prime access. It is also known as early fringe.

> motion pictures) which must be most relied upon as competition for network-supplied entertainment programs. (Amendment of Part 73, 1970, p. 385)

This means that network affiliates were presenting less than half an hour per day of nonnetwork programming during the most heavily viewed hours of the day. Moreover, the programming that was filling those time periods was programming that used to be on the networks. It was as if the networks were programming the entire prime-time schedule. What this did was force alternative voices off the air during this time period and made the networks more influential.

While the purpose of the Prime Time Access Rule was to decrease the influence of the networks, in reality the networks were strengthened—both financially, through increased advertising rates, and influentially, through the decreased supply of prime-time airtime. *The Economics of Prime-Time Access*, an economic report prepared for the FCC, outlines the many ways in which these rules worked in favor, rather than opposition, of network objectives:

> 1. Overall network power has been strengthened, not weakened, by the prime-time access rule. Network originated programming has become scarce, resulting in greater advertiser demand for commercial minutes within prime-time programming, and ratings are generally better for such programs. It has, in addition, strengthened the network's bargaining position with program producers, who are now required to compete for fewer prime-time hours …
> 3. The rule, by limiting the number of network supplied entertainment hours to three (3) per night, has relieved the networks of making difficult programming decisions for what has been, traditionally, the most difficult programming slot, i.e., 7:30 to 8:00 p.m …
> 4. The decrease in prime-time programming hours has tended to force advertising prices upward …. (Pearce, 1973, pp. 2–3)

The report further demonstrates that the rules benefit the networks through their owned and operated stations. These stations, like other affected stations in the top 50 markets, will have the extra advertising time (up to 5 minutes plus adjacencies, i.e., commercials next to network programming) to sell in the fringe time period. As well, it is unlikely that a syndicated program will be successful without being carried on the owned and operated stations. Therefore, these stations, and through them the networks, have significant negotiating power when it comes to dealing with producers of this programming.

Stations not owned and operated by the networks were not necessarily as pleased about PTAR as larger market stations. In smaller markets, it is often more difficult to sell advertising time, so in some cases it would be financially preferable for a station to have network programming during this time period. Independent stations, on the other hand, were strong supporters of the rule, which strengthened their position versus network-affiliated stations because it put the affiliates and the independent stations on more equal footing in terms of programming during that time period. The FCC economic report stresses, however, that because the affiliates would no longer have network advertising filling this time period, competition for national spot dollars would likely increase. This was thought to perhaps work against the independents, but turned out to be unfounded.[2]

The networks were not the only entity that the Prime-Time Access Rule affected positively. Hollywood producers were beneficiaries, which after all was the point of the rules. The FCC hoped that more producers would lead to more diversity in programming. Prices for off-network syndicated programming increased substantially as less prime-time programming was being produced. Producers may have lost some money by not having as many shows to produce for prime time, but that loss was offset by the exceptionally high profits achieved through selling their off-network shows into syndication. Surprising, given this scenario, the so-called Hollywood majors—MCA-Universal, Warner Brothers, Columbia-Screen Gems, 20th Century Fox, Paramount, and MGM—were opposed to the rule. Although the producers were all for lessening network control, they wanted this achieved by keeping the networks out of the production business, not by limiting network program hours. Syndication made up for part of the loss in prime-time program production, but it did not do so completely; therefore, Hollywood producers lost revenue because of the reduction in original prime-time programming.

The large Hollywood producers were also not interested in producing shows for the prime-access period, though they would not have said so openly. These large producers would have to find a means of producing shows more cheaply for this time period, because licensing fees for these programs were less than fees paid for prime time. Also, multiple copies of programs had to be distributed to stations around the country, adding significant expenditure to production costs. Most Hollywood producers did not want to lower production quality (producing on tape rather than film) to create shows for first-run syndication. They wanted to produce top-of-the-line programming—not taped game shows. These producers were not alone. The majority of small independent producers (85%) were not in favor of PTAR (Pearce, 1973, p. 6). Producers working on tape, which is less expensive, tended to support the rule whereas those working on the more expensive medium of film would have liked to see this rule repealed.

PTAR seems to have had a mixed effect in terms of diversity. Diversity of ownership of programming in the access period increased, but this was deceptive, as many of these producers had been creating shows for other dayparts, such as daytime and prime. An early complaint was a shift away from quality prime-time programming to taped game and variety shows. On the positive side, the rule did generate an increase in foreign programming. There was also some increase in locally produced and originated public affairs—one of the key hopes behind the PTAR. However, this was limited to a few major markets and usually stations that already had a commitment to public affairs programming. These types of programs were not expected to air in smaller markets because production costs were prohibitive.[3] Diversity was

---

[2]Both network and national spot advertising decreased from 1970 to 1971, rebounded in 1972, and have continued to grow steadily ever since (Television Bureau of Advertising: Trends in Advertising Volume).

[3]Several things made these shows less attractive for a station vis-à-vis a game show: more costly to produce, more difficult to sell advertising time, and because these shows are of a topical nature, they cannot be repeated.

negatively affected in that fewer public affairs programs or documentaries were scheduled during prime-time hours.

In summary, when the Prime Time Access Rule was initially instituted, some parties in the entertainment industry were winners and some were losers. This, however, did not determine whether certain factions would be for or against this rule. For instance, the broadcast networks, which turned out to be the surprising beneficiaries of the rule, did not all agree that the rule should exist. CBS, one of the major networks the rule affected, was against it, while ABC wanted to keep the rule. NBC, on the other hand, was neutral. Independent stations saw the rule as a means of improving ratings and, therefore, revenues and wanted the rule to remain in place. The rule most benefited Hollywood producers from an economic point of view, because they received higher prices for off-network syndicated programming. These larger studios did not like the rule because it led to a decrease in the number of quality, that is, high cost, network programs that needed to be produced. It was the smaller producers and importers of foreign series who most wanted the rule to remain in effect.

The conclusion of this economic report was that PTAR was not the most effective method for reducing network dominance. Instead, Pearce, the author of the report evaluating the PTAR, suggested that the networks' strength came from their dominance on several levels and that changing one or more features of the network business would have a greater effect in achieving the Commission's goals. There were three areas that were highlighted in the report. First, the networks were powerful in their ownership of stations, the so-called owned and operated stations. Each network owned five stations, which reached almost 25% of U.S. television households. All had stations in New York, Los Angeles, and Chicago—the top three television markets—as well as owning two other stations within the top 12 markets. Second, the networks were the sole means of distributing programs nationally. Finally, the networks were also producers of television programming. Thus, the networks were vertically integrated companies with significant control over production and distribution of programming as well as the ability to control access to the national airwaves by others. The way to increase access to the airwaves was to affect change at one or more of these points in the networks' structure.

The Financial Interest and Syndication Rules

The FCC attempted to break up the networks' stronghold on national program distribution through rules that were created simultaneously with PTAR. According to the FCC's Fiscal 1971 annual report, "Companion regulations include prohibition against network involvement in syndication businesses and network acquisition of financial interests in the subsequent rights to network programs. The rule was intended to increase program sources in prime time beyond the three major networks" (p. 26). These "companion regulations" were the financial interest and syndication rules.[4]

[4]The Justice Department also brought antitrust suits against the three networks to reduce their dominance in national programming. These suits are outlined later in the text.

The financial interest and syndication rules, also known as the fin-syn rules or FISR, were enacted in 1970 by the Federal Communications Commission and took effect September 1, 1971. The 1970 rules[5] forbade a television network to:

> (i) sell, license, or distribute television programs to television station licensees within the United States for nonnetwork television exhibition or otherwise engage in the business commonly known as 'syndication' within the United States; or sell, license, or distribute television programs of which it is not the sole producer for exhibition outside the United States; or reserve any option or right to share in revenues or profits in connection with such domestic and/or foreign sale, license, or distribution; or
> (ii) acquire any financial or proprietary right or interest in the exhibition, distribution, or other commercial use of any television program produced wholly or in part by a person other than such television network, except the license or other exclusive right to network exhibition within the United States and on foreign stations regularly included within such television network .... (Amendment of Part 73, 1970, p. 402)

Thus, the networks could no longer obtain a financial interest in programming that would appear on their air. As well, the networks could not participate in the syndication business, that is, the selling of television programs to stations in individual markets. The networks were not precluded from syndicating into foreign markets programming of which it was the "sole producer."

Thus did the Commission curb the power of the three broadcast networks, which were perceived at the time as having undue influence over programming. The term "network dominance" became the rallying cry against the monopolistic control the networks demonstrated. The Commission feared that the networks were exercising monopsony power over program producers. Monopsony power is when the buyer(s) in a market have an advantage over the sellers and use that power to receive advantageous terms from sellers. In the case of the broadcast networks, they were using their gatekeeping powers as the only national means of program distribution to extort favorable terms from program suppliers. Program suppliers for the most part could only sell to the broadcast networks. Because the broadcast networks were the only game in town, these networks could ask for what they wanted in terms of acquiring programming, and by and large they got it.

Additionally, the Commission was concerned that the networks were exercising monopoly power against what little competition existed in the form of independent stations. In addition to getting favorable terms from producers, the networks were believed to have denied independent stations the opportunity to purchase popular network programming by refusing to syndicate some network programming that they felt would threaten network popularity. *Hawaii 5-0* is a good example of such a situation. Leonard Freeman owned *Hawaii 5-0* but had to sell it to CBS, that is, give up ownership of the program to get it on the air. It ran on CBS for 13 years, and the network never syndicated it during its network run. The rules were meant to inhibit

[5]The fin-syn rules were revised several times. The 1970 rules are the first.

the networks' ability to continue with this practice, which came to be known as warehousing.

Another goal of the FCC was to open the programming market to more independent producers. Because under the rules the networks were not allowed to own programming produced by others that appeared on their air, and because they could not own syndicated programming, it was believed that more producers would enter the marketplace. This would be so as the producers would have increased access to the airwaves as well as the possibility to achieve economic stability. Finally, the rules were meant to benefit viewers by providing variety in programming. By increasing the number of producers, the Commission believed the public interest would be served because there would be a concomitant diversity in programming.

Though the rules are always talked about as a singular entity, there are in fact two different rules. First, the *financial interest rule* barred the networks from obtaining a financial interest in any program that they did not produce. A financial interest could be anything from subsequent movie or book rights to merchandising rights to rights to distribute the programming. This rule meant that the networks could not ask producers for a financial interest in their programming to put the show on the prime-time schedule. At the time this was common practice. What the networks could do was purchase a licensing agreement to air programming that they did not produce. The rule eliminated the inducement to select programming for the prime-time schedule based on the network having a financial stake in that program.

Separately, the *syndication rule* prohibited the networks from engaging in the distribution of syndicated programming in the United States. The networks could continue to syndicate programming that they produced into foreign markets. This affected the networks in two ways. First, syndication of programming was a lucrative revenue stream that would no longer be available to the networks. Though the networks did not produce a lot of programming prior to the rules, when they could no longer syndicate programming any incentive to produce programming is eliminated. Second, the networks could no longer keep off the market those programs they did not want their competitors to have, the previously mentioned "warehousing." As for producers, the syndication market would become an alternative to network distribution, and new producers would be able to get programming onto the network schedule because network-produced or -financed programming will no longer dominate.

HISTORY OF THE FINANCIAL INTEREST AND SYNDICATION RULES

The financial interest and syndication rules, or some form of regulation that would restrict broadcasters' ownership of the programming they aired, had been an issue before the FCC since the late 1950s. The rules emerged from a FCC investigation begun with an *Order for Investigatory Proceeding* in February 1959. By November of that year, a supplementary order to that proceeding looked into the practices and procedures of the television industry "to determine the policies and practices pursued by networks and others in the acquisition, ownership, production, distribution, selection, sale and licensing of programs for television exhibition, and the reasons and necessity in the public interest for said policies and practices" (quoted in *Mt. Mansfield Television, Inc. v. FCC*, 1971). This order paid particular attention to the economics of the industry, asking whether it was necessary for networks to own programming to remain commercially viable. It also asked how production and procurement of programming may affect the public interest in television programming and "to what extent program choices by network corporations are influenced by their acquisition of financial and proprietary interest and subsidiary rights in such programs" (Lee, 1995, p. 15). However, here as later in the history of the rules, the Commission stressed that it was more interested in diversity than in the distribution of profits. This is outlined in the *Second Interim Report of the Office of Network Study* that was quoted in the 1982 *Notice of Proposed Rulemaking*:

> The dominant position which the networks have achieved in their effective control of the program market has serious consequences for the public interest in the wider and more effective use of television channels and the ability of licensees to serve the public interest in community broadcast service. The public interest in a nationwide competitive television industry requires as broad a base as is feasible from which programs necessary to enable licensees to serve the public interest in television service may be selected. In a healthy, competitive television industry, that base should comprise as many diverse and antagonistic sources as possible, so that the spiritual, cultural, and economic aspirations generated in our society may have the opportunity, in competition with each other, to reach the public and to vie for acceptance in a free market for ideas. Present policies and practices in network television program procurement, particularly in the entertainment area, are not adequate for these purposes. Hence, they require modification so that they may conform to the public interest in network television broadcasting. (Amendment of 47 CFR, 1982, Paragraph 20)

Because the FCC was in agreement that some action should be taken, the Commission issued a *Notice of Proposed Rulemaking (NPRM)*, an initial step in the regulatory process. This *Notice* makes public the intention of the FCC to create a new regulation. The NPRM for fin-syn was filed in March 1965 and outlined the FCC findings that the networks pursue practices which restrict competition, particularly to independent producers, and that the networks control the program supply in both the network and syndicated markets:

> The information and data before the Commission appear to establish that network corporations, with the acquiescence of their affiliates, have adopted and pursued practices in television program procurement and production through which they have progressively achieved virtual domination of television program markets. The result is that the three national network corporations not only in large measure determine what the American people may see and hear during the hours when most Americans view television but also would appear to have unnecessarily and unduly foreclosed access to other sources of programs. (Amendment of Part 73, 1965, p. 2147)

Based on these findings, the Commission proposed a set of rules that would increase opportunities for producers to have their programming presented on network television as well as increase the growth of alternative program sources for both network and nonnetwork outlets. A version of these rules would ultimately become fin-syn.

Several changes in the television industry helped bring the FCC to the conclusion that the networks had achieved a dominant position in the industry. The most significant of these issues was that networks were acquiring programming from producers and then selling time (usually 30- or 60-second commercials) to individual advertisers. Though not a new concept, the extent of its practice had expanded exponentially. Prior to this time, independent producers could deal directly with advertisers who would sponsor an entire program. With this package of program and advertising, the advertiser or their agency would then go to the network and purchase a time slot within which to air the program:

> Normally, television network time is sold only to advertisers. The total potential market available to independent producers of programs for *network* exhibition is restricted to network corporations and network advertisers.
>
> Formerly, many network television programs were developed and brought to the market in "pilot" form by independent producers at their own account and risk. A reasonably broad market was then available to such producers. It was composed of a large number of sponsors and potential sponsors of network programming in addition to the three network corporations. The first-run exhibition rights to many such programs were sold by independent producers directly to sponsors and, subject to network approval as to scheduling, suitability, good taste, decency, etc., were exhibited as network offerings .... Up until six or seven years ago, a third to a half of network evening schedules consisted of such independent programs. (Amendment of Part 73, 1965, p. 2150)

Instead of selling programming to a plethora of advertisers and the three networks, at this time the producers could negotiate only with the networks. The marketplace for television programming, the number of potential purchasers, had thus been significantly reduced. Of note, however, are the limitations on the possibility of diversity within either of these frameworks. The choice is between many advertisers, a group not necessarily known for risky programming, and three networks, a finite group looking to create mass audiences. How truly diverse can programming be within the confines of these choices? Even so, given the FCC's argument, more was better than three, and the elimination of advertisers from the marketplace was an issue.

There is conflicting evidence as to why advertisers no longer sponsored an entire program. It has been attributed to increased production costs, which had become prohibitive partly because of the change from black and white to color as well as less production of live programming in favor of filmed programming, which could then be sold into syndication. Less advertiser-sponsored programming has also been ascribed to changes in marketing techniques, specifically that advertising across many shows was more effective than sponsoring a single program. Mass advertisers needed to reach large audiences with multiple messages, either the same commercial more than once or several products by the same advertiser, such as in the case of a large company such as Kraft, which produces multiple brands. Therefore, it no longer made sense for the advertiser to bring a single show to the network. Finally, as television became a truly mass medium, some advertisers realized that this was not the best method for achieving its marketing goals. This was particularly true of nonconsumer products such as U.S. Steel, which had been an early sponsor of television programming. Whatever the reason for the decrease in single- or dual-advertiser sponsorship of programming, the result was that the percent of all network entertainment programming aired from 6 to 11 p.m. provided by a single advertiser dropped from 39.5% to 10.3% between 1957 and 1964. Over the same time period, programming produced by a packager (an outside producer) and licensed to a network increased from 42.1% to 80.4% (Amendment of Part 73, 1965, p. 2168). Ultimately that number would drop even further, so that by 1968 advertisers supplied directly less than 4% of prime-time programming (Amendment of Part 73, 1970, p. 390). This situation created the scenario whereby the three networks became the exclusive purchasers of prime-time programming, the funnel through which all network programming would be evaluated.

While the networks increased their control, the independent producers had less control. Not only were the producers trying to sell to three companies rather than numerous ones, but they were also selling to broadcasters who required additional rights from producers to get their show on the air. Previously, sponsors had rarely shared in syndication or other subsidiary rights. Independent producers retained these rights, which contributed to their ability to be economically stable. It was necessary for them to retain these rights, because few made back their money from the initial network airing, but rather they depended on syndication and foreign sales to generate a profit.[6] Thus, there were economic advantages to producers dealing with sponsors rather than broadcasters as well as the ability to be independent.

By licensing programming to the networks, producers gave up certain rights to compensate the networks for taking on the risk of airing the show and having to sell the advertising to support it. While airing any new show is risky (no one has yet determined how to pick a hit), there was minimal risk in generating advertising sales because at the time it was a seller's market. Either way, the network demanded certain compensation from producers for this risk sharing. These compensations are outlined in the FCC's 1965 *Notice of Proposed Rule Making*:

> in the initial bargaining with producers [networks] seek and frequently obtain separately or in combination the right to share (often 50%) in the profits, if any, from the network run; the right to share in profits from subsequent network runs; the right to distribute the programs or series in domestic syndication and in foreign markets; the right to share (usually 50% for a term of years or in perpetuity) in the profits from domestic and foreign syndication sales; exploitation rights and share of profits in merchandising; and the right to share in other non-broadcast interests (e.g., motion

---

[6]Producers do not usually make money in the initial network airing of a show. In fact, they usually lose money. It is not until a show is sold into syndication that a producer begins to generate a profit.

> pictures, books, magazine stories and articles, phonograph records and plays derived from the programs). (Amendment of Part 73, 1965, p. 2151)

Producers' willingness to give up these rights might decide whether their program gets on the air. While the networks denied this, the FCC felt "it must be recognized that financial participation by network corporations in any proposed program may well be the decisive factor in its selection for network exhibition" (p. 2157). Networks not only controlled the financial aspects of programming, but also the creative product itself. Network programming was based on formulas that depended on certain types of characters, themes, and a limited range of subject matter that satisfied tested commercial patterns (Herskovitz, 1997, p. 187). These formulas were necessary to attract a large audience, which would appeal to advertisers. Thus producers were not only limited in their ability to be economically independent, they were restricted in their ability to make creative choices which had not been the case when dealing with advertisers, at least not to the same extent.

Remember, though, it is not the FCC's concern who does or does not make money in the overall television marketplace. What is of interest to the Commission is serving the "public interest" and specifically in this instance, making sure of an affiliate's ability to "serve the needs and interests of their communities" (Amendment of Part 73, 1965, p. 2148). As part of a station's license agreement with the Commission, the station is required to provide programming that meet the needs of the community in which it serves. The networks have no such requirement, and the FCC has no jurisdiction to regulate the networks, per se, though they can regulate the agreements between networks and their affiliates as discussed previously. As networks provided more and more programming to affiliates, which by definition would be nationally oriented, these stations had less opportunity for local programming that might serve the specific needs of its market. As the FCC claimed, "The ability of licensees to obtain programs necessary to serve the needs and interests of their communities depends in large measure on the schedules offered them by the network corporations" (p. 2149). The affiliate, therefore, was dependent on the judgment of the network programmers to provide programming that would fulfill its obligation to the community in which it broadcast. From the FCC's view, it was unlikely that network programming would be equally suitable to the needs of all 200+ markets. After all, can programming that serves the needs of New York City be as relevant to the needs of the citizens of Des Moines or Dallas?

The review of this material led the FCC to reach the following conclusions about what had occurred as a result of network program practices. These results had been

> (a) to concentrate economic, proprietary and creative control of program production and procurement in network corporations; (b) to concentrate residual rights to television programs in network corporations; and (c) progressively to limit the market available to independent producers of network programs for all practical purposes to the three network corporations and, hence, to restrict the profitability of the operations of independent program producers. (p. 2154)

Thus, the FCC was concerned about network concentration of power on three levels. There was the concentration of economic and creative power at the network level. This concentration led to limiting the prime-time market available to independent producers. At the same time the networks "devised and perfected program production and procurement practices" (p. 2154), they were also increasing their syndication activities in both the domestic and foreign arenas. The networks, therefore, were not only controlling their own airwaves: they were also affecting the programming that appeared on alternative outlets.

Local stations depend on syndicated programming to fill their schedules. If the station is independent, the majority of the day is filled with syndicated programming (what is not syndicated programming is usually filled with local news and public affairs programming). Network affiliates depend on syndicated programming to fill limited time periods not occupied with network programming. If the networks programmed their schedules and were a significant source of syndicated programming, for affiliates it would be as if the network were programming the entire broadcast day. This would be particularly true for the network owned and operated stations (O&Os), which would have a vested interest in supporting the network.

Some statistics support that the networks' entry into the syndication business was growing rapidly. For the three networks combined, the percentage of hours in which they had a syndication interest in a show they aired increased from 45.5% to 72.2% from 1957 to 1964. Over the same time period, the number of mass-appeal series released on a first-run syndication basis dropped from 20 to 1. These numbers suggest that off-network syndication, much of it controlled by the networks, was taking over the market and forcing first-run syndication virtually out of business. Though syndication only made up a small percentage of the networks' overall revenues (less than 1%), there was potential for significant growth in this area particularly in overseas markets.[7]

It makes sense that the off-network syndication market would begin to expand at this time. Wide use of television did not occur until the mid-1950s. During this time period, more network programs were being produced. Prior to the 1960s, there would not have been a "catalog" of off-network programming available simply because the industry was young. By the mid-1960s, programming no longer appearing on the networks would have become more abundant simply as a function of time. Therefore, it was possible for an off-network syndication market to development. Equivalent half-hours of off-network programming first introduced into domestic syndication grew from 484 in 1957 to 2,312 in 1968. Total new off-network series introduced into the syndication market over that time period was 277 (Little, 1969, p. 70).

---

[7]The networks provided syndication figures to the FCC. The Commission had serious doubts about their accuracy, as the networks appeared to have provided the FCC with one number and their shareholders with another. This would be a continuing theme throughout the history of the rules.

In summary, there were several changes in the television marketplace that led the Commission to propose a new rule. First, programming was becoming increasingly concentrated in the hands of the three broadcast networks. This was "inherently undesirable because diversification of economic interests and power in this area was a cardinal principle of the public interest standard found in the Communications Act" (Amendment of 47 CFR, 1983, p. 1024). This concentration of power came about because of the growing syndication market, the change in the economics of program production, and the reduction of single-sponsor television programs. Second, the networks' control over prime-time and syndicated programming precluded others, specifically independent producers and syndicators, from having access to the market.

The limit on the number of producers was of interest to the FCC for two reasons. First, the Commission believed more producers meant more diverse programming and second, because it was felt that the success of independent producers would have a significant impact on the success or failure of the burgeoning UHF stations, most of which were independent stations. Finally, the networks' increasing financial participation in the programming they aired was seen as a conflict of interest. Economic concerns have historically guided network programming decisions; however, as networks continued to increase their ownership in prime time, it was believed that economic concerns would take precedence in determining programming choices.

For all these reasons, the Commission sought to increase competition—both creative and economic—in program production and procurement. Therefore, in 1965 the FCC proposed the financial interest and syndication rules. These proposed rules, not the final ones, were the FCC's suggestion for achieving the intended goals of expanding the competitive market of television programming by:

> (1) eliminating network corporations from the syndication business within the United States and from the sale, licensing and distribution of independently produced television programs in foreign markets; (2) prohibiting network corporations from acquiring distribution or profit-sharing rights in syndication and foreign sales of independently produced television programs; and (3) limiting economic and proprietary control by networks corporations of the programs included in their schedules in desirable evening network time. (Amendment of Part 73, 1965, p. 2158)

The first part of the rule eliminated the ability of the networks from syndicating programming produced by independent producers. The second part expanded the independent programming market. By taking networks out of the profit-sharing business, producers other than the networks would have an equal footing when trying to get onto the network schedule. This proposed rule did not preclude the networks from producing their own programming. What it did do was limit the amount of this type of programming during the evening hours to no more than 50%, or 14 hours, whichever was greater. (This rule became known as the 50/50 rule.) This limitation did not include news programming, whether special events or sustaining programs and would allow half of the prime time schedule to be unaffected by whether the network had a financial interest in a program. In response to the rulemaking, comments were received from the three networks and their affiliates as well as industry, public groups, and individuals.

In September 1968, the FCC issued an *Order for Oral Argument and to Invite Further Comment*, which reiterated the proposal in the rulemaking—restrict financial interest in prime-time programming, prohibit syndication by the networks, and require the networks to divest themselves of their present syndication and financial interests. The networks responded to the order and, not surprising, they opposed the restriction of their businesses. The networks responded with a report by Arthur D. Little, Inc. outlining network financial information and industry practices, which were primarily in response to the Westinghouse proposal. This almost 200-page report, consisting almost exclusively of charts, attempted to show that the networks did not monopolize the syndication or the prime-time programming market. This was April 1969.

The next significant event in this history was the appointment in September 1969 by then President Nixon of two new members to the FCC.[8] Nixon's appointees were approved in October of that year. These appointees included Robert Wells and Dean Burch, who would act as the Chairman of the FCC. Dean Burch was a lawyer, a former Republican National Committee chair and manager of Barry Goldwater's presidential campaign. He was young, 41, and a committed Republican. He would chair the Commission until 1974. Robert Wells, also a Republican, was an officer and minority stockholder in television stations. These new members did not change the balance of the FCC in terms of political affiliation. Republicans replaced Republicans. The makeup of the Commission remained at three Republicans and four Democrats ("Nixon ready," 1969, p. 21). However, Burch would come to be a henchman for the wishes of the president throughout his tenure. (This will be discussed more fully later in this chapter.)

The *Final Report and Order* on the financial interest and syndication rules occurred on May 4, 1970, and was based on the concerns the FCC had discovered coming out of the 1965 *Notice*. The Commission had determined that "the public interest requires limitation on network control and an increase in the opportunity for development of truly independent sources of prime time programming" (Amendment of Part 73, 1970, p. 394). In this *Report and Order*, the FCC did not adopt the 50/50 rule, but did institute the Prime-Time Access Rule.

In addition to adopting the Prime-Time Access Rule, the FCC also adopted the syndication rule, which was the same as it was in the original proposal. As such it was "designed to eliminate the networks from distribution and profit sharing in domestic syndication and to restrict their activities in foreign markets to distribution of programs of which they are the sole producers" (Amendment of Part 73, 1970, p. 397). The FCC also adopted the financial interest rule. According to this rule, the FCC prohibits

[8]The seven (it has since been changed to five) FCC members are appointed by the president and must be confirmed by Congress. The president determines the chair of the Commission.

networks from acquiring subsidiary program rights and profit shares, as little would be accomplished in expanding competitive opportunity in television program production if we were to exclude networks from active participation in the syndication market and then permit them to act as brokers in acquiring syndication rights and interests and reselling them to those actively engaged in syndication. We also believe that the prohibition of network domestic syndication of their own programs will serve a salutary purpose in making for fairer competition. (Amendment of Part 73, 1970, p. 398)

One aspect of the financial interest rule also considered the FCC's concern about warehousing of programming. By controlling programming, the networks could decide when to put programming into the market and when to withhold it. Therefore, the rule contained a provision such that "if the network does not make timely use of the program the producer or other person from whom the right or license was acquired may reacquire it on his timely offer reasonably to compensate the network" (Amendment of Part 73, 1970, p. 399). These two rules—the financial interest rule and the syndication rule—work in concert. First, the rules do not allow the networks to have a financial stake in programming, so the temptation to show favoritism to one's own programming is eliminated, which opens up the prime-time programming marketplace. Second, the rules get the networks out of the domestic syndication business altogether—prohibiting them from syndicating programming either that they produce themselves or could acquire elsewhere. This opens up the nonnetwork program market, because the networks could not force programming into the marketplace. This was something that was readily possible given the networks' advantage over other syndicators, that is ready access to a system of television stations, their owned and operated and stations, as well as their affiliates, on whom they could force programming.

As it relates specifically to the financial interest and syndication rules (as opposed to the PTAR), the *Report and Order* reiterated many of the concerns of the *Notice of Proposed Rulemaking*. Notably, the FCC was concerned with the networks' financial interest in procured programming, especially programming purchased from the major motion picture studios.[9] While the networks claimed at this time, and throughout the life of this regulation, that the "majors" were large corporations with the ability to negotiate favorable terms for themselves, the information before the FCC did not bear this out, at least not at this time.

In 1964 these eight companies sold 27 series to the networks which provided some developmental financing for 17 such series (63 percent). The networks acquired shares in the producers' profit derived from the first network run in all 27 such series (100 percent); networks obtained domestic syndication distribution rights in four series (14.8 percent), and shares in profits from domestic syndication in 23 series (85.2 percent). Perhaps more significant are the figures which show that for the six seasons (1959–64) these majors sold 152 series to networks which provided some developmental financing in 70 (46.1 percent) of the cases, but obtained first-run profit shares in 146 (96.1 percent) of these series, domestic distribution in 13 (8.5 percent), domes-

[9]The eight majors were MGM, Paramount, Screen Gems (a subsidiary of Columbia Pictures), 20th Century Fox, United Artists, Universal Pictures, Disney, and Warner Brothers.

tic profit share in 118 (77.6 percent), foreign distribution in 19 or 12.5 percent and foreign profit shares in 111 (73 percent). (Amendment of Part 73, 1970, p. 388)

There are several interesting things to note about these statistics. First, there is no one-to-one correlation between a network providing developmental financing and having a subsequent financial interest in a program. The networks provided developmental funding in 63% of the cases but acquired shares in the producers' profit in 100% of the cases. Second, from these numbers there is no evidence of the major studios having any type of upper hand in bargaining with the networks. The networks were able to acquire financial interests, including syndication rights, from producers at a very significant level, upwards of 80%. Whether the major studios wanted to do this or not, cannot be determined from these numbers. The producers were as likely to be strong-armed to give away their syndication rights as they were willing to give up these rights to shift risk to the networks. Finally, it should be noted that the area of greatest financial opportunity is in profit sharing of domestic syndication. Most programs do not make a profit during their first network run, so that figure carries little significance. Moreover, domestic distribution, where the company actually takes on the responsibility of distributing the program to individual stations but does not necessarily have a share in the profit from the syndication, is usually done for a flat fee. In fact, the majors had their own syndication arms, and it would not make sense for someone else to distribute shows for them. This is why the percentage for network interest in domestic distribution was so low. The most upside profit potential was in profit sharing of the syndication. This is where the networks had an interest in almost 78% of the programs. Table 2.1 dramatically demonstrates the difference in fees related to syndication by showing revenue made by the networks from programs that they have licensed from an outside company.

TABLE 2.1

Money Generated for the Networks From Syndication of Packager-Licensed Programs

	Distribution	*Profit Share*	*Total*
1960	328,000	566,000	894,000
1964	894,000	4,189,000	5,083,000
1967	2,627,000	3,639,000	6,266,000

Note. Adapted from A. D. Little (1969). Television Program Production, Procurement, Distribution and Scheduling, pp. 68–69.[10] Reprinted with permission.

[10]I can only speculate as to the swings in this chart's numbers. Between 1960 and 1964, both network- and advertiser-produced programming decreased while the percent of packager-licensed programs increased. This would, in part, explain the increase in money from syndication of these programs. The 1967 figures are harder to explain. The increase in the distribution figure may be due to off-network half-hours (not series) almost doubling. The networks may have been charging higher fees for distribution because of this increase.

It is clear to see from these numbers that the majority of money generated from syndication is derived from profit sharing and not from distribution itself. These differences are important to bear in mind. Often the networks would say they did not syndicate the shows that appeared on their air, when what they meant was that they were not responsible for distribution of the show but might in fact have an interest in the profit sharing of that program.

Though these numbers show the networks making money from syndication, it is not a significant part of their profits. However, these numbers are self-reported and may or may not reflect what was reality at the time,[11] which brings up something interesting. The FCC sorely depends on the organizations that it oversees to provide the information on which it bases its regulatory decisions. The networks provide one set of numbers and the producers present another. Another common problem that regulatory agencies face is the voluminous amount of information placed before them upon which they must make their decisions. It becomes clear throughout the history of the financial interest and syndication rules that this is one of the most information-intense rulemaking processes that the FCC will ever decide. This can be attributed to the voluminous amount of information from both sides, much of it contradictory. Not only do both sides contradict each other, but the FCC also finds the networks often contradict themselves. The example that appears most often in criticism of the networks is that they cry "wolf" to the FCC and then tell the financial markets that profits couldn't be better. The inconsistency between the two sides contributed to the continued contentiousness of this issue.

The 1970 *Report and Order* reflected additional concerns of the FCC as it related to the program marketplace. One was the increase in the number of off-network syndicated programs that were being scheduled during nonnetwork hours and the fact that much of this was being sold by the networks themselves. This was because the three networks accounted for almost 25% of syndication sales, making them among the leaders in the business. This increase in off-network programming was eliminating the first-run syndication market. The airing of first-run syndicated programming in prime time was, the FCC felt, crucial to the nascent independent UHF stations, and thus crucial to diversity. Another concern was the networks' ability to control the content and creative aspects of programming in which they had a licensing agreement.

Third, the change in the advertising marketplace that had been a large part of the 1965 *NPRM* was still an issue in the final analysis. By 1970, 90% of advertising was sold as commercial spots, which were increasingly 30-second, rather than one-minute, commercials. More and more individual advertisers were replacing single and dual sponsorship of programming. As mentioned previously, fewer and fewer advertisers were buying programming and bringing it to the networks. Rather the networks were becoming the only buyers of prime-time programming:

> The overall result is that, save for about 6 or 7 percent of their schedules which were the result of direct dealing between the independent producers and sponsors, networks accepted virtually no entertainment program for network exhibition in a 5-year

[11]I will demonstrate in the 1990s when the networks do just this—plead poverty to the FCC but tell Paine Webber that the network business is stronger than ever.

> period in which they did not have financial interests in syndication and other subsequent use. (Amendment of Part 73, 1970, p. 393)

Finally, and certainly the pressing issue as it relates to the rules is that "a direct relationship appears to exist between new programs chosen for network schedules and network acquisition of subsidiary rights and interests" (Amendment of Part 73, 1970, p. 393). This was based on the statistics stated above that outlined the extent of the networks' interests in the programming, which appeared on their air.

The 1970 *Report and Order* affirmed the financial interest and syndication rules. The intent behind the regulations was twofold: "to lessen the bargaining power of the networks, and to remove the possibility that acquisition of subsidiary financial and syndication rights would become a prerequisite to network exhibition" (Amendment of 47 CFR, 1983, p. 1025). By lessening the power of the networks, the FCC hoped to create an opportunity for alternative program production and thus enable licensees (the focus of the FCC's attention) to have more control over what appeared on their air. The Prime-Time Access Rule would also open one hour of top-rated airtime to nonnetwork programming.

The networks petitioned the court attacking the rules (including PTAR) as violating the First Amendment by restricting the networks' ability to select programs to broadcast and as an example of the FCC overstepping their authority by regulating network activities. In *Mt. Mansfield Television, Inc. v. FCC* (1971), the Court of Appeals for the Second Circuit upheld the rules as "reasonable," claiming that they worked to promote diversity which is a fundamental precept of the First Amendment. In addition, as in *Red Lion*, the court found that placing certain restrictions on broadcasters was not a violation of the First Amendment because of the particular nature of the medium. "Technological factors in the broadcast industry make it impossible for all who wish to be broadcasters to do so, even when they have the means to make the substantial capital investment that is necessary in most cases" (*Mt. Mansfield v. FCC*, 1971). Given its findings, the court determined

> that the FCC was reasonable in its 1970 findings that: (1) both the financial interest and syndication rules were necessary to restore to the independent producer those rights which they uniformly were forced to bargain away due to network control of the airwaves, and (2) the financial interest rule was essential to effectuate the syndication rule since only together could these rules preclude networks from getting an interest and thus controlling the product. (Kintzer, 1984, p. 525)

With the *Mansfield* case resolved in 1971, the financial interest and syndication rules were finally official after 12 years.

NETWORK CONSENT DECREES

The FCC was not the only government body concerned with the stronghold the networks had over television programming. The United States Department of Justice filed antitrust suits against the networks in April 1972 after several years of having investigated the networks. They had found that

> (a) ownership and control of television entertainment programs broadcast during prime evening hours were concentrated among the three networks;
> (b) competition in the production, distribution, and sale of television entertainment programs, including feature films, has been unreasonably restrained;
> (c) competition in the sale of television entertainment programs to the three networks by outside suppliers has been unreasonably restrained; and,
> (d) the viewing public has been deprived of the benefits of free and open competition in the broadcasting of television entertainment programs. (FCC Notice of Proposed Rulemaking, 1982, paragraph 7)

In *United States v. National Broadcasting Co.*, the government specifically accused the National Broadcasting Company (NBC) of restraint of trade as it related to purchasing programs from independent producers and of using its network power to monopolize prime-time programming production of shows broadcast on the network. The Department also claimed that NBC, with CBS and ABC, was trying to develop a monopoly over the television program market.

To settle these antitrust suits, the networks signed consent decrees.[12] These consent decrees mirrored many of the restrictions imposed by fin-syn but also limited the number of hours of prime-time programming that the networks could produce. Any programs that the networks produced had to be sold to a syndicator for a one-time payment thus eliminating their financial interest in the program after its initial network airing. NBC was the first to settle its antitrust suit and did so in 1978:

> Among the provisions of the consent decree, effective until 1990, are financial interest and syndication rules virtually identical to the 1970 FCC rules, a limitation on internal, in-house production by the network [the decree allowed NBC to produce 2.5 hours of in-house programming per week], and a variety of other restrictions dealing with everything from options to exclusivity rights. (Glovinsky, 1984, p. 598)

CBS and ABC did not enter into their consent decrees until 1980. The CBS and ABC decrees were slightly more advantageous to the networks than was NBC's. NBC (and CBS) had a favored-nations clause in its decree. This meant that NBC was entitled to receive the same treatment as the other networks. For example, the ABC decree allowed the network to gradually increase the number of hours of in-house programs it could produce for prime time. Since ABC was permitted this programming, so must the other networks be allowed to do the same.

Both the networks and producers objected to the consent decree. Producers did not want the networks to have any production capabilities; the networks claimed the decree protected the producers over the networks and was therefore anti-competitive. For the networks, however, it was sign the consent decree or face the

---

[12]A consent decree is an agreement with the Court to abide by certain restrictions in the decree. It does not, however, require the accused to assume guilt for prior acts.

antitrust suit and, realistically, this was a case the networks were not likely to win. Ultimately, the consent decrees, in conjunction with the fin-syn rules, made the television networks simply distribution mechanisms for programming. Network production was so restricted as to be negligible.

Thus far, we have looked at what the financial interest and syndication rules are, why they were instituted, and why they were instituted when they were instituted. We have also examined what the Federal Communications Commission's role has been in the creation of these rules. To add depth to understanding why fin-syn was created, the next section will evaluate the people and politics that were influential when these rules were created. No regulation is created without people behind it. People with agendas that may have little to do with "serving the public interest." Both in the 1970s and throughout the remainder of the history of these rules, the president, Congressional leaders, and members of the FCC were all significant players instrumental in affecting the outcome of the financial interest and syndication rules. Here we will look at the political figures involved in the 1970s. When we get into the 1980s, industry figures as well as those outlined above begin to play an ever more dominant role in repealing these regulations.

NIXON AND THE MEDIA

The relationship between the federal government and the communications industry and the balance of power between these two institutions, are key determinants in how the flow of information is regulated in the United States. Usually, the relationship between the government, including the president, Congress, and the FCC, and the broadcast television sector, has been a synergistic one. This is true for a number of reasons. In terms of the FCC, the Commission and the industry interact on a day-to-day basis. Because of this, the agency comes to see regulatory issues from the perspective of the industry it is regulating (Krasnow, Longley, & Terry, 1982, p. 48). As for Congress, the relationship between industry and government is a sympathetic one, which has been attributed to Congressional members having financial interests in broadcasting (p. 89). However, the late 1960s, when the fin-syn rules were being created, was a time of conflict between the government and the broadcast industry.

As we have seen, in the late 1960s three major broadcast networks dominated the television landscape with over 90% of the viewing audience during the prime-time hours. Only 7% of households had cable. The average number of channels in the home was seven (Moser, 1997, p. 15). In rural areas, the average number of channels was closer to three. In terms of programming, the most popular shows included *Bewitched*, *Gomer Pyle,* and *Hogan's Heroes*. In terms of news, there were no television alternatives to the major broadcast networks.

Richard Nixon was president of the United States. His relationship with the press was tumultuous throughout his career but particularly so during his first term when he was dealing with a country divided by conflicting ideologies about the war in Vietnam. Because of his animosity toward the broadcast networks, Nixon used his presidential power to constrain and punish the broadcast networks:

> it was Vice President Agnew who maintained the critical pressure against the networks; it was a Nixon appointee, FCC Republican Chairman Burch, who interested himself conspicuously in network analysis of presidential speeches; and one reason for the house Commerce Committee's sweeping subpoena of material from *The Selling of the Pentagon* [a CBS documentary which questioned the military's expenditure on public relations activities for the war effort] appears to have been administration pressure on ranking Republican committee members. (Dunham, 1997, p. 124)

It is evident from this quote that Nixon used all branches of government available to him to put pressure on the media to do his bidding, or at the very least scare them into not presenting disadvantageous materials.[13]

Richard Nixon had a love-hate relationship with the media throughout his political career. Beginning with the famous "Checkers" speech through the Watergate scandal, Nixon learned to use the press, and in particular television, to suit his purposes. The Checkers Speech was one of Nixon's love experiences with the media and may have been the source of his belief that by going directly to the people he would always be able to persuade them to his point of view. Nixon was Eisenhower's vice presidential candidate during the 1952 and 1956 presidential campaigns. During the 1952 campaign, he was accused of financial improprieties. To save himself politically, Nixon made a speech on national television claiming his innocence. Yet, he said, there was one gift that he did get that he was not returning and that was the family dog, Checkers. The speech won him the sympathies of the American public and Eisenhower continued to support him as his running mate.

The Kennedy-Nixon debates, on the other hand, were not so successful for Nixon. Nixon looked sickly and sinister. He had lost 10 pounds and his clothes hung on him. He had recently been hospitalized for a knee infection, that led him to wiggle his leg, visually suggesting to television viewers that he was ill at ease. This impression was furthered by Nixon's profuse perspiration that led him to wipe his brow during the telecast. Kennedy, on the other hand, looked tanned and poised and confident.

Whereas the Checkers speech had saved Nixon politically, the Kennedy debate seriously hurt him. The Checkers speech was the most watched speech of the entire campaign, drawing a larger audience than any by Eisenhower or Stevenson, and ultimately making the vice presidential candidate instrumental in attracting votes for his ticket. The Nixon-Kennedy debate has been suggested as a contributing factor in Nixon losing the 1960 election:

> In the aftermath of the closest election in American history, his [Nixon's] appearance seemed a likely reason for his defeat .... If Nixon's image in the first debate had been the only reason for casting one's vote, Kennedy would presumably have won by a

[13]Additional evidence of Nixon's manipulation of the press is outlined shortly.

> landslide instead of just squeaking by .... What television contributed was something, seemingly trivial, to ponder in an otherwise issueless campaign: visual image as a reason for supporting a candidate. (Culbert, 1983, p. 202)

The medium that had once saved Nixon's political career now had been instrumental in putting him on the side lines.

After the 1960 debate, Nixon became less enamored of the press and television and after he was elected president in 1968 he developed a strategy for using the press to his advantage. In *Presidents and the Press*, Joseph Spear (1984) outlines Nixon's methodology for manipulating the press during his presidency. It was a plan whereby his communications people would constantly feed press releases about insignificant matters to reporters to keep them busy researching inconsequential events. For the important issues, Nixon would go on prime-time television and address the nation directly. Additionally, if reporters wrote or said anything unkind about the administration, the president and his advisors would no longer be available to talk to that particular reporter.

The time when the debate around fin-syn was coming to a head, late 1969, was turbulent. The Supreme Court was demanding school integration. The Chicago Seven were on trial. Simmering underneath all of this was the tension around the war in Vietnam. Sit-ins and demonstrations were taking place in high schools and colleges around the country. A moratorium was declared against the war, and demonstrations were held in Washington, DC and New York City, where people lay end-to-end in Sheep's Meadow as a metaphor for the war dead in Southeast Asia. In particular, the events that took place from mid-October to mid-November 1969 act as a microcosm for understanding the relationship between Nixon and the media, most specifically the broadcast networks.

The first moratorium took place in Washington, DC, on October 14, 1969. On October 13, Nixon announced that he would make an address on November 3 to present his plans for Indochina. Given the tension surrounding the Vietnam issue, much of the press in anticipation of the address speculated that Nixon would outline a specific plan for troop withdrawals. The following excerpt from *The New York Times* of November 2, the day prior to the speech, was typical of the thinking at that time:

> Though no one knows what he will do next about Vietnam, everyone has known for a month that he feels he needs to do something at this stage of the game. So there has been lively speculation that President Nixon may throw the long desperation pass and risk everything on a major new offer to Hanoi, or that he may sweep around the outside of the problem and set a firm deadline for the final peace. But the odds, and the pressures on the President, are greatest for a run right up the middle, to gain some yardage and time for further maneuver. ("The Vietnam Speech," p. 2)

The war in Vietnam had been going on since the Kennedy administration. It was such a political hot potato that Lyndon Johnson did not seek a second term as President. By the time Nixon inherited the war, troops in Vietnam numbered more than half a million. Nixon wanted to win the war, or at least have "peace with dignity." Many Americans, on the other hand, were tired of Vietnam and wanted the war over with. The country was divided between those who sided with Nixon and those who believed that Americans were fighting for a losing or immoral cause. It was felt that if Nixon would present a plan for troop withdrawals that it would go a long way toward healing a divided nation.

Following the moratorium in Washington, Vice President Spiro Agnew gave a speech in New Orleans attacking the war protesters. In that speech, he branded those who supported the moratorium "an effete core of impudent snobs who characterize themselves as intellectuals." He went on to denounce politicians who supported the moratorium and threatened suppression, saying, "Will we stop the wildness now, before the witch-hunting and repression that are all too inevitable begin?" ("President 'Proud,'" 1969, p. 25). The press was surprised at Agnew's speech and even questioned whether the vice president was speaking solely his opinion or if he was also speaking for the president. However, insiders stated later that there was no way that anything the vice president said was done without the president's approval.

Inside the White House, memos about how to deal with the press were being circulated. Jeb Magruder, Nixon's Deputy Campaign Chief, forwarded a memo entitled "The Shot-gun versus the Rifle" to H. R. Haldeman, White House Chief of Staff. From the memo, it is apparent that individual efforts to control the press were being made.

> It is my opinion this continual daily attempt to get to the media or to anti-Administration spokesmen because of specific things they have said is very unfruitful and wasteful of our time ....
>
> The real problem that faces the Administration is to get to this unfair coverage in such a way that we make major impact on a basis which the networks-newspapers and Congress will react to and begin to look at things somewhat differently. It is my opinion that we should begin concentrated efforts in a number of major areas that will have much more impact on the media and other anti-Administration spokesmen and will do more good in the long run. (Spear, 1984, p. 113)

Magruder goes on to list a variety of ways in which the Administration might curtail the media. These included:

> that the Federal Communications Commission set up an official monitoring system to keep track of network news coverage; that the Justice Department's anti-trust division "investigate various media"; that the Internal Revenue Service "look into the various organizations that we are concerned about"; and that the White House "begin to show favorites within the media." There was also this suggestion: "Utilize Republican National Committee for major letter writing efforts of both class nature and a quantity nature. We have set-up a situation at the National Committee that will allow us to do this, and I think by effective letter writing and telegrams we will accomplish our objective rather than again just the shot-gun approach to one specific Senator or one specific news broadcaster because of various comments." (Spear, 1984, p. 113)

Implementation of these ideas did not proceed until after the November 3 speech, which came to be known as the "silent majority" speech. "So tonight, to you, the great silent majority of my fellow Americans, I ask for your support" ("Text of President Nixon's Address," 1969, p. 16). This silent majority were the many people who supported Nixon and his war efforts or at least did not entirely oppose them but were not getting the sort of media attention garnered by the antiwar movement. It was a not so subtle dig at the media. The most significant aspect of the speech, however, is what it did not do. It did not say anything about troop withdrawals. What Nixon did mention was that troop withdrawals would be done in an orderly manner and on a secret timetable—in essence nothing.

Immediately following the speech, the networks had a roundtable of reporters comment on the speech. This was known as "instant analysis."[14] Most commentators that night mentioned that there was nothing new in this highly anticipated speech. ABC's Tom Jarrell, that network's White House correspondent, said that the speech "had 'offered no quick solutions' and perhaps had 'polarized attitude in the country more than it ever had been into groups who are either for him or against him'" ("The Analyses," 1969, p. 50). On NBC, anchor man John Chancellor stated, "that 'the essence of the speech has been a defense of his [Mr. Nixon's] plan to end the war which he thinks is working. His critics think it's not working and it's making the war go on longer, and they will be after him again'" (p. 51). Marvin Kalb, CBS's diplomatic correspondent, commented on a letter from Ho Chi Minh that was mentioned in the speech, which had been written in response to a letter from Mr. Nixon. The president categorized the letter as reiterating public propaganda. Mr. Kalb disagreed saying that "critics of Mr. Nixon 'may disagree with the President's judgment that the Ho Chi Minh letter was a flat rejection of his own letter. The Ho Chi Minh letter contained, it seems, some of the softest, most accommodating language found in a Communist document concerning the war in Vietnam in recent years'" (p. 51). But even while the network reporters did not agree with the president's remarks, the American people seemed to. In a Gallup poll following the address, 77% of the public supported the president's course of action ("Gallup Reports," 1969, p. 24). This figure needs to be taken with a grain of salt, however, because there is a rallying effect that occurs in response to a presidential speech.

Nixon felt that the comments following the November 3 speech were "'biased and distorted' and interfered with the president's privilege 'to appeal directly to the people,' a right he considered to be 'of the essence of democracy'" (Spear, 1984, p. 39). Pat Buchanan, then one of Nixon's aides, came to the president with a scheme to retaliate against the networks. Buchanan had drafted a speech to be given by Vice President Agnew attacking the network news organizations. This speech would be given in Des Moines on November 13. The speech outlined the reporters' offenses:

[14]Unlike today when reporters and pundits comment on every political event, in 1969 this was a new program development. Speeches did not usually run a full half hour and any time that was left over came to be filled with this "instant analysis."

> One commentator twice contradicted the President's statement about the exchange of correspondence with Ho Chi Minh. Another challenged the President's abilities as a politician. A third asserted that the President was following a Pentagon line. Others, by the expression on their faces, the tone of their questions and the sarcasm of their responses, made clear their sharp disapproval. ("Transcript of Address," 1969, p. 24)

The speech described further the networks as "nothing more than liberal think tanks, filled with 'nattering nabobs of negativism,' 'elites,' 'effete intellectuals' from the Northeast engaged in 'querulous criticism'" (Kalb, 1994, p. 205). The speech also "charg[ed] the television network news operations with unfairness to the President, accusing them of a liberal bias and an Eastern parochialism and reminding broadcasters—ominously, some felt—that they operate on government-licensed frequencies" ("Nixon Comments," 1969, p. 28).

Agnew's speech was not the only means that the administration used to retaliate against the networks. The administration's response to the instant analysis was unprecedented. Dean Burch, the Nixon-appointed chair of the FCC, called the networks demanding transcripts of the commentaries following the address. "Mr. Burch said that he had 'received complaints about the discussion programs following the President's speech,' but he declined to say who had made the complaints" ("Burch Supports Agnew," 1969, p. 20). Burch admitted years later to doing this at the request of the White House (Spear, 1984, p. 160).

Burch's call from the FCC was a veiled threat to the networks. Other actions were more blatant. According to Marvin Kalb (1994), then a reporter for CBS:

> CBS feared that the newly appointed head of the Federal Communications Commission, Dean Burch, would cancel or rearrange radio and television licenses. Millions of dollars hung in the balance. In addition, Nixon aides visited CBS headquarters in New York to complain about Dan Rather's reporting from the White House. (pp. 205–206)

The networks had every reason to fear. The Nixon Administration was not only unhappy with the coverage of the November 3 speech. They were also angry about what they considered to be the unbalanced political coverage during the election night, the night after the "silent majority" speech. Again the administration planned to call on Dean Burch to get their message across. Charles Colson, Special Counsel to the President sent a memo to Bob Haldeman outlining what their course of action should be:

> Our analysis of the election night coverage on NBC confirms just what we thought: it was terrifically slanted toward the Democrats.
>
> Dean Burch has agreed to convene a meeting with the three network presidents together. He will call them to task on their coverage and advise them that steps have to be taken on their own to deal with this problem or the FCC may have to consider regulatory remedies. (Oudes, 1989, p. 171)

Calls from the FCC, visits from White House staff, threats of revoking broadcast licenses are the strongest actions an administration can make against a broadcast network. It is one thing for the government to attack the press in speeches or through the press. That is what the First Amendment is all about. However, when the government uses its power to threaten the press for presenting an opinion, these steps were unprecedented in terms of a president's actions to censure the national press and the broadcast networks.

It was within this antagonistic atmosphere between the federal government and the media that the financial interest and syndication rules were enacted. There is no direct evidence linking the passage of fin-syn with Nixon's wishing it were so. Nevertheless, given the president's dislike of the media, some would even say paranoia, there is every reason to believe that Nixon or people high in his administration maneuvered to aid the passing of these rules. There is no evidence that the networks suspected that Nixon was behind the creation of fin-syn. The networks, however, suspected that the Nixon Administration was behind the Department of Justice antitrust suits, and they were correct in their suspicions. "[Nixon] had discussed proposed antitrust suits against the networks with Haldeman on April 21 [1971], saying they would 'screw the networks,' but he decided they should not be bought up now ... [but] under no circumstances is it to be dropped" (Dunham, 1997, p. 111). In December of the same year, Herbert Klein, White House Director of Communications, threatened each of the network heads that if their news coverage did not change antitrust suits would be filed (p. 184). The networks had every reason to believe that Klein was speaking as the voice of the president.

Interestingly, both Burch and Wells, Nixon's two appointees to the FCC, dissented against the majority opinion in the 1970 *Report and Order.* However, they were dissenting to the Prime-Time Access Rule and not fin-syn specifically. Burch's objections were that "the public in the top 50 markets will be deprived of significant amounts of popular high quality network fare in the prime viewing hours ... in the smaller markets, ... there will be a similar deprivation ... [and] the rule will hurt, not help, UHF [stations]" (Amendment of Part 73, 1970, p. 414). Economically, Burch's argument makes a lot of sense. Independent producers will create inexpensive, tried and true programming for the prime-time access time periods, because they will have to be sold into syndication, that is market by market, and there are no guarantees that every station will pick up the program. Smaller markets are affected, because the networks will not produce programming to run in the 50-plus markets. Economically, it does not make sense. Therefore, these smaller stations have to purchase programming for that time period, which will likely be some type of inexpensive programming since these smaller markets can ill-afford high quality programming. UHF stations will be hurt, because they will be in competition for syndicated programming against the better-funded VHF stations. Burch explains that it is all a matter of economics and blames the lack of diversity on the limited number of channels for program distribution, "so long as a broadcaster has only one channel on which to operate, his economic requirements will tend to make him program that one channel for a mass audience. Accordingly, minority needs or tastes will be denied or underserved" (p. 416). According to Burch, the Commission should have looked at alternative methods of distribution, such as subscription television and cable, as a means to promote diversity. As has been demonstrated, however, more outlets does not necessarily mean more diversity.

Again, however, this dissent does not mention the financial interest or syndication rules, which more directly affected the networks from an economic perspective by denying them access to the syndication market. Perhaps Burch and Wells were still acting in the interest of the president even while dissenting, because the rules that were the most harmful to the networks—Nixon's nemeses—were still in place. The Commissioners had not defeated the rules, only objected to a certain portion of them, which did nothing toward having them repealed in any case. It is also possible that they knew the rules would pass even with their dissent, so they could vote their consciences. Either way, the rules were passed and it was likely, given the networks' displeasure, that Nixon was pleased with the ultimate outcome.

CONCLUSION

The fin-syn rules were enacted because at the time of their inception the networks were an oligopoly and as such had unlimited control over the national airwaves. The FCC found that "the networks have gradually—since about 1957—increased their economic and creative control of the entire television program process. Between 1957 and 1968 the share of network evening program hours (entertainment and other) either produced or directly controlled by networks rose from 67.2 to 96.7 percent" (Amendment of Part 73, 1970, p. 389). In the 1960s, the three television networks were the only means of national program distribution and because of the limited number of stations on the air were by default the primary provider of television programming. In selecting that programming, it seems, economics took precedence over other factors. Cantor and Cantor (1992) state that "the networks had accepted virtually no entertainment programs for network exhibition unless they were given a financial interest in those same programs" (p. 45).

The broadcast networks controlled the pipeline to the American viewing public. The fin-syn rules eliminated the networks' stranglehold on the industry and limited them to making money from advertising and from selling the rights to what limited programming they could still produce for a single payment.[15] Specifically, the FCC instituted fin-syn in order to achieve three goals:

> 1) enhancing the profitability of program producers; 2) restraining or diminishing the networks' bargaining power, allegedly derived from their control over access to affiliated stations and employed to extract syndication and other financial interest from producers; and 3) preventing networks from favoring programs in which they had these interests. (FCC Network Inquiry Special Staff, 1980, p. 725)

In the next chapter, we will begin to see to what degree the financial interest and syndication rules were effective in achieving these goals, and the implications for this on the rules being repeal. Before repeal would occur, however, political figures, industry leaders and FCC Commissioners would play a decade long game of tug-of-war over fin-syn.

---

[15]All the networks divested their syndication divisions. ABC and CBS, however, continued to produce prime-time programming and made-for-television movies.

3

The Financial Interest and Syndication Rules (1977–1995)

THE END OF THE BEGINNING

The battle over the repeal of the financial interest and syndication rules began in the late 1970s. It pitted the broadcast networks and their affiliates against independent producers, independent television stations, and the MPAA among others. Ten years after the rules were enacted, the television landscape had changed, and the networks began to argue that they were being unfairly crippled by the FCC regulations. The FCC itself began to move toward repealing the rules. In October 1980, an exhaustive study commissioned by the FCC, the Network Inquiry Special Study, "concluded that 'the financial interest and syndication rules can only be characterized as misguided at best'" (Colvin, 1983, p. 120). The Federal Communications Commission had been on a deregulation trend since the Carter Administration in the late 1970s. Many of the regulations that had been created by Presidents Johnson and Nixon in the early 1960s and 1970s were eliminated less than a decade later. The deregulation trend continued in the 1980s, fueled by Reagonomics. Mark Fowler was the chair of the FCC. To call Mark Fowler a staunch supporter of deregulation is to underplay just how passionate he was about this ideology. The Justice Department consent decrees, which had been left hanging since the early 1970s, were completed by 1980. With the occurrence of these events, the networks had added motivation and saw an opportunity to get the rules repealed and began lobbying toward that end. Thus the stage was set for one of the most divisive debates in recent entertainment and FCC history, pitting television executives against television producers, government departments against the president, and the FCC against Congress.

THE REPEAL OF FIN-SYN — 1983 TENTATIVE DECISION

The contest over the financial interest and syndication rules began in earnest with a study of the network television industry by the FCC's Network Inquiry Special

Staff (NISS). This study initiated a FCC reexamination of the rules which would look at the regulation with the serious consideration that they be eliminated. The FCC initiated this study in 1978, during the Carter administration, with a *Further Notice of Inquiry* requesting information about the network programming business.

The *Further Notice* had been preceded by a *Notice of Inquiry* in early January of 1977. This *Notice* was instigated in part by the Westinghouse Broadcasting Company, which submitted a petition to the FCC calling for a review of the three broadcast networks, and in part because the Justice Department consent decrees, initiated in 1970, had yet to be completed (Commercial Television Network Practices, 1977, p. 549). (As previously noted, the networks did not enter into final plea agreements until 1978 for NBC and 1980 for the other two networks.) As with the PTAR, Westinghouse claimed that the networks controlled the broadcast schedule. This was still possible because even though the financial interest and syndication rules might have reduced the power of the networks, they certainly had not made them docile competitors in the marketplace. One way the networks exerted control over the program market was through their owned and operated stations. These stations are very influential buyers in the syndication market—they can make or break a show—because they were in the largest television markets. The networks still determined what appeared on the network schedule even if they could no longer own an interest in it.

At the same time, the networks were being accused of reducing compensation paid to their affiliates. Affiliate compensation is the fee that networks pay to their affiliates to air network programming. The affiliate is not required to run everything the network provides, but the station is given incentives by the network for these program clearances. Incentives can include things like advertising space adjacent to network programming, but is usually in the form of payments, known as affiliate compensation. Fees paid to affiliates vary from station to station, but factors that go into evaluating compensation include market size and station popularity.

According to Westinghouse, compensation as a percent of network revenues decreased from 23.1 to 13.4% between 1964 and 1975 (Commercial Television Network Practices, 1977, p. 553). While this may be true, over the same time period network revenue increased from $928.7 million to $1.67 billion. So while the percent of compensation decreased, the actual dollar figure increased by 4%. However, network profits increased significantly from $156.5 million in 1964 to $208.5 million in 1975, an increase of over 33%. Thus, while the networks did not decrease compensation, they did not increase it at a rate of growth commensurate with the growth in network revenues. This ultimately allowed the networks to increase profits at the expense of their affiliates. To make up for the "decreased" payments from the networks, the affiliates had to increase the costs of their national advertising spots, which cut into revenues and ultimately local service (p. 556).

The networks' increasing profitability was just one element covered by the 1977 *Notice of Inquiry*. As with previous investigations, the FCC focused on whether the networks were using their influence in the marketplace to exert anticompetitive practices, thus maintaining a dominant position in the television industry. Overall, the inquiry focused on three specific areas: network-affiliate relations, network-program supplier relations, and the relationship between network owned and operated stations and program suppliers (Commerical Television Network Practices, 1977, p. 553). The proceedings were suspended, however, to allow for the new incoming Carter Administration.

When proceedings resumed in October 1978, the FCC issued a *Further Notice of Inquiry.* This *Further Notice* reiterated the Commission's two main goals for the investigation. These goals were: (1) to provide the public with the best possible programming and (2) to discover if the networks were limiting access to the airwaves and thus acting in an anticompetitive manner (Commercial Television Network Practices, 1978). This *Further Notice* reviewed the same issues outlined above in the initial *Notice.*

The FCC added another layer to this investigation. The Commission was cognizant of rapid changes that were affecting the television industry and for this reason they also wanted to take into account what might happen in the future. This led to including issues such as satellite technology, improved television receivers that would allow for better reception of UHF stations, VCR usage, and increased demand for advertising in their analysis. These changes in technology might possibly lead to an increase in programming choices that would affect how the FCC might evaluate the existing rules. Though none of these technologies were making significant inroads into the television marketplace at the time of the investigation, the FCC believed they might ultimately have an impact on "network dominance" and so should be considered in any investigation. The questions outlined in this *Notice* became the basis of the NISS Report.

In 1980, the Network Inquiry Special Staff (NISS) issued its final report—*FCC Network Inquiry Special Staff, Final Report: New Television Networks: Entry, Jurisdiction, Ownership and Regulation* (1980). The report was a complete turnaround from what had been expressed by the FCC prior to this time. Based on an economic—and thus theoretical—perspective, the *Study* concluded that market forces were the most efficient method for creating diversity within the program marketplace. One of the codirectors of the Network Inquiry Special Staff, Thomas Krattenmaker, stated in his testimony before the Senate, "For reasons difficult to identify, the Federal Communications Commission has spent very large sums of money for the past 15 years mediating a garden variety, penny ante commercial dispute between two groups of firms I should have thought were perfectly capable of protecting their own pocketbooks .... With respect to the television networks, ABC and CBS and NBC will gain little from repeal of the rule" (*Competition in Television Production Act*, 1983, p. 50). The NISS concluded that the rules did not achieve their objective and that the rules were not even warranted when they were initially adopted.

The NISS based its findings on the changes in the marketplace brought about by changing technology, in particular the increasing prevalence of cable in American homes.

> The very appearance of new viewer options through an increase in the number of full-time networks, whether employing conventional or unconventional technology, mitigates the concerns expressed by the Commission in the promulgation of these

> rules .... Whatever "dominance" the three commercial networks possess in the network and syndication markets will automatically be reduced by the appearance of new networks. (FCC Network Inquiry Special Staff, 1980, p. 514)

The increase in the number of viewer options, in this case cable channels in addition to broadcast networks, would better serve to fulfill the FCC mandate of increasing diversity in the television marketplace, according to this report. Thus, the NISS made recommendations to the FCC that the fin-syn rules be repealed. At the very least, the financial interest rule had to be eliminated or radically revised (FCC Network Inquiry Special Staff, 1980, pp. 517–518).

The FCC never officially endorsed the NISS Study. As a staffer at the FCC told me, "The Commission did not endorse that study. That's why it was released as a staff study. I think the intent was to adopt it by the Commission, and they didn't" (personal interview, July, 1999). What the FCC did do was release a *Notice of Proposed Rule Making* on July 21, 1982, regarding repeal of fin-syn. This was not yet an official endorsement for repealing the rules. Rather it was a renewed evaluation on the part of the FCC particularly in light of the conclusions of the NISS report and its claims of a changed television marketplace:

> The market for television programming has undergone significant change since adoption of the syndication and financial interest rule .... Therefore, our concern over the abilities of the networks to act as monopsonists in the purchase of television programming may no longer be justified .... In 1964, only 26 percent of all television households received seven or more signals and 78 percent received four or more. Today, 90 percent of all television households receive four or more television signals. Nielsen figures indicate that 65 percent of all television households receive seven or more signals .... In 1964, there were 1,200 operating cable systems with 1,085,000 subscribers. Today there are nearly 4,800 systems serving 23 million subscribers .... Subscription television is now available on 27 stations in the United States .... In addition ... there are an estimated 2.1 million homes with video recorders, approximately 2.6 percent of U. S. households. Some observers expect this to rise to 50 percent by 1990 .... Applications are also pending to provide direct broadcast satellite (DBS) service to the entire country .... (Amendment of 47 CFR, 1982, paragraphs 32–37)

The FCC suggested that these new competitors in the television marketplace were not only providing opportunities for diversity in programming for consumers, but also were beginning to "take their toll on the networks in terms of audience loss," which was evident in network shares declining from 88% in 1979 to 81% in 1981 (paragraph 38). The networks were not only losing audience share. They were also beginning to lose broadcast income (something that would turn out to be short lived), and pay programmers were beginning to be able to outspend the networks to acquire the rights to present feature films, one of television's most popular offerings.

Separate from these marketplace considerations, the FCC questioned whether the fin-syn rules were the best method for achieving the goals of diversity and a fair and open program marketplace given the Special Staff's report. To determine if total elimination of the rules was justified, the FCC solicited comments on several issues related to this question. The FCC called for comments regarding competition, particularly in light of the fact that the top 10 prime-time producers were large corporations including Universal, Paramount, Warner Brothers, and Twentieth-Century Fox, corporations who did not need protecting by the FCC. The FCC was also seeking comments on how the rules might be affecting the networks' ability to negotiate in a more competitive marketplace where the networks had restrictions that their nonnetwork counterparts did not. In considering all of the above, the FCC began to conceive that "it is now possible that the syndication and financial interest rule, adopted in the past to protect the public interest of television viewers by promoting competition, may operate against those interests by unnecessarily restraining the networks' abilities to compete" (par. 42).

While the FCC studied the marketplace and evaluated the need for the rules (particularly focusing on fin-syn), the networks were rallying the troops in support of repealing both fin-syn as well as the Prime Time Access Rule. CBS was the first network to involve their affiliates in repealing both fin-syn and PTAR. On October 25, 1982, CBS management presented their views to their affiliates and left it up to them to put it to a vote. The affiliates supported the repeal of fin-syn but with the qualification that the PTAR stay enforced. This was because the affiliates did not want to return airtime, and thus ad revenue, to the network. The affiliates had come to depend on the considerable advertising dollars generated during the half-hour access period (Pearce, 1973, p. 4). The affiliates felt the PTAR alone was enough to keep the market competitive. Because the networks realized that they needed affiliate support to eliminate the rule, they quickly backed down from their initial position of attempting to eliminate both PTAR and fin-syn. The networks put their full attention on the financial interest and syndication rules convincing affiliates that the elimination of these rules would be beneficial to both interests ("CBS-TV Affiliates Throw Support," 1982, p. 48). The affiliates agreed to support the elimination of fin-syn. They were willing to do this because they perceived it was to their advantage to keep the network viable and content. According to James G. Babb, Jr., the chair of the CBS affiliate board, "'As joint ventures with the network, the affiliates are intimately concerned with the long-term vitality and quality of network programing [sic]. In this instance the rules [fin-syn] impose across-the-board costs and constraints, which in our view needlessly inhibit the network's competitive capability'" (p. 48). Shortly thereafter, NBC and ABC followed suit of the rules repeal.

A *Tentative Decision and Request for Further Comment* followed the 1982 *NPRM* in August 1983. A tentative decision is just that: tentative. It suggests that the Commission is still deciding what it considers to be the best course of action. This is why it calls for further comment.

The Commission determined that the rules were ineffective in achieving its stated goals:

> The financial interest rule has failed to increase the independent program supply, has no effect on program diversity or quality, has not decreased network control over program content or creativity, does not represent an inherently undesirable conflict, and

> appears to present no threat to the well-being of the independents. (Amendment of 47 CFR, 1983, pp. 1096–1097)

Changes in the marketplace suggested to the Commission another reason for the rules to be revised. An increase in programming outlets had changed the networks' ability to dominate the program marketplace. The increased competition in the television marketplace meant that the networks no longer had monopsony power, that is, the ability to act as a single buyer in the market. The marketplace conditions no longer existed that would allow this to occur:

> In order for these concerns to be realized, two conditions regarding network behavior must be met. First, the three networks must be able to act in concert, either tacitly (by parallel behavior) or collusively (by active conspiracy). Second, the three networks together must comprise the sole purchasers of the program producers' product. If either of these conditions is not met, it is not likely that the networks could exert power over program producers. This is so because, if adequate alternative program purchasers exist, any producer who may be dissatisfied with the treatment he receives by *a* single broadcast network has the option of offering his product to a different network or some other program purchaser. (Amendment of 47 CFR, 1983, p. 1063)[1]

The FCC concluded there were new competitors for the networks because of the increase in new technologies, particularly the increase of homes passed by cable from 15.3% to 54.2% from 1970 to 1980 (p. 1058). As well, there had been an increase in viewing share of the independent stations (many of which were UHF stations whose transmission was greatly enhanced by cable). Prior to this time, the lack of available spectrum space, and therefore stations, had prohibited the introduction of broadcast alternatives. New technologies, such as cable and direct broadcast satellite, would create new competition not possible in simply a broadcast arena.

Given these changes and the ineffectuality of the rules, the recommendation of this *Decision* was to abolish the financial interest rule totally and greatly reduce the power of the syndication rule by specifying a "narrow" rule:

> the rules are in need of very substantial revision.... First, it does not appear that it is necessary to control the ability of the networks to bargain for and acquire passive "financial interests" in programs purchased or produced for network exhibition. Second, we will continue to prohibit network participation in the domestic syndication of prime time entertainment program series. Thus, the scope of the syndication prohibition would be narrowed to include only participation in *domestic* syndication markets and to cover only *prime time series* programs .... Third, programming in which a network retained any continuing off-network "financial interest," would in every case have to be made available for syndicated sale within six months after the end of the network exhibition "run." Moreover, for series that run for more than five years, the

---

[1]There is some fundamentally flawed thinking in this argument. The primary flaw is in thinking that alternative outlets have the same ability as the networks to pay for programming. This is not the case.

> network would have to make the series available for syndication no later than the end of the fifth year of the network exhibition. We also believe that it may be appropriate to "sunset" the syndication restrictions that are maintained, in 1990 .... In short, our tentative decision is to eliminate the financial interest rule while narrowing the syndication rule to ensure against possible network incentives to restrict the availability of the most critical off-network programming for independent television station use. (Amendment of 47 CFR, 1983, pp. 1022–1023)

The new rules would allow the broadcast networks to negotiate for financial interest in independently produced programming. As well the networks would be allowed to syndicate programming into foreign markets.

Domestic syndication, however, was another story. The networks would be allowed to negotiate for syndication rights but with a few caveats. The FCC believed that there was a continued need for some type of syndication rule because the agency was still concerned that the networks would warehouse programming if allowed back into the syndication business:

> To reduce any possibility of warehousing, a network will be required, within six months of a series completing its network exhibition run, to transfer all rights in that series it may hold relating to its syndication, to an unaffiliated syndicator. In addition, no later than the end of the fifth year of a network series run, the network will have to transfer all syndication rights for programs in that series to an unaffiliated syndicator. (Amendment of 47 CFR, 1983, p. 1098)

These rules would force the networks to release programming into the syndication marketplace. The rules would make the networks passive participants in the syndication business. They would have no say over the terms and conditions of syndication. In addition, the networks would be required to file notice with the FCC that the sale or transfer had occurred and that it met with the FCC rules. This would allow the FCC as well as the Department of Justice to track any possible competitive infractions. This new limited rule, it was hoped, would prevent the networks from warehousing programs. The decision also contained the sunset provision whereby whatever remained of the rules would be abolished by August 4, 1990.

These suggested rules were based on conclusions of the NISS Study. The NISS had found that "the financial interest and syndication rules might well be disrupting an efficient risk-sharing arrangement between the networks and their program suppliers.... With the rules in place, network fees to producers were reduced, thus forcing the producer to shoulder a greater financial risk initially" (FCC *Tentative Decision,* 1983, p. 1027). This assessment of risk sharing was one expressed by other economists at the time (Fisher, 1991; McGowan, 1967). Without the rules, the networks paid a higher price for a show because they also acquired financial interests in the program, syndication opportunities, and subsequent licensing of show merchandise. With the rules, the networks could not acquire additional interest in the show and therefore would only pay for what they received, that is, an opportunity to air the show. When the networks could invest in programming, their input helped to spread the risk between networks and producers. Fin-syn was accused of "disrupting the efficient risk-sharing arrangement," because they forced the producer to take on more of the risk. Economically, the networks are in a better position to bare the burden of risk than producers are. The reasons of this require some explanation.

Creating programming for prime time is a very risky business enterprise. Several hundred scripts are developed, perhaps a hundred pilots are produced and only a handful of those shows ever make it onto the prime-time schedule. According to many economists as well as the writers of the FCC Study, the networks are in a better position to absorb the risk for a number of reasons. First, the networks know better than anyone what type of programs they need to fill their network prime-time schedule, giving them an advantage over independent producers in knowing what types of programs to develop. They can develop programs that will "take advantage of the audience-flow effects that result from planning an entire network schedule rather than having random placement of programs" (Fisher, 1991, p. 293). Also, the networks can spread risk over many programs while producers can only spread risk over as many shows as they produce. This puts small independent producers at a distinct disadvantage, often forcing them to align with larger production companies, which are in a better position to absorb the risk. (Larger producers have as good an ability to spread risk as their network brethren as long as they have access to the market.) Finally, networks are in the best (some would say only) position to exploit a program promotionally, which ultimately impacts future syndication values.

Remember, of course, that this *Tentative Decision* was not a final report, but an opportunity to suggest new rulemaking and asked for comments. Little did the Commission suspect the battle that this *Decision* would engender.

THE BATTLE BEGINS

The *Tentative Decision* acted as a starting point for the networks and the Hollywood studios to begin a decade long battle in "what may have been the most heavily lobbied proceeding in history" (Fisher, 1991, p. 294). Both sides made massive efforts to sway the Federal Communications Commission to their side. Along the way, various government agencies would align themselves with one side or another. Several federal agencies (the Department of Commerce, the Federal Trade Commission, and the Department of Justice) came out in support of repealing or at least narrowing the rules along the lines of the *Tentative Decision*. This was a huge show of support for the Big Three Broadcasters. The Hollywood producers steadily continued their efforts with the support of the many diverse groups within the "Hollywood creative community" as well as others who considered fin-syn essential to the welfare of the creative community. This group would ultimately include the president of the United States.

The *Tentative Decision* generated strong reactions from the parties concerned, that is, the networks, the producers and ultimately Congress and the president. The networks were disappointed that the rules were not completely abolished. The idea of warehousing was particularly bothersome because it was something the networks claimed they never did, nor would they have an economic incentive to do so.[2] The networks had lobbied hard and, in their minds, the FCC had come up short.

On the other side were members of the Hollywood community, who considered the proposal unacceptable. This Hollywood group formed a coalition representing diverse interests which was called the Committee for Prudent Deregulation (CPD) (Colvin, 1983, p. 120). CPD was made up of "independent producers, independent television stations, television performers, program directors, writers, syndicators, and distributors favoring retention of the rules which have helped them prosper" (Glovinsky, 1984, p. 590). The Committee was created to enable the Hollywood community to speak as a united force against the lobbying efforts of the broadcast networks, one of the strongest if not *the* strongest lobbying group in Washington. This group proved to be a viable opponent in combating the networks. Especially vocal in the group was Jack Valenti, President of the Motion Picture Association of America, who was supporting the major Hollywood studios, suppliers of approximately 70% of the prime-time programming. As a unit and individually, the studios lobbied the FCC.

In speaking with the FCC and the Congress, the CPD argued that the rules had been successful and that networks would revert to prior bad practices if the rules were repealed. They called the *Tentative Decision* "Fowler's compromise," which they claimed was "'nothing more than repeal in sheep's clothing'" ("Networks win," 1982, p. 28). The CPD's response to the *Decision*, and more specifically the NISS Study, was a report by an independent firm called ICF, Incorporated. This report was actually made up of two papers:

> [The first paper] examines the importance of diversity as an FCC regulatory goal and illustrates the potentially serious impacts on the diversity of programming available to the television viewer that repeal of the Rule would have. The second paper focuses more narrowly on the issues of competition and economic efficiency and concludes that repeal of the rule creates considerable potential for network control of the market for off-network syndicated programs. (ICF Incorporated, 1983, p. i)

This report systematically refuted the claims of the NISS Study. The ICF Report claimed there was no real proof of new technologies eroding network television's market. Instead, the rules had increased competition because of increased numbers of independent television stations, independent producers, and distributors, exactly what the rules were created to achieve. While the networks claimed poverty, the CPD presented the Commission with reports on how even with the fin-syn rules the networks had not suffered. In fact, network profits increased 550% from 1970 to 1980. Finally, the report claimed that the NISS was misguided in its evaluation of diversity:

> The Network Inquiry Report employs a limited definition of diversity: "three different, but related, dimensions: the types of programs, the sources of programs, and the

[2]This was not true. See the *Hawaii 5-0* example mentioned in the previous chapter.

> number of choices of outlets available to viewers at any one time" .... But there are many other aspects of diversity.... Diversity as a policy goal must be considered broadly as the opportunity for diverse viewpoints to reach viewers. (ICF Incorporated, 1983, p. v)

ICF believed the only way to achieve this diversity was through government regulation.

The CPD's most persistent argument was the possible stranglehold that networks would have on independent producers and independent stations. For producers, they feared that the networks would revert to prior bad acts. After all, in the 1960s, less than 7% of the network schedule was without network financial interest. For independent stations, they were concerned that the networks would sell programs to their affiliates who would feel compelled to buy them to protect their network affiliation, thus putting independent television stations at a distinct disadvantage. The ultimate result, according to the CPD would be that

> viewer access to popular programs would be diminished, independent station competitive strength would decrease, and advertisers and consumers of advertised products would pay the price of diminished competition in the supply of television advertising. ("Syndication, Financial-interest Comments," 1983, p. 30)

According to the CPD, it was a lose-lose-lose situation if the rules were repealed, and they had the support of the independent stations and the advertising community to back them on up on their argument.

The networks, on the other hand, argued that the marketplace had changed since 1970 and that they were now at a disadvantage in a highly competitive marketplace. New programmers—both cable and broadcast—created increased competition for viewers. They also increased competition for programming. For example, the networks felt they could not compete when it came to bidding for shows against the pay networks, or premium channels, such as HBO or Showtime that consumers pay extra for—an area that was not regulated at the time. Also, the competition (at this time cable and independent producers, but would later also include Fox) had the right to sell its programming and merchandise related to their programs, which gave them additional revenue and additional advantage in the marketplace.

The networks responded to the ICF with a report of their own called *Economic Effects of the Financial Interest and Syndication Rule: Comments of the ICF Report*. This report was commissioned by CBS and was an economic evaluation of the industry. Step-by-step it pulled apart the ICF Report claiming that its methodology was faulty and must be wrong because it disagrees with other previous work. The *Economic Effects* report concluded "that the broadcast networks would not have the power or the incentive to engage in warehousing.... This report also concludes that the repeal of the rule will, if anything, have a positive effect on television diversity, contrary to the allegations of opponents of deregulation" (Crandall, Noll, and Owen, 1983, p. ii). Crandall et al. stated that warehousing would not happen because it had not occurred before the rules were in place so it would not happen now.

Diversity, according to this report, had decreased because of concentration among suppliers, that is producers, due to the inefficiency in risk sharing caused by fin-syn.

In this report and elsewhere, the networks claimed it was the major program suppliers who had all the rights and that the rules had created an anticompetitive environment, at least for the networks. In this expanded marketplace in which the networks were excluded, the producers could hold the networks "hostage" to successful programming. The way the contracts were designed, the networks could only license a show from a producer for up to 4 years. If the show was successful enough to merit a fifth year or more, the networks were hit with stiff renewal fees in the fifth year. Another claim of the networks was that because they had no financial interest in programming, they were risk averse when it came to creative programming. If they made their airtime available to a particularly unusual show, they wanted to know they could achieve profits from other markets if the show was not profitable on the network. Finally, the networks claimed that the number of independent producers had decreased rather than increased with the creation of the rules. This worked exactly against what the rules was supposed to achieve. After all the debating and all the bickering on both sides, in the end, the *Tentative Decision* was never adopted because of intervention on the part of Congress, even more so on the part of the president.

THE REPEAL OF FIN-SYN—CONGRESSIONAL INTERVENTION

The debate had gotten so heated that the Congress got involved even before the FCC came to a Final Decision, which would be the next step after a Tentative Decision. Representative Henry Waxman, a democrat from California, "introduced a bill (H.R. 2250) that would prohibit any change in those [financial interest and syndication] rules or in the commission's accompanying prime time access rule for five years" ("Congress Takes Up Financial Interest," 1983, p. 34). Representative Tim Wirth, a Colorado democrat, chairman of the Telecommunications Subcommittee and one of the bill's sponsors, voiced his concerns about deregulation for deregulation's sake. "We must only deregulate when it is warranted by the level of competition—and the level of competition in the video marketplace simply does not justify lifting those rules which were carefully designed to protect the public interest from the lack of competition now facing the networks" (p. 34). This bill passed the House ("Hollywood's Short-Lived Win on Fin-syn," 1983, p. 28). Ultimately the bill was revised to delay the rules for 6 months rather than 5 years. The time period was reduced to 6 months because, "there was a feeling among some Committee Members that a 5-year moratorium ... may be premature without further study. To provide the Committee with sufficient time to review the issue, the committee agreed to adopt a 6-month, instead of a 5-year moratorium, to ensure that any FCC final action would not become effective in the immediate future" (*Television Network Financial Interest and Syndication Rules*, 1983, p, 4). By reducing the time of the moratorium, the committee enabled the passage of the bill, which allowed for Congress's continued jurisdiction over the FCC on this issue. This bill passed the House in November.

At the same time, the Senate introduced a bill, S. 1707, the Competition in Television Production Act, a parallel bill to the one in the House. As well, "the Senate Appropriations Committee attached an amendment to a fiscal 1984 supplemental appropriations bill prohibiting the FCC from spending funds to implement repeal until May 31, 1984" (Fisher, 1991, p. 296). It was obvious that Congress was doing all it could to put the breaks on what it saw to be runaway deregulation.

The proceedings of these hearings, as well as a 1989 Senate hearing on media ownership, are instructive in understanding the relationship among the FCC, Congress, the industry, and the president. As Krasnow, Longley, and Terry (1982) concluded in *The Politics of Broadcast Regulation*, "although the FCC may initiate policy, the fate of such policy is often determined by others" (p. xiii). Just as no regulation is created in a vacuum, no regulation is repealed in a vacuum either. Fin-syn was certainly no exception. Both the House and the Senate believed the FCC was pushing repeal of fin-syn through too quickly. This was attributed to Mark Fowler, a staunch deregulator who never met a regulation he didn't want to repeal. While it is often the case that political figures do not want to attack the networks for fear of being denied access, particularly come election time, this did not appear to be an issue with fin-syn. After all, the Senate was willing to withhold funding to repeal the rules, possible evidence of their true wish to constrain the networks or at the very least the FCC. As far as President Reagan was concerned, as with Nixon, we see that who is in the White House can have a significant impact on communication policy. The 1983 Senate hearing turned on the intervention of President Reagan. While Fowler, the president's man at the FCC, was pushing for deregulation (something Reagan supported in most areas of public policy), the president called for retention of the fin-syn rules. As will be explained in detail shortly, this can be attributed to Reagan's Hollywood past and his continuing connections to people in that community. Ultimately, the president stepped in and ordered the Departments of Commerce and Justice to change their opinions about repeal of the rules ("The President's Priorities," 1983, p. A22).

In the House, Representative Waxman had introduced H.R. 2250, which was cosponsored by more than 100 other congressmen. The bill was introduced to rein in the FCC. As Mr. Waxman said during the hearings held June and August 1983, "we in Congress are faced with the reality that the FCC may make this change [to the fin-syn rules], which is one of the most important and significant public policy changes that has been made in the television broadcast industry since the 1934 act" (*Financial Interest and Syndication Rules*, 1983, p. 6). The congressman softens his rhetoric slightly when he claims that he is not judging the future but rather limiting the FCC's ability to make changes while the industry is in flux. It was important for Waxman to not appear too antinetwork. As a democrat from California, he obviously had a need to support the Hollywood community, as this was a significant constituency. However, the networks to a lesser extent were also a part of that constituency.

As alluded to earlier, these hearings were the occasion for several prominent organizations to come out on either side of the fin-syn repeal issue. Action for

Children's Television (ACT), an advocacy organization, wished to maintain the rules for the sake of program diversity, particularly that directed at children. The Department of Justice (DOJ) was overall in agreement with the FCC's *Tentative Decision* but suggested minor changes that would "give the networks some measure of control over off-network syndicated programming" *(Financial Interest and Syndication Rules*, 1983, p. 714). The Department of Commerce, like the DOJ, recommended repeal of the rules. "The Department of Commerce believes strongly that the Commission should not seek to regulate the contractual arrangements between program suppliers and the networks" (p. 734). The Department of Commerce also suggested that it was the DOJ, not the FCC, that was better suited to deal with the issue of antitrust, which Commerce perceived as being the pressing issue. The National Telecommunications and Information Administration (NTIA), the Executive agency responsible for telecommunications policy, also supported repeal of the rules. They perceived the rules as intrusive, with little to no impact toward furthering the public interest.

In addition to these agencies, many other important figures in both the business and creative sides of the television industry testified in front of the committee. Representatives of the networks, Jack Valenti (an omnipresent figure in the deregulation of fin-syn, primarily because the MPAA was coordinating and financing much of the public relations efforts behind the scenes), representatives from advertising, independent broadcasters, and minority owners of independent production companies (including Sidney Poitier), all presented their case in front of the committee. Most groups other than government agencies were aligned with the studios, not the networks.

Senate hearings were held regarding the financial interest and syndication rules on November 2, 1983. Barry Goldwater was the chairman of the Subcommittee on Communications of the Committee on Commerce, Science and Transportation. The bill, S. 1707, was called the *Competition in Television Production Act* and was sponsored by Pete Wilson of California with the support of nine other senators including Goldwater. Like the House bill, S. 1707 would "prohibit the Federal Communications Commission from taking any action prior to July 1, 1988 to repeal or modify any of three of its present rules relating to the ownership and distribution of television programs. These are commonly known as the financial interest, syndication, and prime time access rules" (*Competition in Television Production Act,* 1983, p. 1). Going into these hearings the House had passed the 6-month moratorium on modifying the rules and the Senate had passed a bill that would prohibit the FCC from using funds to repeal the rules through May 1984. These actions strongly suggest that Congress was taking serious measures to curtail the FCC vis-à-vis these rules. As well, Congress was putting some restraint on deregulation, which was running rampant at that time.

Goldwater outlined the issue as a fight of David versus Goliath. If David, in the form of independent producers, needed protection, then it was up to the government to provide that protection. Second, Goldwater brought up the issue of quality. However, he qualified the need for government intervention based on this issue. "I ...

have grave misgivings about the Federal Government attempting to impose its judgment as to what should be quality television programming. Apart from those misgivings, however, the issue can be raised about whether the public is better served" (CTP Act, p. 4). If the two groups are equal in bargaining power and the public is served equally with or without the rules, then the rules should be repealed according to this thinking.

These hearings had a bit of glamour to them because some of the Hollywood luminaries attended the proceedings. In addition to testimony from federal departments and agencies as well as the networks, there was testimony from independent producers, including Mary Tyler Moore and Norman Lear. As with the House hearings, the majority of those in attendance were in support of retaining the rules.

The hearing started with the Senators' presentations, none of which was particularly unusual or very different from testimony previously heard in front of the FCC—until Pete Wilson read a letter from Edwin Meese III, the Counselor to the President. This letter was in response to a letter the senator had sent to the president.

> The President has asked me to respond to your letter of July 20, 1983, expressing your concern regarding the syndication and financial interest rules in the television industry. We appreciate your views and have since been in the process of examining all sides of the issue.
>
> As you know, the President has consistently favored Government efforts to promote vigorous competition. However, he has determined in this instance in light of changing market conditions in the television and program production industries that additional review of the consequences or repeal of the rules is necessary. Accordingly, after careful consideration of this matter, the President has decided to support a 2-year legislatively mandated moratorium on any change in the syndication and financial interest rule. A 2-year moratorium would allow us to give the issue further study and monitor future changes in the marketplace, while at the same time ensuring continuing healthy competition within the industry. (CTP Act, p. 9)

This was a huge bombshell. The president of the United States, the promoter of deregulation, was supporting continued regulation of the television industry.

The president's decision has been attributed to a conversation that Reagan had the night before the hearings with Lew Wasserman, the chairman of MCA/Universal and Reagan's former agent. He was accompanied by Nancy Reynolds, a member of the lobbying firm hired by CPD and a friend of the first family (Colvin, 1983, p. 120). As appeared in the press years later, "Many credit Wasserman for keeping the networks out of the profit patch. Wasserman, after all, had been Reagan's Talent Agent and Hollywood's leading statesman to the outside world" (Harris, 1995, p. 86).

Although we do not know what exactly happened in that meeting, it is likely that Wasserman persuaded Reagan to support his old buddies in Hollywood. This is likely to have transpired because Reagan's letter was dated November 2, 1983, the same date as the hearing during which the letter was read. Had the president made a decision before that time, the letter would have had an earlier date. It was not as if Reagan did not know when the Senate hearings were occurring, and it was not as if he had not been approached on the matter. Pete Wilson's letter soliciting an opinion from the president had been sent four months prior. Something forced him to make a decision, and the conversation with Wasserman appears have been that something. By sending this letter, Reagan took the wind out of Fowler's sails.

Fowler was not experienced in dealing with Congress and was in conflict with them through much of the first 2 years of his chairmanship. "Fowler tended to side with ideological friends in the Senate [which was Republican controlled] and then get caught up in the conflict between the Senate and the House [which was controlled by the Democrats] … there was also an element of the Fowler FCC thinking that it could somehow stampede the House Democrats into accepting more deregulation than really wanted" (Tunstall, 1986, p. 245). It was under these circumstances, without the benefit of the support of the White House, that Fowler spoke in front of the Senate committee.

Fowler testified that independent parties had questioned the rules from an economic standpoint almost from the time of their inception. With the addition of the NISS's conclusions, the FCC decided to reevaluate the rules. Rather than asking for a full repeal of the rules, the Commission was looking to repeal the financial interest rules, modify the syndication rules, and leave the prime-time access rule untouched. Fowler justified the Commission's actions explaining that the record for this matter was "voluminous" and had been "exhaustively reviewed." Fowler requested that the Senate allow the FCC to come to a final decision rather than evaluate the tentative decision.

However, after the president had said he did not want the rules repealed, what was Fowler going to do? Senator Hollings questioned Fowler about his interactions with the president regarding fin-syn:

> Senator HOLLINGS. What was the vote on the tentative decision? Was it just a split vote?
>
> Mr. FOWLER. It was a complicated vote, but essentially it was three to one for the tentative decision.
>
> Senator HOLLINGS. And right now with respect to pressures being brought, what contact, directly or indirectly, has President Reagan had with you on this score?
>
> Mr. FOWLER. I briefed him several weeks back, sir, at the White House. I had offered some time ago to provide him with a briefing on the various communications issues before the agency, and he took me up on the offer ….
>
> Senator HOLLINGS …. When did this occur, this briefing, approximately?
>
> Mr. FOWLER. September 28….
>
> Senator HOLLINGS. And my question was what other contact, directly or indirectly, had the President had with you on this score other than September 28?
>
> Mr. FOWLER. None.
>
> (*Competition in Television Production Act*, 1983, pp. 29–30)

Though it is possible and even likely that Fowler did not speak to the president again about fin-syn, it seems unlikely that he was not contacted by some other members of the administration, given their severe separation on the issue. In any case, Fowler's testimony had been significantly deflated by the Meese letter.

Fowler's testimony was followed by presentations by the Commerce Department, the Justice Department, and the FTC, which like Fowler, supported eliminating the rules. These presentations were followed by those in favor of retaining the rules. First, Jack Valenti presented (again!). He was followed by Mary Tyler Moore, who presented as the board chairperson of her production company, MTM Enterprises.

> There is absolutely no reason why those who create programs must be forced by the networks to relinquish their ownership rights and their ability to market and profit from their creations after the network run in order just to get into the network theater.
>
> But this is what happened to me, Norman Lear and to many others in the independent production business before the FCC promulgated the rules they now wish to repeal. Domestic and foreign distribution rights to *The Mary Tyler Moore Show*—that was the first creative venture of MTM—were taken, not purchased, by CBS when the program was first developed in 1969. Norman Lear was required to do the same thing when he created *All in the Family* just prior to the rules. (CTP Act, p. 63)

Ms. Moore did not only argue for the right of producers to own their programming. She also presented the issue of developing programs presenting women and minorities. These shows had been championed by independent producers, not the networks. As Ms. Moore explained, "I want to underscore this, that in the history of television, there have not been and there are not now any women holding positions of significant power at the networks who are involved in the inner sanctum of network decisionmaking" (CTP Act, p. 63).

While the networks talked about money, the independents focused on programming that could educate as well as entertain. But the producers had to countermand the networks' financial claims, and they did so using specific examples of network leverage over producers. *Hill Street Blues*, an MTM production, typified producers' experiences with the networks. As in the past, they explained the concept of deficit financing and how particularly with a successful show like *Hill Street Blues*, the networks were making substantial revenues, while producers hoped and prayed their show stayed on the air long enough to get into syndication. And, even if it did get into syndication after 5 years and 100 episodes, the producer was in debt to the tune of several million dollars. In the case of *Hill Street Blues*, the figure was estimated at $6 million. In effect, the producers were subsidizing the networks, while they got a return on their investment immediately through the sale of advertising.

Another interesting presenter that day was Dean Burch, who had been chairman of the FCC when the rules had been initially enacted. Mr. Burch was not testifying to support his earlier decision, though from his comments he was ready to support them if asked to. Rather he was there as co-counsel for the Committee for Prudent

Deregulation, and more specifically as counsel for the Association of Independent Television Stations (INTV). The fin-syn rules affected programming on the networks, but it also affected the viability of independent television stations. Having been aware of what occurred prior to the institution of the rules, Mr. Burch presented with great authority:

> If the networks become dominant in that [syndication] marketplace—and I see no reason to think they would not become dominant. After all, they are the only three entities through which all programming, all off-network programming must go and if a network as a reasonable, profitmaking corporation, determined that it was in its interest, first of all, to show the program on the network, then to make it available to the owned and operated stations, and then to make it available on a first basis to the affiliates of that network, I do not think that requires either collusion or frankly that it is a violation of any antitrust law. The independents would be disserved throughout that process [punctuation is as it appears in the original text]. (CTP Act, p. 86)

The concern here was that while some government agencies, particularly the Department of Commerce, claimed that the rules were unnecessary because they were really covering for antitrust issues, Mr. Burch was claiming that this was not the case. In fact, the Justice Department referred to many borderline collusive practices on the part of the networks as "parallel practices," meaning that when one company changed its way of doing business the other networks would follow. In this way, the networks while not directly colluding, were still controlling the market. Since this was not collusion, however, it could not be prosecuted.

The networks followed the producers with their testimony presenting information that was virtually a reverse image of that presented by the producers. The networks claimed that the studios held all control and had even begun producing programming for pay services, thus presenting the best programming on channels that consumers had to pay for. This was anathema to the idea of free broadcasting. The networks also claimed that they would never take all the profits from syndication, because the producers wouldn't let them. They claimed that warehousing was a myth. The networks had never engaged in warehousing, there was not one shred of evidence in the FCC decision that showed that it had and economically it would not be beneficial. They also claimed that they were fierce competitors, not colluders. Finally, the networks claimed that they would not have creative control over programming, because that was a combined effort between the networks and suppliers.

Everett H. Erlick, presenting as executive vice president and general counsel of ABC, used a particularly weak example in supporting the network cause.

> There has been a lot of comment that independent producers were somehow victimized and bulldozed and tread upon in all sorts of horrible ways by the networks … it may be that those producers felt that somehow their rights were infringed upon and that they were treated horribly, but strangely enough, they came back to produce other shows for the network. Strangely enough, they wanted to continue to deal with us. (CTP Act, p. 107)

The question Mr. Erlick did not answer is where would the producer go instead.

All in all, these hearings were a win for the CPD, as appeared in *Variety*, the entertainment industry bible, on November 2:

> No Rules Change for 6 Mos., Coast Jubilation
>
> The House Commerce Committee Tuesday (1) unanimously approved legislation barring the FCC from revising its financial interest and syndication rules until next June 1. The measure is a compromise aimed at moving a bill through the full House next month .... The new formula's support in the panel, combined with Senate passage last week of a similar plan, would appear to assure Hollywood of some additional time to press its case against revision of the regs. ("Hollywood wins," 1983, p. 1)

Though they did not get the 5-year moratorium that they wanted, the producers did get a reprieve, with any changes to fin-syn delayed for 6 months. Ultimately, they won more than that. As it would turn out, the networks would have to wait more than 5 years to present their side of the story again.

REAGAN AND THE MEDIA

As with Richard Nixon before him, Ronald Reagan had a long history with the media prior to becoming president. Reagan's experience was decidedly different from that of Nixon's, however. Reagan had started his career as a sports announcer on radio. On a trip to California, he was signed by Warner Brothers and began an almost 30-year career as an actor, working in both television and film. In the late 1940s and early 1950s, he was president of the Screen Actors Guild, the actors' union covering those who work in film and filmed television programs. Switching from acting to politics in his mid-50s, Reagan was elected governor of California in 1966 and served in that position for 8 years. After two failed attempts at the presidency, Reagan was finally elected to that position in 1980. Reagan's experiences in front of the camera obviously served him well. During his presidency, Reagan came to be known as the Great Communicator for his ability to present, and more important, sell his ideas to the American public.

Reagan came to power under the ideology of deregulation, the idea that less government was better than more government. Less government also meant less expensive government, which presumably would mean fewer taxes and more money in voters' pockets.

Reagan did not create deregulation, or unregulation, as it was sometimes called. Deregulation of the communications industry had begun in the latter part of the 1970s. It was a rejection of policy put in effect during the Nixon and Johnson administrations (Tunstall, 1986, p. 3). While deregulation did not start under Reagan, his administration became flag wavers for this type of government. The New Right had become a force to reckon with during the Reagan years, and they had set their sights on the communications industry. According to Tunstall:

> Two interconnected aspects of the New Right ... are especially significant for communications deregulation. One is that American business has geared itself up much more systematically in the last decade to influence politics .... The second is that the New Right, believing the media in the past to have been leftist, oppositionist and concerned with "bad news values," has targeted the mass media as a key territory to be conquered, second only to direct power itself. (p. 12)

Thus, deregulation was not just about getting the government out of industry; it was also about influence at the highest, and possibly widest, levels.

During the Reagan administration, fin-syn was not the only television regulation up for renegotiations. Advertising rules affecting the number of minutes per hour were eliminated. Ownership rules were relaxed, specifically allowing ownership of 12 AM, 12 FM, and 12 TV stations covering 25% percent of the country where the previous limit had been five of each type of station. Equal opportunity hiring provisions for women and minorities were cut back (Tunstall, 1986, p. 147). These were just some of the FCC requirements that were eliminated or severely relaxed during the 1980s. Others included easing of content rules, easier franchise renewal for incumbents, and increased licensing of stations. Given this era of relaxing many broadcast requirements, it becomes surprising that the financial interest and syndication rules were retained—except for what we know or can surmise about the politics surrounding these rules.

In June 1983 Mark Fowler, Chairman of the FCC, offered to meet with White House staff members to brief them on matters pending before the Commission. In September of that year, senior staffers took him up on the offer ("Networks nervous over Reagan," 1983, p. 42). Mr. Fowler, with his administrative assistant Willard R. Nichols, went to the White House, prepared to brief the group on a broad range of issues. To their surprise, President Reagan attended the meeting, which turned out to be a conversation predominantly about fin-syn (p. 42). Fowler had never briefed the president before, which raised suspicions from both sides of the debate. First, it was inappropriate for a president to implicate himself in the workings of the FCC, an independent agency, particularly by meeting in the privacy of the White House. At the very least, the meeting should have been held publicly so that there would be notes in the record. Second, the networks in particular were nervous because "the President maintains close ties with members of the motion picture industry who have denounced the commission's tentative proposal to liberalize the rules" (p. 42). However, the president did not make a final decision about fin-syn without further investigating the matter. He heard presentations from pronetwork sources, such as Secretary of Commerce Malcolm Balridge and the Justice Department's antitrust chief William Baxter (Kintzer, 1984, p. 553).

Reagan's involvement with the financial interest and syndication rules is unprecedented in terms of a president's attention to a single FCC regulation. First there was the September 28 "private" meeting with Mark Fowler. Later, both the president and the chairman were denounced by a House oversight subcommittee for this meeting. According to this subcommittee report, Reagan

> "undermined the fairness and integrity of the rule-making proceeding" by privately involving himself in the affairs of the FCC, an independent agency. Instead, the Reagan-Fowler conversation should have been recorded on the public record .... Fowler insisted that there was no impropriety in not placing his conversation with the President on public record because "it was a straight briefing to the President on this issue [FISR] and other communications matters" and because the President "did not try to influence the FCC's position." (Kintzer, pp. 554–555)

The Reagan/Fowler meeting was followed by a Cabinet council meeting on October 20 to discuss the rule ("Reagan Upstages the Networks," 1983, p. 51). On November 2, the day of the Senate hearings and the Meese letter, Reagan called for the Justice and Commerce Departments to change their decision to support the FCC repeal of the rules. "An embarrassed Assistant Commerce Secretary calls for a two-year moratorium on the change, explaining, 'Our boss has decided that there's an Administration position on this issue, and the Administration's position is our position'" ("The President's Priorities," 1983, p. A22). In this same editorial piece, *The New York Times* accused the President of ignoring more pressing government issues, including foreign policy concerns and possible bank failures, to focus on fin-syn. In fact, it was the president's interest in these regulations that made fin-syn such a hot issue. It might have stayed under the radar, so to speak, if Reagan had not gotten involved.

As Congress and the FCC were at odds (in no small part perhaps because of presidential intervention), they decided to put the responsibility in the hands of the networks and the CPD. The day after the president's announcement, the two sides began negotiations, which were described by an insider as a "shotgun meeting" ("Hollywood Wins," 1983, p. 1). Both sides were to report their progress to the FCC by January 31, 1984. Congress agreed to stay out of the picture until March as long as both parties bargained in good faith. Negotiations did not go well, and talks broke down by mid-January when ABC and NBC walked out. CBS continued to try and negotiate, but they too had walked out of talks with the studios by mid-February.

Between President Reagan and Congress, the FCC had nothing to do but let the matter drop. By January 1985, revisions to the financial interest and syndication rules were deemed a "dead" issue, and Hollywood had Ronald Reagan to thank. As one producer told me:

> The brazen attempt at deregulation that was unsuccessfully launched by the networks in 1980 simply failed to factor the personal experience of the president. Not six months after agreeing to the Consent Decree, the networks plotted their assault on the new FCC. But they failed to realize that Ronald Reagan knew the inner workings of Hollywood first hand. Given his past professional experience, Reagan wasn't about to let the networks off the regulatory leash. (Leonard Hill, personal interview, July 24, 1999)

THE BEGINNING OF THE END

A group of executives from the networks and from the production community, at the behest of Congress, continued to negotiate throughout the remainder of the 1980s but with no movement evident one way or the other. Jack Valenti described these "negotiations" as "the longest floating crap game since the one conducted by Nathan Detroit in GUYS AND DOLLS" (Valenti, 1989a, p. 274). They met bimonthly, with little movement one way or the other. Leonard Hill told me about his involvement with these meetings:

> The producers' representatives were a diverse group. Bob Daly, Barry Myer, Gary Nardino, Rich Frank, and Jack Valenti represented the big studios. Jerry Leider, Len Hill, Chuck Fries, Mel Blumenthal, Russell Goldsmith, and Ken Ziffren spoke for the indies. After a number of frustrating meetings, one of our group proposed a very easy solution. Candidly, it was my suggestion: Let the networks own a financial interest in everything that's put on their air. Daly thought I'd lost it. But the proposal was simple. Let the networks own a flat 25% interest in everything. The proviso being that in return the networks can't produce anything themselves or through a related entity. The syndication rules are retained. Competition would be served because the networks would then have an incentive to put on the best shows regardless of ownership. The studios rejected the proposal. It was DOA. Perhaps they were concerned that the independent companies were inherently more efficient than the studios. In retrospect, it would have been a great deal for everyone. (Leonard Hill, personal interview, July 24, 1999)

This passage suggests that there may have been disagreement among the production community as well as between networks and producers. Even so, the production community began to feel the heat again in 1989, and they knew they had to do something about it.

In 1989, a group of Hollywood producers and organizations came together to create the Coalition to Preserve the Financial Interest and Syndication Rules. This was a sort of new version of the old CPD. The new group included 207 producers as well as organizations such as the Screen Actors Guild, the Caucus of Producers, Writers and Directors and, of course, the Motion Picture Association of America, which had been in the middle of the fin-syn fight from the beginning. The purpose of this group was to inform Congress, the Administration, the FCC, the Departments of Justice and Commerce, and the general public about the financial interest and syndication rules so that they could understand why it is important that they not be repealed. The creation of this organization was likely prompted by two things: (a) the November 1990 expiration of the portion of Justice Department consent decrees, which prohibited the networks from producing programs for their air; and (b) the upcoming hearings of the Senate Commerce Committee Subcommittee on Communications.

Senate hearings, entitled *Media Ownership: Diversity and Concentration*, were held throughout June 1989 to evaluate changes in the media marketplace. The Senate wanted to evaluate the level of concentration in the media industry and to determine if it warranted government intervention. Much of the initial days of the hearing were devoted to the cable industry, its programming practices, and its impact on the broadcast industry, which was spurred by the impending merger of Time-Warner. The broadcast industry was very concerned about the concentration and possible deregulation of the cable industry. However, when the conversation turned to the financial interest and syndication rules and whether their existence continued to serve the public interest, particularly as it relates to competition, the networks did not express the same concerns about concentration of the industry.

The by now usual suspects appeared to plead their case to the Senate. Jack Valenti, speaking for the Hollywood studios, continued the argument they had been presenting all along, that the networks were powerful institutions with a unique advantage of determining television programming. Because of this ability, they had used that power to extort money from program producers and would do so again if the rules were repealed. Included in the argument was the fact that the rules had worked. There had been an increase in the number of independent television stations (from 71 to 320 from 1970 to 1989) as well as the creation of "hundreds" of independent programming companies (Valenti, 1989b, p. 156). This might all be adversely affected when the networks would be able to produce and own all of their prime-time programming starting November 1990. In anticipation of this change, the networks had already begun to increase their ownership in the 1989/1990 season (see chapter 6 for details). Valenti's impassioned speech is best presented in the following extract:

> What Americans know, see and hear of news, education, entertainment, and sports is preeminently borne to the home through the television screen. Therefore, unless we knowingly abase the essentials of a free and loving land, *our government must, at all costs and in spite of all pressure, never allow a tiny group of corporate entities, no matter how seemingly benign the management, to establish dominion over this most pervasive of all human influences*. The networks' monopoly troika cannot be permitted to insert itself into control of national prime-time television, else we squeeze the life out of competition and turn over sovereignty of the prime-time airwaves to three corporate chief executives. (Valenti, 1989b, p. 159, emphasis in the original)

The goal of the rules was to stimulate competition, and they had been effective in achieving this goal according to Valenti. To eliminate the rules was to subject the American public to the views of the limited few. This viewpoint was supported by the testimony of Steve Cannell, producer of shows such as *The Rockford Files* and the *A-Team.* He stated in his testimony, "Let us just realize that their [the networks'] intention certainly is to dominate all of the programming themselves, own it, distribute it, control it. That is their plan, and they are gearing up to accomplish it. And if they succeed, everything that you see on television will be controlled by the minds of three people" (*Media Ownership: Diversity and Concentration*, 1989, p. 629). To support his point, Cannell uses the examples of Norman Lear and *All in the Family* and Carsey-Werner and *The Bill Cosby Show.* In both cases, the issue was that because these producers were not owned by a network, they could shop their shows around until another network picked them up. Without fin-syn, according to Cannell, producers are only able to sell to one network. Under such conditions, a show such as *All in the Family*, for example, would be sitting in a dead script file at ABC because Lear would have been under exclusive contract to that network. As Cannell states, "A new form of television was born, the socially relevant comedy"

(p. 629), suggesting that only independent producers, and not networks, produce this type of programming.[3]

Valenti continued by tearing apart the networks' argument that they need additional revenue. Between the network and their owned and operated stations, each of the networks produced a significant profit during 1988. As well, network profits were rising despite huge license fees paid for sporting events[4]—programming for which the networks claim to lose money. Increased competition was not biting into network profits either. While cable had grown to reach more than 50% of the country, the networks still presented 84% of national advertising. Not only this, but all three networks were owned by large conglomerates with significant investments in other media as well as nonmedia enterprises.[5] Being part of diversified companies allowed the networks to be protected against any sudden changes in the advertising marketplace.

The speech also cast doubt on the idea that the networks are at a competitive disadvantage. The FISR restricted the networks from doing only two things: (a) requiring an equity stake from producers to get their shows on the prime-time schedule, and (b) participating in the syndication market. Apart from these regulations, the networks are also not allowed to own cable systems (though they can, and do, own cable networks). None of these restrictions seriously hampered the networks' ability to compete in the media marketplace.

The speech concluded by suggesting that the networks had not been negotiating in good faith because they expected to be able to do an end run around the FISR. Starting in November 1990, the networks would once again be permitted to produce and own programming that appears on their air. This was an element of the Justice Department consent decrees, which had an expiration date. As Valenti (1989b) states, "the networks do not want to achieve any concord in negotiations with producers. Why should they? They will either succeed in demolishing FISR officially, or devastating it unofficially. Why make a deal, when you can't lose?" (p. 174).

The networks, on the other hand, saw the studios as stonewalling. According to Bob Wright, president and chief executive officer of NBC:

> The studios simply have no incentive to seek any compromise solution that would involve a change in the *status quo* so beneficial to them ... Unlike the networks, they are unwilling to test their arguments against repeal in the marketplace. Their response is

[3]This may be true in a rare case such as *All in the Family*. However, with the exception of perhaps *Wiseguy*, it is hard to make a similar claim about Mr. Cannell's programs.

[4]NBC had paid $500 million for the Olympics, and CBS had spent twice that for Major League Baseball.

[5]At the time, ABC was owned by Capital Cities, which had many media interests including newspapers, magazines, and cable stations; NBC was owned by General Electric, which was third on the Fortune 500 list and had interests in 14 businesses including being a major defense contractor; Loews Corporation was CBS's major stockholder, which had interests in insurance, hotels, and cigarettes, among others.

> to form "The Coalition to Preserve the Financial Interest and Syndication Rule"—hardly signalling a willingness to negotiate in good faith or to compromise. (*Media Ownership*, 1989, p. 465)

One idea espoused by Bob Wright was a proposal to have fin-syn only apply to 50% of the prime-time schedule, or 11 hours per week. "The 11 hour limit would cap networks' ability to acquire financial interest and engage in in-house production. We could engage in foreign syndication, but in domestic markets, could syndicate only programs produced by our owned television stations" (p. 464). Wright suggested that the regulated versus the unregulated part of the schedules could be evaluated—competition versus regulation. If the rules were no better than competition, then the rules should be repealed by 1995. It is understandable why the studios would reject such a proposal. The effects of ownership would take time to evaluate. It would be impossible to know after only 2 years, for instance, if the networks were going to warehouse a show or what they would do in terms of syndicating their own shows because it would take at least 5 years to put a show into syndication. This proposal in effect cut off the independent producers from half the network schedule, something which it could be expected would cut heavily into producers' opportunities to remain viable competitors.

Speaking for the networks at the same Senate Committee hearing, in addition to Robert (Bob) C. Wright, were Laurence (Larry) A. Tisch, president and chief executive officer of CBS, Inc., and Thomas S. Murphy, chairman and chief executive officer of Capital Cities/ABC. The networks' argument centered around the idea that the networks need to be able to compete on a level playing field and that regulation, when instituted, needs to be fair, that is, it must apply to everyone or no one. Although the networks have been operating in an ever-more competitive market, they do so without the ability to be a fully integrated organization, which puts them at a distinct competitive disadvantage. (What they fail to mention is their competitive advantage in having been given the best space on the radio spectrum, but then this never comes up in the networks' arguments.)

According to the networks, fin-syn should be repealed for a number of reasons. First, it is not possible for networks to dominate the industry, if they ever did. Networks compete with independent stations, cable, VCRs, satellite dishes, and even a new upstart network, Fox, rather than just one another as was the case in 1970. The networks also claimed to face competition in the advertising market, from cable and independent stations, and in the program acquisition market, where multinational corporations can sell their programming to a variety of outlets. Second, the growth of independent stations is more attributable to economic recovery than it is to the rules, something the proponents of the rules had been espousing. Third, although the networks have the burden of proof of showing that repeal would serve the public interest, they explained as the providers of free programming that they were serving the public interest in a way that cable and other technologies could not. The financial interest and syndication rules were hindering the networks from fully participating in the television business and thus affecting the future potential of broadcasting. Additionally, they used the 1983 *Tentative Decision* to suggest that the FCC and the Justice Departments are in agreement with the networks. Fourth, they claimed that the fact that the networks' parent companies are successful in other business has no bearing on the argument.

The ultimate concern is the viability of over-the-air broadcasting and its importance to the public interest. This was the trump card in the argument and was well expressed by Larry Tisch:

> Out of the array of video technologies that now compete for television viewers' attention, only one is free to the consumer and only one is universally available—broadcasting. And only broadcasting has accepted the responsibility to provide a national and local program service responsive to the needs and interests both of the nation as a whole and of local communities across the country. The preservation of this unique broadcast system that allows virtually every household free access to a distinctive blend of national and local public service should, in my view, remain a fundamental government policy. (Tisch, 1989, p. 311)

The issue, according to Tisch, was no longer simple competition. It was the actual viability of the networks. Citing a now often used example, the networks claimed they were being outbid by pay cable services. Pay services have the ability to generate revenue from a variety of revenue streams, while the networks are limited to one—advertising. By limiting the networks' ability to make money, they are limited in their ability to bid for quality programming against the competition. "If you, the Senate, do not take off the restraints, we cannot stay in business and therefore no longer provide this free and important public service," was the networks' refrain. Bob Wright (1989b) further supported this argument:

> [Free television] is of particular value to the 45% of TV viewers who do not subscribe to cable, many of whom are poor, elderly or rural citizens. Those Americans unable to afford the pay media depend on the free networks for high quality entertainment programming, for national and international news and for major sporting events.
>
> Networks are the backbone of our system, because of the relationship they have to over 600 local affiliated television stations across the country. There is no way these stations, particularly those in markets below the Top 100, could in any other way acquire the kind of programming they now receive for free from one of the three networks. The communities in which these stations are located are too small to be of primary interest to the national program suppliers or syndicators that sell programs market by market.... (p. 352)

The networks even used this argument to justify their expenditures on sports programming as part of their efforts to serve the public interest. For example, a small pay service would only provide major sporting events—like the Super Bowl, the Olympics and the World Series—to a limited few who could afford to pay for it. The networks, on the other hand, pay huge license fees for the rights to air these events of "universal significance" because they "bring us together as a people and ... [because] the public has come to expect [them] to be universally accessible on free broadcast television" (Tisch, 1989, p. 313).

Because of the need to serve the public interest, it was important for the networks to be able to provide quality programming. Thomas Murphy suggested that the increased competition was eating into network revenues, which in turn affect these companies' ability to provide such quality programming to viewers.

> Advertising revenue is ... ultimately a function of audience size. And even though network programming is a staple of all media, our audiences have diminished significantly. The three networks' combined share of the prime time audience had declined from more than 90 percent in 1970 to approximately 67 percent in the season past .... The reduced audience level we live with inevitably act as a kind of cap on what advertisers will pay for time on the network. (*Media Ownership*, 1989, pp. 502–503)

There are two flaws in this argument. Advertising rates are based on ratings, not on shares. It does not matter from an advertising perspective how large an audience the network is reaching versus its competition. Second, CPMs, or cost per thousand, is based on factors unrelated to audience size. Finally, as we have seen in recently years, the networks' reduced audience size has had little to no impact on advertising revenues.[6]

One example that Bob Wright presented was effective in supporting the networks' position that the rules economically hampered the networks' ability to present innovative programming. He claimed that the rules inhibited the amount of money the networks can spend on programming. This was true because the networks had to structure a deal that would allow them to turn a profit on the airing of the program. The advertising generated by the program had to at least cover the cost of the program because there was no other way in which the network could recoup its expenses. Wright used the example of a program called *The Days and Nights of Molly Dodd.* This was a critically acclaimed, "innovative" program which originally aired on NBC.

> NBC cancelled the show after one season because its ratings, which were mediocre, did not generate sufficient advertising revenue to make renewal economically sensible. The program was picked up by the Lifetime Cable Network which, because it is not subject to the Financial or Syndication Rules, was able to structure a deal with the

[6]The networks provided these numbers as net advertising revenue: 1985: \$6.5 billion, 1986: \$6.7 billion, 1987: \$6.7 billion, and 1988 \$7.3 billion (p. 519). The Television Advertising Bureau (TVB), an industry group which aids local stations in selling advertising, reports very different numbers, compiled by McCann-Erickson (a major advertising agency). Advertising revenue in 1985 was \$8.1 billion, 1986 was \$8.3 billion, 1987 was \$8.5 billion, and 1988 was \$9.1 billion (Television Advertising Bureau, 1999). These independent numbers show a continued advertising growth rate. They show the industry making almost 25 percent more revenue than what the networks self reported. This suggests some continued need for skepticism when evaluating numbers provided by the vested interests on either side of the argument.

> producer whereby Lifetime shares in both the cost of production and the future profits of off-cable syndication. Lifetime acknowledges that it will run "Molly Dodd" on its cable network at breakeven, but can look to future syndication revenues for its returns. (Wright, 1989b, p. 355)

This example suggests that the cable networks can afford to put on innovative programming, but the broadcast networks cannot because they do not own a piece of the show. According to this argument, the networks' inability to present this type of programming is directly tied to fin-syn. Wright continued: "Without the Rules, networks could invest more money in a greater number of programs, structure arrangements with suppliers that would permit more innovation and risk-taking, and enhance our service to the viewer" (p. 356).

The networks' final attack was, of course, aimed at the Hollywood studios. "The only entities served by the Rules today are a few large, vertically integrated Hollywood studios, who want to continue to be the sole source of program financing, and the foreign investors who have bought or want to buy these program financiers" (p. 359). According to the networks, these large corporations have alternative outlets through which to sell their programming if they are unhappy with a network agreement. Examples given include *Cosby* being rejected at ABC and ending up at NBC; NBC rejecting the terms on *Roseanne* which ended up at ABC; no network agreed with the terms Paramount wanted for *Star Trek* so it landed in first-run syndication.

As in most arguments, both sides of the story have elements of truth; however, there is also some guilt by omission. Each side, of course, tried to paint the other side as the bad guy, and both seem to have legitimate arguments. However, even the FCC commented on the contradictory information presented to it when putting together the 1991 rules, which ultimately followed these proceedings. On the surface the networks' arguments seemed specious. Their complaints of increased competition, especially from independent stations and newcomer Fox, were a hollow argument given that this competition had done little to eat into profits even though they had begun to reduce audience share. Larry Tisch in his comments complained about the increase in availability of first-run syndication—an example of how effective the fin-syn rules had been. Also, while the networks were claiming poverty in Washington, they were proclaiming plenty on Wall Street. Finally, nothing in the networks' argument suggested that they would not revert to past practices once fin-syn was repealed. Bob Wright simply suggested it would not happen now, because it did not happen before. He rebutted the evidence before the FCC in the 1970s:

> The FCC found no evidence of "extraction" of profit shares or syndication rights when it adopted the Rules. In fact, the networks paid suppliers for financial interest and held such interests only in about half the programs licensed (not the 93% often erroneously cited by the studios). There was no evidence the networks biased their program selection in favor of these shows, or held programs in which they held syndication rights off the market to advantage their affiliates ("warehousing"). (Wright, 1989b, pp. 361–362)

Wright, however, does not provide verification for ownership figures or any substantiation for suggesting that the networks were not biased to programming in which they had a financial stake. An exchange between the three network chairmen and then Senator Gore demonstrates the networks' less than forthright manner.

> Senator GORE. Well, we heard testimony that no new programming has broken into the ranks for the top ten, or the most popular programs on cable, unless the cable MSOs had received an equity interest in it. Do you think this is an example of abuse?
>
> Mr. TISCH. I do not know if it is abuse, but it is certainly happening …
>
> Mr. WRIGHT. Well, I think the facts probably speak for themselves. I do not think in the last two or three years there has been any service lost that has not had substantial equity ownership by cable companies. It is a very competitive business. It is very hard to get on the systems.
>
> Senator GORE. Well, is that not an example of an overconcentration of power, that the cable industry is able to wield over the programmers?
>
> Mr. WRIGHT. Well, it is certainly an area that can be fraught with abuse. I mean, there is simply no question. The reality is that people are not running out launching new services on a standalone basis.
>
> Mr. GORE. Is it not very similar to what happened when—before the syndication rule, where networks required an equity interest in programming before it could get on the networks?
>
> Mr. MURPHY. I was not in the network business when that happened …
>
> Mr. TISCH. I am not so sure that—and I was not there, so that is why I say am not sure that the broadcasters, the networks required a financial interest to put something on the air. (*Media Ownership*, 1989, pp. 595–596)

Here the networks were being squeezed by the cable operators (because they owned cable networks they wanted to have distributed), and they barely admitted this was so. But, if an equity stake was required for carriage on a cable system, the networks did not admit to the parallelism between that situation and what went on at the broadcast networks with program producers.

Even more pointed was the following exchange between Senator Gore and the chairmen of the networks:

> Senator GORE. Now, you are an extremely successful businessman, and if you are confronted with two programs one of which can go into a particular slot in your network slot, you own one of them and you do not own the other.… If they have an equal chance in your view of being a hit and one of them is going to make you a ton more money than the other one, as a businessman you are going to choose the one that makes you a ton more money, are you not?
>
> Mr. TISCH. No.
>
> Senator GORE. Oh, Come on. Your stockholders are listening to this.
>
> Mr. TISCH. Let me tell you what just happened on our own schedule …. We had a half dozen marginal programs that we looked at, all the same, all terrible. We decided to go

> with our own terrible program there because we knew the program did not have a chance [against hit series *Roseanne*] …
>
> Senator GORE. Is this an example designed to counter the hypothetical I offered?
>
> Mr. TISCH. Yes, it does counter it.
>
> Senator GORE. I do not think so … choosing been alternative sacrificial lambs is very different between trying to pick alternative cash cows …
>
> Mr. WRIGHT. Can I take a shot at that?
>
> Senator GORE. Say, one of them is going to make you a lot more money than the other one. You are not going to take that into account, Mr. Wright?
>
> Mr. WRIGHT. If it were exactly the way you described it, that would be correct, but it never is. The fact of the matter is that there is never equality balance or I have never seen it in our situation …
>
> Senator GORE. I understand that, but I just think it is strange, with all due respect, and I have deep respect for all three of you. I just think it is with strained credulity to ask us to believe that you are going to ignore the fact that you make a lot of money. (*Media Ownership,* pp. 598–599)

Senators were not the only ones who had difficulty believing the networks' testimony. Testimony from James Kellner, President of Fox Broadcasting Co., was particularly damning to the networks. He said in part:

> Rumors to an end to network domination of this market place, I think are greatly over-exaggerated. I have just gone into this business 3.5 years ago trying to start a national program service. And after listening to these gentlemen, I should be depressed to think about the business I have gone into, except I know better. I know what a good business it is despite the appeals for more profits from our competitors. (*Media Ownership,* p. 635)

Fox did have an ulterior motive in trying to keep the rules in place, since this emerging network was unaffected by them. Mr. Kellner's testimony, however, did call the other networks' claims into question.

While these Senate hearings did not affect the fin-syn rules per se, they did start a new round of discussions about the rules.

THE REPEAL OF FIN-SYN

International Issues

International issues had come into play, which put additional pressure on the FCC to reevaluate the rules. Large multinational corporations had begun to purchase Hollywood studios. This meant that much of the programming on American television would be produced by foreign entities. This matter became a bone of contention between the networks and the MPAA. In a November 6, 1989, letter to John Dingell, Chairman of the Committee on Energy and Commerce, Bob Wright (1989a), wrote:

In March of this year, Time, Inc. and Warner Communications announced a merger that created the largest media and entertainment company in the world. Subsequently Qintex of Australia and Rupert Murdoch's News Corporation, which already owns the Twentieth Century Fox Studios, the Fox stations and the Fox Network, each made competing bids for MGM/UA. And then the Sony Corporation announced its bid to purchase Columbia Pictures Entertainment. If all these acquisitions are consummated, four out of seven major domestic theatrical and television production studios, accounting for almost 25% of the entertainment series programming currently seen in network prime time, and 35% of major studio revenues, will be controlled by foreign-owned companies. But our own government's regulations handicap American networks in their pursuit of similar global opportunities in video production and distribution. This puts the absurdity of those regulations—the Financial Interest and Syndication Rules—into stark relief. (p. 123)

If the networks were prohibited from participating in the domestic syndication market, that was one thing. Not to be allowed to engage in sales into the foreign markets was an example of the FCC regulating where it had no true jurisdiction. After all, the FCC had no authority to regulate programming or diversity outside the United States. This was another way for the networks to pick apart the fin-syn rules and give Congress, and the FCC, a reason to think about eliminating them.

Multinational, vertically integrated companies were becoming the basis for the structure of the entertainment business. The networks were put at a severe competitive disadvantage versus these new competitive behemoths. As Wright (1989a) continued:

The effect of these Rules today is not to curb undue network power, which, if it ever existed, has been shattered by competition from cable, new networks and home video. The anomalous effect is instead

- to give a few powerful studios, almost half of which will soon be foreign-owned, protection by these U.S. companies—the networks—in the production and financing of television programs;
- to limit the ability of American companies to play on a global scale equal to News Corporation or Sony;
- to weaken the capacity of American free television to compete against cable for attractive and popular programs, and of local affiliates to continue to provide their communities with news and public affairs service;
- to funnel the revenues generated by this nation's largest export into the plus column of other countries' balance of trade ledgers.

Whatever public policy rationale the Rules enjoyed twenty-five years ago, it has long since evaporated. There is no reason to tie the hands of America's potentially strongest international competitors. The risk to our country's position in the worldwide media marketplace is too great to permit these rules to remain on the books. (pp. 125–126)

The MPAA, of course, would not let this letter go unanswered. Jack Valenti (1989c), sent a letter to John Dingell on November 22. It said in part:

> The NBC letter, alas, is awash in misstatements and omissions so obvious that anyone with professional knowledge of our business would find it, alternately, amusing and sad …
>
> 1. Of the some 211 television producer/programmer companies—independent companies, large, medium-sized, small who are banded together in the Coalition to Preserve the Financial & Syndication Rule—only *two* (Columbia and MTM) are foreign owned. The rest are American based and American owned.
> 2. The networks are not prohibited from buying a studio, such as Columbia …. Networks can purchase a movie studio right now. The only inhibition is they could not be in the syndication business, but they would be able, as they are now, to sell all their TV programs to syndicators, and reap their profits up front. I might add that Sony, under current rules, cannot purchase a network or a TV station.
> 3. Please recall that the *first* entertainment company to sell out to the Japanese was CBS. It sold CBS records to Sony, when other American companies were anxious to purchase CBS records. NBC's voice was not raised then in either anger or despair.
> 4. It was NBC who energetically sought to partner with an Australian concern to buy MGM/UA. (pp. 127–128)

Valenti continues in the letter to demonstrate why fin-syn is a much-needed regulation. His main point is that the impetus for the creation of the rules still exists—the networks remain the only game in town.

> Let me put it this way: If *all* the TV production companies in the US merged into one giant enterprise, that behemoth would have to approach the networks, as a supplicant, to get a show on prime time. And if the networks said "no," that giant newly merged company would be exiled from prime time public view. (p. 129)

Attached to the letter is a fact sheet entitled "Facts about the television marketplace and the power of the three national networks." This sheet outlines the fiscal strength of the broadcast networks. Advertising revenue is up; stock values are increasing; a strong growth trend is predicted for the next five years. Also, the initial erosion of cable into network viewing shares had begun to level off by this time, with no single cable network attracting an audience anywhere near the size of that watching a broadcast network. Finally, networks continue to have an advantage vis-à-vis program producers. Producers must take on deficits to produce their shows in hopes that it will go into syndication. Networks make up their license fee expenditure from airing the programming, if not in the first run then in the second (pp. 132–133).

Valenti (1989c) followed up this letter with another one dated December 6, 1989. It begins by telling about a December 2, 1989, *Washington Post* article that explains that General Electric, NBC's parent company, is about to join with the Japanese in producing supersonic aircraft. This while NASA is trying to maintain U.S. dominance in aircraft production. It appears to Valenti a bit disingenuous for GE to go into business with the Japanese while NBC complains about Columbia Pictures doing the same thing. More important, he also highlights another story from the same newspaper:

> The POST reports that a Chicago TV station, owned by General Electric, reported a failure by GE to certify the unworthiness of airplane bolts so substandard they are a threat to air safety. When this news report reached the news division of NBC, that part about GE's negligence was censored from the news reported on the TODAY Show, NBC's national network morning program.
>
> What these POST stories confirm is that the three national networks possess a vast embrace of power that is accessible to no others ... That's why they have to be held in check so that some fragile balance can continue to exist in the marketplace.
>
> ... both [articles] are pertinent to the networks' insistent they would always act in the public interest if only they were rid of this terrible Financial Interest and Syndication Rule. (Valenti, 1989c, p. 135)

This international issue would certainly strike a chord with Congress—not so much the foreign ownership of American companies, which Valenti demonstrated was not in fact the dire situation that the networks had presented. Rather, the ability of American companies to export product would be of interest. American films had been a major export for decades, as had American television programming. New overseas television markets, however, were opening up with more commercial opportunities, as opposed to government owned entities. Given this opening up of foreign market opportunities, the idea that the American government would be able to say that they had a system open to foreign countries when they approached these countries for access to their airwaves would be very important in the negotiating process.

The Repeal of Fin-Syn—1991

A confluence of events led the FCC to renew its interest in the financial interest and syndication rules and review them once again in the early 1990s. First, there was the development of Fox as a viable network alternative and their petition to the FCC for relief from the rules (riling the existing broadcast networks, which claimed that the FCC was showing favoritism). On January 29, 1990, Fox filed a *Petition for Resumption of Rulemaking and Request for Temporary Relief* with the FCC, asking for a review and modification of the fin-syn rules. Fox was a new broadcast network—the first new network in 50 years. As an emerging network, Fox claimed that fin-syn discouraged diversity because broadcasters would hold back programming so as not to be subject to the rules, for example, networks would program less than 15 hours per week in order not to be defined as a network under the rules. By limiting the amount of programming on the network, diversity was being hampered because fewer producers have outlets for their programming. The FCC issued Fox a one-year waiver allowing the network to exceed the fin-syn programming limits. The Fox petition provided the impetus for the FCC to review the fin-syn rules yet again.

Another reason for the FCC's renewed interest in the rules was the increase in international ownership of companies producing programming for American television, which the networks claimed gave international companies a competitive advantage over the American networks that were wrongfully constrained by the fin-syn rules. In particular, they were talking about Sony's ownership of Columbia, the only studio owned by a foreign entity other than MTM. By November 1990, the consent decrees would also no longer keep the networks from owning and producing 100 percent of their prime-time programming. This concerned for the Hollywood studios that felt that without this part of the consent decree, the networks would be able to circumvent the fin-syn rules. If the networks could produce all of their own programming, even if they could not syndicate it, they could and would use that leverage to again extort financial interests from independent producers. Finally, with Reagan out of the White House, the networks saw an opportunity to finally get fin-syn repealed. Here's how Leonard Hill, a television producer, described the shifting political winds:

> The networks knew that they could not move under Reagan. But when Bush was elected, they pounced. Deregulation had become a Republican mantra. White House Chief John Sununu was very receptive to the networks' lobbying efforts. Unlike Reagan, Sununu was not informed by any personal experience. For him it was all ideology. And Sununu was in a perfect position to stack the FCC with Commissioners who would be in tune with the White House point of view. He not only controlled the appointment of the three Republican Commissioners, he was able to control the reappointment of one of the two Democrats. Jim Quello had long supported regulation of the networks, but I believe the White House made it clear to Quello that the price of his reappointment would be a conversion to the orthodox school of deregulation. Quello didn't have a lot of volts left in his battery, and he dearly loved the perks of being a Commissioner. With Quello in his pocket, I believe Sununu felt confident that he had a 4-to-1 vote on virtually any issue the White House endorsed. (personal interview, July 24, 1999)

The repeal of fin-syn would not happen quite so quickly, however.

In response to Fox's petition, the FCC issued a *Notice of Proposed Rulemaking.* This *Notice* asked for comments on proposed revisions to the rules. These proposals included: (a) keeping the existing rules, (b) eliminating the financial interest rule, but not the syndication rule, (c) eliminating the financial interest rule and modifying the syndication rule per the *Tentative Decision,* (d) keeping the existing rules, but make an exception for emerging networks (Evaluation of the Syndication and Financial Interest Rules, p. 3097). Then there was a *Further Notice of Proposed Rulemaking* in October 1991. Out of this *Notice* and from subsequent hearings, the Commission derived what would become the revised 1991 fin-syn rules.

All parties expected that these 1991 rules would be a giant step toward deregulating the networks, particularly given the make up of the FCC as primarily Republican with a Democrat swayed to the Republican side. There seemed to be increasing evidence that the changes in the marketplace might justify such changes in the rules. The FCC had found that:

- The number of independent stations has increased from 65 in 1970 to some 340 in 1990, 130 of which obtain a significant portion of their programming from an emerging broadcast network (the Fox Broadcasting Company).
- Programming services originating on cable have grown substantially, with over 90 national programming services available today.
- Almost 60 percent of all American television households now subscribe to cable services.
- The networks' aggregate share of the nationwide prime time viewing audience has declined from roughly 90 percent in 1970 to around 62 percent today. (Evaluation of the Syndication and Financial Interest Rules, 1991, p. 3108)

Even with these changes in the marketplace, however, the FCC would not eliminate fin-syn but made only minor changes in the rules. The Commission still had concerns about the networks' ability to control the program marketplace even with the increased competition.

> [the networks] still retained an ability to manipulate the prime time entertainment and first-run programming market to the detriment of program source and outlet diversity. Consequently, it was still necessary to impose modified restraints on network acquisition of financial interests in programming and on network syndication activities. (Evaluation of the Syndication and Financial Interest Rules, 1993, pp. 3284–3285)

Lobbying by the Coalition to Preserve the Fin-syn Rules may have helped persuade the FCC away from a complete repeal of the rules. As well, it seems that an *en banc* hearing was persuasive in moving the FCC away from a full repeal of the rules. Leonard Hill, an independent producer and active participant in trying to retain the rules, described the hearing in which he was a participant:

> We put a group of together [to testify at the *en banc*] that I thought represented the true diversity of the independent community. Specifically, the group consisted of Thomas Carter, Marian Reese, Steve Cannell, Jerry Leider and me. Generically, the group was composed of a black director, a white female business owner, a Republican writer, a veteran producer and an ex-network-executive-turned-supplier.
>
> Neither Marian nor Thomas were very excited about testifying. Thomas was particularly concerned that he didn't know the details of regulatory policy and might not make a good impression. He was very wrong, but his worry wasn't without foundation.
>
> Thomas had started in the business as an actor on the series *White Shadow*. When he decided he wanted to learn directing, he was mentored by the show's producer, Bruce Paltrow. When Paltrow felt Thomas was ready, he hired him to direct an episode. Paltrow never checked with the network. He worked for MTM, a terrific independent company that zealously guarded their creative autonomy. Thomas went on to distinguish himself as one of the most celebrated directors in the medium.

> Thomas understood that his career was directly attributable to the protections granted by the rules that allowed strong independent companies to flourish. But he still was concerned his lack of fluency in regulatory matters would make him ineffective. Thomas was confident he could deliver his prepared remarks, but he was worried about follow up questions. I explained that we had nothing to lose. We were facing the prospect of a 5 to 0 defeat. Even the one uncompromised Democrat, Ervin Duggan, seemed frightfully conservative.
>
> So we showed up at the hearing, gave our prepared remarks and waited for questions. And, naturally, the first question was addressed to Thomas. He wasn't happy with this turn of events.
>
> "Mr. Carter, can you tell me where you went to college?" asked Duggan.
>
> Thomas is caught off-guard by the question. No, he didn't go to Harvard or to the American Film Institute or some other fancy place. Thomas gives me a look that, roughly translated, says "Why is this guy picking on me? What business is it of his if or where I went to college?" But after collecting himself, Thomas answers simply, "Southwest Texas State."
>
> Duggan takes a beat and then asks Thomas, "Do you know any other distinguished alum who graduated from your alma matter?"
>
> By now I can't offer Thomas any reassuring looks. I am as puzzled as he is. What's going on? The FCC has convened a public hearing to talk about deregulation of an entire industry and Erv Duggan is making small talk. There is silence.
>
> "Yes," Thomas finally answers.
>
> "And could you give me that man's name?"
>
> "President Johnson. Lyndon Johnson went to Southwest Texas State." The direct answer doesn't disguise the expression that says, "So what?"
>
> Duggan sits back in his chair. He looks pointedly at his fellow Commissioner, Andrew Barrett. In his prepared remarks, Thomas had recounted his career and how the rules had served to foster competition and diversity. He hadn't talked about his education. Was he hiding something? What was going on?
>
> "Mr. Carter," intones Duggan, "I worked for President Johnson. And I know that the thing that made him proudest of his presidency was the passage of the Civil Rights Act of 1964. I assure you, Mr. Carter, that somewhere in this room is the spirit of President Johnson-and your presence here today is a source of great satisfaction to the spirit of the man I was priviliged to serve." And the room went silent.
>
> Then the network presidents came up to begin their testimony. Four white men in their fifties or sixties ... (personal interview, July 24, 1999)

Coming out of these hearings, there was a modification of the rules rather than a full repeal. These became known as the "1991 Rules."

In 1991, the FCC issued a new *Report and Order* that reflected the Commission's reevaluation of its programming diversity mandate in the current video marketplace. "The Commission has studied, in particular, the continued efficacy of restraints on television network acquisition and syndication of programming in an age when new programming outlets seem to abound and yet the broadcast networks uniquely remain, both for viewers and producers, the outlets of choice" (Evaluation of the Syndication and Financial Interest Rules, 1991, p. 3095). So, though new outlets existed, the networks remained the preferred place of program viewing. This put a twist on what the NISS had reported would happen in its report. More outlets were supposed to mean more opportunities for producers and more choices for viewers. This, however, was not turning out to be the case. It appears that because of this, the FCC was reluctant to repeal fin-syn completely. The "1991 rules," also known as the compromise rules, were a narrowing rather than a complete repeal of the regulations. The 1991 *Report and Order* amended the rules in the following way so as to:

> (1) delete restrictions on network ownership and syndication of network programming as to all dayparts and all programs other than prime time entertainment programming; (2) allow networks to retain all rights in all "in-house" productions; (3) permit networks to fill up to, but not more than, 40 percent of their prime time entertainment schedule with "in-house" productions; (4) allow networks to acquire rights, including financial interests, domestic syndication rights and foreign syndication rights, in outside productions, subject to certain safeguards; (5) allow networks to engage in foreign syndication without limitation; and (6) allow limited network participation in first-run syndication. The *Report and Order* also adopts a new definition of "network" and imposes certain reporting requirements. (Evaluation of the Syndication and Financial Interest Rules, 1991, p. 3095)

Some of these amendments were fairly straightforward. Previously, the fin-syn rules applied to the entire broadcast day. Now, only prime-time programming would be affected. Previously, the networks could sell only their own programming into foreign markets, now they had no restrictions on foreign syndication. Other aspects of the rules, however, either made fin-syn more complex or added restrictions that had not been part of the original rules. The overall effect was for the new rules to allow the networks back into the syndication business, with restrictions, as well as allowing them to acquire financial interests in programming that they aired.

While networks could retain rights to in-house productions, the FCC created a definition of what exactly "in-house" meant. "We will define 'in-house productions' as those network programs which are: (1) solely produced by the network; (2) co-produced by the network with foreign production entities; (3) co-produced by the network with outside domestic production entities that initiate such arrangements" (p. 3117). Since the FCC was allowing the networks to syndicate product produced by others, it only made sense that they should be allowed to retain the rights to production that they had produced themselves. However, the FCC was concerned that the networks would program only their own shows at the expense of outside producers. This is why the Commission instituted the 40% schedule cap, something that had not been part of the original rules.

The new safeguard that the FCC created to keep the networks from extracting financial interests from outside producers "require(d) the networks to wait 30 days after negotiating the basic licensing contracts (for network airing) before negotiating for interest and backend rights" ("New Fin-Syn Rules," 1991, p. 32). This 30 days was meant to be a "cooling off period during which the outside producer can decide to nullify or commit to the network co-production arrangement" (Evaluation of Syndication and Financial Interest Rules, 1991, p. 3119). In conjunction with this safeguard, the network had to file in the public records of its owned and operated stations that it had compiled with this 30-day requirement and that the network had not made acquisition of rights a condition for a spot on its schedule. It was hoped that separating the time periods during which these two issues were negotiated would keep the networks from putting undue influence on producers when negotiating for the initial airing of the show. The FCC's thinking was that by separating these elements when negotiating for the rights to the show the networks would not be able to strong-arm a producer into giving away financial interests and syndication rights in the show as a condition for inclusion on the prime-time schedule.

This was the one area in the revised rules where the Commission conceded that the networks still had a competitive advantage over other players in the television marketplace. That advantage stemmed from their structure—owned and operated stations in the largest markets, a stable affiliate structure and the ability to reach 98% of television households—which was historically based. Even with the introduction of new technologies, the networks still maintained their unique role as the dominant procurer of entertainment programming. As well, the networks' ability to present and develop shows, which were capable of being syndicated, remained an ability unique to the broadcast networks. All of this suggested that there was still little, if any, substitutability between having a show presented over the broadcast networks in prime time and having it air on alternative outlets.

The FCC was also not ready to let the networks advance fully into the first-run syndication market. Issues regarding their control over affiliates caused the Commission to continue restrictions in this area. They permitted

> a network to produce entertainment programming for first-run syndication and to retain a financial interest as well as foreign syndication rights in such programming "solely produced" in-house. However, due to previously discussed concerns regarding the unique nature of the first-run syndication market, we will require that such programming be syndicated domestically through an independent syndicator .... We also clarify that network-produced first-run programming shall be considered network programming for purposes of the prime time access rule. (Evaluation of the Syndication and Financial Interest Rules, 1991, p. 3141)

With all of these changes, the networks would be back in the syndication business albeit with some seriously misguided constraints, the most glaring example being the 30-day delay for negotiating syndication rights. It makes no sense to separate the negotiation of licensing and syndication. One number affects the other. If the network gets a piece of syndication, it will pay a higher fee in licensing with the expectation of reaping syndication dollars on the backend. If there is no financial interest, the network will pay less money in license fees. Also, what is there to prove that the two negotiations remained separate? The paper the networks would put in the public files of their O&Os? Did the FCC really think this would keep the negotiations honest? The Commission obviously thought so:

> We conclude that these reporting requirements will deter possible anticompetitive behavior by the networks and will assist the Commission and interested parties in confirming network compliance with our modified financial interest and syndication rules. In addition, the information submitted in the networks' semi-annual reports will enable the Commission to monitor the efficacy of its various safeguards and to oversee the networks' conduct in the program acquisition and syndication markets. (Evaluation of the Syndication and Financial Interest Rules, 1991, p. 3155)

The final change that the 1991 rules made was to change the definition of a network. Previously a network was defined as "any person, entity or corporation which offers an interconnected program service on a regular basis for 15 or more hours per week to at least 25 affiliated television licensees in 10 or more states ...." This was changed to "any entity providing more than 15 hours per week of prime time programming on a regular basis to interconnected affiliates that reach, in aggregate, at least 75 percent of television households nationwide" (Evaluation of the Syndication and Financial Interest Rules, 1991, p. 3147). The difference in the two rules was that the new rule applied to 15 hours of *prime time* programming and expanded the amount of national coverage from a number of stations reached to a percentage of the country reached. This definition was a means of protecting Fox from the rules. While Fox by this point had reached more than 90% of U.S. television households, Fox had not yet met the programming limitations on this rule, and so they would not be affected by the fin-syn rules unless and until they reached that programming threshold.

Another way that the FCC protected the Fox network was to include "transition rules." These were created in order to give Fox, and other subsequent emerging networks, time to develop. The FCC justified this in that a new broadcast network seemed to be the best real competition for the existing broadcast networks. The transition rules allowed an emerging network to take 3 years to comply to the remaining fin-syn rules once they had reached network status. It was assumed that the type of organization most likely to become a network was one that was already vertically integrated in production, syndication, and broadcast station ownership. It would take time for a company of this type to divest itself of its existing program contracts that might not be in compliance with the rules.

While those opposed to the rules wanted a sunset provision, that is a date when the rules would expire, the Commission did not believe this was prudent. Since the FCC wanted to monitor the effect of changing the rules on the industry, they would not put in such a provision. They did, however, put in a scheduled review so that the rules would be evaluated again 4 years hence.

Once again history repeated itself. Neither side of the argument was happy with the revised rules. Program suppliers were concerned about competition and particularly about the networks getting back into the production business. The networks were still looking for a total repeal of the laws. Even though the networks could produce first-run syndication, this was still considered network programming and therefore could not be scheduled during prime access. Alfred Sikes, Chairman of the FCC in 1991, was in agreement with the networks and gave a dissenting opinion about the decision to maintain fin-syn. He blamed the majority for not focusing on the facts that were placed before them from the many previous studies presented, particularly information that suggested that the three networks were not a single entity, but three individual and fierce competitors. He hit hard on the diversity argument, using it as a reason to deregulate fully. He explained:

> Time and again over the last decade, the Commission has furthered the aim of increased diversity in broadcast programming by allowing free competition in the broadcast marketplace. Time and again the Commission has found that diversity in a competitive mass media environment is furthered by *removing* regulatory restraints, not by erecting new ones. (Evaluation of the Syndication and Financial Interest Rules, 1991, p. 3172)

Sikes, however, did not take into account what the rest of the Commission does. Specifically, the networks have some historical structural advantages that keep them a dominant force in the industry. In his argument, Sikes unknowingly supports this point. He explains that cable networks have begun to bid against the broadcast networks for programming. Premium pay channels, such as HBO and Showtime, were able to offer comparable licensing fees as the networks. Nevertheless, the cable networks were unsuccessful in acquiring these shows instead of the networks. Why, if they were offering the same amount of money would this be true? Why wouldn't the producers gladly put their show on HBO rather than CBS? The reason is simple. The long-term viability of a show is in syndication, and the networks were still the only place in town where a show would be developed long enough and find enough of an audience for it to ultimately make money in syndication.

This time, not unexpectedly, the White House was unhappy with the outcome of these revised rules. The administration, like the networks, were looking for "complete repeal of the original and near-absolute fin-syn restrictions" ("New Fin-syn Rules," 1991). Ronald Reagan had even gotten involved again trying to use his influence to sway the Bush White House, but to no avail ("Chief to Chief," 1991, p. 6). John Sununu, Bush's Chief of Staff, "stressed the administration's commitment to deregulation by saying, 'the President expects his appointees at the departments and agencies to carry out these principles in their particular spheres to the extent they can do so consistent with the legal framework enacted by Congress'" (Covington, 1994, p. 8).

The Repeal of Fin-Syn - Really

All of this to-do was just so much political posturing, because the 1991 rules turned out to be short lived. By late 1991, the rules had been turned over to the U. S. Court of Appeals in Chicago for review. The networks petitioned the Seventh Circuit Court of Appeals to invalidate the rules, claiming that given the changes in the structure of the television marketplace, it was unjustifiable to leave the rules essentially unchanged (*Schurz Communications, Inc. v. FCC, 1992*).

It was not just the increase in competition from cable that was forcing the networks to push hard for the rules to be repealed. When the marketplace changed, the distribution of capital in the marketplace changed. In 1992, according to the *Wall Street Journal*, network television was barely profitable. It was a time when the networks were being called "dinosaurs." But the domestic syndication market was at $4.3 billion and foreign sales had hit $2.64 billion according to Paul Kagan, an industry analyst (Jensen, 1992a, p. B1). Even with the repeal of the rules, the networks would have to rebuild their production units, and even with a prime-time hit, it would be 5 years before they would be able to syndicate off-network programming.[7] Also, cable was not increasing the total number of advertising dollars to television, but rather was taking ad revenue from the broadcasting networks. Because the broadcasters' single source of revenue was being competitively eroded, the networks needed to find additional revenue streams.[8]

For of all these reasons, the networks wanted immediate repeal of the rules. Judge Posner, the federal judge responsible for writing the appeals court decision, agreed. The court felt that the FCC rather than making a decision on one side versus the other, was attempting to split the difference with the new rules, by giving some concessions to each side, with no one ending up with a good outcome. Though the rules were long and verbose, they overlooked evidence and did not explain important concepts. *Schurz* listed its faultfinding of the revised rules:

> First, the court charged the FCC with ignoring the networks' argument that the 1991 rules were unsuccessful because they did not, in fact, increase network access to the programming market .... Second, ... the 1991 rules would not prevent the networks from using their market power to purchase programming at favorably low prices .... Third, ... the 1991 rules limited competition with established networks by stunting the growth of new networks .... Fourth, ... the court asserted that the FCC failed to reconcile its order supporting the 1991 rules with its Tentative Decision [of 1983] .... Finally, the court was concerned that the FCC never defined the word "diversity" as it applied to television programming. (Herskovitz, 1997, p. 197)

Thus in early November 1992, the Court of Appeals struck down the new revised rules and remanded the matter to the FCC for further review. The networks had won an important battle in getting the court on their side. According to *Broadcasting*, "The big three broadcast networks [are] ever closer to becoming full players in network program production and off-network program syndication" (Jessell, 1992, p. 4). Hollywood producers were stunned by the decision and at how quickly the court

[7]At that time, a network show was on the air for approximately 3 to 5 years before it was sold into syndication.

[8]Cable television had an added advantage over broadcasters in that it generates revenue from both advertisers and cable operators who pay to carry a cable network on their system. Additionally, they sell licensed products related to both the network and/or individual programs.

came to its decision (approximately 1 month). As Rich Frank, president of Disney, put it "'For the FCC to have worked seven years on this and then to have a court throw it out in 30 days is incredible'" (p. 8). One reason that the Hollywood community believed that the court was able to come to their decision so quickly was because Judge Posner had written an affidavit for CBS in its fight against the Justice Department consent decrees. Because of this conflict of interest, the Hollywood studios requested Judge Posner recuse himself from the panel. The judge would not remove himself from the panel, and there was nothing they could do.

The FCC interpreted the court's decision to remand as not necessarily meaning that they had to eliminate the 1991 rules. Rather, the Commission needed to do a better job in justifying why they had not given more credence to the networks' arguments in developing the 1991 regulation (Evaluation of the Syndication and Financial Interest Rules, 1993, p. 3291). Therefore, under remand, the rules were revised yet again ("1993 rules"). In April 1993, the FCC eliminated all but one aspect of the fin-syn rules. With these new rules,

> the networks will now be allowed to own a stake in shows provided by outsiders, share fully in rerun sales when the shows move into syndication, and produce and own as much of their prime-time lineups as they want ... the FCC stopped short of letting the networks directly syndicate programs. Instead of selling series reruns—including those they own 100%—to individual stations, they must let an outside company do the selling and then share in the proceeds. (Jensen, 1993, p. B1)

The networks were also prohibited from participating in first-run syndication. These restrictions were minimal in comparison with the 1991 Rules and in fact closely reflected the 1983 *Tentative Decision*. Gone were restrictions on financial interests. Gone were restrictions on non-prime-time programming. Gone were restrictions on production and ownership for prime time. Gone were restrictions on in-house productions and its methods of distribution. Gone were restrictions on foreign syndication, both of off-network and first-run programming. Finally, and what the networks had been pushing for all the way along, these new 1993 Rules provided for the complete elimination of the rules within 2 years. The few restrictions the FCC maintained were supposed to guarantee that the networks would not act in ways detrimental to diversity. The two-year time period would allow for this while not immediately disrupting the marketplace, which might occur if the Commission had simply repealed the rules.

These rules, however, would be useless without the elimination of the Justice Department consent decrees. On November 12, U. S. District Court Judge Manuel Real removed the consent decrees, which "the networks hailed ... as the key to their future" ("Networks Win," 1993, p. 6).

There would be one last attempt to retain the financial interest and syndication rules. The FCC had written into the 1993 Rules that arguments would be heard about retaining the rules 6 months prior to their final elimination. It would be up to the proponents of the rules to convince the FCC that the rules were necessary for promoting competition and diversity. On April 5, 1995, the FCC called for arguments for and against retaining fin-syn.

The FCC issued a *Report and Order* on September 6. The only rules the FCC needed to review at this point were ones related to the networks' entrance into the syndication market. The Commission had allowed the networks to begin syndicating 2 years prior. Starting with the existing record, the FCC believed that the competitive conditions in the market, and the decline of network dominance, called for the repeal of the rules.

The FCC had listed 14 factors that they would use to evaluate whether or not to retain the rules. These included such issues as changes in the number of independent producers, a network's share of the first-run syndication market, network negotiating patterns, mergers and acquisitions within the industry, and growth of alternative networks. The FCC reviewed each of these 14 factors in its 1995 *Report and Order.* Only one factor still concerned the Commission after evaluation of the evidence. That was the increase in mergers and acquisitions of media companies since the 1993 Rules—not just giants like the merger of Viacom with Blockbuster and Paramount but also Disney's acquisition of ABC and Westinghouse's acquisition of CBS. "The Commission will, or course, be reviewing these acquisitions in the normal course of its regulatory business to ensure that they do not undermine the competitiveness of the production and distribution markets" (Review of the Syndication and Financial Interest Rules, 1995, paragraph 25).

The FCC claimed that proponents of the rules were unable to make their case for the continued need for fin-syn. The reasons the FCC gave for rejected the proponents' claims were that they presented (a) either information prior to 1993 or (b) information that the Commission had rejected in a previous hearing. The FCC specifically wanted information from 1993 forward as this was the time period affected by the easing of the rules. The proponents didn't do this:

> Proponents of retaining the rules have not provided persuasive evidence that the established networks engage in, or threaten to engage in, affiliate favoritism to the detriment of non-network stations; that the established networks place or retain programming in their schedules because of their financial interests in or syndication rights to that programming, or for other than legitimate competitive reasons; or that the established networks have reduced the pool of suppliers of television programming through anticompetitive practices. (paragraph 28)

The rules were set to expire on November 10, 1995. On September 6, 1995, however, the FCC decided to accelerate the expiration date. Instead of expiring on November 10, 1995, "the FCC released an order effectuating the rules' demise as of the publication date of the order in the Federal Register" (Herskovitz, 1997, p. 199). Thus, the rules were completely repealed on September 21, 1995. To complete the story, the prime-time access rules were repealed as of August 30, 1996.

IMPACT OF THE REPEAL OF THE FIN-SYN RULES

With the repeal of the financial interest and syndication rules, there was a corresponding change in the structure of the television industry. This change occurred to allow the broadcast networks to take advantage of their ability to participate in the production and syndication markets. Some networks created in-house studios, other networks were purchased by production companies or station owners. Fox expanded its station lineup to include more VHF affiliates, putting them on an equal par with the established networks. New networks emerged, created by production companies looking to guarantee access to the broadcast airwaves. Finally, most of these new vertically integrated companies also included a syndication arm so that these companies would be able to fully take advantage of their new-found freedom in this market.

With the repeal of fin-syn, the networks have become stronger through vertical integration and have begun using their gatekeeper status to request financial interests from producers. These structural changes, however, have had little impact on the diversity of programming content suggesting that yet again, the FCC used an ineffective method to achieve its goal.

4

The Structure of the Television Industry

At the time the fin-syn rules were enacted, the three broadcast networks constituted an oligopoly, that is, more than one company (in this case three) acting under the same conditions as a monopoly. As such, the three networks had virtually unlimited control over the national airwaves, particularly as it related to the selection of programming for broadcast during the prime-time hours. The networks attracted the largest part of the audience because there was little or no competition for viewers except in the very largest television markets such as New York and Los Angeles. Because the networks had the largest audiences, they attracted the bulk of the advertising dollars, which enabled them to produce or purchase the best programming.

The structure of the television industry changed drastically in the 1980s with the advent of cable television and the introduction of a new broadcast network—the first new network in 50 years. Cable not only provided more programming choices through new cable networks, but also improved the distribution of independent broadcast stations. The 1980s also saw the introduction of a new broadcast network, Fox, which became a formidable competitor to the three established networks much to their surprise. No longer were the broadcast networks the only buyers for prime-time programming. Suddenly producers had a plethora of buyers and outlets for their programming.

Outlets continued to increase throughout the 1980s and into the 1990s. Three new broadcast networks were introduced in the 1990s, and digital technologies led to new networks distributed through direct broadcast satellite (DBS) and digital cable. As new technologies changed the structure of the television industry over the past 40 years, who produces television programming and how producers are compensated changed as well. By examining the industry structure over time, we can look at the changing economics of the television industry, the changing makeup of the production community, and begin to see how this affects program content. Woven throughout this changing marketplace are the effects of the introduction and repeal of the financial interest and syndication rules.

TELEVISION INDUSTRY STRUCTURE

Networks and Stations

In the 1960s, the broadcast television industry was made up of three national networks (ABC, CBS, and NBC), network affiliates (local stations that carried network programming), independent stations (local stations with no network affiliation), and late in the 1960s, public television stations. Signals were broadcast over either Very High Frequency (VHF), those channels from 2 to 13 that usually included the three national networks, or Ultra High Frequency (UHF), channels 14 to 69 that tended to have poorer reception than channels delivered over the lower frequencies. Cable television existed in the 1960s, but had very limited distribution. It was primarily used in areas where reception was poor, not to transmit alternative programming sources.

The means for distribution of television programming nationally were the broadcast networks. The three national networks in the 1960s were the American Broadcasting Company (ABC), the Columbia Broadcasting System (CBS), and the National Broadcasting Company (NBC).[1] Under FCC regulations, each network was allowed to own up to five broadcast stations. These stations are known as owned and operated stations, or O&Os. Each network had an O&O in the three major markets—New York, Los Angeles, and Chicago—with ABC also owning stations in San Francisco and Detroit, CBS in Philadelphia and St. Louis, and NBC in Cleveland and Washington, DC.

In addition to the owned and operated stations, the networks distribute programming over affiliated stations. These stations are license holders in local markets that the FCC has authorized to run a broadcast station in a particular market area. These stations enter into an agreement with a broadcast network to air programming the network supplies. The affiliate is not required to run everything the network provides, but the station is given incentives by the network for these program clearances. Incentives include things such as advertising space adjacent to network programming, but they are usually in the form of payments, known as affiliate compensation:

> Traditionally, the networks have paid their affiliated stations for clearing network programming, or more precisely, for clearing the network commercials which are associated with that programming. While the methods used to determine these payments are rather complicated, they are directly related to the size of a station's audience and con-

[1]Only NBC was a subsidiary of a larger company at this time. Radio Corporation of American (RCA) was its owner.

> stitute an important ingredient contributing to the financial health of affiliated stations. (Commerical Television Network Practices, 1977, p. 555)

Compensation provided an advantage to affiliates not available to independent stations—an additional, consistent revenue stream.

Network affiliates usually number between 200 to 215 per network, corresponding with the number of television markets in the United States. These affiliates are often owned by large organizations called station groups, which may own affiliate stations belonging to more than one network. For example, a station group could have an ABC station in Des Moines and a CBS station in Albuquerque. These multiple network affiliations provide station groups with access to important information. Because they know what each of the networks is offering in terms of affiliate compensation, they are better positioned to negotiate contracts for their stations. Major broadcast station groups in the 1960s included Group W (Westinghouse), Metromedia, and Hearst, to name three.

The three national broadcast networks exist as an efficient means of transmitting high-quality programming. Broadcast networks act as consolidators of programming and then distribute that programming to affiliates. For instance, without the networks, each individual station would have to produce its own programming. Or, if the station did not have the capabilities to produce its own programming, the organization would have to purchase programming to air throughout the day. One of two things would happen in this situation. Either, the station would spend significant money producing or procuring quality programs, cutting heavily into its bottom line, or to reduce expenditures, the station would acquire less expensive (usually lower quality) programming to fill the program schedule. But, when affiliated with a broadcast network, stations receive the programming from a single source without having to pay directly for it. The affiliate instead gives the majority of its advertising during those program hours to the network for it to sell to national advertisers. Thus, programming expenditures for independent stations is significantly higher than for network affiliates. Figure 4.1 demonstrates the difference between the average cost of programming for an independent station and a network affiliate.

This figure shows that network affiliates have several advantages vis-à-vis their independent brethren. Through the early 1970s, network affiliated stations paid on average less than half the cost for programming as an independent station did. The affiliate receives compensation from the network, which is a revenue stream unavailable to independents. This compensation is derived from the networks' ability to achieve economies of scale by having a central source of production. This central source also allows for higher quality programming, which in turn attracts a larger audience. The larger viewing audience attracts more and better advertisers both for the network and the affiliates. All of this explains, from an economic perspective, the advantages of the network system as a more efficient method of program distribution.

By the early 1970s, the networks had become so effective as program brokers that network programming had expanded to 13 hours per day during the week, with

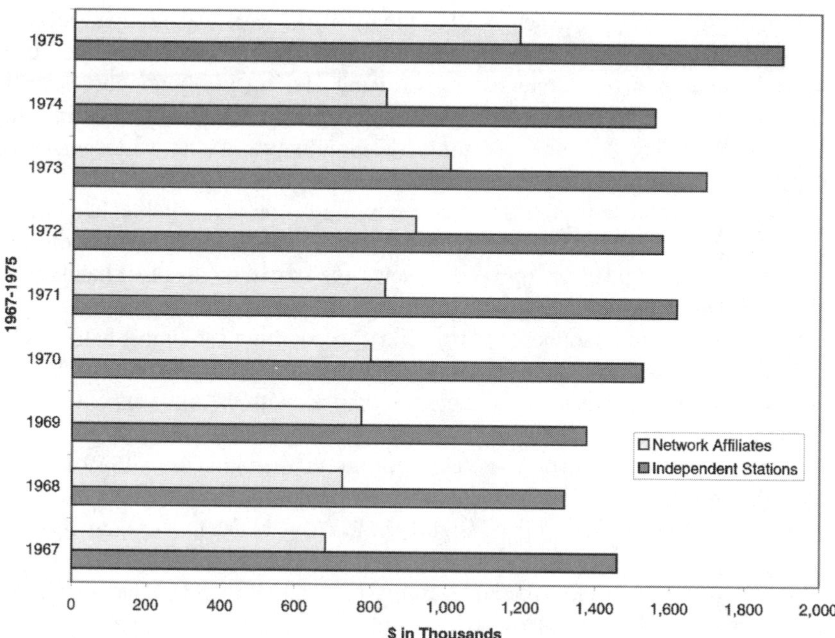

FIG. 4.1. Average program cost by type of station.
Note. Cost information from FCC Financial Data 1967–1975.

additional programming on the weekends. CBS and NBC supplied approximately 70% of the programming on an affiliate's schedule, while ABC provided programming for just over half of the affiliates' airtime (Pearce, 1973, p. 21). Network supplied programming included morning news shows, such as *Today* on NBC; daytime programming, such as soap operas; nightly news programs between 6 and 7 p.m., prime-time programming, which covers the time period from 8 to 11 p.m. and finally late-night programming, such as *The Tonight Show with Johnny Carson*. When not airing network programming, affiliates schedule locally originated programming, such as local news and public affairs programs, and syndicated programming, which in the 1960s and 1970s was primarily off-network syndicated re-runs.[2]

Even though produced centrally, network programming is expensive. In particular, prime-time programming is expensive. In 1972, for instance, the three broadcast networks spent $300 million on news and sports programming, $105 million on daytime programming, $25 million on late-night programming, and a whopping $480 million, more than half of all money spent on programming, on shows for prime time.

[2]Off-network syndicated shows, as the name implies, are programs that originally aired on a network. After roughly 5 years it was sold on a market-by-market basis to stations.

Programming may be expensive, but the networks were well compensated for supplying it, being distributors of programming nationally, and therefore the centralized source for national television advertising. Having this monopoly on advertising allowed the networks to become very profitable organizations during this time period. Taking 1972 as an example, during this year the networks generated over $1.6 billion dollars in revenue from advertising.

Table 4.1 demonstrates that some programming is more profitable than others. Children's programming, for instance, generates revenues over three times the cost of producing that type of programming. News and sports, on the other hand, make only a third more money than it takes to produce the programming. Prime time generates the most significant advertising dollars, accounting for almost half of total revenues but at smaller margins than the other dayparts. This is to be expected because this time period attracts the largest audiences with the most expensive programming.

Overall, the three networks increased program spending from 1969 through 1975. Figure 4.2 provides a historical look at programming costs for the three networks. Program expenses dropped slightly in 1971 but began to rise again in 1972. This in part may be attributed to the fin-syn rules. Because broadcasters were no longer allowed to own a financial interest in a program, they did not pay incremental dollars for those rights. However, as stated, program costs began to increase again in 1972, suggesting that the dip in program spending was an anomaly.

These figures, however, tell only part of the story, because they only take into account programming expenses. In addition to program costs, there are network costs associated with selling and distributing network programs such as general and administrative costs, line charges for feeding programs to affiliates, advertising agency commission, and affiliate compensation. Agency commission at that time was a standard 15% commission of the gross advertising expenditure. Affiliate compensation, the other significant expense after program costs and agency commissions, varies depending on the type of programming. For example, networks pay affiliates more compensation to air prime-time programming than any other

TABLE 4.1

Three Network Total Programming Costs and Revenues, 1972

	Program Costs	*Advertising Revenues*
News and Sports	$300 million	$400 million
Prime Time	$480 million	$800 million
Daytime	$105 million	$300 million
Late-Night	$ 25 million	$ 58.5 million
Children's	$ 25 million	$ 80 million
Total	$935 million	$1638.5 million

Note. Information from Pearce (1973). *The Economics of Prime Time Access*, p. 23.

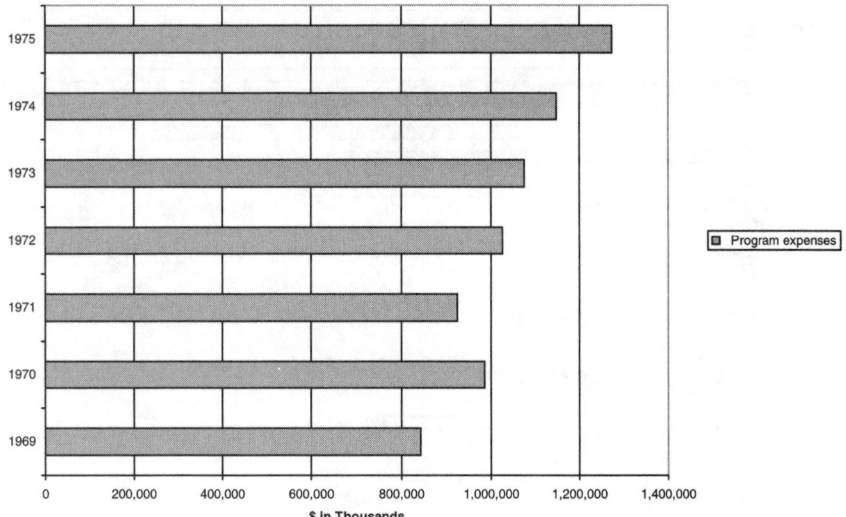

FIG. 4.2. Network program expenses.
Note. Financial data different from Pearce data, because FCC information did not separate technical expenses from programming expenses, these figures are higher. Cost information from FCC Financial Data 1969–1975.

type because the network wants the widest distribution for this programming as possible to maximize clearance for national advertisers. Also, there are more administrative fees associated with prime time programming (programming personnel, promotion, and advertising expenditures, etc.), which reduces the profitability of this daypart. Even with these associated expenses, prime time can still generate a significant profit given its substantial revenues. Overall, however, late-night, daytime, and children's programming were the most profitable for the networks.

After paying for programming, administrative costs, advertising commissions, and affiliate compensation, among other miscellaneous costs, the three networks combined generated a pretax profit of $110.9 million in 1972 (FCC, 39th Annual Report 1973, p. 223). Figure 4.3 provides a history of network income from 1966 to 1975.

As Figure 4.3 demonstrates, broadcast networks do not just receive income from national advertisers; they also generate revenue from their owned and operated stations. Therefore, in 1972, though network income from advertising was almost $111 million, total income (advertising plus moneys from owned and operated stations) was more than $210 million. In addition, the chart shows significant fluctuations in total network income from 1966 to 1975. For instance, 1969's $226 million level was a record to that date. Most of that income came from increased profitability at the network. Income for 1970 was down almost 25%, to just under $170 million. Looking at this legislatively, it is surprising for two reasons. First, cigarette advertising was to be banned from television as of January 1, 1971, which would intuitively lead one to think that cigarette advertisers would spend heavily in their final year on television to

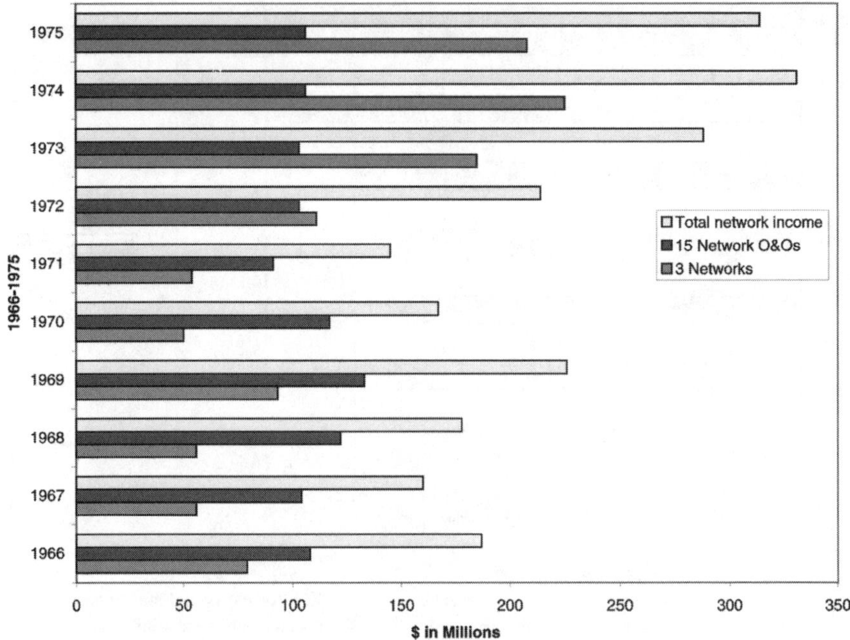

FIG. 4.3. Network income—1966–1975.
Note. Network income is income before federal income tax. Information from FCC Financial Data 1966–1975.

compensate for the future loss of this medium. The numbers suggest otherwise. Second, fin-syn and prime-time access would go into effect in 1971. This would have affected income in two ways—without PTAR, there was more prime-time programming and therefore more advertising to sell and one would expect more revenue (though the subsequent analysis proved that this was not the case). As well, because fin-syn was pending, it would have made sense for the networks to spend less money on programming because they could not buy into the subsequent financial interests. This would have increased income at the network level due to reduced expenses. None of these scenarios appeared to have occurred given the significant drop in network income. Income continued to drop in 1971 but came back to a new all-time high in 1972 and continued to increase thereafter. Any fears of fin-syn's impact on network profitability could be eliminated based on this historical trend. Rather than regulation, economics may have been the culprit behind the change in advertising expenditures. Advertising spending is heavily correlated with the economy. When sales start to fall, the easiest thing for a company to do is reduce its advertising budget. The early 1970s were a time of recession in the United States, which may account for the fluctuations in advertising.

The relationship between the networks and their owned and operated stations gives the networks a very powerful position in the programming marketplace. The owned and operated stations at that time reached between 20 and 25% of U.S. television households. As noted earlier, this coverage included the three top markets for all of the networks as well as additional owned stations in other top-12 television markets. The networks' ability to distribute programming efficiently as well as the strength of the O&O's made the networks the primary provider of programming for syndicated as well as networked distribution. As Pearce (1973) states:

> It was the market as it developed that determined the amount of programming that was network originated, and the amount that was affiliate originated. The market, however, has been weighted in the networks [sic] favor, since the networks are few in number, and have the most powerful groups of owned and operated stations forming the backbone of their network strength. (p. 30)

The networks are able to use their clout as program providers and as station operators to force programming into the marketplace. For example, to be successful, a syndicated show must to be sold into the largest markets. All three networks had O&Os in the top three markets, New York, Chicago, and Los Angeles, virtually guaranteeing the ability to successfully launch a syndicated show and equally the ability to keep competitors out of the market.

Through program development at the network level and as a purchaser of programming through their owned and operated stations, networks had significant control over program selection and distribution. As the only means of national program distribution and as the de facto primary program developer, the networks became the gatekeepers for information and entertainment for the American viewing public.

Independent Stations—The Alternative to Network Television

Independent stations are just what their name implies—independent. That is, these stations are not affiliated with a broadcast network. Few independent stations existed in the late 1960s and early 1970s. This is because the radio spectrum had been divided with the networks getting the majority of available space, particularly in the Very High Frequency range, the part of the spectrum through which the networks were able to send a clearer signal. Most independent stations were in the UHF part of the spectrum. This situation put independents at a technological disadvantage versus the networks, because they could not send a high-quality signal into most homes. Also, a majority of television sets—four out of five—were not equipped to receive UHF signals. The All-Channel Television Receiver Act gave the FCC the power to require all TV sets be equipped to receive UHF signals, thus aiding independent stations in their ability to reach viewers. The Commission believed these stations were the key to creating diversity in the television marketplace, as they equated more outlets with more diversity.

Even with these new TV sets, however, independent stations were only available in the very largest markets, such as New York or Los Angeles. In these big markets, the independents were able to attract only a very small part of the audience due in part to the poorer quality of their broadcasts. While specific market-by-market ratings are unavailable, we do know that the network share of the viewing audience between 1965 and 1975 fluctuated between 90 and 95% of the national audience. This means that the independent stations split the remaining 5 to 10% of the audience among themselves as well as with any public television stations. (It would not be until the 1990s that the network share would significantly decrease. The change was attributed to cable in addition to independent stations and new networks.)

The number of UHF stations grew from 176 to 218 between 1970 and 1980. The largest growth in UHF occured between 1985 and 1990, when figures increased from 363 to 545 (Media Dynamics, 1998, p. 20). Not all UHF stations, however, are independent stations. Looking specifically at independent stations, the number of stations grew from 90 to 120 between 1970 and 1980 (Amendment of 47 CFR, 1983, p. 1057). They continued to grow throughout the 1980s, when independents grew from 129 in 1980 to 380 in 1992 (Evaluation of the Syndication and Financial Interest Rules, 1993, p. 3305). Proponents of fin-syn attribute this growth to the regulation. Those opposed claim it has more to do with the growth of cable, because the issue of UHF versus VHF is eliminated with this newer technology. Whatever the reason for the growth in independent stations, they were decidedly not a competitive threat to the broadcast networks at the time when fin-syn was under consideration.

A key difference between network affiliates and independents is the method by which they acquire programming. Affiliates, during the 1960s when fin-syn was under consideration, had approximately 13 hours per day programmed for them by the network. This meant there were only a limited number of hours during the day when the local affiliate would determine what would appear on their air. Independents, on the other hand, are not required by contract to put on any particular programming and so the station manager scheduled the entire broadcast day. Both affiliates and independents fill the open time on their schedule with local programming, usually in the form of a local newscast in the early and late evening, and syndicated programming.[3] (Independents also programmed local sports, which was a key competitive advantage for these stations.)

Network affiliates purchase fewer syndicated programs, because a large portion of their schedule is provided by the network. Independent stations, on the other hand, must depend almost exclusively on syndicated programming. It is economically infeasible for a local station to produce its own programming 24-hours a day and have it be of any quality.

Stations rely on syndicated programming for one very good reason. It is less expensive to purchase programming than it is to try to produce it on one's own. Like network programming, first-run syndicated programming is centrally produced. By producing a show in a central location and then selling it to tens or even hundreds of markets, the syndicator achieves the economies of scale that the network does by producing its shows. In the case of off-network programming, the show has already been produced and the syndicator merely needs to distribute the program.

---

[3]See programming section below for a detailed explanation of syndicated programming.

Because independents and affiliated stations were in competition when buying syndicated programming, the FCC was concerned that the affiliates would have two advantages over independents. First, the affiliates tended to be more economically sound than the independents thus making them more able to pay for the best, syndicated programming. Second, if the networks were the syndicators, the concern was that they would steer the best programming to their affiliates. These two things added to the affiliates' ability to trounce the independent competition. Finally, the FCC was concerned about warehousing, which was keeping popular shows out of the syndication market. This was done specifically so that independent stations would not have access to these programs (though the networks denied they ever did this).

Independent stations are not, however, helpless entities in the broadcasting industry. While independent stations are not affiliated with a network, they may be part of a station group. Station groups are companies that own more than one station throughout the country. These stations can be network affiliates as mentioned earlier, or they may be independent.

Station groups benefit from economies of scale. Groups can buy programs, equipment and supplies in bulk. In terms of programming this is particularly advantageous, because station groups can negotiate better deals with syndicators as they provide these producers with access to multiple markets. Station groups also act as powerful competitors to the networks' owned and operated stations.

Another key difference between affiliates and independents is how they make money. Affiliates have a dual revenue stream of affiliate compensation from the network and local advertising dollars. Independents are solely reliant on local advertising dollars for their revenue. As we saw in the previous section, independents also pay more money for programming than affiliates do. Therefore, from an economic perspective, network affiliates tend to be more efficient and more profitable than independents.

Over time, this more efficient network system combined with changing technology, led to the virtual demise of independents. Today, there are only a handful of independent stations, because of the increase in broadcast networks. These new networks gained distribution by turning formerly independent stations into affiliates. While they may not look like the old broadcast affiliates, they don't look like independent stations either. "Independent stations ... operate as a hybrid of a network affiliate and their former selves" (Blumenthal and Goodenough, 1991, p. 21). They still have their own local newscast at 10 p.m., but the prime-time programming will come from one of the newer networks, like Fox or the WB. These new broadcast networks have turned the majority of independent stations into local affiliates.

Whether it was the financial interest and syndication rules or the introduction of cable, independent stations had flourished in the 1970s and 1980s. That changed in the late 1980s, when Fox began turning independent stations into Fox affiliates. With the creation of the WB and UPN networks in 1995, independent stations were virtually eliminated. The development of independent stations had been one of the goals of the financial interest and syndication rules. The belief was that the more voices there are in the marketplace, the more opportunity there was for diversity. With the eradication of the fin-syn rules, a corresponding eradication of independent stations occurred. Yet these stations have become part of new broadcast networks, which initially contributed to increasing diversity because of targeting different audiences than those served by the three major networks. The caveat, however, is that that differentiated programming has been short lived. Fox no longer targets an urban audience, and The WB has relegated its urban-targeted programming to one night per week.

Technology Changes Everything

The television industry changed significantly between the 1970s and the 1990s. The biggest change, which no one will dispute, is the introduction of cable into American households, not merely as a method for improving reception, but as a means for providing alternative programming choices. There were now a plethora of cable networks presenting everything from news to sports to music. These channels target specific audience segments appealing to teens (MTV) or women (Lifetime) or men (ESPN). Cable not only carried these cable networks but also was required by law to carry the broadcast networks in the area that it served because of the so-called must carry rules. Therefore, competition for the broadcast networks was coming from new cable networks as well as other broadcast stations, most of which had improved reception because of the advent of cable systems.

The introduction of these competitors was a blessing and a curse. On the one hand, many broadcast networks did what any smart marketer (and good monopolist) would do. They bought their competition. That is, broadcast networks bought cable networks. Suspecting that the broadcast segment was going to start losing audience to cable, better to lose it to yourself, that is cannibalization, than to a *real* competitor.

The new cable channels were also outlets for off-network programming. General interest networks, such as USA and Nick at Nite, filled their schedules with off-network shows. There were two good reasons to do this. First, it was a way for a new network to establish an identity, or brand itself—"that's the network that plays XYZ program." Second, just like the independent stations, the cable networks, at least in the beginning, could not afford to produce original programming. So, from a program seller position (which the broadcast networks were and were hoping to do more of), the introduction of these new competitors was not necessarily a bad thing.

On the other hand, however, new advertising dollars were not coming into the marketplace. Broadcasters (who at the time relied solely on advertising support) and cable networks were all pursuing the same advertising dollars. Over time, cable got very good at presenting its advantages over the broadcast networks. Its most compelling argument was its ability to sell a concentrated audience of a particular demographic without the audience you, the advertiser, do not want to pay for. For example, if Gillette is trying to reach men to introduce a new razor, the company can advertise on ESPN, which delivers an audience predominantly made up of men. They can be sure that the majority of people seeing the commercial are part of the target they want to reach and only that target. This is known as efficiency, and it is what the cable networks sell.

In the late 1980s, cable was still in its nascent phase. In 1980, cable was in only 18% of households. By 1997, cable penetration reached more than 67% of households and has hovered around that number since then (NCTA, 2002). Also by the 1990s, cable had moved much further along its growth curve so that it was able to compete more effectively against the broadcast networks, both in terms of audience reach and advertising dollars. While no one single cable network was able to reach the same size audience as the broadcast networks (and still has not), as an aggregate they have been able to significantly erode the networks' share of audience. By the 2001–2002 season, prime-time network share of the four major networks was at an all-time historic low of 47%, the first time the network share was below 50% (McClellan, 2002b, p. 6). Much of that loss is attributed to cable's growth and popularity. As well, cable networks were able to compete in the advertising marketplace and charge a premium for the audiences they delivered due to the efficiency of cable.

Know too that advertising is not cable's only revenue stream. In addition to advertising dollars, cable networks (at least the more established ones) receive money from cable operators. For example, a cable system operator may pay a cable network 50 cents or more per subscriber per month to transmit their programming. The more popular a network, the more money the cable operator will pay to keep it on the system. Newer networks do not have this advantage because the size of the bandwidth only allows for a certain number of channels on a cable system, which can be anywhere from 30 to 150 or more. Most systems do not have room for 150 networks, so as more and more networks wanted to be included on a system, cable operators began to charge the networks to be included on the system instead of the other way around.

With the combined revenues from advertising and cable systems, cable networks were able to begin producing original programming. Some of this programming was more successful than others. Even truly successful shows still did not generate broadcast network size audiences. The exception to this is "event programming," specials like the *MTV Video Music Awards*, which has mass appeal and is only available on cable.

More important, however, is that most of the programming produced for cable was produced by the networks themselves. Using MTV as an example again, the network created most of its nonmusic video programming in-house. This includes shows such as *MTV Sports*, *Rock 'n Jock,* and *MTV News* as well as its awards programming. The opportunity to merchandise these shows has been lucrative for cable. These companies produce everything from tee shirts to watches to movie spin-offs in association with their programming.

So too, production companies or media conglomerates with a production subsidiary own many cable networks. These parent companies use their cable properties as an outlet for their products. The best example of this is AOL/Time Warner and its many cable outlets, both premium networks such as HBO and basic networks such as TNT, TBS, and CNN. Warner Brothers films are shown on HBO. The Cartoon Network is programmed with shows from Hanna-Barbera and Looney Toons, both AOL/TW company divisions. TNT presents *ER*, an off-network program syndicated by Warner Brothers Television. Being part of a larger organization has given many of these cable networks an opportunity to grow and the clout to negotiate for space on local cable systems. This type of synergy is what the networks wanted—the ability to create programming, air it on the network, and exploit it for its full profit potential. If cable networks were able to do this, why were the broadcast networks being excluded?

More Networks

The biggest change in terms of the broadcast networks has to be the introduction of the Fox network, the first new broadcast network in fifty years. At the time, everyone said it couldn't be done, but everyone was proved wrong.

Fox was successful because this upstart network did not try to be like the other broadcast networks. From the beginning, the network positioned itself as a place for programming that is younger and hipper than its broadcast alternatives. The network's signature shows were *The Simpsons*, an irreverent adult cartoon, and *Married with Children*, a show about a very dysfunctional family with highly sexual overtones. The network built on these successes by adding more programming that appealed to younger audiences. These included shows such as *Beverly Hills 90210* and *Melrose Place*, prime-time soap operas with a strong appeal for women, and *The X-Files*, a science fiction series primarily focused on aliens and governmental conspiracies, which tends to attract a younger male audience. These programs became viable threats to the established networks, attracting similar size audiences. By the late 1990s, Fox's prime-time ratings were within 2 to 3 rating points of the established networks, and Fox continues to be only slightly behind in household numbers even today (McClellan, 2002b, p. 7).[4] More importantly, Fox attracts the coveted 18 to 49 adult audience, the audience for which advertisers are willing to pay a premium. Fox has been so effective in attracting this audience that currently the network is consistently second only to NBC in delivering this demographic (Kissell, 2002, p. 21).

Fox changed the structure of the television industry in another important way. In 1994, Fox "signed up a group of 12 top stations around the country that were previously affiliated with the three older networks. The ensuing scramble by all networks to lock up affiliates ... made it clear that the longstanding loyalties that kept affiliates bonded to the old-line networks were fraying" (Jensen, 1994, p. R3). This was important for two reasons. First, for Fox to build up its network initially, it had

[4]Fox was actually almost tied with ABC in the 2001–2002 season because ABC had a particularly bad year. The network does lag well behind CBS and NBC.

to do so with UHF stations. In a cable household, the difference between a VHF and UHF station is indistinguishable. However, in noncable homes, UHF stations continued to have poorer reception than VHF. The new stations Fox affiliated with were VHF stations. Therefore, in several key markets Fox was able to upgrade its ability to delivering its programming. Second, the majority of the stations Fox bought were CBS affiliates. This meant that CBS would have to find other stations in these markets with which to affiliate. This sent a rumbling throughout the network broadcast industry. If CBS was looking for affiliates, they might take an NBC affiliate or an ABC affiliate. The networks began negotiating deals with their affiliates to keep them as part of the network. The last thing a major network wanted was to become Channel 65 on the UHF band because no other VHF stations were available in a market. Fox's realignment of station affiliations cost the established networks dearly—in order to keep their station affiliations, these networks had to pay significantly increased compensation.

Fox was not the only new broadcast network. In January 1995, there were two new broadcast network contenders, The WB—a broadcast network started by Warner Brothers, and UPN—Paramount's entrant in the broadcast competition. The introduction of these networks can be directly attributed to the repeal of the fin-syn rules. Both Warner Brothers, a division of AOL/Time Warner, and Paramount, a division of Viacom, were (and still are) leading producers of prime-time television programming. As such, the companies wanted to ensure that they would have an outlet for their shows. Both companies owned cable outlets but also understood the need for having a broadcast network as a launching pad for off-network syndicated programs. With the major networks back in the programming business, there was no doubt that the number of prime-time slots available for independent producers would decrease. Creating a network was a means for increasing, or at least maintaining, production opportunities.

The success of these two networks has been mixed, with The WB being more successful than UPN. Both of these program outlets took a cue from the Fox handbook and realized that they needed to differentiate themselves from the other broadcast competition. Both targeted young audiences, as had Fox, and both initially targeted an urban audience, the industry code for an African-American audience. As well, these networks face some of the same disadvantages that Fox initially faced as a new network, that is, limited or poor distribution. Cable has been a means for the networks to subsidize viewership unattainable by over-the-air broadcasting. For instance, WB created the WeB cable channel. This channel is a cable version of the broadcast network and allows viewers who do not get The WB Network by broadcast to get it through cable (Blumenthal & Goodenough, 1998, p. 10).

Over the years, some differences have developed between the two networks. While The WB started out more urban, it moved toward producing more one-hour dramas with teen appeal. This led to shows like *Buffy the Vampire Slayer*, a science fiction, tongue-in-cheek horror program that is set in a California high school; *Dawson's Creek*, a show about a group of teenagers dealing with adolescent issues; and *Felicity*, a fictionalized version of life at the University of New York. These shows were so successful with audiences and advertisers that the network has added more of this type of programming to its schedule. In the 2002–2003 upfront buying season, the network generated $575 million in advertising revenue ("NBC has record," 2002). This is about a quarter of what NBC, the winner in the upfront, generated but very respectable for a network entering its seventh full year of programming.

Paramount, on the other hand, has had only limited success. UPN initially was building the network around a single show, *Star Trek Voyager*, a new spin-off of a Paramount syndicated franchise. This show was successful, but not necessarily the program to build a network around. The network did develop some minor hits with urban appeal. These included shows such as *Moesha*, starring pop-music star Brandy, and *Malcolm & Eddie*, starring Malcolm-Jamal Warner, an actor who had achieved fame as the son on *The Cosby Show*. However, the network has been ill defined, in part because of changes in program management. By the late 1990s, the network had installed a new head of programming, revamped its entire lineup and rapidly, perhaps too rapidly, expanded from 3 to 5 nights per week of programming.

UPN may yet become a more fully functioning network due to changes in network ownership and changes in the ownership of many of its key stations. At its inception, UPN was created as part of Paramount and was owned by Viacom and Chris-Craft. In 2000, Viacom bought CBS. In the same year, Viacom bought out Chris-Craft to become sole owner of the network. While under dual ownership, the network floundered. Now, the network has put management of UPN under Les Moonves, CEO of CBS, which indicates the company's commitment to supporting this entity. Further, News Corp., owner of Fox, bought Chris-Craft giving the company ownership of ten new broadcast stations eight of which were UPN affiliates ("News Corp. Buys," 2000).[5] Because of these affiliations, Fox has a vested interest in seeing that UPN is successful. Many of these affiliate agreements are up for renewal, which makes Fox a powerful factor in UPN's programming decisions. The full effects of these changes are yet to be seen. In the 2001–2002 season, UPN stole *Buffy* away from The WB, which did help improve the network's numbers. However, the network still relies on a *Star Trek* spin-off and the WWE for much of its audience. Estimates for the 2002–2003 upfront are only between $225 million and $250 million, less than half of what The WB is expected to make ("NBC has record," 2002).

For all three networks — Fox, The WB and UPN — the question remains as to whether having their own broadcast network is worth the money and effort it takes to have an assured outlet for their programming. While this will be analyzed more extensively in the next chapter, a look at the 2002–2003 season is instructive for where each of these networks currently stand. UPN will program only 10 hours in prime time, 8 p.m. to 10 p.m., Monday through Friday. Out of ten shows on the net-

[5]With the purchase Chris-Craft, Fox had 13 stations in the top 10 markets including duopolies in New York and Los Angeles, making the company even more powerful in the advertising marketplace. The FCC first allowed duopolies, ownership of two stations in a market, in 1999.

work, six are connected to the parent company being produced by either CBS Productions, Paramount, Big Ticket, or as co-ventures with other companies. These 6 shows represent 4 hours of programming or 40% of prime time. The WB programs 13 hours in prime time, of which seven and a half are produced by Warner Brothers or Turner Television, an AOL/Time Warner subsidiary. Warner Brothers Television is producing a total of 18 hours of prime-time programming, so almost two thirds of its shows are appearing on competitive networks.

Fox, throughout its history, has produced a significant proportion of its prime-time schedule. This network has the most hours of programming in that the network airs 15 hours in prime time. This is 8 p.m. to 10 p.m., Monday through Saturday and 7 p.m. to 10 p.m. on Sunday. Out of 20 shows that it airs, 11 are produced fully or in part by 20th Century Fox and 2 are produced by Regency, a Fox Television production unit. These shows represent 9 hours of programming or 60% of the prime-time schedule. With these shows, 20th Century Fox Television is now the leader in producing shows for prime time with 19 hours of programming scheduled for the 2002–2003 season.

All three "emerging networks" have taken advantage of the synergies possible from being vertically integrated. Only a few years ago, UPN and The WB were only producing a handful of shows for their networks. Today, after much internal pushing for integration between divisions, all of these networks are producing significant percentages of their schedules internally. Currently, Paramount, Warner Brothers, and 20th Century Fox are still successfully producing programming for the established broadcast networks. These companies perhaps believe, and rightly so, that for now they would do better to sell their programming to both the older networks as well as emerging ones, particularly because UPN and The WB need to become more established.

It is important to note that a seventh broadcast network came into existence in late 1998 and has been trying to establish itself ever since. It is called the PAX Network and the network positions itself as a place for family programming. This is not surprising given that the majority of stations that make up the network were once part of a Christian broadcasting network. What is interesting about the network is that it is using a completely different programming strategy than that used by other new entrants into the broadcast arena—family programming versus urban, young-adult skewed fare. Thus far, the network has had only limited success with this strategy. In 1999, NBC made a strategic investment in the company taking a 32% stake in the company with the option of purchasing a controlling stake by February 2002 (Byrne, 1999). It was reported that NBC bought into PAX to have a second outlet for programming (there has been sharing of programming between the two networks) and to gain access to PAX's stations. In November 2001, however, NBC proposed that it would purchase Telemundo, a Spanish-language broadcast network with 10 broadcast stations. That purchase cleared the Federal Trade Commission, and the FCC in April 2002 approved it as long as the company divests one of its Los Angeles television stations. Without the sale, NBC would retain a triopoly in that market (Albiniak, 2002). Bud Paxson, owner of PAX, claims this purchase is in violation of the existing agreement between PAX and NBC because it will create "triopolies" in five major markets. NBC is claiming that the agreement to purchase PAX is valid until 2009. Either way, NBC's purchase of Telemundo does not bode well for the long-term viability of PAX.

The Old Networks

It was not just the industry around the networks that had changed. The networks themselves began to change their structure with the changing of the industry. As mentioned above, the broadcast networks began to buy or create cable networks. NBC and ABC were more successful initially in this horizontal integration strategy than CBS. NBC developed CNBC, the leading business news network, and MSNBC, a joint venture with Microsoft which presents news 24-hours a day on cable and on the Internet. The network uses these cable outlets as additional means for distributing and "repurposing" programming, that is, using programming more than once. A good example of this is *Dateline*, NBC's newsmagazine. This show will appear on the broadcast network first, and then segments from the show will subsequently appear as news pieces on MSNBC. ABC has one of the top-tier cable networks in ESPN, the leading sports network on cable, A&E, one of the top entertainment channels as well as other cable properties. (These will be outlined more fully below in the section on program producers.) CBS tried on several occasions to develop a cable franchise. It owned CMT and TNN and tried to launch a 24-hour news channel called Eye on People but sold the venture to Discovery Networks, a cable programmer, when they could not establish the network. As an individual company, CBS was not successful with this strategy. However, when Viacom bought CBS, it combined the network with such cable properties as MTV, VH1, and Nickelodeon among others.[6]

Ownership of the broadcast networks changed throughout the 1980s and 1990s. NBC, which had been owned by RCA almost from its inception, was bought by General Electric in 1987 (MacDonald, 1990, p. 242).[7] General Electric is a multinational conglomerate with subsidiaries that produce everything from nuclear power to medical equipment to airplanes. The company has no other media division other than NBC.

Westinghouse, a station group owner, bought CBS in 1995. The combined company's revenue was $13 billion. The FCC allowed the merger to occur even though the combined company would have ownership in stations above the legal limit at the time. No company could own more that 12 stations covering 25% of the country.

[6]Viacom also owns UPN, thus having a single company owning two broadcast networks. Though FCC regulations forbid this, the Commission ultimately allowed Viacom to keep the network in the interest of diversity.

[7]RCA had originally been formed as a subsidiary of GE in 1919. To increase the company's abilities in radio, patents needed to be acquired which were owned by other companies. This meant selling stock in the company to Westinghouse, AT&T, and United Fruit. GE, however, remained the major share holder (MacDonald, 1990, pp. 21–22).

Westinghouse/CBS would own 15 stations reaching more than 32% of the country (Ledbetter, Borow and Moodie, 1996, p. 30). It was expected, rightly, that the pending Telecommunications Act of 1996 would pass Congress. This bill would raise ownership limits to 35% of the country, thus eliminating any need for the new company to divest any of its current holdings. As mentioned above, CBS was purchased again in 2000. This time by Viacom, a multinational media conglomerate. Viacom, prior to the merger, owned Paramount, a producer of television programs and theatrical films, Blockbuster Video, and MTV Networks, among other properties.

The Disney Company bought Capital Cities/ABC in 1996. Disney is a major supplier of first run as well as syndicated programming through its Touchstone and Buena Vista divisions. Where as Paramount and Warner Brothers started their own networks to guarantee access to network viewers, Disney purchased ABC for the same reason.

The Telecommunications Act of 1996 gave networks the ability to expand their owned and operated stations to 35% of U.S. television households. With this new regulation, the networks are four of the top six station group owners (Trigoboff, 2002).[8]

Thus by the mid-1990s, larger corporations owned the broadcast networks—both new and old. All had cable holdings in addition to being broadcast networks. Some had program production capabilities, or would be building them as quickly as they could. Most would also own broadcast stations, and some would have cable networks. Whatever the configuration, all these companies had become vertically integrated organizations with the ability to control programming from conception to production to distribution in first-run and subsequent markets.

PROGRAMMING

Syndicated Programming

Syndicated programs are shows that are distributed to individual stations throughout the country on a market-by-market basis. While produced at a central location, they are not distributed so as to appear simultaneously throughout the country as with network programming. Rather, syndicated programming is distributed locally with the local station determining when to schedule the show. A current example would be the *Oprah Winfrey Show.* This nationally syndicated talk show airs at 9 a.m. in Chicago and 4 p.m. in New York. The show airs at different times in different markets because the individual station managers have determined the best time for airing the show in their market.

There are two types of syndication—first-run syndication and off-network syndication. First-run syndication includes talk shows, game shows, court shows, and some dramas, such as *Xena* or *Babylon 5*. These are programs that have been specifically produced for the syndication market and have never appeared on a network

[8]The order is Viacom (CBS and Paramount stations), Fox, Paxson, NBC, Tribune, and ABC (Disney).

schedule. Off-network programs, on the other hand, are programs that developed their popularity from initially appearing in network prime time. These include everything from the old *I Love Lucy* show to *Seinfeld.* Movies sold on a market-by-market basis are also considered syndicated programming.

Syndicators are primarily large national (and now multinational) organizations. The station negotiates a price to air a show for a certain period of time, say 2 years, for a certain amount of money per episode. The cost of the license fee depends on the size of the market, the type of show, and the show's popularity. Talk shows and game shows, for instance, are relatively inexpensive to produce, which is why these shows have become a staple of time periods with smaller viewership, that is midday or prime access, 7 to 8 p.m. Once a producer has paid for the set and the talent, it is only a matter of paying for running costs such as cameramen, talent coordinators, and so forth. These shows are the least expensive syndicated product to produce as well as the least expensive to license. On the other end of the cost spectrum are the popular off-network programs. The most expensive of these shows include network hits such as *Seinfeld, ER,* and *Roseanne.* However, not all off-network shows are "mega-hits," and some off-network programming has been on the market for many years. These are also factors in the ultimate cost to the local station.

Like network programming, first-run syndicated programming is centrally produced. By producing a show in a central location and then selling it to tens or even hundreds of markets, the syndicator achieves the economies of scale that the network does by producing its shows. In the case of off-network programming, the show has already been produced and the syndicator merely needs to market and distribute the program.

From the producer's perspective, syndication is the bread and butter of the industry. Producers of prime-time network programming do not make money during the original airing of their program unless the show is a huge success. In fact, they lose money. Rather, the producer recoups their cost, and hopefully even makes money, when the show is sold into syndication after its initial network run.[9] This used to be after 5 years or more, but has been reduced to 2 to 3 years.

After a show has been selected to appear on the prime-time schedule, the networks pay a licensing fee to the producer. This license allows the network to air an episode of a series. In the early days of television, the license covered a one-time airing, but today it is for two. The license fee rarely covers the producer's cost of making the show; therefore, the producer needs to finance the show in its initial run in hopes of making money back from ancillary rights including syndication. This is known as deficit financing.

In the early 1970s, the license fee to play a half-hour series was between \$115,000 and \$125,000. For a one-hour series, the fee would be between \$200,000

---

[9]The average prime-time drama costs \$2–3 million to produce and the average comedy, \$1–2 million. The network pays about half that figure in license fees. For a hit, however, the network will pay the producer enough to recoup and then some. For example, *Law & Order* costs \$2.2 million to produce, and NBC pays \$3.1 million in license fees per episode (Lacter, 2001).

and $249,000. Hollywood producers claimed that one-hour shows cost $250,000 or more to produce, while half-hour shows cost more than $150,000. Of course these numbers could fluctuate significantly if star talent is added to the budget. For instance, Peter Falk is reported to have earned $100,000 per episode of *Columbo*, a 90-minute series on NBC. This fee would significantly bite into the top $450,000 budget supplied by the network (Pearce, 1973, p. 113).

If a show was unable to attract an audience and was not picked up for a second year, the production company stood to lose a lot of money. If the show was renewed, however, "the contract between the network and the producer usually stipulate[d] a cost escalation provision of 5 percent, plus any wage and material cost increases" (Pearce, 1973, p. 114). If a show reached the end of its initial contract and/or it became a long-running series, it could be renegotiated with the network for renewal at a fee that would enable the producer to make a profit.

Once a show had been cancelled by the network, the producer could sell this "off-network" show into syndication. The producer would enter into agreements with individual stations throughout the country. "A flat price is determined for the length of the run based upon past or expected popularity, type and size of the market, expected time of viewing, competition between stations, and economic conditions generally" (Pearce, 1973, p. 115). Producers could also syndicate their off-network shows into foreign markets as an additional revenue stream. For instance, a long-running hit such as *Ironside* generated more than $30 million just in domestic syndication with additional monies coming from overseas markets. It is this type of windfall that a producer is hoping to achieve when he or she enters into creating a prime-time series.

The success of off-network programming helps explain why the FCC was concerned with who controlled the syndication market. If the networks controlled the programming at the network level and that programming was the type that was most successful in syndication, then the networks would have control over all programming, both network and syndication. Also because the most lucrative shows in syndication were at first network series, had added power to the networks' gatekeeper status. Finally, network ownership of stations in the largest markets enabled the networks to make or break the success of a syndicated program. Remember that a syndicated program is sold market by market and the cost of the show is partially determined by the size of the market in which it airs. The bigger the market, the more money the syndicator makes. Being in the top 10 largest television markets is necessary for a show to be successful. (The top three markets alone—New York, Los Angeles, and Chicago—account for more than 15% of television households.) Because the network affiliates in these markets are the owned and operated stations, the network is the one determining if a show is picked up for air. While during the 1960s and 1970s there were independent competitors in the largest markets, the networks affiliates were still the preferred stations on which to air syndicated programs. Being denied access to the network O&O can be devastating to a new syndicated program.

Today, because of the plethora of media outlets and the fragmentation of the viewing audience, producers have more selling options than before. They can sell shows into syndication as was done in the past and achieve substantial remuneration for their initial investment. In the case of *Seinfeld*, a huge network hit, the producers made more than $2 billion in syndication in its initial year in syndication (Schlosser, 1998a). Other options now available allow producers to recoup their money more quickly. They can put their shows into syndication after 2 or 3 years rather than 5 years, they can negotiate broadcast and cable windows at the same time, or they can repurpose their shows, that is create an agreement where a show is aired on network and cable at the same time. For example, *Everybody Loves Raymond*, *Cosby*, and *Spin City* were all sold into syndication while in their third season on a network (Schlosser, 1998b). More recently, cable outlets have become so anxious to get programming that they have been buying network shows after only one or two years on a network (Grego, 2001, p. 40). Another way for producers to recoup more quickly is by selling off-network hits to individual broadcast stations and cable networks at the same time. In the past, this was not done because stations wanted programming exclusivity. With the fragmenting of the audience, station managers have put less value on this requirement. Repurposing, or 'dual window' deals as they were initially called, are becoming more standard in the industry. Repurposing began in 1999 when *Law & Order: SVU* first aired on a broadcast network, and the same episode appeared on a cable network within 2 weeks of its initial airing. The producer makes additional money due to the multiple airings. This trend has been successful enough that the networks are looking for multiple outlets for its programming. In fact, Disney's purchase of Fox Family Channel, now ABC Family, was just for this purpose. Already Disney is airing several of its network shows on the cable network, including *Alias* and *Whose Line is it Anyway?*, and has an agreement with its affiliates to be able to repurpose up to 25% of its programming.

Relationship between Buyer and Producer

Producers—whether they be networks, advertisers, or independents—can produce shows for the networks or the syndication market. Each of these scenarios has advantages and disadvantages.

Logistically, a producer faces many difficulties syndicating a program versus licensing a program to a network. The producer has to sell the show market by market. The producer has to provide individual tapes throughout the country and provide advertising and promotion. All of these things add to the cost of producing a syndicated program. In addition, the return on a syndicated program is usually less than a network program and the networks know this:

> The independent producer ... fears that he will make less money if he sells his program independently, and is forced to deal with the networks. The networks have great bargaining strength in negotiations with the independent producer because they offer the independent producer a wider viewing audience. (Kintzer, 1984, p. 519)

In addition to the added expenses over network programming, the independent producer has to fund a syndicated program him- or herself.

In producing a show for the network, the network assists with financing the pilot and pays for some of the program itself in the form of a license fee. The trade-off here is that the networks then want some creative control and an equity stake for their investment. A producer needs to make a cost-benefit analysis: Are the smaller returns on producing a syndicated program offset by the creative freedom of financing a project on one's own, or are the long-term benefits and the possibility of a large payoff worth what the producer has to give up in creative control?

> Before fin-syn, what the producer had to give up was substantial:
>
> First, a network would take a financial interest in the production. In general, investments in productions not guaranteed to receive good ratings or make money were risky. Second, the network would take a percentage of the money brought in by the subsidiary uses of a program. While it would be to the networks' benefit to air programs in which they had a financial interest, this second interest *assured* them of recovering their initial investment. Unfortunately, it was primarily through subsidiary use of a program that producers could recover their costs and make a profit. Independent producers eager to enter the valuable prime time television market found it necessary to transfer a "substantial part of the potential profitability of their products to the purchasers—the networks"—in order to have their programs aired, or to make any money at all. (Kintzer, 1984, p. 520)

Prior to the enactment of the rules, the producer was paid a license fee for giving the network the right to air the show, and the network got financial interest in the show, as well as a percentage of the syndication rights. The networks believed they were entitled to this because they had taken on the risk of financing the program, even though they had nothing to do with its initial creation or development. The networks were indeed taking a risk. If the show was not a hit and did not produce 80 to 100 episodes (the number of episodes needed for a show to be syndicated), then the syndication rights were worthless and the network would lose money in production and distribution costs. The networks' risk, however, was offset by their ownership of backend rights on multiple programs on their air and revenue from advertising sales.

The networks' ability to control creativity and ultimately the financial future of a prime-time program gave producers pause when approaching these broadcasters with their work. Unfortunately, once advertisers were no longer in the television production business, they had nowhere else to go. While fin-syn did eliminate some of these issues, producers still needed to sell their programs to the networks. Reviewing the financing of prime time is important for understanding what was at stake in the relationship between the networks and producers, as well as being integral to what types of programs get on the air.

Financing Prime Time Programming

While producers may (or may not) have to wait to recoup their costs, networks make their money back almost immediately by selling advertising on the programming that they purchase. They can even recoup much of the money they spent on development by airing the pilot, a sample of the show the producer uses to sell the show to the network, as the first episode of the series. In the 1970s, pilots were produced as two-hour movies.[10] This way, even if a show was not picked up as a series, the network would recoup its costs by airing the pilot as a movie of the week. It may also have been a means for determining audience reaction to a show. If the pilot/movie got a good rating, the network may decide to pick up the show as a series.

By broadcasting the show, the network gets to sell advertising during the airing of the program. Most of the advertising inventory (approximately 70%), is sold during the upfront season. This season is actually a one -to two-week period in the beginning of June. The remainder of the inventory is sold in the scatter market, that is, whatever is left is sold throughout the remainder of the year. Unlike in other industries, broadcasters must sell their product by a specific time. If they do not sell a commercial that is to air today, they cannot hold it until tomorrow to sell. Because of this, commercial prices come down as the airdate approaches. To keep prices high, the broadcaster wants to sell the commercial as early as possible.

Pricing for advertising is based on network estimates. Pearce (1973) explains how these prices are determined:

> Advertising pricing and the sales levels of such advertising are dependent upon the overall strength of the economy, the program and other costs, station clearances, and competitive counter-programming from the other networks. Although these estimates are almost exclusively based on past performances of essentially similar (some would say, identical) programs, they are necessarily subjective since they deal with an uncertain future. (p. 31)

The key factors that determine the price that advertisers will pay for commercials are ratings and the marketplace. The money an advertiser will pay for a commercial is based on the rating multiplied by the CPM, cost per thousands, of a certain demographic. This is why ratings are so important. For example, if the CPM for women 18 to 49 is six dollars and a show delivers five million women, then the cost for a commercial on that show for that advertiser is \$30,000 (\$6 × 5,000). Therefore, it is easy to see that if the audience size increases, the advertising rate increases accordingly. Networks can also ask a premium over the CPM for especially popular programs. Because so many advertisers want to get into the most popular shows, the networks can bump up the price according to what the market will bear.

The average household CPM (the only demographic for which historical ratings are attainable) for nighttime programming in 1970 was \$2.10. This number decreased slightly in 1971 and 1972 but rebounded in 1973 and grew steadily till the early 1990s (Television Bureau of Advertising, 2002). To look more specifically at CPMs, it is instructive to look at an example in the 1990s for which more statistical data is available. The average prime-time household CPM for the networks in 2000 is estimated to be \$13.42. For comparison, daytime CPMs are \$4.35 and Late Night

[10]An alternative under consideration at the networks in recent years is that the producer would create a 10-minute presentation rather than a full-fledged pilot in order to keep costs down. This, however, has not become the norm.

are $9.15. Therefore, it is more expensive for an advertiser to reach an audience during prime time than it is at other times during the day. These numbers, however, are household numbers and, as mentioned, advertisers rarely if ever purchase households. They purchase specific demographics. Many advertisers want to reach women between 18 and 49. The CPM for this target in prime time on one of the networks is $26.25. Because it is a more specialized audience than households, it commands a higher price. Even more expensive, for example, is the male 18–34 audience that commands a CPM of $57.50. This is because men, particularly young men, watch less television and are more difficult to reach. Today, it is standard thinking that the most desirable audience is adults between the ages of 18 and 49. This was a new concept in the 1970s, and it changed the way that commercials were sold (and likely the types of programs selected to reach this audience).

It could be argued that advertisers, even more than broadcasters, have the strongest impact on what is presented to the viewing audience. Broadcasters are attempting to draw an audience that is most attractive to advertisers. Advertisers are interested in presenting their sales message to people who can afford to buy products. Therefore, premium brands and male-targeted brands rely most heavily on network television. Female-targeted brands use network television but rely more heavily on less expensive syndication and cable options. Additionally, the number of advertisers who purchase network television is very concentrated. Two hundred advertisers, representing approximately 3,500 brands, account for 90% of television advertising (NBC Business Development, 1996). This is further concentrated by the fact that large brand companies use large advertising agencies that purchase for multiple companies. That marketers of mass-produced products want to attract a mass audience cannot be disputed, and this certainly seems to have implications for program content diversity. According to Cantor (1988):

> Because the executives are committed to making a profit and to serving the largest possible audience, they, from all reports, seem to cater to pressure groups and to advertisers who are afraid of alienating large segments of the buying public. This can determine content .... (p. 87)

Taken to the extreme, networks are even creating shows specifically for advertisers. A recent example is Disney producing *The Disney Paint Program* for Home Depot, a company that has committed to spending an estimated $100 million dollars with the company (McClellan, 2002c, p. 12).

Another factor that affects content diversity now that did not exist in the 1970s is that networks are producing their own programming. While this will be analyzed at length in the following chapter, it is important to note here that economics plays an important role in deciding what programs will appear on the prime-time schedule. Executives are not only concerned about whether or not it will sell to advertisers. They are also acutely aware of how expensive a show is to produce and how quickly can it go into syndication or be repurposed.

Program Producers

In the late 1960s and early 1970s, there were three types of television program producers—the networks themselves; advertisers and their agencies, who acquired programs from producers and brought a package of programming and advertising to the network; and independent producers. This last group could be anything from one of the major Hollywood production companies (what we would think of today as a media conglomerate) to a midsize independent, publicly owned company to a small individually owned company that tended to produce live-on-tape, that is, cheaper programs, using another company's facilities.

Each of the networks was involved in television production, but to different degrees. ABC had minimal involvement in television production except to use its facilities for shows that appeared on the networks and to produce made-for-television movies. ABC at the time was the largest theater owner and had been producing theatrical films until an antitrust suit was brought against them. It made sense with this in-house expertise to apply their theatrical experience to films for television. These movies were, not surprisingly, shown on ABC. CBS, like ABC, produced movies to air on its network. Both CBS and NBC were more involved in producing series for their prime-time schedule than was ABC (see Table 4.2).

It makes sense that ABC produced less series programming as this company was still a burgeoning network and would not truly come into its own until the 1970s. NBC produced less programming than CBS in 1964, but by 1968 the two networks were producing the same amount of programming for the evening hours.

Advertisers and their agencies used to be major suppliers of prime-time programming. Examples that many people may remember are shows like *Texaco Star Theater* or the *Kraft Music Hall*. These were programs that would be developed by a producer. The producer would approach an advertiser, who would in turn approach the network to see if the program was something the network would accept for their schedule. After all, the advertiser would not want to invest in a program only to have the show be rejected by the network. On the other hand, the advertiser approaches the network from a position of strength, because it is bringing revenue as well as

TABLE 4.2

Number of Network Supplied Program Hours for Prime Time

	ABC	*CBS*	*NBC*
1964	3.75	6.5	4.75
1965	2.25	7	4.5
1966	2.25	5	5.5
1967	3.5	6.5	5.5
1968	3	5	5

Note. Adapted from A. D. Little (1969). Television Program Production, Procurement, Distribution and Scheduling, pp. 2–4.

programming to the network. This is as opposed to a producer who is looking for the network to finance his or her show. Sponsor programming was a common means of program development until the early 1960s, but its popularity waned significantly throughout this decade. In 1957, for instance, advertiser-supplied programming accounted for over 25 hours of programming on the prime-time schedule of the networks. By 1960, that number was down to 11 and by 1968, this type of programming was almost gone representing only 2½ hours in all of prime time.

As the 1970s progressed, Hollywood production studios became the principle suppliers of television programming. This became true over time as the studios began to see television as a necessary evil. With the introduction of television, Hollywood had to compete for its audience's leisure time. They had to provide a product compelling enough to induce an audience to (a) leave the comfort of their living room, and (b) pay for their entertainment. By the early 1970s, television had become a major competitor with motion pictures and most movies were losing money in domestic distribution. Some incremental revenues could be gotten from international markets and from selling the rights to broadcast their films on television, which initially had been a concern for Hollywood because they believed they would be competing against themselves. Rather than fight television, it became obvious that getting into the television production business itself could be a way for Hollywood producers to benefit from this medium.

There were eight major motion picture companies at this time. These were Columbia-Screen Gems, MGM, Paramount, 20th Century Fox, United Artists, Universal, Warner Brothers, and Disney. Some were more successful than others in creating programming for the television market. United Artists had gotten out of television production. Warner Brothers had disappeared from the business in 1965, but reentered in 1969. MGM, 20th Century Fox, and Screen Gems had various levels of success in television, but it was Universal (owned by MCA), Disney, and Paramount (owned by Gulf & Western) that were the leaders in television program production (Pearce, 1973, p. 102).

Universal had become so skilled at television production that by 1972 two-thirds of its film revenue was derived from television (Pearce, 1973, p. 102). This studio's hits included *Ironside*, *Marcus Welby M.D.*, *Columbo*, *Macmillan and Wife*, and *Adam-12*.

Paramount remained a force in motion pictures even while creating a series of hits for television. At this time, Paramount had just produced *The Godfather*, the top grossing movie of its day. For television, the studio was producing *Mannix*, *Mission Impossible*, *The Brady Bunch*, and *The Odd Couple* as well as made-for-television movies.

Several smaller producers were as successful, if not more successful in television production, than some of the major studios. Quinn Martin Productions, for instance, produced 4 one-hour dramas for television including *The FBI* and *Barnaby Jones*. Equally productive were Tandem Productions, producers of *All in the Family* and *Maude*, and MTM Enterprises, producers of *The Mary Tyler Moore Show* and *The Bob Newhart Show*. Many small producers worked with the major studios or used network facilities to produce their programming and offset their production costs. This structure of large companies and small independents producing programming for prime time would be transformed by the 1980s.

Changes in regulation and technology throughout the 1980s and beyond led to the consolidation of the media industry. So much so that it is difficult to talk about simply program producers. There are virtually no independent production companies and even the Hollywood "majors" have become part of multinational media conglomerates. Most of these companies are household names like AOL/Time Warner Inc., The Walt Disney Company, and Viacom. None of these organizations is just in program production. They are in television, both broadcast and cable, and the Internet and magazines and music and retailing among other enterprises. Of the Top 25 media groups as compiled by *Broadcasting & Cable* magazine, seven produce television programs for the broadcast networks ("Big Deals Alter the List," 2002, p. 42). These are AOL/Time Warner Inc., Vivendi Universal, The Walt Disney Company, Viacom, Sony, News Corp. Ltd., and General Electric (NBC). Within these seven, each of the six broadcast networks is represented. Table 4.3 provides a quick reference as to these companies' entertainment and media revenues and major television holdings.

Today, the production companies are the broadcast networks. Studios and conglomerates have swallowed up the broadcast networks (Disney and Viacom). Studios without networks created them (Fox, Warner Brothers, and Paramount). And, the one unattached network, NBC, created its own studio. In effect, there has been a merging between what had been three gatekeepers (the networks) and eight producers (the Hollywood studios) to six vertically integrated gatekeeper/producers.[11] Most of these companies became vertically integrated in the mid-1990s, so they are only now starting to fully take advantage of the synergies that these companies hoped for when they took on this organizational structure. With this broad structure in mind, we will now look more closely at each of these individual companies and how they developed through the late 1980s to their current situation.

AOL/Time Warner is the largest media conglomerate. Time Warner Inc. was created in 1989 out of the merging of Time, Inc., the publisher of magazines such as *Time*, *Life*, *Fortune*, and *Sports Illustrated*, with Warner Brothers, a company most known as one of the original major Hollywood studios as well as a producer of television programming. This already large institution grew even further in 1996, when Time Warner purchased the Turner Broadcasting System, owner of significant cable networks, most notably CNN and the TBS Superstation. The company grew once again in 2000 when AOL, the country's largest Internet Service Provider, purchased Time Warner. This merged company has interests in publishing, music, the Internet, film, and retailing in addition to its television holdings. On the television side, Time Warner owns cable networks such as TBS, TNT, CNN, and HBO; cable

[11]These six companies, however, are not yet equal in the broadcast arena. The three major networks, plus Fox, have the most power in terms of generating advertising dollars and in terms of delivering the largest audiences, which has long-term syndication benefits.

TABLE 4.3

Corporations That Produce Programming for the Broadcast Networks

Company	*Revenues–2001*	*Television*	*TV Production*	*Other TV Interests**
AOL/Time Warner	$38.2 billion	WB TV Network 12.7 million cable subscribers	Warner Bros. TV Castle Rock TV Witt-Thomas Prod. Telepictures Prod. WB Distribution WB Animation	TW Cable, CNN, Court TV, Cartoon Network, HBO, TBS, TCM, TBS
Vivendi Universal	$31 billion	USA Networks	Universal TV Group Brillstein-Grey Multimedia Ent.	Home Shopping Network
Walt Disney Co.	$25.3 billion	ABC Network 10 Stations	Buena Vista TV Touchstone TV Walt Disney TV	ESPN, SoapNet, The Disney Channel, equity in Lifetime, E!, History Channel, Classic Sports, A&E, ABC Family
Viacom	$23.2 billion	CBS, UPN 15 stations	Spelling Ent. Viacom Prod. Paramount TV Viacom television	MTV Networks (MTV, VH1, Nickelodeon, Nick at Nite, TV Land), Showtime, The Movie Channel
SONY	$17.1 billion		Columbia TriStar (Television and Distribution)	Game Show Network
News Corp. Ltd.	$13.8 billion	Fox B'casting Co. 32 stations	20th Television Fox TV Studios	Various sports cable channels, Fox Family Channel, FX, Fox News Channel
General Electric	$6.7 billion	NBC Network 13 stations Pax Comm. (32%) Telemundo	NBC Studios	MSNBC, CNBC, Court TV, equity in A&E, Bravo, AMC, Prime Network, and regional sports

Note. Revenue information from "Big Deals Alter the List," (2002). Ownership data from Columbia Journalism Review (n.d.) and company websites.
*This is a list of the other *major* television holdings.

systems, including the system that services Manhattan; and broadcast network, The WB. In addition, Time Warner produces programming for both cable and broadcast as well as syndicating this product after its network run.

Television production is created under a number of separate divisions, including New Line Television and Turner Television, but the primary producer is Warner Bros. Television, which produces programming for the broadcast networks. In addition to first-run network programming, Time Warner is also in the syndication business. Since its inception, The WB has launched nearly a dozen off-network syndicated series. The company's real syndication success, however, is in its off-network programming from the major networks. This includes programs such as *ER*, *Friends*, and *The Drew Carey Show*. In addition, Time Warner is a leader in first-run syndication with shows such as *Jenny Jones,* a talk show, and *Extra*, a tabloid news program.

In 1998, Warner Brothers Television changed network television when it negotiated for $13 million per episode for *ER*, a first-run drama that airs on NBC. *ER* was entering its fifth year on the air and therefore was up for renegotiation. NBC was in a difficult position in that it needed to protect its Thursday night franchise. Thursday nights have traditionally been NBC's strongest night. In fact, the network has led in the ratings on this weeknight for more than 10 years. *ER* was the 10 p.m. anchor program for the night. The other highly rated show on that night, *Seinfeld*, was not returning in the 1998–1999 season. NBC could not afford to lose its other key program for the night. *ER* could have been offered to another network, which was NBC's biggest fear.

This type of issue is just what the networks wanted to avoid by owning their own programming. If they produce programming themselves, they do not have to worry about a stiff increase in the license fee when the show reaches its fifth year. While *ER* helped Warner Brothers in the short term, long term it has put added incentives on the networks to produce in-house and to produce less expensive fare, such as game shows and reality programming, to compensate for exorbitant licenses on long-running hits.

Vivendi Universal, prior to its buyout of USA, was more active in motion picture production and the international television market than in US distribution. The wish for additional American holdings is what prompted the buyout of USA, which includes USA Network, Sci-Fi, the Home Shopping Network, TicketMaster, and Studios USA (now Universal Television). Even before this purchase, the company was in the syndication business offering older off-network programming such as *Murder, She Wrote*, *Miami Vice,* and *Magnum, P.I.* As a major motion picture producer, Universal has created past hits such as *Out of Africa* and *Schindler's List*, as well as recent releases such as *American Pie 2*, *Jurassic Park III*, *Gladiator*, *Erin Brockovich,* and *The Mummy Returns*. With the purchase of USA, Vivendi is setting the stage to become a more active producer for the American market. The question also remains as to whether USA Networks, as a general entertainment network, might be merged with one of the major broadcast networks, because this is a trend in evidence with Disney's purchase of ABC Family, Fox's ownership of FX, and Viacom's relaunch of TNN from The Nashville Network, a music channel, to The National Network, a general entertainment network.

In terms of production, Universal Television is a major supplier of programming to network prime time through its *Law & Order* franchise, which includes the original *Law & Order*, *Law & Order: Special Victims Unit*, and *Law & Order: Criminal Intent*. The studio changed network prime-time financing when it created "repurposing," which started with *Law & Order: SVU*. The show first aired in prime time on NBC and was followed by an airing nine days later on USA Network. This dual window did not seem to hurt ratings on either network and appears to be reaching an unduplicated audience. In addition to *Law & Order*, the company produces *The Agency*, *The District*, and *RHD/LA* for CBS, as well as *Just Shoot Me* for NBC.

Universal is also a producer and distributor of syndicated programming. The company produces talk shows such as *Jerry Springer* and *Maury*, as well as dating shows, *Blind Date* and *The Fifth Wheel*. The studio also produces and distributes *Crossing Over with John Edward*, a show that purports to send messages from relatives who have passed away.

The third largest media corporation is The Walt Disney Company. It is the first on the list to own one of the three major broadcast networks, ABC. In addition to broadcast, Disney owns cable channels, ESPN and the Disney Channel; theme parks; and television and film production units. The current company was formed by the merger of The Walt Disney Co. with Capital Cities/ABC in 1996. The Disney Company had the production and film experience while ABC had the distribution channels, through both broadcast and cable outlets.

Disney's television production is carried out under the Touchstone and Imagine names, while its syndication business is under the Buena Vista banner. (Touchstone and Imagine are under the banner of Buena Vista Television Productions.) Disney currently produces a number of shows for network television including *Alias*, *According to Jim*, and *My Wife and Kids* for its own ABC network, as well as *Scrubs* for NBC.

In the late 1990s, the fact that the production unit was not creating more shows for ABC had been a bone of contention within the company. Because of this situation, in July 1999, the network announced that it was combining its network program development area with its TV production unit, Buena Vista Television Productions (BVTP). In an article in *Broadcasting & Cable*, a weekly trade publication, then ABC Television Network President, Pat Fili-Krushel, was quoted as saying "There are two goals in consolidating these efforts. One is to produce creative results that will [get] more Disney product on the ABC Television Network. The second is that it allows us to achieve some economies of scale" (Schlosser, 1999, p. 10). It did do just this. It has also meant less product produced for other networks. In the same article, one network executive was quoted as saying, "That [the combining of the two divisions] sounds pretty dangerous to me .... I think it's going to make it really hard for other studios to think seriously about selling to them." This was not unpredicted. Herskovitz wrote in 1997:

> The problems presented by such a merger [Disney with ABC] are twofold. First, the opportunity for independent program producers to provide programming to ABC has now been severely curtailed. The chances of an independent production gaining a schedule slot ahead of a Disney production are measurably lower. Second, other net-

> works and independent stations have been effectively cut off from a large supplier of programming, both for original programming and for acquiring syndication rights. Disney most certainly will favor supplying programming to ABC over other outlets, and would be foolish to sell syndication rights of popular programs to independent stations or other networks over ABC affiliates. (p. 182)

I would add to Herskovitz's concern an additional concern about quality. Because the studio will no longer have to sell its programming to someone else, they may not need to produce as high a quality product. Of course, everyone wants to do a good job. However, it is very different to sell to an outside company when you are in competition with others than it is to sell to yourself without anything else to compare your work against.

Even before this merger of production and development, Disney was already providing programming to ABC at more favorable terms than it would to an outside buyer. Disney's Touchstone produced the top-rated show, *Home Improvement.* The studio extended the license fee for a sixth and seventh season. If the network was forced to purchase the show from an outside company, they would have had to renegotiate much like NBC had to do with *ER*. No such hard-ball tactics occur when you are negotiating with yourself. It is not just television programming that is given a sweeter deal; movies also enjoy these rights. Disney sold the rights to air *The Lion King* to ABC. One can guess it was a better deal than if purchased by a company outside the Disney family. The company wins overall. The movie was a ratings success, and they did not have to pay an outside company for the right to air it (Roberts, 1998, p. 54). Creators of the work, however, are the losers in this situation. Most creative people have a stake in the backend rights, which are based on profit. This type of internal deal making significantly reduces their share of the profit. Because of this, Matt Williams, producer of *Home Improvement*, took Disney to court. The case was settled for an undisclosed figure.

The merger that created Viacom happened earlier than the other companies mentioned. Viacom was a big player in the off-network syndication business, and in fact was the syndication arm that CBS had to spin off when the financial interest and syndication rules were introduced in the early 1970s. Viacom also had interests in cable systems as well as cable programming. To become a more diversified corporation, Viacom bought Paramount, one of Hollywood's major studios, as well as Blockbuster Video, the leading distributor of video rentals in the country. This strategy allowed the corporation to be fully integrated into the motion picture business. (In addition to its production and video store holdings, Viacom owns movie theaters throughout the United States and Canada, as well as in nine other countries.) To complete its integration on the television side, Viacom launched UPN with Chris-Craft in 1995.

By the 1990s, this media mega-giant owned film and television production units, broadcast television stations, basic and premium cable channels, as well as Blockbuster, retail outlets, movie theaters, theme parks, and publishing. Films are produced and distributed through the company's Paramount division. Broadcast television production is through the Paramount Network Television. Cable channels include MTV, VH1, Nickelodeon, and Showtime, all of which have their own in-house production units. As well, Viacom owned the broadcast network, UPN.

While Viacom had been very successful in its cable business, particularly with its MTV Networks division, this had not been the case with its broadcast network. As noted previously, UPN has been without direction since its inception. The company's inability to make UPN successful is likely one of the reasons for the purchase of CBS in 2000.

The combined television holdings of the merged Viacom/CBS are extensive. The combined company has both broadcast and cable networks. These include the CBS and UPN networks; MTV Networks, which includes MTV, VH1, Nickelodeon, TNN among others; BET; and Showtime Networks, the company's premium cable networks. On the production and distribution side, there is Paramount television, which includes six production units, including Paramount Network Television, Viacom Productions, Spelling Television, and Big Ticket Television, and CBS Enterprises, the company's syndication arm. Finally, the company owns the Viacom Television Station Group, which has 34 local stations including 16 CBS owned and operated stations.

Like Warner Bros. TV, Paramount is a leader in prime-time program production. The company produces shows such as *Frasier* and *ED* for NBC, and *JAG* and *Becker* for CBS. Viacom Productions creates *Sabrina the Teenage Witch* for The WB. *Star Trek* and its many iterations are a staple of the production company and the show, in one form or another, has been an anchor for UPN. Under its Spelling Productions banner, programs such as *7th Heaven* and *Charmed* are created for The WB. Paramount also produces for cable with *Any Day Now* on Lifetime. Big Ticket Television, yet another production unit, produces both network and syndication programming. *The Parkers* is produced for UPN within this unit. This division also produces first-run syndication shows, *Entertainment Tonight, Judge Judy, Judge Joe Brown,* and *Judge Mills Lane,* as well as the various incarnations of *Star Trek*.

Prior to the merger with CBS, Paramount had only limited success in syndication. Now the company syndicates such off-network hits as *Spin City, Everybody Loves Raymond, Frasier,* and *Nash Bridges*. The company is also successful in first-run syndication through King World Productions Inc., a company CBS purchased in 1999. This division sells shows such as *Wheel of Fortune, Jeopardy!,* and *The Oprah Winfrey Show.*

News Corp. Ltd. is so enormous it would be unwieldy to present a thorough history of how the company came to exist as it currently does. As an Australian company, it has various media interests in that country as well as the United States, the United Kingdom, and cable and satellite interests throughout Asia. The company is far more global in its reach than any of the other companies.

For the purposes of this work, an overview of News Corp.'s American history will be provided. Though other companies were created through huge mega-mergers, Rupert Murdoch, the chairman and CEO of News Corp., was more measured in his growth strategy. Murdoch purchased Twentieth Century Fox, producer of film and television, in 1985. In 1986, Murdoch purchased six television stations in large markets. That same year, the Fox network was launched, though prime-time programming did not begin until 1987. The next event that influenced Fox television's fortune was the 1994 purchase of NFL broadcast rights. Also in 1994, Fox shook up the industry by signing 12 New World affiliates to the Fox network (see earlier discussion). That same year, Fox started its cable ventures with the creation of FX, an entertainment channel, followed by the Fox News Channel 2 years later and the purchase of the Family Channel the year after that.[12]

In terms of supplying programs to the industry, 20th Century Fox TV has become the leader in the industry (this distinction had previously belonged to Warner Bros.). Not only a leader in production, but a leader in terms of hit programming. Most of those hits appear on its own Fox network, including *The Simpsons*, *Bernie Mac*, *24*, and *King of the Hill*. Even with this success, Murdoch mandated that the number of shows produced in-house increase. Hits the studio has produced for other networks include *The Practice* for ABC, *Yes, Dear* and *Judging Amy* for CBS, and *Buffy the Vampire Slayer* for the UPN.

Fox's Twentieth Television syndication division has also been very successful and is the leader in off-network syndication. Much of this success is attributable to concerns surrounding the consolidation of the media industry, specifically that program producers will funnel their programming to their own stations or cable networks. *King of the Hill*, a show that debuted in 1997, was sold into syndication for fall 2001. The 22 Fox owned and operated stations purchased the show. Another Fox-produced hit, *Buffy the Vampire Slayer*, was also sold for 2001. FX, the Fox-owned cable network, purchased it. As early as 1993, Fox was being accused of steering its programming to its own affiliates. Tribune Broadcasting and Chris-Craft/United Television Group leveled charges of favoritism against the company. The CEO of Tribune, Jim Dowdle "maintains that the Tribune stations in markets where Fox owns stations were never given a fair shot at the show" ("Fox Denies," 1993, p. 23). Even so, Fox funneled many of its network hits onto the fledging cable network, including *The Practice* and *Ally McBeal*. Fox, however, seems to be reevaluating this strategy due to lower than expected ratings.

In terms of first-run syndication, the studio has not had anywhere near the same sort of success as it has had with network programming. In 1998, it had an embarrassing flop with the late night talk show, *The Magic Hour*, hosted by NBA star Earvin "Magic" Johnson. The company has two daytime first run shows, *Texas Judge* and *Divorce Court*, neither of which is a definitive hit.

In terms of cable franchises, Fox is playing catch up in comparison with its global media rivals. Fox purchased The Family Channel with Saban Entertainment and turned it into the Fox Family Channel. While the network was well distributed with more than 80 million subscribers, it never achieved the same cache as most of the more established cable networks and has struggled to build a loyal audience. That is why Fox decided to sell the network to Disney in late 2001. The company

[12]This network has since been sold to Disney in 2001 and is now called ABC Family.

also owns FX, another general entertainment network. While this network carries high-profile programming such as *The X-Files* and *NYPD Blue* as well as repurposing shows like *24*, it has traditionally been hampered by its limited distribution. Even while the network has grown to reach more than 70 million subscribers, it has not been able to break through to attract a sizable viewing audience.[13] Fox's most recent entrée into cable is Fox News Channel (FNC). Coming in as the newest 24-hour news channel (after CNN and MSNBC), FNC initially had to work hard to draw viewers who have already established viewing habits with other news networks. That was until the terrorist attacks of September 11, 2001. By January 2002, the network had surpassed CNN as the leader in prime-time news viewership on cable and was reaching four times the audience of MSNBC ("Cable News Wars," 2002).

The synergy Fox is able to achieve is best exemplified by its hit series, *The X-Files:*

> As "X-Files" winds through Murdoch's News Corp. empire, for example, just that one hit will generate an estimated profit of $1.4 billion to $1.5 billion over the expected eight-season life of the show .... That's because the Fox-produced show runs first on the Fox network, reruns are syndicated by Fox and cable rights go to a Fox cable network. The domestic and foreign ad revenues, licensing and syndication fees and video and merchandise sales all go to Fox. And a feature film based on the series produced an additional $72 million or so. (Roberts, 1998, p. 55)

Fox seems to be the most successful of the broadcast networks in exploiting its creative properties in this way. It is likely that this is true because they have been able to do so for a longer period of time than any other network. Fox was never restricted by the fin-syn rules and has always had a production unit to supply programming to its network. That competitive advantage, however, has been shrinking over time and now News Corp is competing against other fully integrated production and distribution companies.

Of the top media companies being discussed, Sony has as many interests outside of media as it does inside. (One other company being evaluated, General Electric, has media as even a smaller percentage of its overall business. NBC is but one of many divisions, the rest of which have nothing to do with media.) Sony bought Columbia Pictures in 1989. Like the other mergers, this included a major Hollywood studio with its accompanying television production business. Unlike any of the other producers, Sony is only a content provider. In addition to its Columbia TriStar Motion Picture Group, which includes Columbia Pictures and Sony Pictures, Sony owns the Columbia TriStar Television Group, Columbia TriStar Home Video, as well as music interests including Columbia and Epic Records. Finally, the company is probably most known for its electronics. An area that straddles the electronic/content divide is video games, an arena in which Sony excels.

---

[13]The network is starting to have some success with original production, specifically *The Shield,* which won an Emmy award for its leading actor.

Columbia TriStar produces programming for all the major networks. The company produces *King of Queens, The Guardian,* and *Judging Amy* for CBS, and *Dawson's Creek* for The WB. While Columbia is an equal opportunity distributor, it has been at a disadvantage due to not owning its own network. According to *Variety,*

> Columbia TriStar TV often has to cede partial ownership of its shows to get the on the air. That was the case with its promising frosh series "King of Queens."
>
> CBS demanded ownership in the show at the 11th hour in May in exchange for a pickup. If the show goes the distance, Sony will have to share the profits with the Eye web. (Hontz & Littleton, 1999, p. 12)

Combined ownership also exists with the other shows Columbia produces for the network. It is just this situation that led to the company to get out of the prime-time production business except on a very limited basis. According to Sony Pictures Entertainment President Mel Harris, "the traditional network business model doesn't make sense anymore for independent suppliers." (quoted in Adalian, 2001, p. 19). This is not to say that the company is out of production all together. Sony will continue to manage its existing hits, produce more programming for cable networks, produce and distribute syndicated shows, and develop relationships with advertisers to bring shows to the networks, the strategy that existed back in the 1950s and 1960s.

Columbia will continue to produce programming that has been successful for them such as daytime drama and syndication. Columbia produces *Days of Our Lives* and *Young and the Restless*, two of the most-watched daytime dramas. In syndication, the company distributes *Seinfeld*, which alone would make the company a leader in the industry. The show is expected to generate $1 billion in its first 10 years in syndication. The company also distributes recent off-network shows, *The Nanny* and *Party of Five*. The company's first-run syndication programming includes *Ricki Lake, V.I.P.,* and *Judge Hatchett.* The best hope for expansion is in supplying programming to cable. In this area, Sony currently has shows on TBS, Lifetime, and Showtime and will have first-run series on at least three other networks in the near future.

General Electric, through its NBC division, produces programming for the network through NBC Studios, which was created in September 1995 to take advantage of program ownership. NBC has produced late-night programming and daytime programming for decades. When the network first moved into prime-time production, the studio primarily focused on made-for-TV movies. As the division began its foray into prime-time series, the programming was spotty at best. In 1998, the network produced *Conrad Bloom*, which did not even last the season. Even worse, the NBC Studios-produced *Wind on Water* aired only once.

Since then, NBC Studios has had some success particularly with situation comedy, *Will & Grace*, which is in its fifth season and has won the Emmy award for best comedy. Also produced internally was *Providence*, a drama that enjoyed four seasons on the air. Perhaps the biggest success particularly from a financial standpoint is the game show, *The Weakest Link*. Not only did the show air twice a week, NBC sold a weekday strip version of the show into syndication. In the 2002–2003 season, NBC Studios or the NBC news division will produce 11 programs representing 9½ hours out of 22 hours of prime-time programming.

In addition to these large fully integrated media giants, there are several smaller players, relatively speaking, in the television production business. The largest and most successful of the independents is Carsey-Werner. Two of this company's biggest hits were *The Cosby Show* on NBC and *Roseanne*, which aired on ABC. Currently, this production company has two shows on the air, *That 70s Show* and *Grounded for Life,* both on FOX. Another independent producer is DreamWorks, a film and television production company that was started several years ago by the entertainment triumvirate of Steven Spielberg, Jeffrey Katzenberg, and David Geffen. While the company had two shows on the air, *The Job* and *Spin City* on ABC, last year, they have only one show, *Boomtown,* a show it is producing with NBC, that will be on the air for the 2002–2003 season. All other independents currently producing for the networks have a more limited track record. These companies either produce a specific genre of programming, like reality series, or they produce a single network series and then disappear.

The Effect of the Introduction of Fin-syn/PTAR

One of the primary objectives of the financial interest and syndication rules, as well as the Prime Time Access Rule, was to weaken the networks' strength in program development. This did not happen, according to Pearce (1973):

> Network control over the program production industry was strengthened, not weakened, by the prime-time access rule in a very important respect. The network's bargaining position with Hollywood program production houses was strengthened because the market for expensive television programming had been reduced by roughly 16 percent without any commensurate reduction in the number of production houses, especially since the vast majority of those production houses found that competing for programming slots in the prime-time access periods at the local station level was uneconomic. (p. 38)

If a production house wanted to create high quality (in terms of production values) programming, the networks were still the only game in town.

Another unexpected consequence of the rules was the networks' increased advertising revenue from prime-time programming. Whereas before PTAR the networks programmed 3½ hours during prime time, after the rules they only programmed 3. In giving back a half-hour of programming to affiliates, they also gave back the advertising within that program. One would think that this would have reduced the networks' prime-time advertising revenues. Instead, what occurred was a simple change in supply and demand. By reducing the number of prime-time hours, the rules also decreased the supply of prime-time advertising available. This reduction in supply increased the price for prime-time advertising.

Looking back at the chart at the beginning of the chapter, which outlined network profits, a significant increase in network profits is evidenced from 1972 to 1973. In fact, those profits increased from $110.9 million to $184.8 million.[14] "Not only are prices per minute higher—an all-time record of $120,000 to buy a one-minute commercial in CBS's *All in the Family*—but sales for the [sic] 1973 are up … about 15 percent in prime-time" (Pearce, 1973, p. 40).

With the reduction in prime-time hours, documentary and public affairs programming decreased significantly in the prime-time hours. By the 1973–1974 season, only NBC had regularly scheduled prime-time public affairs programming, *America* and *NBC Reports*. The rules also affected children's special programming. These shows began later in the evening in compliance with the regulation. Also, the networks accepted fewer children's specials, because there was less time within which to place these programs.

The prime-time access rule did not appear to be the boon to independent producers that the FCC might have thought. Though the rule was designed to stimulate diversified program production, "most producers felt right from the start that it would be of no help to them because of the cost factors involved" (Pearce, 1973, p. 118). While prime-time license fees for a half-hour show could be as much as $125,000 (with this not covering all of the producer's costs), that fee would be approximately $70,000 in prime access. The producers would have to come up with a way to produce a show that was less expensive than what they produced for prime time. This alone would mean a reduction in production quality. As well, there are additional costs associated as previously discussed. Economics forced the type of programming that ultimately appeared in this time period—inexpensively produced game shows and tabloid news programs. The FCC may have hoped for increased public affairs programming or more locally produced fare, but because they did not define diversity within the regulation, audiences got what the market would most efficiently provide. Table 4.4 demonstrates that prior to PTAR, drama, comedy, variety, and game shows were presented in the access time period. In 1972, game shows became the predominant form of programming during this period.

The PTAR reduced the network schedule by 12 hours per week. At the time, 10 of those 12 hours were produced by Hollywood. Because it is not economical to produce prime-time-like programming for the access period, most large production companies stayed away from this type of programming. Thus, they lost in the vicinity of $2 million per week with the creation of these rules. Because of this, the Hollywood studios were not in favor of these rules. They were not the only producers against the rules; even some of the producers who were helped by the rules would rather see them eliminated. The goal of these producers was to be creating "network-calibre programming, not first-run syndication programming" (Pearce, 1973, p. 125). Even some small production companies felt that the rules were misguided in their thinking. By reducing the number of opportunities in

[14]PTAR started in 1972. It appears it took the market a year to adjust to the change in advertising supply. That the growth trend continues after this year supports this hypothesis.

TABLE 4.4
Access Period Programming Other Than Movies 1970–1972

	1970		*1971*		*1972*	
Program Type	*# of ½ hours*	*% of Total*	*# of ½ hours*	*% of Total*	*# of ½ hours*	*% of Total*
Game	170	11.1	294	22.8	672	48.6
Drama	712	46.3	357	27.7	228	16.5
Variety	265	17.2	225	17.5	255	18.4
Comedy	334	21.7	242	18.8	24	1.7
Other	56	3.6	169	13.2	204	14.8
Total	1537	100	1287	100	1383	100

Note. Adapted from Pearce (1973). The Economics of Prime Time Access.

prime time, the FCC reduced the number of opportunities for a small company to get on the schedule.

The financial interest and syndication rules were instrumental in changing the structure of the television industry. Looking historically, the creation of the rules appeared to cause an increase in the number of program suppliers. According to *Broadcasting* magazine:

> The number of producers supplying networks with prime time programming increased from 23 in 1970–71, to 29 in 1981–82. The number of distributors increased at an even faster rate, from 122 to 184. And where 10 producers were providing first-run programming for the half-hour period made available for nonnetwork programming by PTAR, in 1971, the number had increased to 42 last year. ("Producers, Stations Ban Together," 1982, p. 41)

Although PTAR did not work to weaken the networks' strength in programming, the fin-syn rules were at least successful in creating some additional competition in the production marketplace.

Effects of the Repeal of Fin-syn/PTAR

As throughout the history of television, a handful of companies determine what will be seen by the American viewing audience. In terms of broadcast television, that number is now six, with four being more powerful than the other two. The difference now, versus in the 1970s, is that these six companies are vertically integrated from program production through to distribution and syndication. These companies represent a merging, or consolidating, of the industry between the networks and the Hollywood studios. Most of those companies have stated that they plan to increase the synergies within their own company, which means increased in-house production. More in-house production means less production by independent producers (if there are any of these left).

Almost as important as the expansion of in-house production was the development of network syndication units. ABC had the advantage here with Touchstone and Buena Vista already existing in the Disney corporate structure. CBS developed Eyemark as its syndication arm, which became involved in both first-run and off-network syndication. Much of the first-run syndication, such as *Martha Stewart*, were programs developed to be run on CBS owned and operated stations. CBS also purchased the leader in first-run syndication, King World Productions, the producer of such monster hits as *The Oprah Winfrey Show, Jeopardy,* and *Wheel of Fortune*. Their newest program hit is *The New Hollywood Squares*. NBC initially allowed other companies to syndicate its program product domestically and expanded its abilities to distribute internationally. More recently, the company has geared up to syndicate what it produces.

Increased competition between networks or between network and cable has not significantly impacted the distribution of wealth within the television industry. Though there is increased competition for advertising dollars, the three major networks still garner more than 60 percent of the advertising dollars in the marketplace (Media Dynamics, 1998, p. 34). Only 25 percent of the remaining available dollars come from cable revenues, and those moneys are split among hundreds of cable networks. Because the networks maintain dominance in their ability to attract advertising dollars, it is difficult for alternative outlets to compete for programming in the marketplace.

Financially, the networks remain the powerhouses in the business because the pricing of network television advertising has not followed the laws of supply and demand. The broadcast networks have experienced continually increasing revenues as they have delivered an increasingly smaller audience (and presumably an inferior product to advertisers). These revenues have allowed the networks to remain dominant in the industry, because even while the advertising pie has been increasing at less than 10 percent a year, cable's percentage of that pie has remained the same (Media Dynamics, 1998, p. 30). Therefore, the incremental advertising dollars are going to the three major networks and the three mini-nets. The only way this might possibly change is if another medium *could* deliver the same size audience as the networks do. Thus far, no other medium has come close.

In the 1960s and 1970s, the three broadcast networks consistently delivered 90% of the prime-time television audience. By the 2001–2002 season, that percentage had dropped below 50%. This means that in 30 years, the broadcast networks have lost 40% of the viewing audience.[15] Supply and demand would suggest that as broadcasters deliver a smaller audience that advertisers would pay less money for

[15]In the same period of time, the number of television households have increased from 60 million to 98 million, which means in absolute numbers, the networks are delivering the same number of households they did 30 years ago. However, they are not delivering the same number of young people.

that audience (after all, they have alternative suppliers from whom they can purchase a similar audience at a cheaper price). However, this has not been the case. Rather, what the networks have to offer—mass audience—is in smaller and smaller supply. Therefore, demand—and price—continues to increase. So even while the networks' audience is declining, their ability to attract a substantial audience makes them more and more attractive. As Glovinsky (1984) puts it:

> the competition presently offered by new video technologies is not sufficient to counter the dominance of the networks. Repeal of the [fin-syn] rules in the context of the present and projected television marketplace would therefore achieve a paradoxical result in allowing the networks to solidify their position as dominant participants in the home entertainment industry, while at the same time weakening the power of independent producers who have served as a partial check to network dominance. (p. 606)

Glovinsky was writing in 1984, but his argument rings true even today. What he had predicted has come to pass. The networks continue to be the dominant force in the television industry, both from a viewership perspective as well as economically. That dominance has been solidified by the networks' ability to be both vertically as well as horizontally integrated. There really are no independent producers anymore. They can no longer afford to create programming on their own. Even a major producer such as Columbia TriStar had to associate with CBS to improve their chances of distribution, and failing that, they have pulled significantly out of the business until a new revenue model can be determined.

Vertical integration has led to concentration, which has in turn limited the diversity in program suppliers and program outlets, at least in terms of the largest outlets.

> The rise of vertical integration is transforming the television business, influencing what shows get on the air.... It's also heightening turmoil in Hollywood, where independent producers contend that, as they'd predicted, the tightening stranglehold on distribution has all but driven them to extinction. Many Hollywood creative types decry vertical integration, seeing it also as a major reason for the decline in the quality of TV shows. "The more interesting, innovative shows aren't coming from these big groups with so much already to protect," says Gary Goldberg, a creator of the ABC hit "Spin City," which the network partly owns. "You see this blandness and similarity to the shows. Consumers are the ones who get hurt." (Roberts, 1998, p. 55)

Vertical integration was only made possible by the elimination of the financial interest and syndication rules.

This concentration of power denies access to viewpoints that communicate a different perspective of the world. Increasing the number of distribution outlets has not been the answer to this problem, because these new outlets are owned by the existing integrated companies. This integrated structure makes it virtually impossible for an independent company to succeed because of exceedingly high barriers to entry. Even if they could overcome these barriers, there is tremendous pressure to serve mass audience tastes to attract advertisers. Thus, increasing the number of outlets is not the answer to increasing diversity, even though the FCC has seen this as a panacea to limited diversity for years. In the next chapter, I will argue that increasing the number of producers is no more effective than increasing outlets in providing a multitude of voices in the media marketplace.

5

Fin-syn's Effect on Industry Structure and Diversity

INTRODUCTION

Having presented the economics of the television industry and the background for the financial interest and syndication rules, I now turn to the question of how the regulation has had an effect on diversity. As was discussed in the opening chapter of this book, the FCC has maintained diversity as a fundamental policy goal. The FCC, however, often fails to define what diversity means. Is it more diverse content? More outlets? More sources of programming? The underlying goal of the fin-syn rules was to increase content diversity. However, the Commission did not regulate the content itself. Rather, they put restrictions on who could and could not own programming. The following analysis will demonstrate that this sort of structural regulation is not an effective means of achieving the ultimate goal of content diversity. To demonstrate this, diversity will be examined in terms of (a) content diversity (types of programming) and (b) marketplace diversity (suppliers of programming).

Analyzing Diversity

By looking at the content of programming over the periods surrounding the introduction and elimination of the financial interest and syndications rules, I will be able to make some conclusions regarding the predominance of certain content trends, as well as the level of diversity available to television viewers through the broadcast networks. In particular, this analysis focuses on how programming was affected by the presence or lack of financial interest and syndication rules, which perforce requires examining the networks as economic entities, though much of this was covered in preceding chapters. Dominick and Pearce (1976) provided such an analysis from 1953 to 1974. They explain that the "product of an oligopoly [like the networks] is essentially homogeneous (although a great deal of money is spent to advertise minor differences) .... Considering the networks as economic institutions indicates that there would be significant influences on content choices available to the American public" (pp. 70–71). These content choices are significant because, according to Gerbner (1967), they determine where a society's attention is placed. Maxwell E. McCombs and Donald L. Shaw (1972) called this agenda setting. Agenda setting suggests that the mass media affect the level of importance that the public attach to an event, issue, or person. Further, the theory suggests that while the media do not tell people what to think, it does steer them in a direction in terms of what to think about. Intuitively this makes sense in that if the media does not present an issue, it will fly under the radar of the viewing/reading public. Recent terrorist events would certainly confirm this idea. Though agenda setting specifically looks at politics, the theme can be applied to entertainment programming as well. Messages presented through entertainment are no less significant in many ways than those presented in a evening news broadcast.

In evaluating the content of programming, determining an appropriate taxonomy that remains valid from decade to decase is a particular stumbling block. While the 1960s were full of musical and comedy/variety series, the 1990s and 2000s have "reality series." Reality shows include *Survivor, Cops,* and *America's Funniest Home Videos,* all of which were unheard of in previous decades. For this study, two types of categorizations were used. The first was from a study by L. W. Lichty who evaluated programming from 1947 through 1974 (Sterling & Kittross, 1978, pp. 528–531). This study was selected because it provided the most thorough analysis of programming during the initial evaluation period (1969–1973). The second category was developed from three different sources. One source was a study conducted in the 1960s called *The People Look at Television.* In this study commissioned by CBS, Steiner (1963) created program categories based on how viewers actually watch television versus how networks or producers categorize programming. The second source was the Dominick and Pearce (1976) study, and the final source came from analyzing programming on the prime-time schedules for the past 10 years. The first taxonomy was applied across the entire period studied. The second code, which was specifically designed to take 1990s genres into account, is applied to that later time period only.

Previous researchers used various numbers of program categories from five to fifteen (Dominick & Pearce, 1976; Steiner, 1963; Wildman & Robinson 1995). This research uses 22 categories in both cases in order to be precise about types or programming particularly within the drama category. While drama is one of the predominant program genres, certain subcategories within this segment attract more attention than others, and these categories change over time.

Fall program schedules were taken from McNeil (1996) for the 1960s and 1970s, as well as for up until 1995. Subsequent years were from *Broadcasting & Cable* and *Variety,* major industry trade publications. Midseason replacements were only considered if they were part of the schedule the following year. Only regularly scheduled programming was considered, thus eliminating specials from this analysis. Movies were grouped together, because more fine-grained distinctions would require a special study. Shows were categorized based on descriptions in McNeil and in later years from *zap2it.com* (and its predecessor, *ultimatetv.com*), a website that includes show descriptions and press releases containing descriptions of television programs, as well as network and program distributor websites.

The time periods evaluated were determined around the creation and elimination of the financial interest and syndication rules. The initial period of study was 1966 to 1974.[1] This time period allows for 4 years of data prior to the start of the rules, the actual year the rules went into effect, and 4 years of data following its enactment. The time period evaluated allows for any changes in program selection to appear on the schedule and any fluctuates that may be due to "natural" programming trends versus the repeal of the rules. The second time period covers 1989 to 2002. Remember, changes were first made to the rules in 1991, then again in 1993 and were finally repealed in 1995. Therefore, this time period covers 2 years prior to any rule changes through the years of the rule changes up until the present time. For reasons previously discussed, only prime-time programming will be evaluated.

Time, rather than shows, was used as the basic unit for analysis. This was to account for the variety in show lengths in the earlier evaluation period. Some shows were 45 minutes, some 90 minutes, in addition to the 30 or 60 minute shows we are used to today. Therefore, quarter hours were used as the time period of analysis. More programming was evaluated in the seasons prior to 1971. After 1971, program hours in prime time were reduced significantly due to the introduction of the Prime Time Access Rules.

Three types of data were analyzed. First, I looked at program content in the two time periods. Changes over time were evaluated using simple percentages of the various program genres and the percentage of time these genres appeared on the program schedule during each season.

Next, I looked at diversity in the program schedule in several ways. First, I used Dominick and Pearce's diversity indicator:

> This is an index of the extent to which a few categories dominate prime time. It is derived by summing the percentages in the top three categories per season and subtracting from 100. It can range from zero (all content is accounted for by only three or fewer categories) to 79 (content is divided equally into 14 categories). A low score would indicate a restricted range of choices for the audience. (p. 73)

With 22 categories, the numbers could range from zero to 86. This index is helpful in evaluating changes in the types of programming that may dominate the prime time schedule. Next, I evaluated the diversity of programming on the schedule overall, for example, how concentrated programs were within particular genres. This is known as vertical diversity and is measured using the Herfindahl Hirschman Index.

[1]Throughout this chapter, individual years represent the beginning year of the broadcast season, therefore 1966 represents the 1966–1967 season, 1974 represents the 1974–1975 season and so on.

Economists use this index to determine the amount of concentration in an industry. It has been adapted by social scientists to determine diversity in program content. This analysis builds on the Dominick and Pearce index by taking all of the schedule into account and not just the top 3 categories. Vertical diversity, however, does not provide a complete picture of what is available to the viewer at any particular point in time. Therefore, horizontal diversity was evaluated as well. The horizontal diversity index evaluates the number of different types of programs available to the viewer during a particular half-hour period.

The final area of analysis was the suppliers of prime-time programming. This was done to determine if there is a correlation between the types and diversity of programming and the producers of that programming—an area that is overlooked in most diversity research. Here, too, changes over time were evaluated using simple percentages. For example, how much prime-time programming does Warner Brothers produce and how has that changed over time? Has this number been affected by the change in the fin-syn rules? Does the company produce more programming now that they own a television network? Percentages were also used to determine the amount of concentration in production of prime-time programs over time.

Measuring Program Diversity

Figure 5.1 shows the percentage of time the three broadcast networks devoted per week to each of the program genres from 1966 to 1974. Figure 5.2 presents the same information from 1989 to 2002. (The categories have been collapsed for easier presentation. For a full listing of the categories and percentages by type, see the appendices.)

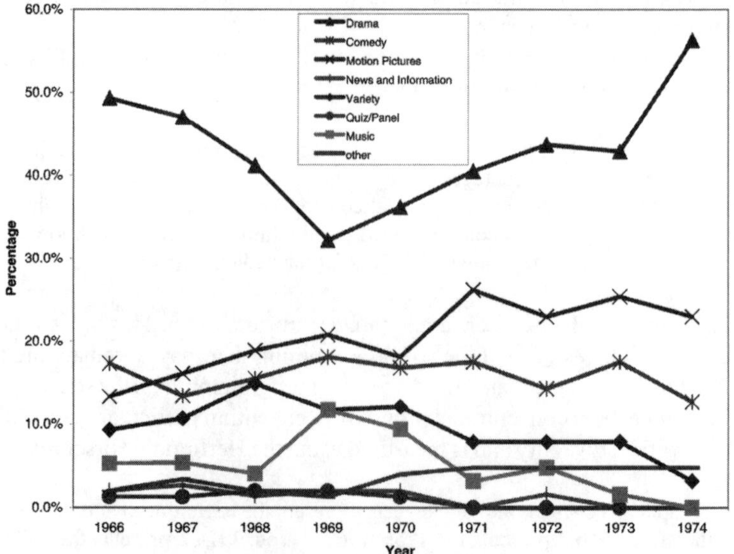

FIG. 5.1. Program genres by %—1966–1974.

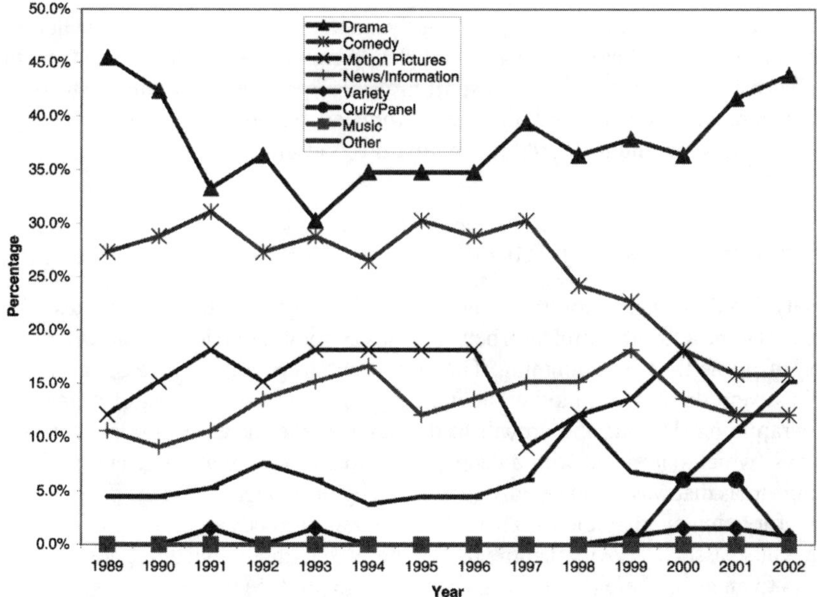

FIG. 5.2. Program genres by %—1989–2002.

It is clear to see that certain types of programming went in and out of style during this time period. In the 1970s, the largest growth was in dramas and motion pictures, accounting for 56% and 23% of prime-time programming hours, respectively, by the 1974–1975 season. Quiz and panel shows had disappeared by the early 1970s, likely due to continued fallout from the quiz show scandals in the late 1950s. Music and variety series had lost significant appeal by the mid-1970s, with only long-time favorite, *The Carol Burnett Show*, keeping the genre alive. Documentary series, part of news/information, had disappeared from regular prime-time programming by 1973. The increase in "other" programming is attributable to the introduction of *Monday Night Football* in the 1970–1971 season. Situation comedies remained a steady percentage of the prime-time schedule throughout the time period.

Looking at the 1990s and beyond, a couple of interesting trends emerge. First, there was a significant increase in situation comedies over the previous time period. Whereas, comedies accounted for between 13 and 20% of the schedule during the 1960s and 1970s, for much of this later time period that number hovered around 30%. In 1998, situation comedies began to decline until they are now back in the 15 to 20% range. News and information have increased significantly versus the previous period. Quiz and panel shows made a bit of a comeback in 2000 and 2001 but have disappeared from the schedule again in favor of reality series. Motion pictures were on a steady growth path in the early 1970s but declined through much of the 1990s and are flat entering the new century. Dramas also appeared to be declining early in this time period, but there has been a steady growth trend since the beginning of the 1990s. Dramas have particularly taken off within the last two years. Variety programming has disappeared from the prime-time schedule, at least from the networks' perspective. The recent spurt in "other" programming can be attributed to an increased hour *of Monday Night Football*, an extended hour of the *Wonderful World of Disney*, and an increase in reality programming.

Programming and Regulation

Analyzing these data according to the presence or absence of the fin-syn rules, there appears to be a strong correlation between the economics of television and the selection of prime-time programming. The only program genres to increase during the 1970s were dramas and motion pictures, certainly not the cheapest of prime-time programming. Driving the growth in dramas was the increase in crime/detective shows (which correlated with a decline in action/adventure and western programming, areas that was being heavily scrutinized by the Congress and the public at that time for being overly violent). There does not appear to be any economic or regulatory cause associated with that trend. The increase in motion pictures, however, belongs to an area where the networks continued to produce their own programming. Remember that both ABC and CBS had been producing made-for-television movies in-house.

Even without the financial interest and syndication rules, the prime-time landscape began to change in the late 1960s and early 1970s. Pearce (1973) wrote:

1. There has been a shift away from the half-hour situation comedy series, and half-hour series generally.
2. Dramatic programs have become increasingly one-hour, 90 minutes, or even two hours. This is known as the "long form."
3. Fewer original programs are being ordered by the networks. Ten years ago, a typical season was 39 originals and 13 repeats. Today it is likely to be 23 originals and 23 repeats, or, at best, 26 originals and 26 repeats. When 23 originals and 23 repeats are ordered, making a total of 46 weeks of programming, the remaining weeks are often used for news or entertainment specials, including pilots.
4. A new program form, the mini-series, has evolved. These mini-series usually have fewer than 20 original programs in any one season, for example, NBC's popular *Columbo* series has only eight original episodes in any one season, and this mini-series rotates with other mini-series on the network. (p. 34)

Several factors contributed to these programming changes, the most important being the escalating cost of programming. Program costs increased approximately 60% from 1965 to 1972. This is while the cost of living rose by 33%. These costs can be attributed to the introduction of color television, the production of which is more expensive than black and white. A half-hour pilot increased from $72,000 to $250,000 between 1960 and 1973, while program costs increased from $50,000 to between $115,000 and $135,000 (Pearce, 1973, p. 35).

Two types of programming that the FCC tends to take an added interest in—public affairs and children's programming—began to decline in the early 1970s. This can in part be attributed to the Prime Time Access Rules. With fewer hours in the prime-time period, the networks put on more programming that would attract the most advertiser dollars—a category in which public affairs does not tend to rank high. In fact, public affairs and documentary programming virtually disappeared from the prime-time schedule in the early 1970s, when regularly scheduled prime-time public affairs programming dropped by 30%. This type of programming did increase during the 1973–1974 season, but this was an anomaly because of the significant amount of prime-time coverage given to the Watergate hearings and the presidential election during that season. Only NBC maintained a weekly series of this type, *America* and *NBC Reports,* during the 1972–1973 season. By the following season, no network had a weekly public affairs program in prime time (Pearce, 1973, p. 43). As for children's programming, it was the time of day that hurt this genre. Because of PTAR, these shows could not begin until after 8 p.m. Where 80% of these shows used to begin at 7:30 p.m., by the 1972–1973 season only 25% of this type of programming would begin at this early time period, prompting many angry calls to the FCC. All of these factors suggest that it was not fin-syn that contributed to the change in program content and ultimately diversity.

The early 1990s show an increase in programming that is either less expensive to produce and/or more easily sold into syndication. Reality programming and newsmagazines are the cheapest types of programming that a network can produce. Reality programming, such as *America's Funniest Home Video*, is actually made up of footage submitted by the viewing audience. Even a program such as *Survivor* has minimal upfront expenditures on the part of the network, because there are no writing or talent costs.[2] Likewise, versus fictional programming, newsmagazines are inexpensive to produce. The industry figure is approximately $400,000 per one-hour show (versus $2 million for a one-hour drama). Also, networks themselves produce newsmagazines. They do not have to pay an outside production company. Talent costs are amortized over many programs. This programming is also repackaged on other network-owned news entities, providing added opportunities to amortize the cost over several airings.

Two types of inexpensive programming made a comeback on network prime-time—game shows and variety programming. ABC had such a successful run during the summer of 2000 with a game show called, *Who Wants to be a Millionaire?*, that the network aired the show four times a week during the 2000–2001 season. This show alone was responsible for pulling ABC from last place to first in the Nielsen ratings race. The other networks, hoping to replicate ABC's success, came out with new game shows, such as *Greed*, *The Amazing Race*, *Fear Factor*, and even remakes of old shows, such as *21* on NBC. Some game shows were more

---

[2]A downside to reality programming is that no one knows what the syndication market for these types of shows will be like. Whether people will watch *Survivor* in reruns is still a big question for the show's producer.

successful than others. Only NBC was able to replicate *Millionaire's* success with its game show, *The Weakest Link*. These shows are very attractive from an economic perspective. First, production costs consist primarily of editing, talent costs, and prize money—miniscule in comparison to costs associated with a scripted program. Second, a successful prime-time game show can be repackaged as a syndicated "strip" show, which *Millionaire* and *Link* have both done. Another genre making a minor comeback on the schedule is variety programming. Thus far, only *Whose Line is it Anyway?* exists in this category, but it has the same economic advantages as game or reality programming.

Comedies are more expensive to produce than reality or game shows, but they have proven to be the best genre for sale into the syndication market. First, affiliates and independents like to program this type of show during the prime-access and late-night time periods. Second, they have the added advantage of being less expensive to produce initially than drama series. While comedies were 13% of the schedule in 1974, by 1989 comedies accounted for more than 27% of the schedule. This genre represented almost a third of the schedule through the 1990s, when it began to decline in 1998. This is likely because the schedule had become so flooded with look-alike shows that the networks had to admit to themselves that they had overdone it with this type of programming. So, while the fin-syn rules did attribute initially to an overabundance of situation comedies, the networks have pulled back because it does not make economic sense for them to overproduce one type of programming.

Music and movies have decreased on the schedule due to the increased availability of cable. With networks such as MTV, VH1 and CMT, cable can provide music in a way that broadcast networks are not able to. Cable is also better at providing movies with premium channels such as HBO and Showtime that present movies without commercial interruption.

A recent anomaly bears comment, and that is the recent increase in drama programming—a genre that is neither cheap nor particularly successful in being sold into syndication. One reason for this increase is the elimination of Sunday night movies. The networks used to program this night with either blockbuster movies or made-fors or miniseries. Since the networks have gotten out of the movie business, this frees up some money to produce more original programming. Another possible reason for the move toward dramatic programming is the increase in repurposing. Repurposing occurs when a show is aired on a broadcast network first and then airs on a cable network either later in the week or the following week. This practice started in the late 1990s as a way for producers to more quickly recoup their investment. It has since become a way for networks to do the same thing. Repurposing started with *Law & Order: Special Victims Unit* in 1999. The show would air first on NBC and then on USA Cable Network 9 days later. USA Network, owned by the same company as Studios USA (now Universal), is the producer of *Law & Order*. In this way, repurposing acts as a double whammy for USA. They make money from selling the show to NBC, and then they get to sell advertising within the show when it appears on USA, not to mention that they have a new, highly produced program at significantly reduced cost. Other companies have gotten onto the repurposing bandwagon. *Once and Again* aired first on ABC and then on Lifetime—from production to double distribution, all owned by Disney. *Alias*, which Touchstone produces, airs first on ABC and then on ABC Family. Expect this trend to continue as it has become part of the "new economics" of the broadcast television industry.[3]

Program Diversity Analysis

Figure 5.3 is based on Dominick and Pearce's (1976) diversity indicator. This index demonstrates the extent to which a limited number of categories dominate prime time. "It is derived by summing the percentages in the top three categories per season and subtracting from 100" (p. 73). With 22 categories, the numbers could range from zero to 86. The lower the number, the less diversity.

Diversity in this sense was at its peak in between 1968 and 1970. However, diversity began a downward trend beginning in 1971, the first full year of the fin-syn rules. Remember, the lower the number, the less diversity in programming. Thus, more time was being devoted to fewer types of programming. The 10-point decline in diversity from 1970 to 1971 can be attributed to an increase in motion pictures on the prime-time schedule. Twenty-five percent of program hours made up of movies

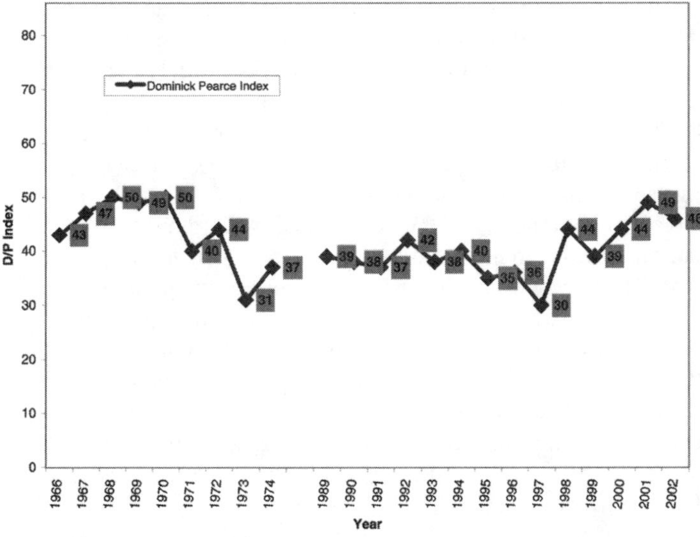

FIG. 5.3. Dominick and Pearce diversity indicator.

[3]Because this phenomenon is so new, no one knows what the long-term syndication implications are from repurposing.

became the norm for several years. Crime/detective programming also became a major staple of prime time. In 1973, when diversity was at its lowest during that period, three categories—motion pictures, crime/detective dramas and situation comedies—accounted for 69% of network prime-time programming. It is likely that the increase in motion pictures can be attributed to the introduction of fin-syn. Because the networks couldn't participate in programming, they put on programming that would not benefit other television producers. However, cable was not yet highly distributed, and Hollywood was only just starting to release films to the networks, so these situations too may have contributed to the increase in this type of programming. Certainly the increase in crime/detective programming is difficult to attribute to economics or regulation. It may have been that the networks wanted to create a situation whereby they could say to regulators that diversity decreased when they were no longer allowed a stake in the programming. Nevertheless, no evidence, other than speculation, supports this theory.

By the 1990s, diversity had recovered from its 1970s low of 30 to rebound to almost peak levels by the 2001–2002 season (see Fig. 5.3). Early in the decade, diversity hovered in the 30s. Some of this may be attributable to the repeal of fin-syn. Throughout this time period, the networks would begin to produce their own programming and to look for long-term syndication opportunities. This need to exploit economic opportunities led to the increase in situation comedies and an abundance of newsmagazines throughout the decade. Motion pictures, sitcoms, and crime/detective shows accounted for the three top programming slots through most of the decade.

A pivotal year during this time period was 1997. After diversity had remained constant for 8 years, it fell sharply in 1997 and then rose even more sharply thereafter. The flood of situation comedies on the networks saw its peak in 1997, with 40 comedies on the air representing 30% of prime-time programming. The same year, crime/detective dramas represented 25% of programming. That is 55—more than half of all programming—was represented in only two genre categories. Even the networks realized the mistake of overloading the schedule with too much of the same kind of programming, and they pulled back accordingly.

The current diversity trend can be attributed to the changing economic structure of the industry. The networks have a handful of expensive programming they have had to balance with less expensive programming. This has led to the "new" genres, such as game shows, reality programming, and even comedy variety programming coming back to prime time. While game shows appear to have been a short-term fad as their disappearance from the schedule and an accompanying decrease in diversity attest, other shows, particularly reality programming, seem to have staying power.

To ensure the coding was not skewing results based on categories not existing in the 1970s, the programs were also coded using an index geared toward 1990s programming. The prime time schedule in the 1960s and 1970s was filled with westerns and variety series—programming that has disappeared from prime time in the 1990s. Similarly reality programming and newsmagazines are genres that did not exist, or only existed on a limited basis, in the earlier time period. By creating a code

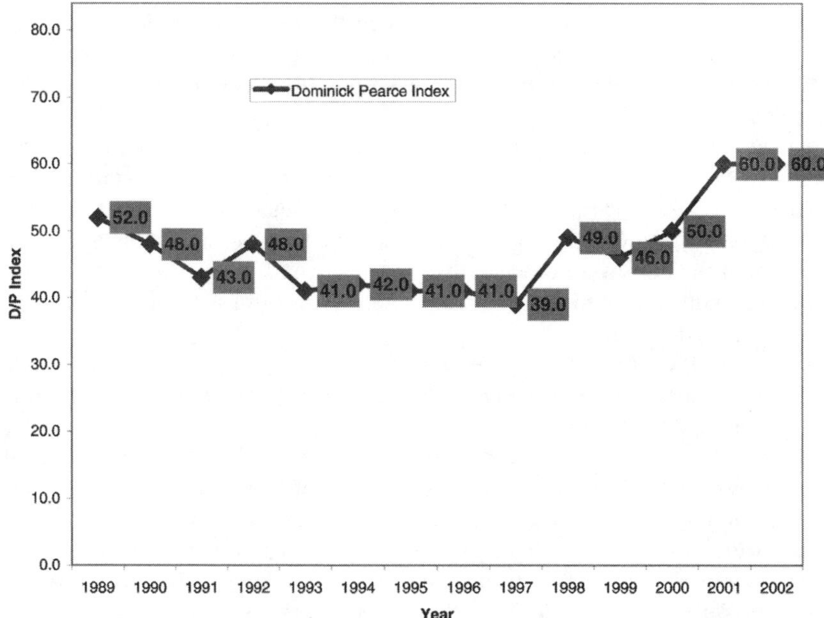

FIG. 5.4. Dominick Pearce Index.

for the later time period wherein the categories aligned with the current schedule, a more fine-tuned analysis of the latter time period could be done (see Fig. 5.4).

The pattern follows a trend similar to that using the codes from the 1970s. Diversity is at its highest during the 2001–2002 season and continues into the 2002–2003 season. The lowest point is during 1997, when the schedule was dominated by situation comedies. This coding does suggest that the programming is more diverse than when using the coding from the earlier periods. Whether we believe this or not, the similarity in trends further supports how ineffective the fin-syn rules were in achieving their diversity goal.

Though diversity initially dropped, particularly in the years immediately following the rules' repeal, diversity has most recently increased to pre-fin-syn levels. This is not to say that there is a breadth of diversity—the scale reaches to 86 and the diversity score never got above a 50 in either decade. The bottom line is this: diversity *increased* after the repeal of fin-syn. Whether or not it is quality programming is another matter. It is, however, more varied.

An alternative means for looking at diversity is the Herfindahl-Hirschman Index (HHI). The Herfindahl index is calculated by summing the squares of the percentage, or share, of each program type. This index measures "the size distribution of programming .... The higher the Herfindahl index, the greater the concentration of programming into a few program types, and hence the less the diversity" (Litman, 1979, p. 403). Thus if we can equate high concentration with a limited number of program genres, then we can use this index as a determinant of lack of diversity.

While this index measures diversity in much the same way as Dominick and Pearce's diversity index, it goes one step further by taking into account all program types and not merely the top three. Figure 5.5 provides the Herfindahl indices for the years being studied.

As with the Dominick index, the 1970s showed a marked decline in program diversity on the networks suggesting a strong concentration of programming into a few program types. The Herfindahl index follows the same pattern as the Dominick Pearce index. The pattern is consistent around the time of the elimination of the rules—after the rules were enacted, diversity decreased. When the rules were repealed, diversity increased. It is possible, therefore, to correlate the regulation to diversity in programming.

Using 1990s coding, again we see a now familiar pattern—programming at its most concentrated during the 1997–1998 season (see Fig. 5.6). With this coding, the increasing diversity trend continues into the 2002–2003 season. Remember with the Dominick Pearce index, diversity remained flat. Because the Herfindahl index shows increasing diversity, it demonstrates that past the top three categories of programming, there is more variety for the television viewer.

While the two previous methods evaluate programming vertically, that is, across the entire programming schedule, another means of looking at diversity is to measure it horizontally (see Fig. 5.7). A horizontal index evaluates what is on the three networks at any given point in time, so it more truly evaluates the diversity of pro-

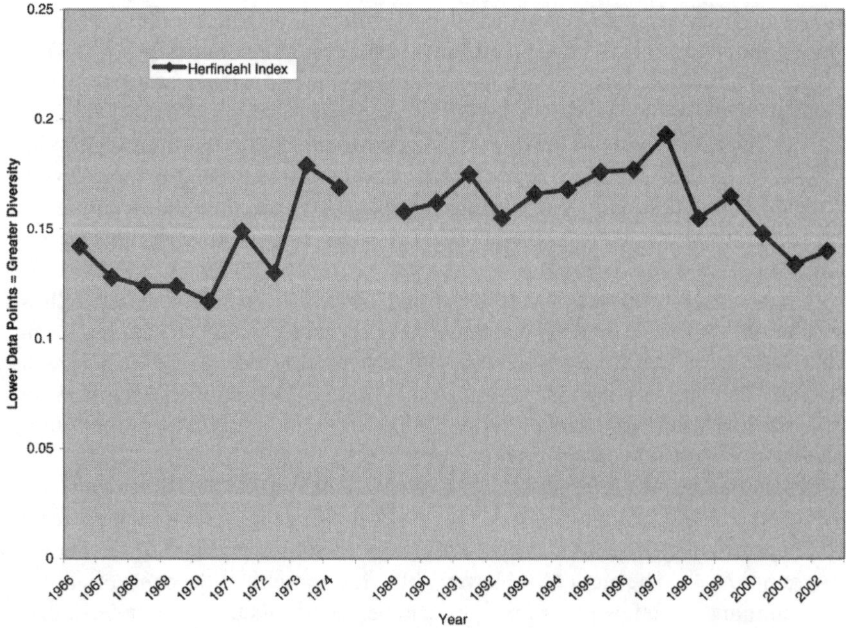

FIG. 5.5 Herfindahl Index.

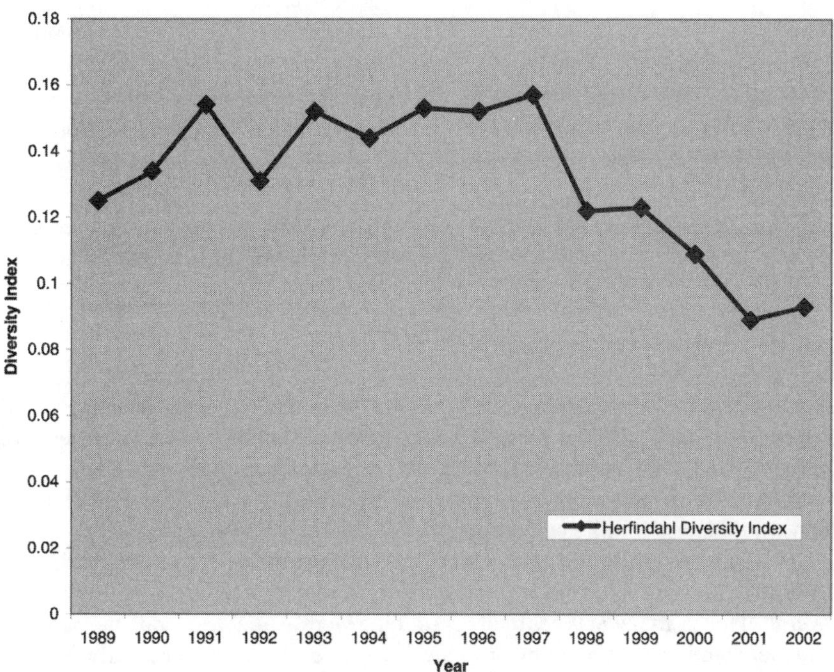

FIG. 5.6. Herfindahl Index—1990s code.

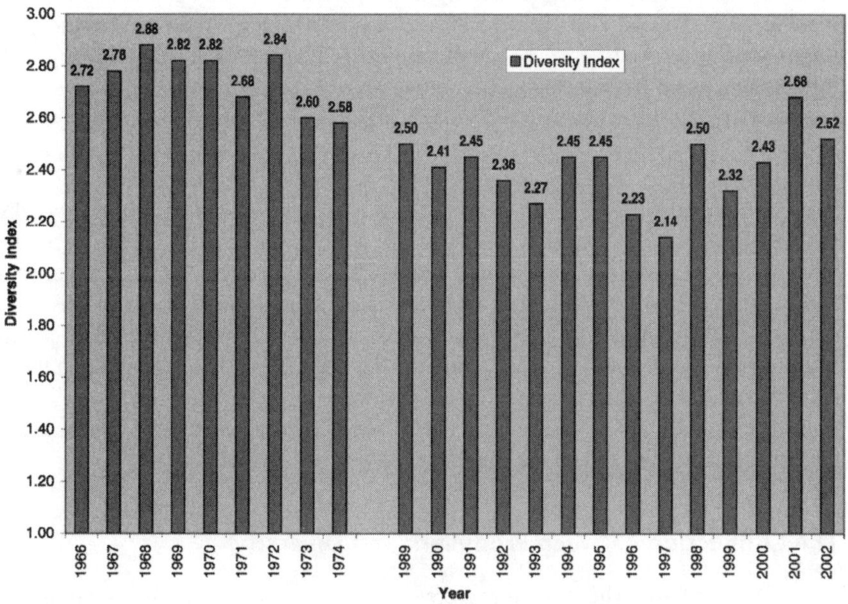

FIG. 5.7. Horizontal Diversity Index.

gramming a viewer has available to him or her at any particular half-hour period. This is an important distinction from a horizontal index. Litman (1979) provides the following example:

> assume each of the networks decides to offer a new documentary program in its schedule. This would increase the "vertical" diversity in each network's schedule; however, if these new documentaries are broadcast opposite each other, then the viewer has no choice at that point in time. Hence, changes in vertical network diversity may not fully translate into increased viewer options. (p. 403)

A horizontal index is calculated by counting the number of program genres available during each half-hour period of the prime-time schedule. This number is divided by the total number of hours or prime-time programming. This figure determines the average number of program types during prime time. Perfect imitation would equal 1 while perfect diversity would equal 3 (p. 404).

This index tells a slightly different story than the other two. In the early time period, the fluctuations in horizontal diversity reflect the fluctuations in diversity overall. That is, as fewer types of programming were available overall, the networks had more similar programming on at the same time. However, this is only on a very limited basis. Perfect diversity is a 3. Until 1974, the diversity index does not go below 2.6, suggesting that the networks are counter-programming to pull viewers from their competitors. In the 1990s, horizontal diversity on the networks is significantly reduced. This makes sense in light of the new program options available to most viewers. The networks may feel less of a need to diverge from one another, but rather, want to diverge from cable. For example, one reason variety/music programming disappeared from the schedule in the 1990s is because these programs were available on a 24-hour basis on individual cable networks such as Comedy Central and MTV. These program types are no longer viable options for the networks, so instead they produce more comedies and drama, which is their forte and something they can better afford to do. Economics comes into play here as well as the networks produce fewer types of programming overall, which we saw from the two previous indexes. The types of programming the networks are producing are less expensive and/or more able to be syndicated. Not surprising, horizontal diversity had its lowest point in 1997, just as programming reached its lowest level of diversity. It is also not surprising to see this index rebound during the 2001–2002 season when there were many more new genres available for viewers.

As we have seen with the previous charts, recoding the information has little impact on the diversity index (see Fig. 5.8).

The Connection Between Producers and Diversity

The FCC's contention has been that there is a correlation between who the suppliers of programming are and the diversity of programming that they produce. This is true based on the Commission's minority policies as well as the fin-syn rules, which

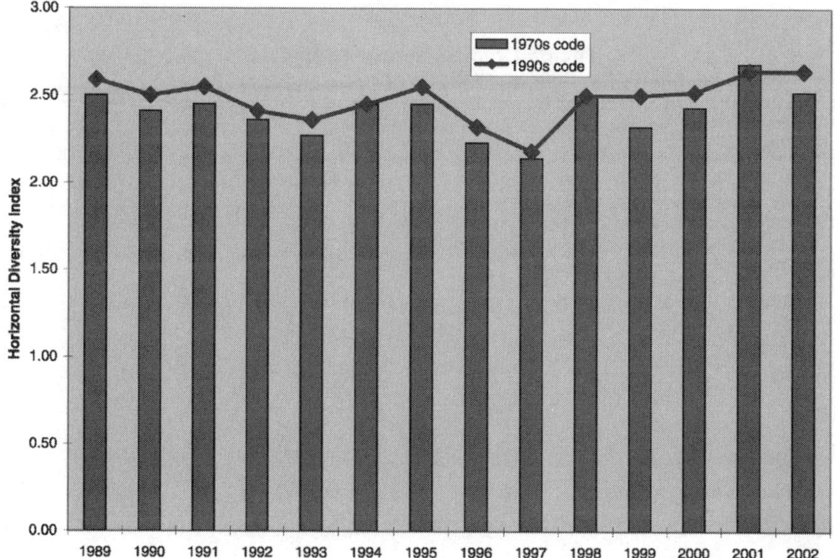

FIG. 5.8. 1970s vs. 1990s code.

suggested that more producers, and specifically not networks as producers, would create more diversity for prime-time network viewers. To test this theory, who the program suppliers were in the two time periods surrounding the introduction and repeal of fin-syn was assessed. Changes over time were evaluated using simple percentages. This information was then compared with the program diversity information. By looking at who the producers are and comparing that information with the level of diversity, we can see whether the FCC's hypothesis is correct.

The FCC has also been concerned about the level of concentration within the television industry. One of the major effects of the repeal of the fin-syn rules was the change in the structure of the television industry. This change led to extreme concentration in the supply side of the television industry as well as increased vertical integration of the broadcast networks. Examination of program suppliers would not be complete without examining the effect of this significant change. As mentioned previously, many media scholars have decried the effects of media consolidation as anathema to diversity. This research will suggest otherwise.

Unfortunately, information for the earlier period was intermittent, so the analysis there is limited. There is enough, however, to evaluate who the major suppliers were and how many there were. Information on the 1990s and beyond was plentiful and provides a thorough picture of the interaction between supplier and content.

Table 5.1 shows the share of programming by the leading prime-time program suppliers during the 1970 and 1977 television seasons. It provides data for a year before the fin-syn rules and for a year after the rules had been in effect for a number of years. Though in both years the top 10 included many of the major studios, such

TABLE 5.1

Twenty Leading Network Suppliers: Prime Time, 1970, 1977 Share of Programming Hours (%)

Supplier	*1970*	*Supplier*	*1977*
Universal	12.8	Universal	18.4
Twentieth-Century Fox	7.3	Warner	6.7
Paramount	6.4	Spelling/Goldberg	6.1
Columbia	6.1	Lorimar	5.4
MGM	4.5	MTM	5.3
Filmways	3.6	Columbia	3.6
ITC	3.0	MGM	3.5
Harbour	2.6	Paramount	3.5
Spelling/Thomas	2.3	Aaron Spelling	3.2
Talent	2.2	Twentieth-Century Fox	3.2
Teleklew	2.0	Walt Disney	2.9
CBS	1.9	Tandem	2.9
Walt Disney	1.9	Quinn-Martin	2.7
Leonard Freeman	1.8	Tat	2.4
NBC	1.8	Toy	2.2
Sullivan	1.8	CBS	2.0
Peekskill	1.7	Four D	2.0
Xandu	1.7	Whacko	1.7
Van Bernard	1.5	Schick-Sunn Classics	1.6
Glenco	1.5*	David Gerber	1.6
	66.9		80.9

Note. FCC Network Inquiry Special Staff (1980).
*Others with 1.5 market share: Barnaby.

as Universal and Warner Brothers, several independent companies accounted for significant percentages of the prime-time schedule. In 1970, major studios held the top five slots, and independent studios held the next five. Eleven of the top 20 suppliers were independent production companies. Also of note is that the top 20 suppliers accounted for almost 67% of prime-time programming. In 1977, independent producers were still well represented in the top 20. Spelling/Goldberg, Lorimar, MTM, and Aaron Spelling were all independent producers in the top 10 in 1977. Eight out of the bottom 10 suppliers were also independent companies. Overall, then, 12 out of the top 20 suppliers during 1977 were independent companies. However, the program supply market was beginning to consolidate, which is evidenced by the fact that the top 20 suppliers in 1977 accounted for almost 81% of prime-time hours versus 67% only 7 years before.

By the 1990s, I could not even evaluate based on the top 20 because there were not enough suppliers to fill that many spaces, so the top 15 were analyzed for 1995, and 10 for 2002 (see Table 5.2). (Totals do not equal 100% because of mov-

TABLE 5.2

Fifteen Leading Network Suppliers:
Prime Time 1989, 1995, 2002 Share of Programming Hours (%)

Supplier	*1989*	*Supplier*	*1995*	*Supplier*	*2002*
Lorimar	12.9	Warner Brothers	18.9	CBS	28.0
CBS	7.6	CBS	12.1	ABC	21.2
Columbia	7.6	NBC	8.3	NBC	14.4
Universal	6.8	ABC	7.6	Warner Brothers	9.9
Warner Brothers	6.8	Paramount	6.8	Universal	6.8
ABC	6.1	Universal	5.3	20th Century Fox	1.5
MGM	4.5	Columbia	4.5	Bochco Prod.	1.5
Paramount	4.5	Disney/Touchstone	4.5	Endemol Ent.	1.5
Stephen J. Cannell Prod.	4.3	20th Century Fox	3.0	Hallmark Ent.	1.5
Disney/Touchstone	3.8	Steven Bochco Prod.	3.0	Next Ent.	1.5
20th Century Fox	3.8	Carsey-Werner	2.3		**87.8**
NBC	3.0	Brillstein-Grey	1.5		
Viacom	3.0	Cosgrove/Muerer	1.5		
Carsey-Werner	3.0	Gothic Renaissance	1.5		
New World	2.3	Castle Rock Ent.	0.8		
Castle Rock Productions	1.5		**81.6**		
Cosgrove/Muerer Prods.	1.5				
GTG Productions	1.5				
Alien Productions	0.8				
Steven Bochco Prods.	0.8				
Carson Productions	0.8				
MTM Productions	0.8				
	87.7				

*1989 = 1989/1990 season.
**Lorimar attributed as part of Warner Brothers as of 1990.
***Spelling and Viacom counted as part of Paramount as of 1994.
****Witt Thomas attributed to Warner Brothers as of 1995.
*****1996–Disney/Touchstone attributed to ABC and Castle Rock to Warner Brothers.
If a broadcast network owned any part of a show, the show was credited to the network.

ies on the schedule, that is movies represent 12.2% of the 2002 prime time schedule.) In 1989, there were still a number of independent companies—Lorimar, which was the leading supplier that year; Cannell Productions; Carsey-Werner; New World and a handful of smaller companies like Alien Productions and GTG Productions. ABC and CBS had already cracked the top ten while NBC was at Number 12.[4] This was likely in anticipation of changes to the fin-syn rules. Consolidation of top suppliers continued with 15 suppliers accounting for 80% of prime-time programming. By 1995, the three broadcast networks were the second, third, and fourth leading program suppliers for prime time, together accounting for 28% of prime time. Only Warner Brothers produced more programming than the networks. While there were six independent companies within the group of the top 15 suppliers, they accounted for just over 10% of programming. By this time, the top 15 accounted for more than 80% of programming. By 2002, the three original broadcast networks are the top three program suppliers, accounting for almost 64%, or two thirds of all of prime time. In fact, the top six (which by this point consisted of the six broadcast networks and Universal) accounted for 82% of programming. The leading six suppliers accounted for less than 50% only 11 years earlier (see Table 5.3).[5]

Breaking this down a bit further, because the financial interest and syndication rules were concerned with maintaining the vitality of the independent production community, an analysis was done of the percentage of programming by type of producer (see Fig. 5.9). Producers were categorized as network (this includes only the three major networks for this analysis), Hollywood major, what I termed a mini-major (companies such as Lorimar, Orion and Viacom), independents and movies. Movies were evaluated as a separate category because their suppliers are varied, but their presence on the prime-time schedule is significant.

As the chart clearly demonstrates, the mini-majors have all disappeared by the end of the decade, having all been acquired by a larger corporation (the exception being Viacom which acquired CBS and thus no longer qualifies as a "mini" anything). Independents have fallen from supplying 15% to 6% of the prime-time schedule from 1989 to 2002. It appears the major studios have lost the largest share, going from a high of 48.5% in 1990 to 18.2% in 2001. This is deceiving, however. Instead of three networks and eight major studio producers, we now have six combined network/producers. These studios have not disappeared, but rather have merged with networks to become vertically integrated corporations. Because of this, the big winners have been the three major broadcast networks. These three companies went from a low of 13.6% in 1990, just prior to the changing of the

---

[4]The fin-syn rules did not forbid the networks to produce their own programming. It was the consent decrees that limited this production. By 1989, the networks could produce 4 hours of programming per night and by 1990, that restriction would be eliminated.

[5]Twentieth-Century Fox appears to be underrepresented in this chart. That is because most of its programming appears either on the Fox network or the mini-nets, or shows are produced in conjunction with a network as is the case with several Fox shows that appear on CBS.

TABLE 5.3

Six Leading Network Suppliers:
Prime Time, 1989, 1995, 2002 Share of Programming Hours (%)

Supplier	*1989*	*Supplier*	*1995*	*Supplier*	*2002*
Lorimar	12.9	Warner Bros.	18.9	CBS	28.0
CBS	7.6	CBS	12.1	ABC	21.2
Columbia	7.6	NBC	8.3	NBC	14.4
Universal	6.8	ABC	7.6	Warner Bros.	9.9
Warner Bros.	6.8	Paramount	6.8	Universal	6.8
ABC	6.1	Universal	5.3	20th Century Fox	1.5
Total Top 6	47.8		59.0		81.8

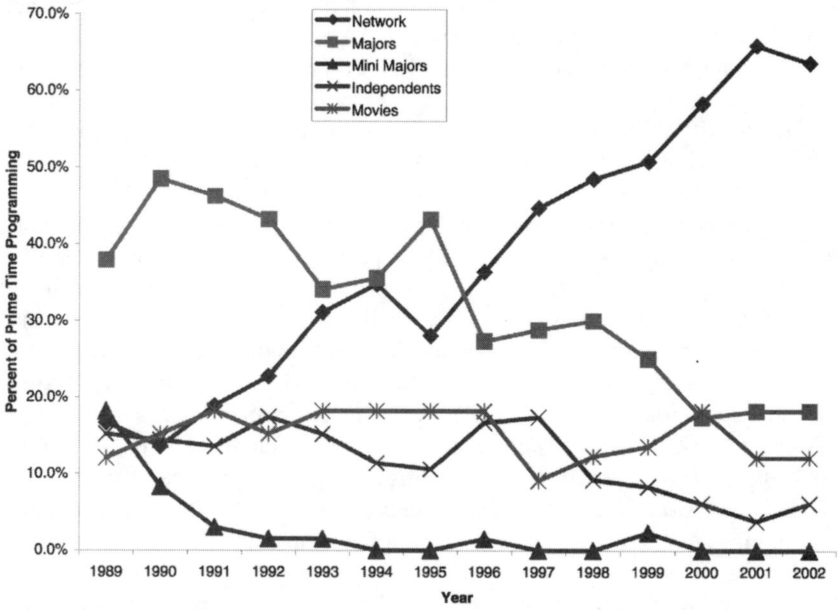

FIG. 5.9. Prime time programming producers—1989–2002.

fin-syn rules, to a high of 65.9% in 2001, with a slight drop in the 2002 season. However, that is a jump of more than 450%.

Based on the diversity analysis earlier in the chapter, diversity was at its peak between 1968 and 1970. Based on the current analysis, we saw that the industry was the least consolidated in 1970. Therefore, we might make the statement that the number of suppliers in the industry has influenced the diversity of programming (both horizontal and vertical). However, that trend does not continue into the 1990s. Though programming was in the mid-level of diversity, between 35 and 42 on an

86-point scale up until 1997, by 2001 diversity is at its highest (49) even while the industry was its most consolidated.

In looking at the consolidation of the supply market for prime-time programming, the changed structure of the industry has to be taken into account.[6] Until this point, only the three original networks have been considered as networks. However, this is not the reality anymore. Fox is considered by all in the business, as well as outside of the industry, to be a full-fledged network. The weblets, UPN and The WB, have also established themselves as full broadcasters—The WB more so than UPN, as previously discussed, but this too may change with Viacom's increased interest in the network and Fox's purchase of a number of UPN affiliate stations. When we take this into account, the distribution of program supply changes a bit, as Table 5.4 shows.

This table analyzes the percentage of prime-time programming supplied to the networks as a formulation of the supplier. This is done in three different ways. First, suppliers are calculated simply based on the three original broadcast networks. Then, Fox is added to the original broadcast networks, making it a four-network analysis. Finally, all six networks are considered as part of the network group.

There is little difference in the percent of production by the networks when analyzing a three- versus four-network universe. If we look just at the three broadcast networks, they account for 63.6% of programming. When we add Fox, that number increases slightly to 64.2%. However, add UPN and WB and the number increases to nearly 75% of the prime-time schedule being supplied by these six companies. This increase occurs because not only do UPN and WB get added to the network total, but Warner Brothers (WB's parent company) is eliminated from the major studio figures. The only majors not associated with a network, Columbia and Universal, account for 5.3% of programming. From a diversity standpoint, independents are given more opportunities when the three newer networks are added to the analysis. Independents account for only 4 hours, or 6.1%, of programming on the three original broadcast networks. When all six networks are analyzed, independents account for 9 hours, or 8.7% of programming. Though not significant in comparison to what the major studios are producing, it is significant in relation to what they produce for the Big Three. Even so, the six vertically integrated network/producers create and distribute three-fourths of all prime-time programming. This means that only 25% of prime-time programming is being supplied by companies other than the six networks themselves and almost half of that percentage is movies, not regular prime-time series.

Having said all of this, it is important to bear in mind the previous diversity analysis. While many media critics have decried the consolidation of the media industry

[6]Many programs are produced as collaborations between networks and studios, networks and producers, or producers and studios. In the present analysis, the network was considered the producer if they had any financial stake in a show. The network was given primacy to show the impact of fin-syn.

TABLE 5.4

Suppliers of Prime Time Programming–2002
As 3 Networks, 4 Networks, and 6 Networks
% by Supplier in Hours

	3 Networks		*4 Networks*		*6 Networks*	
	# of Hours	*% by Supplier*	*# of Hours*	*% by Supplier*	*# of Hours*	*% by Supplier*
Networks	**42.0**	**63.6%**	**52.0**	**64.2%**	**77.5**	**74.5%**
ABC	14.0	21.2	14.0	17.3	14.0	13.5
CBS/UPN	18.5	28.0	18.5	22.8	25.5	24.5
NBC	9.5	14.4	9.5	11.7	9.5	9.1
FOX			10.0	12.3	12.5	12.0
WB					16.0	15.4
Majors	**12.0**	**18.2%**	**12.0**	**14.8%**	**5.5**	**5.3%**
Columbia					1	1.0
20th Century Fox	1.0	1.5				
Universal	4.5	6.8	4.5	5.6	4.5	4.3
Warner Brothers	6.5	9.8	7.5	9.3		9.0
Independents	**4.0**	**6.1%**	**7.0**	**8.6%**	**9.0**	**8.7%**
Bochco Prod.	1.0	1.5	1.0	1.2	1.0	1.0
Barbour/Langley			1.0	1.2	1.0	1.0
Carsey-Werner			1.0	1.2	1.0	1.0
Endemol Ent.	1.0	1.5	1.0	1.2	1.0	1.0
Hallmark Ent.	1.0	1.5	1.0	1.2	1.0	1.0
Next Ent./Telepictures	1.0	1.5	1.0	1.2	1.0	1.0
STF Productions			1.0	1.2	1.0	1.0
Titan Sports					2.0	1.9
Movies	**8.0**	**12.1%**	**10.0**	**12.3%**	**12.0**	**11.5%**

due to its negative effects on diversity, this research just does not support that theory. As the industry has become more consolidated, diversity has increased.

Program Styles or Formulas

Researchers have evaluated television program content from various perspectives. They have analyzed the amount of violence during prime time, how gender roles are portrayed, and how specific occupations are presented through this medium. These studies are useful in understanding how television might create certain perceptions. These studies do not give a sense of how that programming is presented, the style of the shows, which I will examine in this section. However, just as the FCC did not attempt to define content or quality, nor will I. Rather, an analysis of program style will provide an additional layer for understanding if there is a difference between the types of programming produced by the networks and those produced by other sources without delving into specific content messages.

According to one of the network executives I spoke with, programs are produced according to certain formulas. "On the dramatic side, most of dramatic television is a franchise of some sort—either a legal franchise, either a law enforcement franchise, a medical franchise, most of its that .... Or there're hybrids, like *Providence*, which is a hybrid of medical and family" (W. Littlefield, personal interview, July 28, 1999). What is true now has been true for the last 30 years. Dramas primarily fall into two categories, medical dramas or crime/legal dramas. The few exceptions to these are sci-fi, action/adventure, and periodically, spiritually themed programs.

But, whether medical, legal, or sci-fi drama, few of these programs are stylistically different from one another. The recent exceptions are well noted: *ER*, *NYPD Blue,* and *Homicide*. *ER* appeals to audiences because of its different style. The show is based on an ensemble cast, there are several story lines working at any given time, and the pace of the show is very quick to reflect the urgency of the setting. *NYPD Blue* and *Homicide* stand out from other standard police dramas. *NYPD Blue* was most noted initially for pushing the boundaries of nudity on television. Since then, the acting, camera work, and story lines, dealing with such topical issues as alcoholism and racism, have differentiated this police show from the crowd. *Homicide* was initially most known for its use of handheld cameras. The choppy, frenetic pace presented through this technology made the show appear different, perhaps more urgent, than others on the air. This show too dealt with sensitive issues, such as religion and homosexuality, not often presented in an intelligent format on the medium. These shows, however, are the exceptions. Most dramas are virtually indistinguishable from one another. Even a critically acclaimed and highly rated show such as *Law & Order* is nothing more than a cop show and a lawyer show put together in one program, sort of a combination of *Dragnet* and *Perry Mason*.

Comedies seem even more alike than dramas. This may be because there are so many of them on the air that they all begin to look the same. It used to be that comedies came from producer's experiences, for example, Gary David Goldberg created *Family Ties* from his experience of having been a hippy and having children more conservative than himself. Now, it seems that comedies stem from the networks' need to present a particular demographic to attract that audience to the network. For instance, when NBC was looking to attract a young adult audience they "put out the message ... we want a photograph of young people, single, who cohabitate. We want to see them living in an urban environment, sharing space, a view of life when you're first out on your own. You know, first job, first this, first that" (W. Littlefield, personal interview, July 28, 1999). This description is what ultimately led to the creation of *Friends*. Because of this show's success in attracting a young upscale audience, *Friends* spawned a slew of look-alike shows in the years after it appeared on the air. Even a show like *Ellen*, which made television history for being the first with a lesbian as a main character, is nothing more than a *Friends* knockoff—a group of friends in their 20s or 30s sitting in Ellen's house talking about life's issues.[7] Hit comedy *Will & Grace* is also a sitcom in this vein even though it presents a gay, male lead character. This group of shows is what I call the "friends as family" sitcom. It is a variation on the theme of the family situation comedy that has populated prime time since *Lassie* and *Father Knows Best*.

More recent sitcoms in the traditional family sitcom vein include shows such as *Everybody Loves Raymond, The King of Queens, According to Jim, The Bernie Mac Show*, the list goes on. Whereas there are minor variations on the theme, the nuclear family of mother, father, and children is predominant. These shows, like *Friends* and its ilk, usually have two primary sets—the home and one other, either a place of business or a local coffee bar. Even a show like *3rd Rock from the Sun*, a "fish out of water" series about aliens coming to earth to learn the customs on this planet, is nothing more than a family sitcom because the aliens disguise themselves as a family to fit in. Ultimately, there is very little difference between these shows and shows from the 1970s, such as *The Brady Bunch* or *The Partridge Family*, except for maybe the hairstyles and the bell bottoms.

The other dominant type of sitcom is the office or workplace comedy. In the 1990s, this included shows such as *Veronica's Closet, NewsRadio, Working, Sports Night*, and *Spin City* to name a few. These shows usually present a lead character who is competent in their work life and a failure in their personal life. *Murphy Brown*, a show that was considered groundbreaking in the 1990s for presenting a hard-nosed woman reporter who did what she wanted, is not stylistically different from *The Mary Tyler Moore Show*, another show about a woman in a newsroom who was trying to make it on her own terms in the 1970s. Or, it can be seen as *Maude* moved into the workplace.

Even these 1970s icon shows, which were considered groundbreaking at the time, were created to deliver a particular demographic. According to Lentz (2000), while Norman Lear's shows such as *Maude* and *All in the Family* were given the label of "relevance," it was that relevance that also gave them appeal for an advertiser-friendly audience. "CBS launched its era of the 'relevant' situation comedies in order to boost ratings among the most highly valued demographic groups" (p. 60). This group consisted of well-educated, politically and socially conscious young adults—any advertiser's dream group. Moreover, these were the Baby Boomers—the largest single demographic group with the potential for the largest advertiser payback.

Programs are based on formulas now as much as they were in the 1970s. Whether sitcom or drama, each show is written to create a problem and solve it within the allotted time period of 30 or 60 minutes. Most characters, no matter what the genre, are in their 20s or 30s and by and large they are white. The formula may have become more refined in the 1990s because the broadcast networks are taking a

[7]*Ellen* did appear on the air a half season ahead of *Friends*. However, the show was retooled after the first season.

cue from the cable networks and defining their audiences more narrowly. NBC pursues an 18–49 adult audience with household incomes of more that $75,000, CBS targets the 25–54 year audience (though the network has been trying to target a younger demographic for years and has made some inroads in that area in the last couple of years), and ABC primarily targets the 18–49 audience, though that varies based on the day of the week. These more refined demographic targets direct the networks to program shows that are created to appeal to these more narrow audiences. Of course, every decade has its standout programs that are the exceptions to the rule, shows such as *All in the Family* and *M*A*S*H* in the 1970s and *Homicide* and *ER* in the 1990s. These shows, however, are surrounded in the schedule by lesser fare, such as *Here's Lucy, Medical Center,* and *Barnaby Jones* in the former case and by *Suddenly Susan, L.A. Docs* and *Nash Bridges* in the latter. These exceptions are no more plentiful in the 1990s than they were 20 years ago.

SUMMARY/CONCLUSION

Diversity was at its peak in the late 1960s before the advent of the financial interest and syndication rules and declined two years after its institution. Throughout the 1990s, diversity has remained fairly constant, at a middle range but increased sharply in the most recent years. It is, therefore, possible to say that based on these numbers that the fin-syn rules detracted from diversity.

The fin-syn rules affected diversity on all of the measurements tested. Based on Dominick and Pearce's diversity index, which is a measure of the concentration of programming in the top three genres, diversity decreased from an index of 50 in 1969 to a low of 31 in 1973 and rebounding to 37 in 1974. This number increased to 39 in 1989, dove to 30 in 1997, but has since jumped to 49—virtually matching the pre-fin-syn high. The Herfindahl-Hirschman index, also a measure of concentration, demonstrated the same pattern of diversity. Based on these figures, it may be possible to say that fin-syn contributed to a decline in diversity, since the drop occurred at the same time as the rules. Similarly, the repeal of the rules, led to an increase in the diversity of genres within two seasons after its repeal.

These indexes analyzed vertical diversity, that is diversity within a single network or throughout the entire broadcast schedule. A horizontal index was used to measure diversity across networks at any given time period. The horizontal index also showed that diversity was flat in the early 1970s and throughout the 1990s and beyond. What this index also demonstrates is that the networks do not schedule the same type of programming at the same time as their competitors. The networks counterprogram against one another. The networks did this in the 1970s, and they continue to do so in the 2000s. Even with three to four dominating program types, it is possible for the networks to put on programs that are different from the other networks in any given time period. And they do.

Looking at program genres, three types of programming dominated the prime-time viewing hours throughout the time period studied. These were dramas, situation comedies, and movies. In both the 1970s and 1990s, drama was the leading program genre. In the 1960s, these dramas were primarily action/adventure shows or westerns, whereas by the 1970s the dramas were in the crime/detective category, and this trend continued into the later period. In the early period studied, dramas were followed by motion pictures and then sitcoms. The order was reversed in the 1990s. The reason for the increase in sitcoms over movies in the 1990s is twofold. First, with the advent of cable, movies became more readily available to viewers. Cable also provided these films uncut, uncensored, and without commercials, something broadcasters could not do. Second, situation comedies are relatively inexpensive to produce with the added bonus of syndication after their network run. Purchasing movies are a sunk cost for the networks while creating sitcoms is a long-term investment.

Recent developments in program diversity may be due in part to the economics of program production. As production costs and licensing fees increased on shows not owned by the networks, other less expensive types of programming were needed to offset these expenditures. To limit program production costs, the broadcast networks began relying more heavily on non-scripted, less expensive programming. The primary example is newsmagazines. In fact, for the first time in 1998 this genre overtook movies as the third most prominent genre in prime time. This was due to economics. The economic efficiency of newsmagazines may derive not only from their lower production costs than scripted programming, but also from the networks' ability to use existing news production assets to generate this type of program. However, even with the addition of this new genre, there was no perceptible increase in diversity, because rather than being an incremental genre, it replaced other more expensive programming genres.

It should be noted here that the increase in newsmagazines can be attributed to the repeal of fin-syn. Before fin-syn, the networks had the most experience in producing news and public affairs programming. While news departments were cut in the 1980s, the networks always maintained these divisions. Thus, the networks were in a position to produce their own programming, for example, newsmagazines, without buying or creating a studio as soon as the consent decrees let them so do.

New genres did not appear until 2000, with the advent of game shows and reality series. No longer limited to the news format, the networks looked to other low-cost solutions programming. Game shows provide inexpensive programming that can be flexibly slotted into the network schedule. Reality programming, depending on the format, can also be slotted as needed. A show such as *Survivor* or *Big Brother* has the added benefit of being produced by CBS News (though they call it something else), allowing what has become a cost center to become a potential profit center.

The conclusion is worth restating. There has been a discernable change in diversity. Yes, there has been consolidation in the production side of the business. Yes, the networks—whether we are talking about three, four, or six—now account for an overwhelming majority of the programming that appears in prime time. However, while that may concern us intuitively in terms of program content, it has been proved through this analysis that *consolidation* is not having an effect on the diversity of content. This was not only true in the case of program genres but also in the case of program styles.

The fears of the Hollywood producers, primarily independent producers, have been realized. The broadcast networks have reverted to their pre-fin-syn ways. The majority of programming not produced in-house is programming in which the networks have a financial interest. Something new in the 1990s is that a majority of entertainment programming is being produced in-house by the broadcast networks. In the 1970s, the networks produced news and public affairs programming and left the entertainment programming to outside suppliers. This in-house production of entertainment has led to a corresponding reduction in the number of studio-produced programs and, in fact, fewer Hollywood production companies altogether.

This analysis suggests that it does not matter who or how many people produce programming for network prime time. Rather, it is economic factors that contribute to the variety of programming that will be available to audiences. As networks needed to be more creative in their financing, they found both new types of program genres and new ways of paying for it. This further supports the idea that something other than who the producer is affects the content and that the medium itself and/or economics may determine the diversity of the product more than the people doing the producing. If this is the case, then the financial interest and syndication rules were not the appropriate means for achieving the goal of diversity.

6

The Program Selection Process

INTRODUCTION

Ultimately what appears on our television screens is the responsibility of a handful of network programming executives. These men, and now women as well, have been using a process for selecting programming that has been in existence almost since the medium's inception. At its simplest, producers come up with a show idea, they pitch the idea to the network and the network says "yes" or "no" to the show. A number of factors determine which shows the executive will accept or reject. Those factors have changed throughout the history of fin-syn, even though the process itself has not.

In the 1970s, what led the FCC to institute the financial interest and syndication rules was a concern that the networks were becoming both too powerful and too demanding when it came to this selection process. Too powerful, in that they were the gatekeepers of news, information, and entertainment for the American public. This was so because of the limits of the radio spectrum, as discussed earlier, which made the broadcast networks the only providers of television programming in most U.S. markets. Too demanding, because networks were requiring an equity stake in a program before it would be accepted as a part of the prime-time schedule. As statistics quoted earlier showed, the networks had ownership in more than 70% of their prime-time schedule by the mid-1960s, up from only 45% the previous decade. This strong arming of producers was a fundamental reason for the creation of fin-syn. Not only was the Commission concerned about network participation in the selection of programming. They were concerned about network input into programming once it appeared on the air.

Since the rules were repealed in 1995, the economic structure of the industry changed drastically. The television networks have become vertically integrated institutions with the ability to produce programming through internal business units. Corporate parents put pressure on the networks to purchase programming internally to achieve synergies and, of course, increase profits. Being part of large media conglomerates, there is added pressure on the networks to be profitable so that Wall Street may find the parent company appealing. This has led to finding new ways to increase revenue and decrease costs. Increased revenue is coming through new methods of syndication and, more recently, repurposing, as well as taking a financial interest in programming that appears on air. Decreased costs are achieved through purchasing more in-house productions, producing more lost-cost programming such as game shows and reality series, and by cutting layers of middle management. These pressures from corporate parents come in the face of ever-increasing production costs, increasing licensing and talent fees, and increasing competitive pressures from new broadcast networks, cable, and DBS.

Based on a series of interviews with network executives and prime-time program producers, it appears the incentives introduced into the program selection process by the repeal of the fin-syn rules have clearly affected the program selection process within broadcast networks. Specifically, the networks have an incentive to select programs produced in-house because of both financial and political reasons. Secondarily, if the show is not internally produced, then the ability to have equity ownership in an externally produced show is expected for inclusion on the prime-time schedule.

What is true now and has always been true is that selecting programs for the prime-time schedule is the most important aspect of a network programming executive's job. Prime-time programming is the lifeblood of the television network, because it fills the most visible and most profitable time period.[1] It is the product that is sold to all constituencies—viewers, affiliates, and advertisers. And while advertisers may be most concerned about the audience a program attracts, affiliates are most concerned about content and how a show will play in their community, and viewers are interested in entertainment and information—the network executive is concerned about all of these things when selecting shows for the prime-time schedule.

Content, audience, and programming mix are just some of the factors that are considered. In addition, network executives have to juggle business relationships that exist between networks and studios and networks and producers. They must also take into consideration test results from audience research on pilots. These things are not new. What is new since 1995 is their incentive to select in-house productions and to obtain an equity stake in programming not produced by the network as previously mentioned. A second change is the evolution of syndication market, which affects programming decisions because

[1]Success in prime-time ratings has traditionally spilled into other dayparts. For example, if people are watching CBS in prime time, they are more likely to watch CBS late night (David Letterman). Also, wherever a television set is turned off is where the set turns on again, so if someone is watching NBC in prime time, they will automatically turn on the *Today Show* the next morning.

executives may be looking for what is going to make money back fastest. It seems the bottom line has become the bottom line.

The bottom line for media critics, however, is twofold. First, with increased vertical integration, independent producers have less access to audiences or they must align themselves with studios or networks to get their show on the air. It has become standard that producers will align themselves with a studio. The ones I spoke with did not necessarily feel that this was a bad thing. Second, more attention to the bottom has led to lesser quality programming. No one that I spoke with claimed that television is of low quality overall. Yes, some shows are very low brow, but taken as a whole, the prime-time schedule could be compared with the Golden Age of Television.

NETWORK PRIME TIME PROGRAM SELECTION TIMELINE

Programs may be developed throughout the year, but the majority of programs are developed using a timeline that has been around since the beginning of television. (This timeline provides a context for understanding the program selection process.) It is a schedule based on the broadcast year of September to May. This schedule is one that most suits advertisers and is not necessarily the best for producing "quality" programming, but every network follows it.

Throughout the fall and after the launch of the new season, programming executives meet with producers and writers to hear new programming ideas. If the network likes a particular idea, they ask that a pilot script be developed. This is known as a script commitment. This script is a sample script, an idea of what the first show will be like. The network will finance this script, which currently costs around \$75,000 to \$100,000. In return for financing the script, the network retains the right to order the pilot (a fully created episode of the show), and if they like the pilot, the show itself. The network may have 100 to 150 scripts written. From these scripts, the network will select approximately 20 to 30 shows to be produced as pilots. The number of shows to reach the pilot stage may be less, depending on the number of shows the network needs to replace in its current schedule.

Once a pilot is approved for production, the producer of the show will be given development money by the network. The amount is approximately \$1 million per pilot[2] and usually covers most of the producer's costs. Often the producer will supplement the money provided by the network to produce a better pilot. This can be a two-edged sword. The producer creates a better pilot so that the show will have an edge over the other pilots in contention for a slot on the prime-time schedule. However, if the producer adds too much money, he may create a pilot that he or she will not be able to replicate on a weekly basis after the show is on the schedule. Thus, the producer gets his or her show on the air, but not for long.

---

[2]This is an average number. Depending on the track record of the producer, whether it is a half-hour comedy or an hour drama, it can be more, though usually not less.

Once the network selects a pilot for its schedule, a licensing agreement is signed between the network and the producer. The network retains the exclusive right to air the series, usually for 5 years, with a network option to cancel prior to that time.

The networks start to make decisions about what will appear on the fall schedule in March, when the networks hold what are known as "development meetings." These meetings are small-scale presentations for the top 100 to 200 advertising clients. There, the top network programming executives say how well the network is doing in the marketplace, but the main reason for the meeting is for the executives to tell the advertisers what they think will be on the fall schedule. No final decisions have been made by this point, but it is an opportunity to begin whetting the advertisers' appetites for the new programming. There is some interaction between the network executives and the advertisers in the form of a question-and-answer period. However, because most of the programming decisions are so preliminary, it is not possible for the advertisers to have input into the programming. Though these meetings are private, soon after, the trade press begins to speculate about what will appear on the fall schedules. It seems silly to have these meetings when the programming is so undecided and the networks are going to give the definitive schedule in 2 months. However, these meetings began out of a need to keep advertisers happy, and so they have continued.[3]

Throughout the remainder of March, April, and May, pilots are created and refined with input from the network programming executives. During the first two weeks of May, pilot screenings are held, where all the top network executives, not just programming executives, evaluate the potential shows. Again, no final decisions are made at these meetings, but everyone's input is taken into consideration. Final pilot decisions are made during the second and third week of May.

Programmers use a number of criteria to determine which shows appear on the new schedule. For returning shows, programmers look at factors such as past performance, age of the show, and how many other shows are not returning to the schedule. For new shows, the programmers think about the track record of the producers of this program, the fit of the program with the rest of the schedule, and if necessary, the fit of the show for a particular day and time. For all shows, programmers consider what type of demographics the show is likely to attract, can the show be used effectively to counter-program against the competition, are the costs reasonable and the talent recognizable or if not, at least likeable (Head, 1989, p. 28).

The final prime-time program schedule is presented to all advertisers during the third week of May in New York City. These presentations are huge "dog and pony" shows and can cost the network upwards of a million dollars or more. From the network perspective, these presentations are worth every dime, as the audience is made up of advertising executives responsible for placing several billion dollars worth of

[3]In 2002 for the first time, as a cost-cutting measure, the networks did not hold these meetings.

advertising time. If they like what they see, it can mean significant revenue for the network.

After the advertiser meetings are held, the networks present the new fall schedule to their affiliates. Next, the networks present the shows to the press at the annual July press tour, where the nation's television press screen the pilots and get to interview the cast and producers of the programs selected. The viewers finally get to see the shows sometime around the third week of September, when the new fall season launches. After the new season starts, the process begins all over again.

This method for choosing programming provides an explanation for why program selection is inefficient. Not only is it inefficient, it leads to at best substandard programming. The unspoken issue around diversity is not so much different as quality. Quality becomes secondary under this system. First, as mentioned, this schedule exists to accommodate advertisers. Of course advertisers would like the networks to produce better programs, but they don't want to have to change the way they do business to get them. Second, because all pilots are being produced at the same time, talent resources are being stretched to their limit. This has been particularly true in the last few years with the introduction of two new broadcast networks, not to mention the plethora of cable options that now also produce their own programming. Finally, the shows are being produced under severe time constraints to meet the May deadline. Between the tight schedule and the battle for talent, it is unlikely that creative people are producing their best work. It is difficult, however, to say how to change the system to satisfy both the entertainment community and the advertisers.

In the remainder of this chapter, network programming executives and prime-time program producers provide additional insight into this process. They discuss the elements that are part of the consideration set when deciding on programs that will appear on the prime-time schedule. These executives had opinions on all of these processes, from how a show is selected to the number of people involved in the process. They are concerned about the networks' increased participation in programming, though more so from a financial standpoint than a creative one. They also had suggestions for changing the process, but they were not overly optimistic that it ever would.

PRIME TIME PROGRAM DEVELOPMENT PROCESS

There are several steps in the selection of programming for the prime-time schedule. The two primary areas are development—that is, the actual nurturing of a show—and selection. I have separated these into two areas for more clarity of the process. As well, while it is the selection process that is of particular interest, it is important to understand how network executives get the pool of programs to select from.

The development of prime-time programming is done primarily by the programming division of the television network. The process is fairly standardized, and the participants were consistent in presenting the process. From the network point of view, the first step in the process is the needs assessment. Warren Littlefield, a television producer, working with Paramount Television, whose show *Do-Over* appeared on The WB for the 2002–2003 season, explained this process to me in July 1999. Prior to his current position, Littlefield had been at NBC for more than 20 years, through the time of *Cosby* and *Family Ties* to *Friends*, *ER*, and *Will & Grace*. He oversaw the development process for nine years as the entertainment president at NBC, a position he left at the end of 1998. "The first thing you do is you look at your schedule. You assess your needs. An example would be if you were at ABC in 1999, all you knew all year long was *Home Improvement* was leaving. *Home Improvement* was leaving! What are you going to do to lead off Tuesday night at 8 o'clock? Well, you have to deal with that. And you formulate based upon the needs of your schedule and the strength of your competition, a strategy. So you look at your assets, you look at your liabilities, you do a needs assessment." Flody Suarez, currently an independent producer and former programming executive at NBC, expanded on this process when we spoke in August 1999: "At the beginning of a development season, development people at a network will sit and look at their schedule and say, 'Okay best case scenario we're going to need this many shows. Worst case scenario, we're going to need this many and this is probably where we're going to need them. What are the kinds of shows that we think can succeed in those time periods? And let's focus on those. What's not on television right now?'"

Once the network has determined the types of shows it needs and the time periods that need to be filled, they must go about getting the programming to fill those slots. This is where the network turns to the Hollywood creative community, which includes independent producers, the major studios, and their own in-house production units. As Warren Littlefield explains, this next step in the process is to open your doors to producers. "'Come bring us your shows.' And in that process you listen to all the studios, as well as your own studio and you constantly are telling the studio community, the agent community, the writer/producer community every forum you can possibly speak to 'here's what we think we need and what do you have?'" Suarez agreed saying, "You put out the word to the town. That's kind of what you're looking for, and you take pitches.[4] Sometimes somebody pitches you something that doesn't fit your model at all, but it's a good pitch, and they're good writers, so you buy it."

As this comment suggests, just because the network has done a needs assessment, it does not mean that that is the only type of programming that the creative community brings to the networks. Nor is it the only type of programming the network looks at. Suarez told me that they look at programming that may not be part of the initial plan but may have an interesting creative element attached to it: "They bring you stuff you weren't looking for. They pitch you writers and you say, 'Okay I like the writer. Let's hear the idea' and then the department ends up buying a slate of projects. A lot of them will be right in that target of what you were looking for and then a lot of them will be these wild cards. These flyer-type projects, which end up

[4]Pitches are meetings where a writer or producer or a studio "pitch" their idea to a network. This may be a phone call or a more formal meeting.

in many cases seeming special and different because you don't have five of them sitting there."

What the executives were explaining is that the process is not science. It is part business, part art, part gut. The networks start with a framework—the needs assessment. They know they need to replace certain shows that are going off the air because they are too old or ratings have not been high enough to warrant that the show return for another season. They understand that there are certain time slots that need to be filled. This could be an 8 o'clock comedy or a 10 o'clock drama. All of these factors will affect what the network asks for from the creative community. However, the needs assessment is not a hard-and-fast rule. It is a game plan from which to work. The executives want to leave themselves open for unplanned opportunities. Most so-called flyer projects that Suarez spoke of come from producers or writers who have a strong point of view about a project. "A lot of things also just come in where simply someone says 'here's my idea. You know, this is my idea. A funny thing happened to me. I want to write about my life experience.' *Family Ties* came out of the life experience of Gary Goldberg being an aging hippy and having kids who were more conservative than he was. *The Cosby Show* came out of Bill Cosby's experiences of being a parent. *Home Improvement* from Tim Allen. So a lot of it in the development process, particularly in a half hour comedy, is creators or talent coming up with a point of view," according to Littlefield.

A strong point of view is fundamental to the pitch and ultimately the long-term viability of a show. In January 2002, Matt Williams, one of the producers of *Home Improvement*, described his development of the show much in the same way as Littlefield talked about it from the network perspective. "I wanted, and my partners wanted, to write a show about an American family and especially a show built around a father. And then we end up, thank God, bumping into Tim Allen through Jeffrey Katzenberg at Disney, and this was a perfect match. So we really took our time and really honed the concept of the show and what that show was about, what we wanted to say and it was driven purely by Tim's personality, Tim's standup, and what we wanted to do about family life."

The pitches described thus far are the simplest—a writer creates a concept for a show and tries to sell it to a network or studio. There is, however, a spectrum upon which shows get picked up and developed, from the simplest to the most complex, particularly from a monetary standpoint. Stephen McPherson is president of Touchstone Television, the production division of ABC Entertainment. McPherson was formerly at NBC as a programming executive. In January 2002, he provided the following analysis of the development process. "The simplest [way for a show to get picked up] is a writer walks in the door and pitches a show to a studio and they go, 'great we'd like to do it.' They then pitch it to the network, they say, 'great we'd like to do it.' He writes a script; it's picked up to pilot; it's picked up to series, and it goes on the air. The most complicated ones are … a British television series exists and you're going to do a remake of it, and you make a deal with the exec producers of the British show to supervise American writers who do it through a studio here, and potentially it's a coproduction because there's not domestic financing. Big stars always make a difference and big properties make a difference and preexisting network commitments and penalties make a difference."

But whether simple or complex, after a show has been pitched and the network has determined that it is interested in a show idea, the negotiation of the contract begins. The contract can be for a script, a demo, a pilot, or a series commitment. The following describes what might be a typical production deal for better-than-average producers. NBC's experience with *Friends* is typical of this. According to Littlefield: "When we bought *Friends* from Warner Brothers, Bright, Kauffman, Crane … were not super hot, but they were fairly hot. And so we had to say based upon their heat, we had to guarantee a pilot commitment. Now, what does that mean? That probably when the deal was all said and done in a negotiation it probably meant if we didn't make the pilot off of what they were writing, we probably would have owed them a couple of hundred thousand dollars. To make the pilot was a million dollars. And so many deals are simply a script, 75,000 plus fringes. Okay, so under 100. Then you get the little more heat, a pilot commitment, so now your exposure is several hundred thousand. And if it's a firm, you gotta roll film, a demo, is 500 thousand, and a firm pilot, you're going to make it, is at least a million and can be for a half hour up to 2 million."

Programming executives at each network go through this process with 20 to 30 producers. That number can be more or less depending on how many shows the network needs to replace. It is not this particular step of the process that regulators take issue with. Rather, it is the actual selection and what goes into deciding what finally ends up on the screen.

PRIME TIME PROGRAM SELECTION PROCESS—FACTORS IN THE FINAL DECISION

Several factors go into making the final decision on what programs will appear on the prime-time schedule. These include relationships between networks and producers, what is going to be most profitable for the network, whether the show is produced internally, how well the show has tested with audiences, and what are its prospects for attracting advertisers, as well as the shows prospects for success in the syndication market.

Relationships

A major factor in the final selection process is the relationship between a network and a studio. If the studio already has a show on the network or has a particularly hot property, it can use it as leverage to sell more programming to a network. This is not an unusual business practice. Other businesses do it all the time. In fact, networks do it themselves when selling advertising time. If an advertiser wants to be on *ER,* for instance, the network will package commercials in that show with commercials in other less popular programs. The implications may be smaller, but the business practice is the same.

Of course, a very important relationship now is the one that exists between the network and its own in-house studio. As explained in the previous chapter, all of the networks have their own in-house studios either through merger, acquisition, or creation. A few years ago, Disney restructured its organization to increase the sale of programs internally. Stephen McPherson, president of Touchstone Television, explained his relationship with the ABC network this way, "We're incredibly close [with the network] ... we try to work as closely as we possibly can and frankly the closer, the better ... We're not obligated to sell everything to ABC. Certainly we try to mine that relationship and it's an important one for us and for them ... we have a vertically integrated relationship with a network but we produce successful material for other broadcast networks as well."

While the implications of the internal relationships will be discussed more fully later in the section about vertical integration, it is important to note here that internally produced programming has the so-called home court advantage when it comes to being selected for the prime-time schedule. In August 1999, Ted Harbert explained why this is so. He is the former chairman and president of ABC Entertainment, a similar position to that held by Littlefield at NBC. Harbert worked at ABC for 20 years, the last four (1993–1997) of which he was responsible for all prime-time and late-night programming. He left ABC and signed a multiyear deal to develop programming with Dreamworks, where he worked on *Arsenio*, a failed vehicle for Arsenio Hall, and *It's Like You Know ...*, another short-lived sitcom. In 1999, Harbert was named president of NBC Studios, the in-house production unit for NBC, which produces for multiple dayparts including prime time. Harbert said: "Michael Eisner is saying okay ABC [and Disney] everybody just get together in the same room and do it together. I think their [Disney's] shows will get on the air. That isn't going to mean that they're better. If you put the network person in charge of both sides of the fence, saying, 'Okay, you're in charge of the studio side, of developing shows from the studio side and you also have to ... choose the shows as the network person that go on the air.' It's impossible to ask the network person to have that much objectivity. To be able to look at the show they've been developing from the very, very beginning and say, 'Oh, no what I've just been working on personally, that I'm personally invested in from the very first moment with the writer, gee that's much lousier than the Warner Brothers show. I'm gonna go with the Warner Brothers show.' I just think it's a virtually impossible thing to ask the people."

Another very important factor is the relationship between a network and an individual producer. These usually exist in the form of a series commitment. This is a contract between the producer and the network, whereby the network agrees to pick up the next project by the producer, virtually sight unseen. Sometimes this works, and sometimes it does not. "Contracts certainly play a big part in [the decision-making process] .... Marta Kauffman, David Crane have two shows on the air that were 22-episode commitments because we had commitments to them," says Suarez, about his experience at NBC. "John Wells has commitments, you know, based on *ER*. And those are good shots to take .... Sometimes it works and sometimes it backfires. Certainly *Frasier* worked. *Wings* was a success ... [*Pursuit of Happiness]* ... was a disaster. But it's not a science. It is an art and you have to treat it as that. When you start treating it like a business, it tends to fall apart."

Series commitments have been a means by which the networks reward producers for having a successful show. The networks are willing to risk acquiring an unsuccessful show, because once a producer has a hit, the other networks want to work with that producer. This is important because historically the success of a producer is a key determinant for the success of a show overall (Biebly & Biebly, 1994). By providing the producer with a series commitment, the network guarantees that the next creation by the producer will appear on that network. NBC did just this with Steve Levitan, producer of such hits as *Frasier* and *Just Shoot Me*. Littlefield explains: "Everybody wanted to be in business with him. So it was going to cost 13 on the air no matter what, so NBC stepped up, made a commitment to 13 on the air. He did a pilot .... Now, if you hate the pilot, you can buy out of it, but it's really expensive, millions and millions. More likely you say, 'Hey, you know what, this is who we said we'd be in business with, let's see what they do.'" A commitment usually consists of 13 episodes, but can be as many as 22 or even higher in very special cases. As Littlefield described, this was the case with *Cosby* on CBS. "*Cosby* I think was a 44. CBS *Cosby* .... But they have the ability to I think probably, they'll end it up with 44 guaranteed fees, but they could have cut back to 22 episodes or something, but anyway, it's quite unique, and that was a time when CBS was desperate for an announcement, so that's the deal they made."

Paul Haggis is an example of a producer who has a series commitment. His commitment is with CBS, which means he must first present his work to the network before he can sell it elsewhere. Haggis is a writer/producer, whose most recent show is *Family Law,* which airs on CBS. He has been in Hollywood for more than 20 years, working as a writer and/or producer on such shows as *thirtysomething*, *Due South,* and *EZ Streets*. While he has a commitment with CBS, he is not tied to a particular production studio, which is the case with many other producers. In February 2002, he spoke about the different ways his shows have gotten onto the network: "I've had a long relationship with CBS. Oh, I guess I've been ... creating series for 10–12 years for them. And I think I've done four or five. I can't remember. I don't like to count the failures. (laughs) [With *Due South*], Jeff Sagansky approached me and said would you create a show about a Canadian Mountie or trapper who comes to Big City USA ... and that show was owned entirely by Alliance Entertainment. [With] *EZ Streets* which was my next show ... I sold the project myself as a writer/producer to CBS and then I sent it out for bids around to the various studios, met with them and finally decided and it got down to either Universal or Paramount, and Universal was willing to put the most money into the budget and so we went with Universal." For this producer, the series commitment could mean ownership by the network or by an outside production company.

Most often with a series commitment the network does not get a financial interest in the show,[5] which is why series commitments are expected to become a thing of the past. The network executives gave other reasons as to why there will be fewer of these types of commitments, but money and ownership are certainly a factor. According to Littlefield, "A lot of shows have gotten on the air because there were series commitments and I would say that that trend will probably fade away. The networks always want to make fewer of those so they're not shackled by them." This is true. Networks want to have as much control over what appears on the schedule as possible. What is also true is that by eliminating commitments, the networks eliminate a lot of overhead.[6]

McPherson agrees with this assessment but explains that the economics of the business has changed networks' reliance on producer commitments. "Giant overall deals [were based on] the model used [by] the movie studios [whereby] your one hit pays for all your failures, and I think there's really a sense that that can't be the way that we operate. We have to do shows for less money. We have to cut down the deficits. As foreign money becomes harder to get, as domestic syndication becomes more cluttered, as there become more channels and choices for everybody, there's less off-network money, so you're really just talking about people looking at the business and saying, 'Ok this didn't make sense. This didn't make sense. How can we save money here, save money there.' Because in the end it all comes down to money."

Money, Money, Money, Money

Perhaps most important, and the factor underlying the other aspects of the decision-making process, is the cost of production, which of course ties into the company's bottom line. The first place where cost cutting occurs is in the pilot stage. There has been some subtle reduction in the number of pilots in recent years. "There's not a dramatic reduction, but there are fewer [pilots]," according to Littlefield, "because the development process is so costly that people have gotten a little more conservative about that." Ted Harbert agreed. "The process hasn't really changed. Yes, there are less pilots made than there were before because networks are losing money, and so they're cutting their budgets so they're making less pilots." It has been reported that Twentieth Century Fox reduced its pilot output by one third in 2002 (Adalian, 2002, p. 8). So far, they are the only major studio to reduce production so dramatically. Recently, there have been rumblings in trade publications about producers creating presentations rather than full-blown pilots. However,

[5]Networks do not receive a financial interest in shows with a series commitment because the producer/studio has the upper hand in negotiating the terms. As Suarez explained it, "NBC ... had a lot of deals that made it impossible to own, you know the John Wells, the Marta Kauffmans, the Steve Levitans, they couldn't force ownership in those."

[6]The networks are not the only ones doing this. Studios have reduced the number of writer/producers on their payrolls as well as a cost-cutting measure.

McPherson attributes this to posturing by the networks rather than a change in the process. "Presentation just means the networks are going to pay less money .... But you have to realize with that, it was studios competing to get on the air and being deficit entities we're going to do everything we can, and everything we can includes spending more money to make the best show we can because it's a sales tool. So by people saying we're just going to do presentations that's just a way of saying we're going to pay less for pilots .... When they [the networks] look at their budget rightfully they say—let's [use] fake numbers—they say, 'Ok, we have 10 million dollars. We're going to do 10 drama pilots. But you know what, we're going to actually do 12 drama pilots but for each of them we're not going to pay a million dollars, we're going to pay 800,000.'"

Rather than spend less on pilots, it seems the networks have become more selective in who they give money to. Certainly the cost of production has increased. In 1988, a half-hour pilot cost between $650,000 and $750,000. A one-hour pilot was more than double that amount (Lewine, Eastman, & Adams, 1989, p. 148). Now, the cost of a half-hour sitcom pilot can go as high as $2 million. When the relationship is important enough, that number can go higher. Warren Littlefield gave me an example of an outrageously expensive drama pilot. "Well, if you want to be as recent as John Wells' 8 o'clock Sunday night, *Third Watch*, I was told that was a little under six million." Pilots have reportedly been created, however, for as much as $10 million (Wild, 1999, p. 76).[7] What all of this suggests is that while the networks are claiming poverty, they will pay for a show that they believe will ultimately make them money on the backend. Few pilots being produced would mean less access for producers; however, there does not seem to be any real consensus that the number of pilots has been going down in any major way.

One way that cost has definitely affected selection is through having a financial interest in programming. This is being done with a vengeance since the infamous *ER* license renewal in 1997. As discussed, NBC was so desperate to retain this show for the network that they ended up paying $13 million per episode. Those kinds of prices on a fifth year renewal have scared the networks away from shows in which they have no control. "Well, the fact of the matter is if you look at the traditional model, the network basically rents for a four, five, six, whatever year period, rents a show in the form of a license fee," explained Littlefield. "It's an unacceptable model. Because in the first 4 years, the network has all the leverage, you build a monster hit or even a modest hit and the lion's share of the profits come to you at the network. However, you have built from nothing this phenomenal asset and then they can turn around and "ER" you. And then the shift changes dramatically and you can eliminate all profitability for a time period. You can destroy your financial equation and you have no participation whatsoever in the lifelong value of the asset when you have done a tremendous amount to help create the asset, so it's just not a model that's acceptable. So what you're going to see is, not 100% ownership of a schedule at a network, but you're going to see more and more ownership or joint

[7]UPN reportedly paid this figure for a series called *Seven Days*.

ownership .... So what you'll see I think is a lot more joint venture deals. You'll see more long-term protection for networks, so that an *ER* can't be repeated."

There is widespread agreement that the *ER* deal was a bad one, particularly from other producers. According to Dick Wolf, producer of the *Law & Order* franchise of shows, "The *ER* deal is the worst deal in the history of show business. And if they had made it a year earlier, it would have been about 3 million an episode. NBC lost football, they lost *Seinfeld*, and this was a perceived emergency. There's nothing on television worth 13 million an hour" (Longworth, 2000, p.17).

The *ER* deal had ramifications beyond just paying such a high fee for one show. It affected almost every other show on the network schedule. Tom Fontana, producer of *Homicide*, was forced to reduce the budget on his show to accommodate the *ER* fee. "NBC's capacity for profit has been basically eliminated. That's not to say they're losing money, but they're not making money. I'm told GE has a policy that, if one of the companies which it owns doesn't earn 10% profit a year of its budget, then they sell that company. Right now, NBC is not going to do that ... so they are in the process of downsizing .... NBC the network airs *Homicide*, and NBC the studio produces *Homicide*, so I have been asked to try to reduce the budget in the eighth year" (Longworth, 2000, p. 44). Not only are existing shows affected, but also newer shows. *ER* has been implicated in the rash of less expensive programming that appears on the prime-time schedule. Reality programming, newsmagazines, and game shows do not carry the high price tag of a prime-time drama and help to offset these expensive shows.

Taking a financial interest in programs has become a way for networks to protect themselves against this type of financial hit. Suarez predicted in 1999 that "it [will] be [no] more than a year of two away when the networks own a piece of every show on their air. Otherwise people can hold them up for ransom the way *ER* did. NBC turned that show into a hit with the producers and with everyone else, but ended up being the only one who had to pay through the nose for it." He was right. With only limited exceptions, all of the networks have some financial stake in the new shows that appear on their air.

Network Ownership's Impact on the Decisionmaking Process

The significant factor affecting program selection was not necessarily whether the network produces a show themselves, but whether they have a financial interest in it. Everyone agreed that the networks were increasing their ownership in programming and that they would continue to do so over the coming years. Some producers and executives were surer than others that the networks would require at least a piece of *every* show that appeared on their air. Some thought it was a bad thing and others were neutral about it.

Network executives feel torn between putting on the best show and putting on the show that is going to make the network the most money. The continued concern about being *ER*ed, for example, being forced to pay higher license fees on successful shows in the fifth year when owned by outside suppliers, plays heavily into the executives' decision making process. "You really do have to focus on one level what's the best show," says Littlefield. "On another level, you have to say, however, it may be the best show, but it could bring about my extinction or it could be part of my extinction. So you're constantly fighting [selecting the] best product, or how do I get a piece of it or how do I protect myself? And that's the age that we're in right now ... you can create a great, great value through network television for the life of the product and enough people still want to do that and you can only do that with a network ... that's what the networks are good for ... to create asset value. So that's why people are willing to say, 'Hey, we'll be in business with networks.' And virtually all the studios are open to some form of a sharing of risk and sharing of equity." So even while the networks must decide between best show versus best buy, they remain acutely aware of their ability to provide something that no other media vehicle can, and that is the ability to create a valuable asset because no medium can provide the kind of exposure and promotion that network television does. This is why producers are willing to accept the new economic realities.

As expected, ownership in programming contributes to one program being selected over another. Shows are also being maintained on the schedule for longer than they might be if the network did not have an interest in the show. Even shows in which the networks did not originally have an interest have had their financing restructured to allow the network to become a financial partner for a show to stay on the air, particularly in that ever-important fifth year. *NewsRadio* is an example of this type of negotiating. Half a season short of syndication, the show was going to be cancelled. The producers gave up 10 to 15% of their syndication profits to remain on the air (Stroud, 1998, p. 26). This type of "negotiation" concerns production executives like Tony Jonas, president of Warner Bros. Television, "'Shakedown' is probably too strong a word, but they should not have the right to insist on ownership just to provide real estate on the airwaves" (Wild, 1999, p. 11).

Giving a piece of the show to the network has become a normal way of doing business since the repeal of the fin-syn rules, because access to the airwaves depends on giving the network a financial interest in the program. Sometimes these requirements are subtle, like requesting that a producer create their show with their studio's production facilities, and sometimes they are quite blatant—your money or your show. While some producers are not happy with this situation, others see partial network ownership as an opportunity to improve the show's chances of getting, or staying, on the air. Suarez in his position as producer says it can actually work in the producer's favor. "We have no problem with splitting ownership of a show with a network. It's the same deal to a producer. I don't care who's paying us to produce the show. And the backend is the backend to us. So actually, I like it because then a network is invested in the show, and they have more at stake and more reason to put it on.... And more reason to keep it on in kind of middling success, because it's harder and harder to launch a show." Rob Burnett, president of Worldwide Pants, an independent production company that produces *Ed* and *Everybody Loves Raymond*, expressed a similar sentiment in March 2002. "For us since we are not big enough, we are not desirous of deficiting shows ourselves necessarily. If we are not set up to deficit and distribute shows, we ultimately need a financial partner. So it makes more sense for us to get a financer earlier in the process .... If we are ultimately going to have to invite someone to the party, you might as well invite them to help set up the party."

The networks have pursued different strategies in their approach to program ownership:

> CBS will have a 91 percent stake in its total network schedule next season, representing 23 shows and 20 hours of programming; Fox will have a 72 percent stake in its total network schedule, or 18 shows representing 13 hours; ABC will have a 62 percent stake in its total network schedule or 21 shows representing 19 hours; and NBC will have a 52 percent stake in its schedule or 23 shows representing 19 hours next season .... UPN has a 67 percent economic stake in its fall schedule, and AOL Time Warner's WB Network has a 47 percent stake in its schedule. (Mermigas, 2002, p. 30)

CBS has been very aggressive in requiring that the company have a financial interest in all new shows that appear on their air. For the 1999–2000 season every new show on the network was partially owned by CBS ("TV Season Preview," 1999, p. A6). That trend has continued. While a few new shows have gotten on the air without the network having an equity stake, these shows are the exception. ABC, as discussed, combined its Disney production division with its ABC programming area in 1999. This was specifically to increase the amount of Disney-owned programming on the ABC schedule and thus far this strategy has been successful. While in 1999, the majority of ABC-produced programming was either newsmagazines or sports, specifically *Monday Night Football*, now the network has 11 shows produced by the entertainment division in addition to these other properties. NBC has been slowly developing its own in-house studio. While they have stumbled in creating their own programming, they have at the same time become financial participants in programming that appears on their air that they do not produce. Thus far, the studio has created only one unqualified hit in *Will & Grace*, a semi-hit in *Crossing Jordan* and some serious missteps in *Emeril* and *Inside Schwartz*. According to Suarez, "There is no set rule, but I think that CBS was certainly incredibly aggressive. They own a part of every show that they put on. NBC was incredibly aggressive but had a lot of deals that made it impossible to own, you know the John Wells, the Marta Kauffmans, the Steve Levitans, they couldn't force ownership in those, but I think they own a good deal of everything else they put on. Which may work or may not. You know it's great to own it because the upside is so huge, and you are spending a lot of time and money to create a hit that you want a piece of that backend. I think ultimately at the end of the day in the next few years, every network will own a piece of every show that goes on their air, and it will just become standard. To be on the air at any network, you're going to give up X% of your show.... Then people won't play this game any more. It's just, 'Okay, you're on with us. We own 50%, you own 50%. Let's call it a day and make a hit.' And there's enough profit there for everyone."

One of the areas most affected by in-house production is the genre of made-for-TV movies. It is an area that the networks have been readily able to enter at the expense of the independent production companies. Movies that are being produced out of house are primarily big-budget miniseries that the networks could never afford to produce on their own. In fact, movies have virtually disappeared from the network schedule, with each network having only one night devoted to this type of long-form programming.

Vertical Integration

Relationships, testing, and profit motive have long been part of the consideration process for network programming executives. Vertical integration, however, is a new element in this decision-making process. Vertical integration exists when a producer of any product owns multiple aspects along the line of production. In the case of television networks, they now can own production (creating the show), distribution (presenting the show to audiences), and ancillary markets (selling the show into syndication). This is only a recent turn of events. With the repeal of fin-syn the market was opened for networks to be unlimited in producing their own programming. This led to considerable consolidation within the industry among producers, networks, and syndicators, thus vertical integration. Now network executives need to keep these multiple aspects of the business in mind when making their program selection.

I asked the network executives if they felt there was a difference in the process of developing programming internally versus externally. They saw little difference between acquiring programming from an in-house studio versus an external source, at least in terms of the actual process. "The selling may be a little different, but essentially what you're always trying to do is package elements," says Littlefield. "We have an idea or they have an idea. Find the writer and then you commit to a script. They come in, they lay out the characters, they lay out the story. You approve the story. They write a draft. You react to that, you give notes and then you say 'let's try it.'"

Having multiple perspectives on this process, Harbert agrees with the assessment of internal programming selection. "Traditionally, even an in-house operation will come in and pitch a show, and it's bought the same way and is selected as a pilot the same way and is turned into a series the same way."

Currently, ABC, Warner Brothers, and News Corp., owner of Fox Broadcasting, have a vertically integrated organization whereby a studio and a network report up through the same management structure but operate as separate divisions of the respective companies. Stephen McPherson at Touchstone explained it this way, "I think vertical integration is both a management thing and a relationship thing, because you can vertically integrate an organization, and if the people managing those various divisions and parts are not working together, then it really doesn't matter. I think you need to make sure that each of the divisions maintains its autonomy, because I think that's what makes them productive and profitable, so it's a constant balancing act, [but in terms of the selection process] certainly vertical integration makes a difference."

Vertical integration is seen as eliminating a valuable step in the development process. First, developing programming is a creative process. When one entity created the programming and another would select it, the two companies would argue and disagree and out of those discussions, the show would often be improved. What has happened instead, according to Suarez is "… you ended up *not* pitching internally. You'd just develop the shows yourselves." So, unlike other executives interviewed, Suarez stated that the process did favor internal shows and eliminated much of the development process altogether. Producers also stated that this process was detrimental to the overall quality of network programming. "I believe the best creative work always happens when there is a creative tension," says Matt Williams. "It used to be, studio executives would go into the network and they would fight like hell because they had ownership of this show, literal ownership, but also they felt proud about a show and they would beat the shit out of the network to get their show. How do you do that when it's the same company? And so what usually happened is out of that tension there was always a better show evolving where you challenged each other."

There are already many examples of network-produced programs that have failed miserably. Shows that were put on the schedule for no other reason than the network studio produced them. In a *New York Times* article, Warren Littlefield, who was then president of NBC entertainment, practically admitted that the network had put *Union Square* on the air because NBC was part owner in the show (Sterngold, 1997, p. D2). "*Union Square* … is even by the admission of some of those involved in the production a work in progress" (p. D1), an industry euphemism for a dog. *Union Square* lasted for two airings. While the selection process is supposedly the same, the in-house shows are more equal than others. Ted Harbert provided some other NBC examples that fall into the *Union Square* category. "[*Wind on Water*] and *Conrad Bloom* are the two best examples. There were just clearly better shows to put on and they didn't. Now I think they've … learned that lesson, so I think they're going to be more moderate in their attempt …. "[8] NBC was not the only network to show favoritism to its own programming. ABC had *Geena* and *Madigan Men,* while CBS produced and aired *Bette* and *Welcome to New York,* none of which lasted more than one entire season.

Some of these issues may be self-correcting by the market. While Disney restructured to be more synergistic that strategy has not proved to be successful for ABC. ABC has been unable to retain a network president and they have been going out-of-house for their programming. So much so that ABC has entered into a first-look agreement with HBO and has begun repurposing *Monk,* a show that airs first on the USA cable network.

Given vertical integration and the combined network/programming departments, all things being equal, an internally produced show is going to get an airing over one in which the network does not have an interest. It is also more likely to get a better time shot and be kept on the air longer. While it is possible that some shows of lesser

[8]I was working at NBC when *Wind on Water* and *Conrad Bloom* were developed. It was evident to me, a nonprogrammer, from the script that these shows were terrible. The fact that *Wind on Water* aired once and *Conrad Bloom* did not last a full season suggests that audiences agreed.

quality are given preference over those produced by outsiders, this is a situation that is not likely to be sustained. Ultimately, the network's job is to make money and the best way to do that is to put on the best shows. Much in the same way that the networks overproduced comedies in 1997, they realized that was not in their best interest and pulled back production of these shows in subsequent years. Similarly, if producing shows internally is not going to make a network profitable, as was the case with ABC, producing shows with external entities will be reinstated.

Pilot Testing

External pressures as well as internal ones are affecting how executives do their job. New competition from cable, and in particular HBO, has become a major issue for the networks. A whole generation has grown up not knowing the difference between a broadcast network and a cable network and doesn't care. Appointment television is virtually a thing of the past,and viewers have a multitude of options and demands on their time. All of this leads to risk-averse program selecting. "You have to have this star," says Paul Haggis. "You have to frontload the project, so if it fails someone can point a finger and go,well, it had all the right earmarkings, it had this actor and this actress and this showrunner and it had a good script and so they can report to their bosses that they did everything they could and it still failed. Rather than taking a flyer on something with some strange idea with a bunch of nobodies in it [and worry that] if it fails [people will] say, 'oh, how could you be so stupid?'" All of this leads to a reliance on research and testing—a quantifiable way to justify decisions.

Testing has long been part of the television industry. In *Inside Prime Time*, Gitlin (1983) quotes network executives in the 1980s who explain that testing is "a tool … which should take a back seat to instincts" (Tom Werner, head of prime time programming at ABC) and "as one of ten things that feed into a [programming] decision" (Barbara Corday, head of comedy development at ABC; pp. 44–45). Producers have complained about testing for 30 years (Cantor, 1988, p. 165), and they continue to do so today. Their concerns are understandable, however, testing for television is no different than testing for any other product. Respondents are concerned about the impression that their answers will have on the person performing the test. Dick Wolf provides the following example, "It's just like when *I'll Fly Away* was the second highest testing pilot in five years because, if you call up a bunch of people on a cable test and ask, 'Would you watch a show every week about the civil rights movement in the sixties?' what do you think people are going to say? 'No, I'm a racist, I have no interest in watching that'? Of course they're going to say 'yes' but nobody watched" (Longworth, 2000, p. 16).

The difference now versus 10 or 20 years ago is that testing methods have become more sophisticated. Cable testing (testing in the home) has replaced auditorium testing, where groups of people rate a show they watch on a theater screen. Cable testing, in some senses, carries a bit more weight because the show is viewed in its "natural" setting and because larger numbers of people are included in the testing sample, which make the numbers more statistically significant. It does still have its flaws. Harbert explains the process. "We put out a show to 15 markets and call up and recruit 30 families a market and get 450 families to watch a show, and then they're called immediately afterwards ... but the big fallacy in that is that not a show goes on the air now without at least a half-million dollars of marketing put into it where the audience is prepared for what they are going to see. The shows shown on cable testing, they're seeing them cold and, again, if the show has any, a lot of edges, anything too different or unusual, the audience will be sort of caught off guard and say, 'I don't like that,' but when they get used to what they're seeing, then they can grow to love it and again those become the biggest hits."

In addition to cable testing, networks use focus groups to assess programming. These are groups of 10 to 12 people who are asked questions about the show and asked to evaluate it after viewing a pilot. Rob Burnett explained the problem with this research methodology. "It does have a terrible averaging effect on what they put on television and what is misleading about it, I believe, is if you have a group of people and you go around the room and rate the show 1–10, and if everyone rates the show a 6, there's your rating. And then you have another show, where 3 people rate it a 10 and 7 people rate it a 0, that rating is a 3 basically for those 10 people in the room, and that 3 won't get on the air. But the truth is, a show that can get 3 people to give it a 10 can be very powerful, because that is a 30 share and you have 3 people that [sic] are very passionate about the show and the other people hate the show, it doesn't matter. There's the other show where everyone is getting 5's and 6's, no one is going to watch the show, because no one cares about the show ... you know it's kind of like if you think of everyone in your house, all 20 people in your house, and you have to decide what to get for food, and everyone is going to vote, and you have to pick something that everyone likes, you know that you are never going to get the crazy Vietnamese-Thai food, that's never going to happen. You are always going to get pizza, every time, and I think that's what happens here."

A story I heard several times was about the testing of *Seinfeld*. This show was one of the worst testing shows ever. Of course, it went on to be one of the most successful shows in the history of television. Unfortunately, even examples like this have not tended to temper executives' dependence on testing.

Research has been called the lamppost to the drunk. It is something that you can lean on to justify your decisions. This is true in many businesses, not just television. However, when large sums of money are at stake, executives tend to rely on research to validate their decisions. This overreliance on testing has been criticized as one of the culprits to making network executives more risk averse and relying on old, accepted program formulas.

Changes in the Syndication Marketplace

With more television outlets and increased pressure to turn a profit, programs are moving into syndication more quickly than ever before. Because syndication is where money is made, the networks are less concerned with competing with themselves than they are with making money. Where networks would warehouse shows so they would not be competing with their own programming, now shows are sold into broadcast and cable outlets at the same time. This is sometimes to the detriment of their current programming.[9] Ted Harbert explains what happened with *Home Improvement.* "Now networks ... can't wait to get a show that they have into syndication to a fault. They want them out there so quickly to try and reap some revenue, but possibly to the detriment of the show that's still on their prime-time schedule. I mean the studies prove that once a show that's on the air goes into syndication, the network ratings come down. The best example, I think, is *Home Improvement*, which is a show that a lot of kids and teens watch. And when it was on the air in syndication at 7 o'clock, there was no reason for parents to let their kids watch it again at 8 o'clock or even when it was at 9 o'clock, actually it was at 9 o'clock then. Kids used to beg to stay up and to watch *Home Improvement* when it was on at 9. When it went into syndication, parents could say, 'Okay you saw it already tonight. Go to bed.' And that hurt the show."

Shows are no longer on a timetable when it comes to syndication. As McPherson explained it to me, a show goes into syndication "whenever that distribution entity feels that it can take advantage of the asset in the most productive way." That "most productive way" is changing due to the proliferation of television outlets. "There's 200 channels, 800 channels, if you get DirecTV, there's many more choices, and there's less of a value to a lot of the programming that used to make up a lot of that air time. There's just much more stuff being done. Disney channel produces for itself. They're not going to take reruns of a family sitcom. As you have this proliferation of choices, there's still going to be a great syndication market for *Friends* or *Seinfeld*, but there's going to be less of a market for a lower level hit, mid-range show that people feel like, 'Well, rather than pay syndication money for that, I'll produce my own.'"

This means that syndication may not be the pot of gold at the end of the rainbow that it used to be. Paul Simms, producer of *NewsRadio,* remarked that "there are so many more channels, but there are also so many more sitcoms now. You make your money back, and you make a good amount of money, but it's not the huge jackpot payoff it used to be. That's going to affect the business. It used to be production companies could say that ten flops are worth it to get one hit; it's getting to be more like it's worth four or five flops to get one hit" (Wild, 1999, p. 29).

A new issue has arisen in the syndication market that is adversely affecting producers to the benefit of the networks and their parent companies. Due to increased vertical integration, more and more companies are selling programs within their own company rather than going out into the marketplace to sell a show. For instance, a network that has its own production company will sell a hit show to its cable network at a below-market rate without opening the show to bidding by other outlets, cable or broadcast. Though this is very lucrative for the company, it is detri-

[9]The exception to this has been *Law & Order,* which saw increased ratings on the network after it began airing in syndication on the cable channel, A&E.

mental to the profit participants in a show—the producers, the actors, and so forth. If the vertically integrated company sells the show internally, it is at a heavily discounted price, which means that the profit participants are cheated out of their rightfully earned money. By selling internally, the companies have almost created a new form of warehousing. Rather than keeping a show off the market, they are keeping the show off the market to competitors.

Highly publicized examples of this are David Duchovny's suit against Fox, also Steven Bochco against Fox, and Alan Alda against Fox (M*A*S*H). In each situation, the profit participant accused the parent company of selling the show internally at less than market value, thus reducing the artist's profit. Matt Williams also had a similar situation with Disney/ABC. Williams' show, *Home Improvement*, was produced by Touchstone and aired on ABC. The show was on the air prior to the time that Disney bought ABC; however, when the show was up for its important fifth year negotiation, Touchstone and ABC were one and the same company. While Williams could not go into details because of the settlement, he did express what some of the inherent issues are when a studio and a network are all part of the same company. "I have to be very careful ... because of the settlement I can't discuss it. The only thing I can say in general is you see the obvious conflict .... When the studio is supposed to go in and combat and beat down the network and squeeze out as much money as you possibly can, when the studio is negotiating with itself it becomes a problem and that's regardless of whether it's a Fox show or *Home Improvement* ... you understand in the most general sense why that's a huge problem from a producer's point of view ... that goes back to, I'm talking creatively now, I'm not talking about lawsuits and finances, that goes back to a general check and balance, because I believe the best creative work always happens when there is a creative tension."

Ted Harbert was not surprised by this occurrence. "The two networks that could be doing the most would be ABC and Fox. ABC could try to put shows on Lifetime, but it's really Fox that would be doing that. Disney/ABC doesn't have the same global domination view that Rupert Murdoch [has] and Rupert Murdoch will absolutely, in my opinion, take the chance of pissing off a profit participant for the chance of making his own cable ventures more powerful. And so I think the Fox deal putting *X-Files* on FX, that lawsuit was bound to happen."

I had this discussion with Ted Harbert before ABC bought Fox Family, now ABC Family. It seems now that ABC is looking to expand its reach in as many ways possible. An important aspect of this, for ABC as well as the other networks, is to present multiple airings of a show, known as repurposing, across both the broadcast and general entertainment cable entities of a company. An example of this is *Alias*. This program is produced by Touchstone, airs on ABC on Sunday night and repeats later in the week on ABC Family. This is just one example of the new face of television economics.

What has made the selection process different versus during the time of fin-syn is plain and simple economics. The marketplace is more complex. Production is more expensive. Syndication is more uncertain. Audiences are more fragmented.

The networks are doing what they can to make money within a very volatile business environment. While no one is ready to hold a charity event for the networks, it appears that the decisions they are making in terms of programming are a direct reflection of trying to create the best programming while balancing that with making the most money. This is not new. It is, however, harder.

How Producers Stay in the Game

In the changing marketplace of program selection, producers have had to become more creative in ensuring that they can make a viable living. In many cases this has meant being aligned with a major studio or, as seems to be the trend, a broadcast network particularly since they are becoming—if have not already become—one and the same thing. This aids in getting a show produced and ultimately on the air. These deals can be structured in a variety of ways, which Littlefield explained. "There's all kinds of deals. Let's go to some examples … 20th Century Fox Studios pays [David Kelley] a lot of money to have the distribution worldwide and the joint ownership with David Kelley of all of his television. David Kelley has series on ABC, CBS, and Fox. So their strategy has not been exclusivity. Their strategy has been … they would go out and sell a couple of series deals here and a series deal there and they spread it around …. Bochco had the opposite concept. He had a deal at 20th Century Fox for many years just like David Kelley, only he would go in and tie up exclusively with a network. Originally with NBC, then with ABC, and then with CBS … He's very frustrated by the stuff he put on CBS, that it didn't get treated differently and Bochco decided to go to a studio and he's not, it would seem now, making an overall network deal, so he's going to spread it around. He's going to do it more like Kelley at a new studio, Paramount … it's safe to say with someone like Bochco, of his caliber, that it's a joint venture. They're probably 50/50 partners. And that gives him a very healthy initial deal to come to the studio and it gives him heavy ownership in what he creates."

Paul Haggis, again, is someone who has a relationship with a network and not a studio. He explained his experience on *Family Law.* "I sold the concept to CBS, I said, 'Here is what I want to do.' The head of drama development and I talked it back and forth. He said, 'That's a great idea where do you want to do?' I said, 'Let's do it at Columbia. They're good people.' And so I took it to Columbia and they said, 'Great. Let's do it.' And then Columbia and CBS got together and said this should be a Columbia and CBSP, or CBS Productions, coproduction, and that was without my input. I didn't disagree, but that's a studio and network decision. I'm a profit participant, I'm an owner of the show, but I'm not, I don't own, the copyright. Producers sign it over to the studios and the studios, in this case, cosign it over to the network."

Most producers are now aligned with a major studio or a network. As discussed here and in other sections throughout this chapter, this does not appear to bother producers I spoke with. It has meant an added level of security in having a vested financial partner early in the process. Though there is no guarantee that these relationships will lead to a show being put on the air—being with a studio/network provides some added security that a show will be picked up particularly if the network has a financial stake in the show.

ONCE THE SHOW IS ON THE AIR

In addition to the selection process, the FCC was concerned about the level of network involvement in a show once it was on the air. Both executives and producers agreed that established producers were left alone by the networks. They also agreed that young talent (when they could get in the door) was heavily managed by the networks. Littlefield gave an example of what happens before a show gets on the air. "When *Will & Grace* was pitched, we had made a deal, I made a deal at NBC Studios for Mutchnick and Cohen .... And so they came in and pitched this huge ensemble of characters and kind of over in the far right-hand corner were the Will and Grace characters. And so what I said to them is 'Well, take those characters, forget all these other people, take these two characters over here in the corner and put them in the center and you've got a show' ... over several meetings and discussions where they came back and refocused the idea, pitched it out again, then wrote a draft, did a couple of rewrites, finally there was a piece of material that I felt was strong enough to go forward. So then I sent it around to everybody else at the network, let them freak out because we're putting gay characters on the air, and then eventually we made it."

Little has changed in terms of network involvement once a show gets on the air. Cantor (1988) described how the network involvement worked in the 1960s and early 1970s. For new shows, a network executive would sit in on story conferences, scripts would be reviewed by the network censor, and the film was viewed for final approval (p. 122). On the other hand, highly rated shows or shows with competent producers were exempt from network supervision (p. 127). Now, the story is very much the same. Once a show is on the air, the network executives agree that many shows need network oversight. The amount of network supervision depends upon the experience of the producer. Again, Littlefield explains, "It varies tremendously based upon who you're in business with ... Think of it as a ... chart that went from 1 foot tall to 6 feet tall, and you have all types of sizes in between, 1 being they're very young, they're very inexperienced, they need a lot of help, and a lot of supervision, then they get a lot of that. That can also be termed interference. But the fact of the matter is there's a lot of people out there, because there are so many networks, because there's such a drain on talent who don't fully know what they're doing and they haven't had the training. And you're paying them enormous amounts of money every week and so they get a lot of involvement where stories have to be approved, directors have to be approved, guest casting has to be approved, every draft is gone through, runthroughs, there's a lot of network and/or studio intervention. Or, there're people like Kauffman, Bright, Crane [producers of *Friends* and *Veronica's Closet*] who are extremely ... competent showrunners. They know what they want to do and probably the greatest thing, with a Larry David and Jerry Seinfeld, the greatest thing you can do is get out of their way. You know, I mean I think our greatest input ever on the *Seinfeld* show was: you need a girl. Okay? We looked at the pilot, it's funny. Get a girl. Okay? That was our contribution. That and we didn't fuck it up. We kept it going."

Ted Harbert's experiences at ABC reflect those of Littlefield at NBC. "There are a lot of producers who have shows on the air that aren't very good, both the shows aren't very good and the producers aren't very good. It requires a lot of network involvement to try to help that producer find out what their show's about, find out how to tell a story that makes sense, and really help in just about every area of the show. There are other shows, like *NYPD Blue* or *The Practice* from David Kelley and Steven Bochco, where there's no network involvement needed at all, because those people are incredibly competent and not only are not looking for network involvement, but also don't need it because they're that good. It goes from 0 to 100 .... Unfortunately we live in this business where we eat up so much volume, we invite a lot of hacks into the room to put on shows that need a lot of editorial restraint and oversight."

"I think it depends on the relationship with the exec producer, frankly," says McPherson. "I think in some shows they're [the network is] incredibly involved and in other shows they're not .... There's only so much a network or a studio executive can impact on a show if you haven't hired someone who has a vision that they can execute on a week in, week out basis. There are very few shows you could point to—I couldn't point to one—where it isn't driven by a singular creative personality who has a vision for the show or a team in Larry David and Jerry Seinfeld, that is executing it day in and day out. Can you help it with promo and make sure they're getting seen? Yes. Can you help with casting? Sure. Can you make sure that the story lines are going in the right direction or what you perceive is the right direction? Yes. But in the end it's about those people doing the shows, and that's why they are such valuable assets. And they are few and far between, unfortunately."

From the producer's perspective the networks are involved in programming on two levels: oversight by a programming executive and review by standards and practices. The producers expect the networks to be involved by providing notes at table readings. "You always have your point person," says Matt Williams. "You always have your executive that comes to the readings. It's not your president of the network or anything, and they make suggestions, and they give script notes, and I'm, at least we, have always made it a policy, we are political and rightfully so. You listen to all notes and then you go off, and if you hear a good idea, fine and good. But there was no one who ever came in and said you must do this, you MUST change this."

Says Haggis: "Well, you know you have a different set of people developing the pilot and then the people who are going to supervise the series on the network level. So your current department takes over after about the sixth episode or so .... And it all depends [on] the personality of the man or woman at the top as to how they supervise those shows and how much they trust the writer/producer .... We had fairly light input as far as criticism, as far as don't do that story and when we did hear don't do that story it was usually because another series was doing a similar story that week and so they didn't want two stories about abortion. One on our show on Monday and one on *Judging Amy* on Tuesday, or any of the other of their shows. And then we would argue, and if we got into a really touchy area, and we did three or four times on *Family Law*, we'd argue it out. It would be either myself and the head of current programming, or myself and the president of the network, would sit down and they would say, 'No, we don't think this is appropriate.' And usually that was an intelligent sort of passionate meeting in which we were discussing is this responsible television or is this not."

Rob Burnett explained it this way, "The network has the control, they in the most classic sense are the client, and we are the producers, the sellers. The client has to be satisfied .... The brightest and best network executives are ones that understand at its core, the writers and producers of a show will have to guide the show and they stay back and can make helpful suggestions ... if you think of a doctor and a patient, I think the writers are the doctors and the networks are the patients. And the patients can say, 'I feel this way, I feel that way,' but they don't really know how to be doctors. So, they can be very useful in sort of suggesting things to the doctor, but they haven't been to medical school .... What makes it very complicated and where I am very sympathetic to the network is most of the doctors out there are pretty bad, and they are key in this analogy, so I think that they are well within their rights to be very hands on and panicky sometimes, because I have seen firsthand a lot of the people that [sic] are in charge of these massive productions, and they are not very qualified to do it, so it's a very difficult dance honestly, but the most successful shows on television, I believe, are ones where you get the right writer, the right casting, and it happens."

It is rare, however, that a network will ask someone to pull a show or drastically change a script concept, although it does happen. Tom Fontana had the following experience while working on *Homicide*:

> The only time I can think of where I pulled a script that we were going to shoot was we had done a story about a SIDS death: it was based on a true story about a woman who had had a number of her children die, and they were supposedly SIDS deaths, but the truth was she had murdered them. Roz Weinman, who is the head of broadcast standards, called me and she said, "Listen, I'm asking you not to do this story, not because I think you've done it badly, but because, for parents whose children have actually died of SIDS, it's such a painful thing to have gone through, that to then have a show with the kind of clout that *Homicide* has, implying that they might have killed their child." She said, "I don't think you really want to do that to these parents." And when she said that, I said, "You're absolutely right." And I pulled the story. But that was the only reason I did it. What was great about it was that Roz and I fight all the time about everything, and I mean everything! And it was the only time she called me not out of a concern for the advertisers or the lobbyists or anything like that. She was coming at it from the same place that I like to think that I come at my writing from, which is the human heart. And I couldn't *not* do it. (Longworth, 2000, p. 48)

Paul Haggis had a similar story from an episode of *Family Law:* "We wanted to do an episode about a woman who was alleging discrimination because she'd had a double mastectomy and was suing her employers because of that. And this woman had been sort of pushed to the edge, and there was a scene in which she stands and she rips her blouse open, because they're accusing her of doing this for cosmetic reasons. She rips her blouse open, and she says, 'Do you think I would do this for cosmetic reasons?' Now, so we went back and forth on that. It was a very powerful scene and we'd had this prosthetic chest made for the actress which was exactly accurate as to what this would be. Do we show it? Do we not show it? So we ended up not showing it. I felt very passionately that we should. The president of the network felt very passionately that we shouldn't. Not because of the reasons that you think. But because she didn't think it was responsible. She thought it might scare other women off from getting a life saving operation .... It wasn't 'oh, don't do that because of some salacious reason' or ... 'do do something because it's going to get us ratings.' They weren't coming to me for those reasons. They were coming for good solid reasons and you have to respect that input."

Even *ER* gets notes from the network, 'Sure [the network may ask us to change] language," says John Wells, the show's producer. Wells continues:

> Not so much with story line, occasionally, but that usually has to do with health care issues. On *ER* it's because they're concerned that we in some odd way provide a lot of health care information to the viewing audience more than anybody else does. So they'll get concerned if they think we're not being balanced in a portrayal of a health care situation. But, sure, on language .... The network, they're genuinely concerned about how far can they push it and not lose advertising. And, at the same time, knowing that you could get beat to death on the other side by cable and by what other people are putting on the air. So they're very conscious of it. It's not just "Oh, we won't let you do this because we're prudish"; it's "How far can we push it to compete with cable, and at the same time not alienate advertisers and some audiences?" (Longworth, 2000, pp. 134–135)

In all of these cases, the network input was from a point of sensitivity to the audience. Not concern for advertiser or ratings, but issues of community levels of acceptance about some very sensitive issues.

From the producer's perspective, similar to that of the network executives, network participation is different depending on how well established the producer is in the business and how well the show is doing. "It depends on how successful the show is," according to Matt Williams. "I'll give you an example. When I was a writer/producer on the *Cosby* show, no one said a word. In fact, I think we saw the network show up once, maybe, and that was usually for a party, so there was no involvement. With *Roseanne*, the same thing. There was some minor involvement early on, saying, 'shouldn't the stories be a little stronger?' ... so at the beginning and this was not imposed, it was suggested, a little bit more traditional story plotting and ok, we listened, but little involvement .... If a show's working, they're all smart enough to keep their mouths shut and just stand back and let it go .... Ironically, on our series that failed, there was much more involvement. 'Can't you emphasize this more? Can you bend the story lines more in this direction?' And I think that usually happens, and this is where I'll take some of the blame, it usually happens if you don't have a really clear, specific premise for your series. If you don't know exactly what the show is about and what it's going to do for 200 episodes, that's when the network will come in."

As Littlefield explained earlier, the networks do have final say in a lot of areas including selection of directors, script review and casting. However, the network input is dependent on the relationship with the producer and most things are negotiable. Suarez says, "Yeah, the answer is ... it's a marriage. You don't always do everything they want. They don't always do everything we want. Good network executives don't try and dictate. They understand it's a process, an evolution ... it's not cut and dry ... do you get a note from a network saying kill off this character? No, no network is going to be that invasive."

Many producers I spoke with and several that have been quoted in other sources have touted the advantages of producing for cable or one of the newer networks because of the freedom that these entities afford a producer. However, Steven Bochco, producer of *NYPD Blue* and *Hill Street Blues* among others, explains how this is not a panacea either, "Anytime you're in business with an entity that has 'above the line' creative controls, it means, in theory at least, you cannot hire an actor without their approval. You cannot hire a director without their approval. You cannot hire a writer without their approval. They have control over final cuts of all your product. So, on the one hand you're gaining tremendous latitude on the page, but you're giving up a tremendous amount of creative control on the other side of it. So, you know, I'm not sure that's such a great bargain, quite honestly" (Longworth, 2000, p. 201).

The FCC's concern about network involvement in programming seems to be unfounded. Of course, the networks are going to be involved in the process at some level. They are paying for the show. They are promoting the show. However, as many of the producers said, they are also not stupid. They hire the best people to do the job that they can and let them do it. There are, however, different levels of competence among producers. The level of network involvement seems to correlate with the level of experience that the producer has. The more experience, the less network involvement.

Blanding the Landscape

The real issue is what appears on our television screens. Many have accused the networks of putting on bland, uninteresting and uninspired programming. While some suggest that the new verticalization of networks and program production is at fault, there are other aspects of the network television business that contribute to what some see as suboptimal quality programming. These factors include: (1) a class of middle managers at television networks whose incentives steer them toward less risky, more formulaic programming; (2) a greater reliance on decision-making-by-committee; and (3) the introduction of marketing and advertising concepts, specifically the need to create new shows for an advertiser-friendly demographic, into the program selection process.

With respect to the role of middle managers at television networks, some critics say that the changing structure of the television industry has led to network downsizing and therefore fewer middle-level executives with more at stake. The remaining middle managers are more afraid of losing their jobs and also continue to face the increased financial pressure discussed earlier.[10] Neither network executives nor producers had anything particularly positive to say about this group of middle managers, though this is nothing new. In the eighties when the network hierarchy was more bureaucratic, these executives had the same sort of mentality.

> More layers in the hierarchy means more executives with the power to say no, and the proliferation of that power means more executive involvement at every stage of decision-making and program production. "There is a curious corporate principle," according to Len Hill, "that says a person with a vice-president's title will find enough work to fill the day. There's a producer's axiom: Beware of networks that have too many vice-presidents." Many producers share this lament. (Gitlin, 1983, p. 129)

Most participants felt that programming executives, while not necessarily uncreative, were too afraid of losing their jobs to make any type of risky decision. As in the past, they considered this a contributing factor to the blanding of the TV landscape. Harbert talks about it this way, "There are also a lot of shows that have too much oversight that don't need it, so that the idea of the network and studio bureaucracies growing to the point where there are just so many people involved in the process that's just counterproductive.... It's very difficult when there's a lot of pressure on their jobs to turn the profitability around, so unfortunately a lot of people interpret that as meaning they have to go increase their involvement. They have to stay on top of it more and give more notes. Well, that will just have an inverse relationship to what they're trying to achieve [good programming]."

"I think as long as you have smart people running the networks, they're always going to try and do great programming," says Haggis. "Nobody sits down to do bad programming, or create a bad show and you always try to get the best writers, the best actors. It's just the decisions. You know when you actually decide, sit down behind closed doors and say, 'this one goes, this one doesn't' .... The business is shrinking, and people are working more out of fear. There are fewer daring network executives. That's not true. There are, Moonves [Leslie Moonves, chairman of CBS], there's no man I admire more than Moonves. Great guy. He's a straight talker and he really loves taking chances. Whether he can or not, something like *EZ Street,* he says he loves the show, I'll program nothing but this. They're not watching what do I do? The answer would be keep it on anyway, and they'll come to you. You hope that they'll still do that. They certainly did it with *Homicide* and a few other shows. That's becoming, that's a story you don't hear as often."

It is not just middle managers who are the issue. More and more programming selection is done by committee. "A television program is selected to go on a network schedule through a committee process," says Ted Harbert. "A low-level executive buys the idea and tells them to go write a script. A script is written. The president of the entertainment division and their staff read all the scripts and decide

[10]Of the four major broadcast networks, only NBC and CBS turned a profit last year.

which pilots to make. The pilots are produced, the pilots are screened for all levels of management at the network including Los Angeles management and New York management. This includes the sales department, the research department, affiliate relations department, and overall network and corporate management. Then, depending on the network, a committee gets together and decides which pilots are chosen to become series and announced for a fall schedule." It is no longer creative people that have input into the decision, but also sales, marketing and other network departments.

Marketing came up as an issue with a number of people that I spoke with. While producers used the word marketing, what they meant was advertising—that is creating a show with a particular, advertiser-friendly audience in mind. Some producers said they would not produce a show for a demographic or a time slot and that the networks did not ask them to. "Your agents or your people or your advisors are always saying, 'they're looking for an 8 o'clock show' or 'they're looking for a 10 o'clock show' or whatever. I've never, they never come to me and say that, but that's what I hear from other writers," says Haggis. "No, it's hard enough finding a good idea. And, if you happen to find one that fits a teen audience or you happen to find one that fits geriatrics if it works, you pitch what's in your soul ... and then you hope it's going to fit." Others, however, admitted to trying to create shows for particular time slots or particular audiences and most of them failed miserably. Matt Williams commented on his attempts to do this. "*Thunder Alley*. *Buddies*. And these were short-lived series. Not that we didn't make some creative mistakes. I'm not passing any blame here. But it truly was, 'OK, this is the approximate time slot, this is the kind of demographics they're looking for, let's create a show for that' and I learned pretty quickly—at least from my perspective, I'm not talking as a marketing expert or advertising or any of that part of the industry, I'm talking purely as a creative individual, it never worked." The advertising structure does affect the content in so far as it promotes lesser quality programs to fit a preconceived idea.

Overall, however, there does not appear to be any consensus about the state of the television landscape—some of it is very good and some of it is not. Rob Burnett described it best when he called it polarized. "I think some of the shows, particularly the one-hour shows are frightfully good. You look at shows like *The West Wing*, *Law & Order*. I think those shows in quality you can put up against a lot of feature films .... I think on the comedy side some of them, like *Raymond* and some others, are also very, very impressive. And then there is a lot of stuff that is horrible, just really, really horrible."

Stephen McPherson had a similar sentiment, though he was more positive about the landscape overall. "I think it's really underrated. If you look at the quality of both comedy and drama work that is done week in week out on television ... between *West Wing* and *Law & Order* and *The Practice* and *ER* and *Alias* .... There's really good drama work .... Comedy wise, *Will & Grace* is as funny as any movie that I've seen lately and great romantic comedy. I think in the family genre, *My Wife and Kids* and *Raymond* are doing as good funny as is out there. The thing is, television constantly gets berated for its quality, and it's such a vast market that by the nature of that there's just going to be crap out there. What happens is that things succeed and then people try to imitate them and those usually fail. But the new stuff, the stuff that sets new kinds of boundaries, those things succeed. People are bitching now about reality. Do we have too much? Well, yeah, we do have too much because we have reincarnations or copycats of two things in *Millionaire* and *Survivor* that were fresh and new and interesting and incredibly entertaining and then everyone tried to do their version of it. And that doesn't work."

It is this repackaging of successes that leads to the blanding of the landscape. It is a risk-averse strategy the film industry uses as well, that is, Rocky 3, 4, and 5.

That, however, does not mean that there is not good television out there. It's just not all great. "I think it's not as good as it was a few years ago, but not as bad as it was many years ago," says Paul Haggis. "I think we really had some wonderful shows appear over the last 20–30 years and this was the second Golden Age of television for a while. It was some really great, great shows and I couldn't wait to watch. I don't see as many of them as I used to .... There's still some great shows on, but they tend to be shows that have been on—*NYPD Blue*, *Law & Order*, shows that have been on for some time .... I couldn't give you a 1 to 10 [rating], because I don't know what 1 is or 10 is, but I think it could be better. It doesn't stink."

CONCLUSION

While the program development process—creating a needs assessment, communicating to the Hollywood community what the network's needs are, committing to scripts and pilots—has not changed, the program selection process has. This process has been most affected by the change in the structure of the television industry, which has changed the economics of the industry. With increased consolidation has come increased alignment of producers with large studios or with the networks themselves. With changes in regulation, there has been the corresponding increase in network participation in the programming on their air, either through in-house production or their profit participation with outside suppliers.

No one seems particularly pleased with the current system, and several participants expressed concerned about the affect of the current system on program content. Producers are concerned about their ability to produce the kind of shows they would like to produce. Some, like Matt Williams, are leaving television and are working in film instead. Others, such as Paul Haggis, are frustrated with the system and are working in both television and film. Haggis explains why he is working in multiple arenas. "The landscape has changed a lot and I'm still pitching television shows. I still have multiple 13 commitments. I still love television. I still want to do it, but the landscape has radically changed.... [with] the market share dropping, the networks seem to be more conservative in what kind of programming they want to choose...You want to sell to the widest possible audience and my stuff tends to be, when I'm doing my best, work that can upset some people, or at least challenge some people ... A long, long time ago, television was where you could do the brave work, the cutting-edge stuff and films were where you did megahits.... Things have sort of shifted in Hollywood where things are happening in films. The independent films have really come into their own in the last 15 years, and they're doing more and more interesting films out there and less and less interesting television. Not that great television isn't still being done. There's terrific television being done, but it's much harder to get it on the air. Where it used to be I'd pitch one idea over the phone and sell it, now I'm pitching four or five ideas before they find something that I'm happy with that they're happy with, so we can go ahead on a series."

Independent producers' wish to produce programming that is different or risky or in any way out of the ordinary is not new. One producer in the 1960s said, "they wanted the series to go a certain way and I another, so they let me out of my contract because I like to do things my way" (Cantor, 1988, p. 128). Established producers were often shut out in the 1980s as well. Herb Brodkin, a producer of both series and miniseries, claimed that only about 10% of his ideas ever got on air (Gitlin, 1983, p. 122). Therefore, it again is unlikely that regulation or media consolidation is responsible for producers not being able to produce what they like or as much as they would like.

Network executives are concerned, however, about the product becoming homogenized because of program selection by committee. "I would just throw everybody else out of the room," says Ted Harbert. " I think it should be the head of the company, the head of the entertainment division and one or two of his or her trusted executives and not a gang.... I would let the research department do their research, but I wouldn't let them participate in the process, because they all too often say a show will never work.... That also goes for the sales department, the affiliate relations department, all these departments that say, 'oh, no my constituency won't like that or will like that.' What that ends up doing is bringing so many voices into the system that it rounds out the selection process so that you have homogenization. Anything with extremes ends up being eliminated and [you end up with] what I call nice shows, nothing wrong with them, but also nothing right with them .... Only when a programming chief stands up and says, 'this is what we're doing' do shows that end up really mattering, doing well, get on the air. And often when the head of programming will take the chance and say, 'thank you all very much for your input, forget it this is what I want to do,' those are the decisions that have led to the most successful programs."

Suarez agreed: "The problem becomes when they're letting the marketing department or the sales department have an equal say in the decision when they're not, when they're not the ones who were involved in the process. Anyone who worked on *Mr. Rhodes* [a show NBC owned] could tell you, 'okay that show's never going to make it. We don't have the writing staff, we don't have a lead actor, I don't care how it tests, there's no show there. It's all smoke and mirrors ... we tricked you, but we knew we tricked you and we can't do that 22 weeks' and that's where the system fails .... We fixed the pilot. You can't do that every week.... And so it went on, and it stayed on for I think 18 episodes and was a failure. And cost the company a lot of money."

Harbert continued by summing up the state of the business as he saw it very well. "The history of broadcasting, and film for that matter, has always rested on the idea that you need a diverse source of ideas to come up with a good schedule. And only being rather focused on picking the best and not letting anything else get in the way is what's led to successful, profitable schedules. Because of the change in the share levels, because of all the erosion and therefore the loss of profitability … and costs continuing to rise, they're searching around for ways to get back profitability …. I'm not a big fan of vertical integration, but frankly no one cares what I think anymore about that and they're going to do it anyway, so I might as well go join them. There's not a lot of choices."

From the perspective of the FCC and the repeal of fin-syn, the issue is what are the networks doing in terms of their relationships with producers vis-à-vis their powerful position as gatekeeper to the American viewing audience. Are they demanding financial interest in the programs that appear on their air? The answer is yes. Are they giving preference to shows that are produced in-house? Again, the answer is yes. Are the networks involved in the creation of the shows once they are accepted for air? Here the answer is a qualified yes. Yes, they are, but not to the point where they are telling producers what to write and not write. More important, what needs to be addressed is the effect of these things on diversity—the FCC's underlying concern. Parallel these changes in selection process with the diversity of programming and again we see that it is not negatively affecting this area. However, what is of issue is the quality of programming—something the Commission does not address. I will do so in the concluding chapter.

7

The Reality of Diversity

INTRODUCTION

Diversity as a communications policy is decidedly flawed. The Federal Communications Commission again and again has tried to create diversity in the television marketplace and has failed miserably. From minority ownership to the cable television acts, no regulation has been successful in creating a multiplicity of voices that satisfies the government, the public, or the critics. The case study of the financial interest and syndication rules clearly demonstrates that structural regulation of the media is simply inadequate to produce an abundance of varying voices available through television, and I would add other media as well.

A key issue behind this failure is the lack of an agreed upon definition for diversity. What is it that the government, the public, and the critics are really talking about when they say they want diversity? On its face, a diversity of programming would mean many different types of programming from many different producers providing a breadth of perspectives. We do have a certain level of diversity now and that has been consistent throughout the time period analyzed for this book. This would lead us to believe that what everyone wants is more diversity. Or, I would even suggest that what these different publics want is better quality, which most people would agree is lacking on much of the television dial.

Does this suggest that diversity should be eliminated as a goal? Yes, if the government is only allowed to regulate structure. The answer is a resounding no, if the government will regulate content. Clearly if you want diverse content then you have to regulate the content, not everything around it.

Though this flies in the face of the First Amendment, it is not unheard of for a democracy to mandate certain percentages of programming while not specifying the content itself. Some Western European countries have done this by regulating the percentage of various program types, that is, cultural, educational, entertainment, and so forth. In the Netherlands, 25% of programming is dedicated to culture, 25% to information, 25% to entertainment, and 5% to education (Brants & McQuail, 1992, p. 159). In Germany, the two public channels and the regional channels "are required by law to offer a comprehensive and integrated programme that is politically balanced" (Kleinsteuber & Wilke, 1992, p. 85). In Ireland, radio stations are required to program news and current affairs as 20% of their programming (Kelly & Truetzschler, 1992, p. 117). England also has some restrictions on programming in that regional companies have to air programming in all of the following categories: drama, entertainment, sports, news, factual, education, religion, arts, and children (Tunstall, 1992, p. 248). While many European countries, most notably Britain, are going through a period of deregulation much like the United States, regulating content within a democracy has historical precedence.

In the United States, content is mandated. The Congress required broadcasters to air children's programming and in fact only the Children's Television Act (CTA) was successful in producing content diversity. That was because it is the only piece of legislation that specifically requires certain content—in this case 3 hours of children's programming—be available through the public airwaves. Why must we limit ourselves to only regulating children's programming? Why not other "special interest" programming? The CTA demonstrates that the First Amendment is not absolute. If we truly want different content, we may have to find a way to regulate that content within a broad definition of the First Amendment.

It is important to remember, too, that broadcasters are public trustees. Through broadcast licenses, they are given the right to use something that belongs to the American public—the airwaves. With the use of those airwaves come obligations. The fact that television licenses exist, and they require that broadcasters serve in the public interest, may allow us some flexibility within the First Amendment, because the programming obligations are attached to public rights.

If specifically regulating content continues to bring up too many First Amendment issues, then certainly the revenue model of the industry needs a second look. I am not saying here to create yet another type of structural regulation. Rather, I am suggesting that advertising is at the heart of the diversity problem, rather than a mere symptom. Television companies exist to make a profit. Programming must be created that will produce that profit. Profitable programming means programming that serves the interests of advertisers. Given these facts, changing ownership, changing television producers, or creating more outlets simply will not change the content that exists. Given the restrictions of the advertising model, limits are placed on the types of programming that will be produced. Programming must fit into 22 minutes, it must be self-contained, and it must not be controversial within the current economic and social frame. If content diversity is the goal, then advertising cannot be the backbone of the television revenue model.

Finally, diversity and consolidation are two separate issues and should be evaluated as such. Somewhere along the way, theorists have tied the two ideas together. Intuitively, it makes sense. As media companies become larger and larger and repackage and repurpose their content over multiple outlets, it is true that there would be fewer options available for consumers. This lack of diversity, however, is, again, a function of reliance on advertising, rather than the mere fact of consolidation. If regulators are concerned about having a viable marketplace and allowing multiple players to make money in the television industry, that is a laudable goal. It should not be confused, however, with diversity as we have seen over and over that different producers do not produce different content because they are tied to a very specific creative frame.

If we remain committed to diversity as a policy, how do we get it? Before answering that question, we will examine the flaws of structural regulation and the current economic structure. By understanding their failure, we can perhaps develop a methodology that will lead to a more diverse television marketplace.

Source Diversity

One of the two structural ways that the FCC has tried to create diversity is through allowing more and different producers of content to have access to the airwaves. This has, however, not been an effective means for creating diversity, and there are a number of reasons for this.

First, there is the assumption that different producers are going to produce different types of content. This has just not proven to be the case. In the case of fin-syn, whether it was Hollywood producers or broadcast networks, the same types of programs were produced. The same is true, at least in television, when it comes to minority management of stations (Mason, Bachen, & Craft, 2001). Minority ownership did not translate into different content for viewers.

The argument that has come up over and over again is, "What about *All in the Family*?" "What about *Hill Street Blues*?" My response is "What about *The West Wing*?" "What about *Alias*?" People bring up these earlier shows as the pinnacle of quality programming, and they are. There are, however, shows on the air now that are just as good. The lack of diversity may not be due to a lack of sources, but rather a lack of talent.

While several producers I spoke with claimed that better programming just wasn't getting through the pipeline, there is just no way to validate this. It may very well be possible that some form-breaking, earth-shattering new show is out there, but I doubt it. There are simply a finite number of truly talented television people. We have had more than 70 years of television and we can count on two hands the number of groundbreaking writer/producers that there are. Norman Lear. MTM Productions. Steven Bochco. David Kelley. Just like there were not several hundred Mozarts running around 300 years ago, there aren't several thousand talented writers and producers of television programming who can fill hundreds of hours of programming on a daily basis.

Television, unlike independent film for instance, requires that a person be able to write a new script week in and week out for at least 22 weeks a year. Using the film analogy, you can write a great independent film, shoot it yourself, and then get a distributor and never have another good idea again. That can't happen in television. If you come up with a great show idea, you better have a concept that is going to carry that show through 200 episodes. Not only do you have to write the scripts, fairly soon after you will be expected to be the "showrunner," the producer who oversees the day-to-day responsibilities of getting the show on the air. What happens in many cases is that someone is good at writing but does not have the talent to produce or simply hasn't been in the business long enough to learn the process properly.

Part of this has to do with the expansion of the bandwidth, that is, the creation of the 500-channel, or at least the 150-channel, television universe. All of those channels need content. When there were only three or four broadcast networks, there was a pool of talent, and people tended to work their way up through the ranks. Matt Williams is a good example. He worked as a writer on the *Cosby* show for three years during which he won an Emmy Award; he then worked in conjunction with Carsey-Werner on *A Different World* and *Roseanne*, where he was the creator and executive producer. In 1989, he created his own company, Wind Dancer, where with his partners he was creator and executive producer of *Home Improvement,* as well as several other network programs. It was only after having many years of experience working on network programs that Mr. Williams became a showrunner himself.

Today, this is the exception rather than the rule. Between 1987 and 1997, the number of comedies increased from 36 to 62, and the number of dramas increased from 33 to 38 (Spring, 1998, p. 9). The analogy that Spring uses is one of expansion teams in baseball. A new team or two is added every 4 to 5 years so as not to "dilute the talent pool." Network television, on the other hand, has increased production by one third in 10 years. It has significantly drained the quality of television, primarily because writers become showrunners after working on a show for only one or two seasons. They are trying to run a show before they understand how to do it. The obvious downside to this is that networks have a tendency to get more involved with shows that have more junior, less experienced staff. Someone may be a talented writer, but that is not enough. They also have to be ready to produce the show as well. Many of the same producers who said great shows were not hitting the air, also said that they saw an awful lot of shows that were very poorly run, so there is agreement at least on some level about the limit on talent.

In this sense, the expansion of the bandwidth is also the culprit in less than quality programming. It is necessary to fill 150 channels with programming 24-hours per day. First, it is not cost effective to produce new programming for every part of the day. Even news channels repeat programming throughout the course of the evening. Content gets repackaged and reproduced to fill all that air time. Programming also has to be economical in general. Costly sports programming has to be offset with news and talk shows. Pricey dramas have to be balanced with titillating game shows. Moreover, and getting back to the original point, there is just not 150 channels worth of talent. Some of the programming is going to be very good and some of it is not. The question in terms of quality is: Is more of the programming good or bad?

In terms of source diversity, what would satisfy all of the players involved? Analyzing this objectively, it is an issue of profits and not diversity of content. It bears restating, *there is no proof that different producers create different content.* Rather, the matter is who is going to make money in the television industry. This is at the crux of the FCC's current reevaluation of the consolidation of the television industry and the renewed called for the revival of the financial interest and syndication rules.

Call for the Return of Fin-syn

In May of 2002, three influential senators asked the FCC to draft a coherent policy regarding consolidation of the media industry so the widespread consolidation of the last decade might be curtailed. As many rules that deal with this issue are up for possible repeal, the Commission is being asked to look at them as a group rather than as individual policies. Hollywood writers and producers have added their voices to this argument and have called for renewal of some type of regulation that reflects the restrictions of fin-syn, which they hope will either ban further consolidation or break up existing media monoliths.

Senators Ernest Hollings, Mike DeWine, and Herbert Kohl sent a letter to the FCC stating, "Given the substantial ongoing consolidation in the media industry and recent court decisions striking down rules that restrain this trend, we are extremely concerned [about] ... competition and [believe] discourse is at risk" (Phipps, 2002, p. 9). These senators carry a lot of weight with the television industry in that they hold powerful positions in the Commerce Committee, which among other business issues oversees matters of antitrust—one of the major concerns behind the concentration of media sources. While the senators have not outlined a specific plan to reinstitute fin-syn, there is every indication that they are leaning in that direction. *Electronic Media*, a major television industry trade publication, has stated that "the legislators have made clear that they want to slam the brakes on media industry consolidation" (Halonen, 2002, p. 1). There are two specific issues the senators have asked the FCC to evaluate. First, are the networks showing favoritism to internally produced programming, and second, can independent producers be viable within the current vertically integrated economic structure.

The emerging debate sounds familiar. Broadcasters are claiming unfair restrictions on their business. They are also suggesting that they will have to start charging viewers for programming and that free over-the-air television will disappear. Cable representatives have gotten into the fight on the side of broadcasters. This is partially because the FCC is looking at the rules as a group, and cable regulations are likely to be evaluated first. It is also because there is a parallel issue between broadcasters' role as gatekeeper for over-the-air television and cable operators' similar role for their systems. In both cases, regulators will be looking at how these companies give preference to programming in which they have an equity stake over independently produced fare. In response, the National Cable & Telecommunications Association (NCTA, 2002), a national trade association for the cable industry has stated, "The past decade has seen the creation of more than 200 new and diverse cable networks, leading to a cornucopia of choices for cable consumers. During the same period, the percentage of programming networks in which cable operators have any attributable interest has fallen from more than 50 percent to less than 25 percent" (p. 37). This may be true, but it would be necessary to evaluate the size of the networks that the cable operators have ownership in versus the ones they don't in order to get a true picture of what is going on in the industry. If history is any indication, expect the networks and cable operators to use this rhetoric as well as claiming poverty as long as this debate continues.

In early June 2002, the Caucus for TV Producers, Writers & Directors, an industry organization that represents more than 200 creative people, added their voice to the fray, "Without specific federal constraints, these 400-pound gorillas will stifle creative innovation, infect the pool creatively and financially with the bottom-line fungus of the myopic" (McClintock, 2002a, p. 1). They stated that they want the FCC to resurrect the financial interest and syndication rules and apply them to cable operators as well as broadcast networks. Specifically they have asked that: Cable systems and broadcast networks be limited to no more than a 30% equity position in a show, that any single entity be allowed to occupy only up to 15% of a cable system's capacity, and cable systems and satellite operators that reach more than 30% of the pay TV audience should be restricted from having an ownership interest in any programming service it carries (p. 22). The caucus' claims include concerns about independent producers getting their shows on the air and their inability to shop their shows around to other networks if an initial network does not pick up the show.[1]

These concerns on the part of the creative community may have as much to do with recent severe cutbacks in major contracts as it does with media consolidation. In the past, it was not unusual for the networks or the studios to sign $2 million per year contracts to have a writer/producer exclusive to their company, even if the writer was only remotely connected to a hit show. The economics of the industry no longer allow for these pricey "above the line" costs. This is not because revenues aren't increasing. They are. However, costs have increased even more, and the backend syndication paydays aren't what they used to be. Foreign markets which have traditionally been a source of ancillary revenue are drying up as producers overseas would rather produce their own sitcoms. Similarly, the domestic market for syndication has slowed down in recent years, and the days of $500 million syndication deals are only available for a limited few mega-hit shows. To help offset these costs, networks are investing $2 million in 10 to 12 writers rather than one (Adalian, 2002, p. 8). This would suggest that more writers are getting opportunities. They are just not receiving windfall profits.

As in the past, the issue is one of a balance of profits in the industry—not an issue of diversity, though that is often how the argument is framed. This is due to the FCC's competing agendas of diversity and competition.

Competition as Opposed to Diversity

What is conflagrating the issue is the Federal Communications Commission's dual goals of promoting diversity, while at the same time ensuring that there is a compet-

[1]The issue of producers being unable to sell a show to a competing network once the initial network passed on the show came up many times in the press both in the 1970s and today. It was not an issue with the producers I spoke with. I have been unable to account for this.

itive media environment, specifically that there is not an overconcentration of ownership within a few companies. But, and this is a big but, there is no proven causality between media consolidation and a reduction in diversity. There are very good market reasons to have multiple players in an industry—more opportunities for more companies, less chances for monopolistic practices, and so forth, but diversity is not one of them.

Antitrust issues center around whether the networks are using their monopoly and monopsony power to keep other players out of the market, by example, showing favoritism to their own programming at the expense of competitors, and whether they are taking advantage of their suppliers by requiring an equity stake to appear on the air. Some of these factors were in effect when fin-syn first came into being and are happening again today. Requiring producers to give up a piece of their show to appear on the networks is now standard practice. The networks each have at least a 50% stake in the programming on their air and some are as high as 70 and even 90% (Mermigas, 2002). The networks could never achieve those kind of ownership numbers without requesting a stake in the programming that appears on their air. It is no secret to anyone that the networks do this. What is less known is that the networks are selling time periods, that is giving the best time slots on the schedule to those who make the best deal with the network. Ted Harbert, former chairman and president of ABC Entertainment, gave me this example. "*The Norm Show* aired Wednesday 9:30 behind *Drew Carey*. ABC made significant demands to Warner Brothers (WB) of what they wanted to keep the show Wednesday at 9:30. WB passed and therefore a 20th Century Fox show got the Wednesday 9:30 time period—and also gave up a significant piece of the ownership to ABC. Whereas *Norm* is now scheduled behind *Two Guys, A Girl and a Pizza Place*, Wednesday at 8:30, a much less preferable time period" (personal interview, 1999).

There is definitely favoritism for internally produced shows over those produced out of house. The numbers speak for themselves. ABC picked up seven new shows for the 2002–2003 season and six of them are produced by Touchstone, another Disney division. NBC only picked up five new shows and four of them are being produced internally. There is a limit to this, however. As one of the producers told me, no one goes out of their way to put on a bad show. So, to that extent they won't put on a bad show that's produced internally over a good show that's not, but certainly if two shows are of equal value the internally produced show will get the time slot.

Are the networks colluding, conspiring to keep others out of the television business? It's not likely. There was no evidence from the conversations that I had with producers and network executives that this was so. However, do network programmers talk with one another? Of course, they do. Most of them have worked with one another from time to time, as these executives move from network to network routinely. Do those conversations include plans to keep smaller competitors out of the industry? While we can't know for sure, I think that's giving them too much credit. Partly this may be so because the vertically integrated structure creates such a high barrier to entry that it is not necessary for these executives to collude. Television was big business in the 1970s and has only gotten bigger and more complex. This complexity has made it almost impossible for new players to enter the market, because they have to do so on so many levels—production, distribution, cable outlets, and so forth. There is not a lot of economic viability for small players in this market. Because of this, independent producers have either been merged into the larger companies or have disappeared. The only major truly independent production company to still exist is Carsey-Werner, a company that started in the 1980s and has a backlog of hit shows, like *Cosby* and *Roseanne*, to sustain it through financial tough times.

The lack of independent producers, and therefore the increased consolidation of the industry, is what leads policy makers to be concerned about diversity. But diversity is not the issue. It is a competitive environment where multiple players can be profitable in this market. That, too, was the fight behind fin-syn. Not diversity, but a battle between who was going to be able to make money within the television production market—Hollywood producers or the broadcast networks. Remember, however, this does not affect content diversity. It affects how much money goes into whose pocket. Regulators assume a causal relationship between competition and diversity which just does not exist. Just as with diversity of content, if you want content diversity regulate content diversity. If you want multiple players in the market, regulate for that, but don't assume that by regulating competition you will *de facto* get content diversity.

Outlet Diversity

Outlet diversity has similarly been a poor replacement for content diversity. When channel capacity into the home increased from an average of seven in 1970 to more than 40 in 1997, there was no corresponding increase in program genres. For example, MTV was a new type of program genre. However, ESPN was sports and sports programming has been a TV staple since the introduction of the medium. As well, some channels, like TV Land, consist entirely of off-network reruns—obviously not a new and diverse program choice. New channels, rather than providing new content, have provided primarily the same content for the entire day. The History Channel presents documentary programming. Nickelodeon provides programming for children that is educational and available throughout the day. The rule is programming that replicates what is on the networks. This is so because the market structure of the industry limits the available programming choices.

The economics of the television industry used to be similar to that of the film industry in that one hit would pay for 10 failures. The networks are not willing to do this anymore, so new ways are being created to ensure a return on the programming investment and to do it as quickly as possible. One way that the networks are ensuring a faster return on investment is by having a secondary distribution channel usually in the form of a general entertainment cable channel. These channels are used as a secondary outlet through which they can distribute their programs. Disney has ABC Family, which repurposes programming from ABC. CBS has UPN. Leslie Moonves, president and CEO of CBS Television, has been given oversight over UPN and has stated in the press that there will be some repurposing between the two networks. Fox has FX, which it uses as an outlet for much of its syndicated programming. The WB has any of a number of Turner properties to choose from. Similarly, NBC recently bought Bravo, where there has already been sharing of programming, and Telemundo, where given the pattern of late this is also likely to happen. Each of these networks present programming on the broadcast network that is then re-presented (or repurposed) on the secondary outlet. This will lead to more redundant programming and less new content through more outlets. Networks are also making their prime-time programming available through video-on-demand and DVD collections (Adalian, 2002, p. 8). With profit margins shrinking, getting as much money out of existing assets is paramount.

The other reason that there is likely not to be more new content also relates to economics. Any individual channel has to determine what is going to be the most economic way to fill the daily schedule. For some, it is going to be with syndicated content, in many cases older syndicated content because it is less expensive. Creating a new show, in most cases, is going to be more expensive than buying a new one. If a new show is produced, in the current risk-averse environment, it is apt to be a copycat show of an existing hit. After the success of *Who Wants to be a Millionnaire*? other networks came out with a slew of game shows. With the success of *Survivor*, reality programming was the hot genre. It also didn't hurt that these programs are relatively inexpensive to produce. This does not only happen at the network level. A prime example from syndication is the judge or court series. After the success of *Judge Judy*, syndicators came out with *Judge Joe Brown*, *Judge Mills Lane*, *Divorce Court*, just to name a few. The sheer expense of the business is driving the limits of diversity in the newer outlets.

Given everything that has been discussed this far, we saw that more producers do not mean more content diversity and we saw that more outlets do not mean more content diversity. This means we have to look somewhere else for the solution to the problem.

Quality and not Diversity—Advertising is the Culprit

The underlying issue here is not diversity, but quality. Defining quality is no easier than defining diversity—something the FCC has admitted to avoiding. However, when critics, the government and the public speak of quality what they mean are "important" shows. Included in this category are children's programming, public affairs programming, arts programming, documentaries, nature programming, in short the types of shows that have been the purview of public television. Public television continues to do well in providing these shows but has been plagued by increasing costs, increasing competition from cable networks and decreasing public spending. Because of this, they have had to turn to advertisers as a source of revenue in addition to individual subscribers and public funds. Dependence on advertising moves public television into the same arena as for-profit broadcasters. No longer shielded from advertiser concerns, public broadcasters must take commercial interests into account when developing their schedule. This means less risky programming, less marginal programming, less diverse programming.

Advertising and the economic structure of the television industry are the reason why we have a mediocre level of program diversity. As long as programming is supported by advertiser dollars, we will continue to get the same kind of programming that we have and have had over many decades. This is so for a number of reasons. First and foremost, any medium that is dependent on advertisers for revenue must either provide a large audience or a very specialized audience to make money. Most media do some combination of both. For instance, a cable network like MTV provides a very targeted audience of teens and young adults that is difficult for advertisers to find anywhere else. Because of this, advertisers are willing to spend a lot of money with the network in order to reach these hard-to-reach consumers. The same is true for most magazines and radio stations. Broadcast networks are the one medium that exists to provide humongous audiences. They are by definition the provider of broad-based programming. In today's market, it is the one thing that gives them an advantage over the competition—they just reach more people than anyone else.

To provide this audience to advertisers, broadcasters must produce programming that is going to attract the largest number of eyeballs. Advertisers don't care if it's a test pattern or *The West Wing*. If a large audience with a lot of money to spend will sit down and watch it, that's all that matters. Quality dramas, like *The West Wing* and *Law & Order* and *CSI*, do generate significant ratings and therefore advertising dollars for the networks. *Survivor* and *Fear Factor*, shows not likely to be part of any critic's quality list, also generate large audiences and, I would add, higher profits because they are significantly less expensive to produce. While millions of people watch these entertainment programs, it has been proven time and again that large audiences do not watch public affairs programming or arts programming or children's programming or any of the other programming that legislators and critics think they should.

Putting aside all issues of source diversity or content diversity or structural regulation, content diversity cannot be changed without changing the economic structure of the industry. Advertising is the tail wagging the dog. Programming must be produced that will generate a large audience, or a wealthy audience or a very targeted audience. The program cannot be too controversial. It should be family friendly and not too intellectual. A new trend, a throwback to the early days of television, is making a comeback. That is, networks (who are now producers) are creating programming specifically for advertisers. Starting with heavy product placement in shows like *Survivor*, which included a Target store logo and mention within the game, and *American Idol*, where emcees are seen drinking Coca Cola, producers are creating full programs for advertiser dollars. Here are two examples of deals that are in the works. One is Disney that signed a $100 million contract with Home Depot and then created a home-improvement show called *The Disney Paint Program* for the advertiser (McClellan, 2002c, p. 12). The other is with the Discovery networks that signed a $50 million deal with Procter & Gamble (P&G). P&G products like Swiffer will be prominently featured on *Trading Spaces*, a decorating show on one of the Discovery properties (Romano, 2002, p. 17). The artificial wall that existed between "church and state" is starting to come crumbling down.

Therefore, there needs to be a space where programming can be created that is untouched by the tentacles of advertisers. Much like public television used to be, there needs to be a place where less mainstream producers can have equal access to present their programming, where programming is not subject to the Nielsen ratings, and the needs of underserved audiences can be met. I will use the children's television marketplace to show how successful this can be.

Children's Television Case Study

There are three primary outlets for children's programming—PBS, Disney, and Nickelodeon. While others provide entertainment programming such as cartoons, these three distributors present educational content that is also entertaining. PBS children's programming is most known for *Sesame Street*. However, the network also airs *Between the Lions*—a reading series targeting children four to seven, *Barney*—a show that teaches preschoolers 2 to 5 years of age basic social skills, like sharing and making friends as well as physical, emotional, and cognitive development, and *Caillou*—a show that targets children from 2 to 6 and lets them see the world through the eyes of a 4-year-old boy interacting with his family. These are just three of the more than a dozen shows that target preschool and slightly older children. These shows are developed and presented with different age groups in mind and geared to their different developmental levels. Though each PBS station is different, it is not unusual for the network to air 7 hours or more of children's programming per week day.

The Disney Channel, not to be confused with Disney Toons, presents an array of children's programming that is based on a "whole child curriculum" (Disney, n.d.). *Stanley,* for example, is a show that teaches children about different animals through the eyes of an inquisitive 4-year-old and his pet fish, Dennis. *Rolie Polie Olie* is a show about a robot boy and his family. The show teaches children about family relationships and being part of a community. *Out of the Box* is a live-action show where two adult hosts sing, dance, and make crafts with their preschool friends. The network programs 12 hours of preschool programming each weekday and 6 hours on the weekend.

Nickelodeon presents programming for children throughout its broadcast day and segments the dayparts based on the target audience. Nick Jr. is presented in the morning and is for preschoolers, there is also Teen Nick and Nick at Nite for adults. Nick Jr. includes among other shows *Bob the Builder*—a show that encourages positive attitudes and teaches children cooperation and other social skills, *Blue's Clues*—which uses various clues to encourage children to develop reasoning skills, and *Dora the Explorer,* a show for preschoolers that teaches problem-solving skills through interaction with the shows characters while at the same time teaching them Spanish; Nick Jr. programs 5 hours of preschool shows per day.

All of the programming that was just discussed is not advertiser supported, at least not directly or exclusively. Also it is interesting to note that each of these outlets has a different revenue structure in general.

PBS, or the public broadcasting system, is funded by a combination of public funds, individual subscriber "donations," and corporate sponsors. The most significant restriction is that corporate messages are not allowed in the middle of the programming but can appear before or after the programs. Also, messages can only be 15 seconds in length, as opposed to the standard 30-second commercial. Restrictions have been reduced significantly in recent years so that sponsors may include product messages, company logos, and a phone number or web address (PBS, n.d.). PBS, particularly with *Sesame Street* and a few noted others, has been the standard bearer for quality children's programming on television. This programming has won numerous awards from educators as well as for its production values.

The Disney Channel was launched in 1983 as a premium cable network, that is, it was only available to cable subscribers who paid an additional monthly fee to receive the network, much like HBO or Showtime. By the late 1990s, The Disney Channel became a basic cable channel but continued with its heritage of no commercials. It also continued its heritage of a more expensive carriage fee that it charges to cable affiliates in order for them to receive the programming. Unlike PBS, which does not have a wealth of alternative revenue sources, Disney does. The company uses The Disney Channel as a loss leader for other products. That is, you get these shows for free, but you'll pay for everything else you want with it. Ancillary licensed products such as videos, toys, books, and CD-ROMs are some examples of alternative revenue sources for the network. Similarly, Disney also has revenue from it other broadcast and cable ventures as well as its other entertainment properties.

Disney is known throughout the world for its high-quality animated feature films. That quality has been translated in a very real way to its cable network. The shows for preschool children are overall highly produced and very educational in content. Certainly the network does promote Disney products in between its programming, including their website and Disney films, but the network is not overwhelmed with commercials for action figures or cereal or other consumer products. (Recently, the network began advertising consumer products on a limited basis, using a system similar to PBS.)

Nickelodeon was launched in 1979. By 1995, the network had established its number one position as the place for kids on cable. "It has a larger kids' audience than the three major broadcast networks combined" (Nickelodeon, n.d.). This cable network was managed for most of its existence by Geraldine Laybourne, a former teacher. The positioning of Nickelodeon is as a place for kids and kids only—no adults allowed. During the morning hours, the network programs shows for preschoolers that is presented without commercials. This is known as Nick Jr. Much like the Disney model, Nick Jr. programming is supported by revenues generated through other areas of the network. Nickelodeon is as successful in generating a children's audience as MTV has been in generating a teen audience.[2] Because of this, the company has been very successful in gaining a large percentage of chil-

[2]This should not be surprising as they are part of the same company. Viacom believes in a cradle to grave strategy. Start viewers with Nickelodeon, then move them to MTV, then to VH1, and so on.

dren's advertising dollars. Licensed products are a large part of Nickelodeon's success. Go to Toys 'R Us, for example, and a whole section will be devoted to Nick products created through the Nickelodeon consumer products group. The company also has a movie division, animation studios, a magazine and publishing group, live tours, and international outlets. Nickelodeon programming is recognized for being fun and educational and has received numerous Emmy awards, the industry's highest honor.

The example of children's programming can show a number of things. First, quality is achieved even while diversity may not be. When you look at the children's programming market as defined here you have quality. You have a segment of programming geared to an importance audience—children. The programming being produced is of the highest quality and has an educational underpinning—all the things that the Congress was looking to achieve through the 1990 Children's Television Act. In addition, the programming is available for as many as 8 hours per day, certainly enough quantity for any child. Second, this programming is produced with limited direct advertising funding. Because these shows do not have the specific need to cater to advertisers, they are freer to create the kinds of programming that will best suit their audiences. Obviously, this is easier with a very defined market like children who have special needs at different age levels, but the model can be applied to other audiences. Finally, three distributors provide a full palette of programming for this young audience. Not ten, not 100, but three. This again suggests that diversity, or diversity as competition, is an inappropriate goal.

As a final thought here, it is important to note that the broadcast networks are not included in this group. The broadcasters are required to air children's programming, and they do on Saturday mornings.[3] But this isolated island of children's programming is not effective in serving the daily television needs of children (and their parents). Broadcasters are meant to serve a wide variety of viewers. They are generalists, not specialists, and that is fine for broad-based, advertiser-supported programming.

Where is This Quality Programming Going to Be?

As part of the Telecommunications Act of 1996, broadcasters were given an additional six megahertz of spectrum upon which to present a high-definition television (HDTV) version of their channel. HDTV is simply very high-quality digital television. HDTV is presented in letter-box format, which is more wide screened and rectangular than current television broadcasting and has four times the clarity. While many people use the terminology interchangeably, digital television (DTV) and HDTV are not the same thing. HDTV is a type of digital television. It is the highest quality type of digital broadcasting and thus takes up the most capacity in

---

[3]CBS's Saturday lineup is made up of Nick Jr. programs. CBS and Nickelodeon are both owned by Viacom.

terms of transmission. SDTV (standard digital television) is any form of digital television.

The Act set up a timetable for the conversion to digital broadcasting. The top 10 market network affiliates were to have digital broadcasting by May 1999 and the top 30 markets by November of that year. All stations are to be digital by 2003 by which time they are expected to be simulcasting a portion of their analog programming in digital. By 2005, all stations are expected to be fully simulcasting their programming on both analog and digital signals. Not all stations are meeting these deadlines. Most of the top 30 markets have complied with 113 out of 119 stations on air. Some of the stations that are not yet digitized are in New York City, where the events of September 11 wiped out some stations' digital capabilities. Many more stations in smaller markets are petitioning the FCC for extensions to these deadlines, because they will be unable to meet them. As of June 2002, 483 DTV stations are on the air[4] (FCC, 2002). While the stations can keep their analog channels until conversion is completed, they are required to return those channels to the government by 2006. A caveat, however, is that broadcasters will not be required to return the analog part of the spectrum that they were using back to the government until the country is 85% digital. Broadcasters would provide both analog and digital signals so that people can continue to receive their programming until the new technology is in the home.

There has been tremendous controversy over HDTV. First, broadcasters were given the digital spectrum for free to compensate for the money they would need to pay to update their equipment. At the time, Senator Bob Dole called this a $70 billion handout to the broadcasters. Many government officials still feel this way and continue to call for additional public service requirements on the part of broadcasters to compensate for this giveaway. Second, while HDTV takes up the full six megahertz of spectrum, a lower quality digital program does not. With 12 megahertz of spectrum at their disposal (six analog and six digital), broadcasters can program multiple channels. For instance, broadcasters can choose to present one form of programming in HDTV and up to six lesser-quality programs, including paging and data transmission, for which they could create additional revenue streams.

No one expects that the broadcasters will ever return the analog portion of the spectrum back to the government. First, after September 11, digital transitions were severely slowed due to the downturn in the economy and in the case of New York loss of some transmission capabilities. Moreover, it is unlikely that the nation will be 85% digital in any of our lifetimes. Thus, with the combination of both analog and digital spectrum, broadcasters have the ability to transmit up to 12 channels of information at any one time.

This additional spectrum was provided to broadcasters under the assumption that they would have certain public interest requirements attached to them. The Gore Commission, a group made up of some of television's most noted luminaries includ-

[4]1688 stations have been granted DTV authorization by the FCC, so only 28.6% of stations are airing digitally.

ing Newton Minnow, former chairman of the FCC, and noted children's television activist Peggy Charren, among others, explored some ideas about what those requirements should be. The Commission on a whole was a failure, because in trying to achieve consensus among disparate groups the recommendations were, on the whole, very bland. Some of the suggestions included requiring the FCC to fashion minimum public service requirements, creating a trust fund to support public television, and requiring broadcasters to use their data transmission capabilities to help schools, libraries, and nonprofit organizations. One of the key recommendations that came out of this Commission was that when the broadcasters turn back the part of the spectrum they are using for analog, that "Congress should reserve the equivalent of 6 Megahertz of spectrum for each viewing community in order to establish channels devoted specifically to noncommercial education programming. Congress should establish an orderly process for allocating the new channels as well as provide adequate funding from appropriate revenue sources" (Current, 1998).

The Gore Commission was on the right track with this idea. More than anything an advertiser-free environment for programming would be the most useful public interest requirement in the current era of consolidation. Expanding on the Gore plan, my recommendation is that each broadcaster would be required to have one channel available for programming by independent producers. As stated, no one believes that broadcasters are going to return the spectrum. If they are not going to give back the equivalent of $70 billion in property, then they should support someone else using a portion of it. In addition, and this is very important in today's overcrowded media environment, broadcasters should be required to promote this channel on their regular network. The Gore Commission made their public service channel local. In some markets that may be feasible. However, in order to have high quality programming, it will need to be done on a national level.

The digital channel could be run by public television executives, or the independent producers could determine who they would like to run the channel or the government could provide oversight in terms of administration of the network. The broadcast network would pay for program development and marketing of the channel. In terms of a producer's ability to make money, if the show is a success, the producer is free to sell it to additional outlets, that is repurpose the show, in the same way that the networks do. They would also retain ancillary rights. In terms of governmental oversight, if they want to use European models of defining percentages of programming that would be appropriate.

In this way program diversity would be expanded because there would be an outlet for more controversial programming and programming that does not appeal to large audiences or audiences advertisers want to reach. In this way, more children's programming, more public affairs programming, perhaps even something we have never imagined could be on the television screen. With six broadcast networks, this plan would create six full-time television stations available for programming throughout the day—certainly enough to provide independent producers with jobs, the critics with important programming and citizens with the information they need.

If it is not possible to eliminate advertising entirely in this scenario, then it would be appropriate to limit it to certain times of the day thereby reducing their influence on the programming. In the same way that Nickelodeon pays for Nick Jr. with advertising in other dayparts, so too these channels could restrict their advertiser-supported programming. When advertising becomes a source of revenue, instead of *the* source of revenue, it is possible that programming can become more varied.

SOME FINAL THOUGHTS

Since the introduction of fin-syn, the television landscape has changed dramatically. There are now six, some would say seven, viable networks instead of three. This is certainly an improvement and provides at least some variety of programming for those unable to receive cable or other alternative television sources. Whether that will continue remains a question.

The question we need to ask ourselves is: What is television meant to achieve and who is responsible for achieving it? The answer will depend on your perspective. For the government and the public, it is a diversity of voices. For television executives, it is profits. The question remains as to whether or not the medium can do both.

Regulation of the television industry has thus far proven to be ineffective in creating diversity. Whether market forces are able to do what regulation has not is yet to be proven. My suspicion is that it will not given the industry's dependence on advertising. What is needed is a new definition of diversity—or perhaps even a new policy goal since diversity is so ambiguous. What is also needed is a space within the media marketplace that is insulated from advertising and its accompanying need to produce large, homogeneous audiences. It is only in this way that we will be able to have content that serves multiple audiences, and puts public interest over profit motive.

References

Adalian, J. (2001, October 26). Sony unplugs TV: Columbia TriStar TV dismantles prime-time unit. *Variety*, 1, 19.

Adalian, J. (2002, June 26). Tube's tied: Flagging fortunes force nets to throw out their old script. *Variety*, 1, 8.

Adarand Constructors, Inc., v. Pena, 515 U.S. 200 (1995).

Albiniak, P. (2002, April 15). OK on NBC-Telemundo deal. *Broadcasting & Cable.* Retrieved July 9, 2002, from http://www.broadcastingcable.com

Amendment of Part 76 of the commission's rules with respect to carriage of digital television broadcast signals (2001). Retrieved January 2, 2003, from www.fcc.gov/bureaus/cable/orders/2001/fcc01022.txt

Amendment of Part 73 of the commission's rules and regulations with respect to competition and responsibility in network television broadcasting, Report and Order, 23 FCC 2d 382 (1970).

Amendment of Part 73 of the commission's rules with respect to competition and responsibility in network television broadcasting. Notice of Proposed Rule Making, 45 FCC 2146 (1965).

Amendment of 47 CFR 73.658(j)(l)(i) and (ii), the syndication and financial interest rules. Tentative decision and request for further comments, 94 FCC 2d 1019 (1983).

Amendment of 47 CFR 73.658(j), the syndication and financial interest rule. Notice of proposed rule making in docket 82–345. (1982).

The analyses that touched it all off. (1969, November 24). *Broadcasting*, 50–51.

Andersen, R. (1995). *Consumer culture & TV programming*. Boulder, CO: Westview Press.

Bagdikian, B. H. (1992). *The media monopoly* (4th ed.). Boston: Beacon Press.

Barnouw, E. (1990). *Tube of plenty*. New York: Oxford University Press.

Baxter, W. F. (1974). Regulation and diversity in communications media. *The American Economic Review, 64*(2), 392–399.

Besen, S. M., & Johnson, L. L. (1984). *Regulation of media ownership by the Federal Communications Commission: an assessment*. Santa Monica, CA: Rand.

Besen, S. M., Krattenmaker, T. G., Metzger, A. R., Jr., & Woodbury, J. R. (1984). *Misregulating television: Network dominance and the FCC.* Chicago: University of Chicago Press.

Bielby, W. T., & Bielby, D. D. (1994). All hits are flukes. *American Journal of Sociology, 99*(5) 1287–1313.

Big deals alter the list of big deals. (2002, May 13). *Broadcasting & Cable*, 42–49.

Blumenthal, H. J., & Goodenough, O. R. (1998). *This business of television.* New York: Billboard Books.

Brants, K., & McQuail, D. (1992). The Netherlands. In B. S. Ostergaard (Ed), *The media in Western Europe: The Euromedia handbook* (pp. 152–166). London: Sage.

Burch supports Agnew; Shift in F.C.C. role seen. (1969, November 15). *The New York Times*, pp. 1, 20.

Byrne, B. (1999). NBC Moves in on PAX. E!Online News. Retrieved July 9, 2002, from http://www.eonline.com/News/Items/Pf/0,1527,5319,00.html

Cable news wars: Behind the battle for cable news viewers. (2002, March). Retrieved July 9, 2002, from www.pbs.org/newshour/media/cablenews

Cantor, M. G. (1988). *The Hollywood TV producer: His work and his audience.* New York: Basic Books.

Cantor, M. G., & Cantor, J. M. (1992). *Prime-time television: Content and control.* Newbury Park, CA: Sage.

Cass, R. A. (1981). *Revolution in the wasteland: Value and diversity in television.* Charlottesville: University Press of Virginia.

CBS-TV affiliates throw support to repeal of financial-interest rules. (1982, November 22). *Broadcasting*, 48.

Chief to chief. (1991, March 4). *Broadcasting & Cable*, 6.

Columbia Journalism Review (n.d.). Who owns what. Retrieved May 10, 2002, from http://www.cjr.org/owners

Colvin, G. (1983, May 2). The battle for TV's rerun dollars. *Forbes*, 116–120.

Commercial television network practices and the ability of station licensees to serve the public interest. Notice of Inquiry, 62 FCC 2d, p. 548. (1977).

Commercial television network practices. Further Notice of Inquiry, 69 FCC 2d, p. 1524 (1978).

Competition in Television Production Act: Hearings before the Subcommittee on Communications. 98th Cong., 1st sess. (1983).

Comstock, G. (1991). *Television in America.* Newbury Park, CA.: Sage Publications.

Congress takes up financial interest, syndication issue. (1983, March 28). *Broadcasting*, 34–35.

Covington, W. G., Jr. (1994). The financial interest and syndication rules in retrospect: History and analysis. *Communications and the Law 16*(2), 3–19.

Crandall, R. W., Noll, R. G., & Owen, B. M. (1983). *Economic effects of the financial interest and syndication rule: Comments on the ICF Report.* Washington, DC: Owen Greenhalgh & Myslinski Economics Inc.

Culbert, D. (1983). Television's Nixon: The politician and his image. In J. E. O'Connor (Ed.), *American history American television: Interpreting the video past* (pp. 184–207). New York: Frederick Ungar Publishing Co.

Curran, J. (1991). Mass media and democracy: A reappraisal. In J. Curran & M. Gurevitch (Eds.), *Mass media and society* (pp. 82–117). London: Edward Arnold.

Current (1998). The advisory committee's 10 recommendations, 1998. Retrieved July 11, 2002, from http://www.current.org/dtv/dtv823g.html

De Jong, A. S., & Bates, B. J. (1991). Channel diversity in cable television. *Journal of Broadcasting & Electronic Media, 35,* 159–166.

Disney. (n.d.). What we're made of. Retrieved July 11, 2002, from http://Disney.go.com/disneychannel/playhouse/grown-ups/phd_about.html

Dominick, J. R., & Pearce, M. C. (1976). Trends in network prime-time programming, 1953–1974, *Journal of Communication, 26,* 70–80.

Dunham, C. B. (1997). *Fighting for the First Amendment: Stanton of CBS vs. Congress and the Nixon White House*. Westport, CT: Praeger.

Entman, R. M. (1985). Newspaper competition and First Amendment ideals: Does monopoly matter? *Journal of Communication, 35*(3), 147–165

Entman, R. M., & Wildman, S. S. (1992). Reconciling economic and non-economic perspectives on media policy: Transcending the "marketplace of ideas." *Journal of Communication, 42*(1), 5–19.

Evaluation of the syndication and financial interest rules. 8 FCCR 3283 (1993) .

Evaluation of the syndication and financial interest rules. Report and Order, 6 FCCR 3094 (1991).

FCC Financial Data. (1967–1975). Washington, DC: Author.

FCC Network Inquiry Special Staff. (1980). *Final report: New television networks: Entry, jurisdiction, ownership and regulation, Vol. 1.* Washington, DC: GPO.

FCC Network Inquiry Special Staff (1980). *Background Reports, Vol. 2.* Washington, DC: GPO.

Federal Communications Commission. (2002). Review of the commission's broadcast ownership rules and other rules adopted pursuant to Section 202 of the Telecommunications Act of 1996. Retrieved July 9, 2002, from www.fcc.gov/Bureaus/Mass_Media/Orders/2000/fcc00191.txt

Federal Communications Commission. (2002). DTV stations authorized to be on the air, June 12, 2002. Retrieved July 12, 2002, from http://www.fcc.gov/mb/video/files/dtvonairsum.html

Federal Communications Commission. (1993) Broadcast signal carriage issues. 1993 FCC Lexis 1835 (1993).

Federal Communications Commission. (1996). Report and order, in the matter of policies and rules concerning children's television programming, revision of programming policies for television broadcast stations. Retrieved July 9, 2002, from www.fcc.gov/Bureaus/Mass_Media/Orders/1996/fcc96335.htm

Federal Communications Commission. (1971). 37th annual report/fiscal 1971. Washington, DC: U.S. Government Printing Office.

Federal Communications Commission. (1973). 39th annual report/fiscal 1973. Washington, DC: U.S. Government Printing Office.

Federal Communications Commission v. League of Women Voters of California, 468 U.S. 364 (1984).

Federal Communications Commission. Statement of policy on minority ownership of broadcasting facilities, 68 FCC 2d 979 (1978), 980–981.

Financial interest and syndication rules: Hearings before the Subcommittee on Telecommunications, Consumer Protection and Finance. 98th Cong., Sess 1 (1983).

Fisher, F. M. (1991). The financial interest and syndication rules in network television regulatory fantasy and reality (1985). In J. Monz (Ed.), *Industrial organization, economics and the law: The collected papers of Franklin M. Fisher* (pp. 289–322). Cambridge, MA: MIT Press.

Fortunato, J. A., & Martin, S. E. (1999). The courts v. the FCC: Diversity and the broadcast provisions of the 1996 Telecommunications Act. *Communications & the Law, 21*(3), 19–41.

Fox denies any 'Simpsons' favoritism. (1993, March 22). *Broadcasting & Cable*, 22–23.

Freer public access to medium sought. (1970, May 25). *Broadcasting,* pp. 28–29.

Gallup reports 77% back Nixon. (1969, November 5). *The New York Times*, p. 24.

Geller, H. (1982). FCC media ownership rules: The case for regulation. *Journal of Communication, 32*(4), 148–156.

Gerbner, G. L. (1967). An institutional approach to mass communication research. In L. Thayer (Ed.), *Communication: Theory and Research*. Springfield, IL: Charles C. Thomas.

Gitlin, T. (1983). *Inside prime-time*. New York: Pantheon.

Glovinsky, E. H. (1984). Stay tuned for new technology: The paradoxes of the proposed financial interest and syndication rules. *Hastings Communications-Communications Entertainment Law Journal, 6*(3), 589–620.

Greenberg, E., & Barnett, H. J. (1971). TV program diversity–New evidence and old theories. *The American Economic Review, 61,* 89–93.

Grego, M. (2001, April 2). Cable on off-net rights tear, *Variety*, 40.

Halonen, D. (2002, June 3). Program stakes in danger. *Electronic Media*, 1, 37.

Harris, K. (1995, September 4). Lights! camera! regulation. *Fortune*, 83–86.

Head, S. W. (1989). A framework for programming strategies. In S. T. Eastman, S. W. Head, & L. Klein (Eds.), *Broadcast/cable programming: Strategies and practices*. Belmont, CA: Wadsworth.

Heeter, C. (1985). Program selection with abundance of choice: A process model. *Human Communication Research, 12,* 125–152.

Herskovitz, M. L. (1997). The repeal of the financial interest and syndication rules: The demise of program diversity and television network competition? *Cardozo Arts & Entertainment Law Journal, 15*(1), 177–212.

Higgins, J. M., & McClellan, S. (2002, February 25). Everything's in play. *Broadcasting & Cable*, 18–23.

Hollywood's short-lived win on fin-syn. (1983, September 26). *Broadcasting*, 28–29.

Hollywood wins D.C. compromise. (1983, November 2). *Variety*, 1, 76.

Hontz, J., & Littleton, C. (1999, January 8). Sony was steady if not stellar. *Variety*, 10, 12, 34.

Hundt, R. (1996, March 28). News flash! FCC wins Oscar for brave-hearted application of anti-trust theory of vertical integration in broadcasting. Speech presented at the American Bar Association, Washington DC. Retrieved July 9, 2002, from www.fcc.gov/Speeches/Hundt/spreh617.txt

ICF Incorporated. (1983). An analysis of the impacts of the repeal of the financial interest and syndication rule: Report to the Committee for Prudent Deregulation. Unpublished manuscript.

Iosifides, P. (1999). Diversity versus concentration in the deregulated mass media domain. *Journalism & Mass Communication Quarterly, 76*(1), 152–162.

Jensen, E. (1992, November 9). Media: Networks gain in syndication dispute, but many see rerun of battles ahead. *The Wall Street Journal*, p. B1.

Jensen, E. (1993, April 2). FCC angers cable firms, aids networks; Rerun profits could enrich big broadcasters. *The Wall Street Journal*, p. B1.

Jensen, E. (1994, September 9). Television (a special report): Where the money goes: Still kicking: A year ago, the networks seemed headed for extinction; No longer. *The Wall Street Journal*, p. R3.

Jessell, H. A. (1992, November 9). Appeals court vacates rules. *Broadcasting*, 4–8.

Kalb, M. (1994). *The Nixon memo: Political respectability, Russia, and the press*. Chicago: University of Chicago Press.

Kelly, M., & Truetzschler, W. (1992). Ireland. In B. S. Ostergaard (Ed), *The media in Western Europe: The Euromedia handbook* (pp.108–122). London: Sage.

Kleinsteuber, H. J., & Wilke, P. (1992). Germany. In B. S. Ostergaard (Ed), *The media in Western Europe: The Euromedia handbook* (pp. 75–94). London: Sage.

Kintzer, E. L. (1984). The proposed repeal of the financial interest and syndication rules: Network dominion or public interest representation? *Hastings Communications—Communications Entertainment Law Journal, 6*(3), 513–620.

Kissell, R. (2002, May 24). Peacock's final flourish, *Variety*, 1, 21.

Kleiman, H. (1991). Content diversity and the FCC's minority and gender licensing policies. *Journal of Broadcasting & Electronic Media, 35,* 411–429.

Krasnow, E. G., Longley, L. D., & Terry, H. A. (1982). *The politics of broadcast regulation.* New York: St. Martin's Press.

Krasnow, E. G., & Berg, M. D. (2002, April 15). Where things stand. *Broadcasting & Cable.* Retrieved April 15, 2002, from http://www.tvinsite.com/broadcastingcable/index.asp?layout=story_stocks&articleid=&doc_id=80906&pubdate=4/11/2002

Krattenmaker, T. G. (1998). *Telecommunications law and policy.* Durham, NC: Carolina Academic Press.

Krattenmaker, T. G., & Powe, L. A., Jr. (1994). *Regulating broadcast programming.* Cambridge, MA.: MIT Press.

Lacter, M. (2001, May 28). Making crime pay. *Fortune*, 158–161.

Lamprecht v. Federal Communications Commission, 958 F. 2d 382 (D.C. Cir. 1992).

Ledbetter, J., Borow, Z., & Moodie, D. (1996, January 16). Merger overkill. *The Village Voice*, p. 30.

Le Duc, D. R. (1982). Deregulation and the dream of diversity. *Journal of Communication, 32*(4), 164–178.

Lee, T. A. (1995). *Legal research guide to television broadcasting and program syndication.* Buffalo, NY: William S. Heim & Co., Inc.

Lentz, K. M. (2000). Quality versus relevance: Feminism, race, and the politics of the sign in 1970s television. *Camera Obscura, 15*(1), 45–93.

Levin, H. J. (1971). Program duplication, diversity, and effective viewer choices: Some empirical findings. *The American Economic Review, 61,* 81–88.

Lewine, R. F., Eastman, S. T., & Adams, W. J. (1989). Prime time network television programming. In S. T. Eastman, S. W. Head, & L. Klein (Eds.), *Broadcast/cable programming: Strategies and practices* (pp. 134–172). Belmont, CA: Wadsworth.

Lin, C. A. (1995). Diversity of network prime-time program formats during the 1980s. *The Journal of Media Economics, 8*(4), 17–28.

Litman, B. R. (1998). The changing role of the television networks. In A. Alexander, J. Owers, & R. Carveth (Eds.), *Media economics theory and practice* (pp. 225–244). Mahwah, NJ: Lawrence Erlbaum Associates.

Litman, B. R. (1979). The television networks, competition and program diversity. *Journal of Broadcasting, 23*(4), 393–409.

Little, A. D. (1969). Television program production, procurement, distribution and scheduling. Unpublished manuscript.

Long, S. L. (1979). *The development of the television network oligopoly.* New York: Arno Press.

Longworth, J. L., Jr. (2000). *TV creators: Conversations with America's top producers of television drama.* Syracuse, NY: Syracuse University Press.

Lopes, P. D. (1992). Innovation and diversity in the popular music industry, 1969 to 1990. *American Sociological Review, 57*(1), 56–71.

Lutheran Church-Missouri Synod v. Federal Communications Commission, 141 F3d (D.C. Cir. 1998).

MacDonald, J. F. (1990). *One nation under television: The rise and decline of network TV.* New York: Pantheon Books.

Mason, L., Bachen, C. M., & Craft, S. L. (2001). Support for FCC minority ownership policy: How broadcast station ownership race or ethnicity affects news and public affairs programming diversity. *Communication Law & Policy, 6,* 37–73.

McChesney, R. W. (1997). Rise of the media giants. *Fair/Extra*! Retrieved January 6, 2003 from www. fair.org/extra/9711/gmg.html

McClellan, S. (2002a, July 1). Fox duops in Chicago, will pay $450M for WPWR-TV, giving it combos in top three markets, *Broadcasting & Cable*, 8.

McClellan, S. (2002b, May 27). Winning, and losing, too. *Broadcasting & Cable*, 6–7.

McClellan, S. (2002c, May 27). Cross-platform construction. *Broadcasting & Cable*, 12.

McClellan, S. (2002d, May 20). Faith, hope and stability: As broadcast nets announce fall schedules, some are more desperate than others. *Broadcasting & Cable*, 16–29.

McClintock, P. (2002a, June 11). Org makes a plea to D.C. *Variety*, 1, 22.

McClintock, P. (2002b, April 3). FCC is told to rethink owner regs. *Variety*, 1, 17.

McClintock, P. (2002c, April 1). FCC lets Viacom doff cap. *Variety*, 1, 15.

McCombs, M. E., & Shaw, D. L. (1972). The agenda-setting function of mass media. *Public Opinion Quarterly, 36,* 176–187.

McGowan, J. J. (1967, Fall). Competition, regulation, and performance in television broadcasting. *Washington University Law Quarterly*, 499–520.

McNeil, A. (1996). *Total television: The comprehensive guide to programming from 1948 to the present* (4th ed.). New York: Penguin.

Media Dynamics (1998). *TV dimensions '98*. New York: Author.

Media Ownership: Diversity and Concentration: Hearings before the Subcommittee on Communications. 101st Cong., sess. 1 (1989).

Mermigas, D. (2002, June 3). Fin-syn repeal has yet to pay off. *Electronic Media*, 30.

Metro Broadcasting, Inc. v. Federal Communications Commission, 110 SC 2997 (1990).

Miami Herald Publishing Co. v. Tornillo, 418 U.S. 241 (1974).

Miller, M. C. (1996, June 3). Free the media. *The Nation*.

Moser, J. D. (Ed.). (1997). *1997 International television & video almanac*. New York: Quigley Publishing Company, Inc.

Mt. Mansfield Television, Inc. v. Federal Communications Commission, 442 F.2d 470 (D.C. Cir. 1971).

Napoli, P. M. (1996, August). Assessing diversity in broadcast syndication. Paper presented at the annual meeting of the Association for Education in Journalism and Mass Communication, Anaheim, CA.

Napoli, P. M. (1999). Deconstructing the diversity principle. *Journal of Communication, 49*(4), 7–34.

Napoli, P. M. (1997). Rethinking program diversity assessment: An audience-centered approach. *The Journal of Media Economics, 10*(4), 59–74.

National Cable & Telecommunications Association (NCTA). (2002, February). Television and cable households, 1979–2001. Retrieved July 9, 2002, from www.ncta.com/industry_overview/

NBC Business Development & International Finance (1996, December). TV ad expenditure trends.

NBC has record $2.74B upfront (2002, June 6). *Broadcasting & Cable*. Retrieved July 7, 2002, from http://www.brodcastingcable.com

Networks nervous over Reagan briefing from FCC's Fowler. (1983, October 10). *Broadcasting*, 42.

Networks win financial interest, syndication battle. (1983, August 8). *Broadcasting*, 27–31.

Networks win, Hollywood winces as fin-syn barriers fall. (1993, November 22). *Broadcasting*, 6, 16.

New fin-syn rules disappoint White House. (1991, April 22). *Broadcasting*, 32–33.

News Corp. buys Chris-Craft. (2000, August 13). *CNN Money.* Retrieved July 9, 2002, from http://money.cnn.com/2000/08/13/deals/chriscraft/

Nickelodeon: The facts. (n.d.). Retrieved July 11, 2002, from www.viacom.com/prodbyunit1.tin?ixBusUnit=20

Nixon comments on news analysis. (1969, December 15). *Broadcasting*, 28.

Nixon ready to move on FCC. (1969, September 1). *Broadcasting*, 21.

Orbit Communication Corp. (n.d.). About satellite-TV. Retrieved July 23, 2001, from http://www.orbitsat.com/AboutSat/higsoty2.htm

Oudes, B. (Ed.). (1989). *From the President: Richard Nixon's secret files.* New York: Harper & Row.

Owen, B. M. (1977). Regulating diversity: The case of radio formats. *Journal of Broadcasting, 21,* 305–319.

Owen, B. M. (1978). The economic view of programming. *Journal of Communication, 28,* 43–50.

Owen, B. M., Beebe, J. H., & Manning, W. G., Jr. (1974). *Television economics.* New York: Lexington Books.

Owen, B. M., & Wildman, S. S. (1992). *Video economics.* Cambridge, MA: Harvard University Press.

PBS. (n.d.). Sponsorship Messages. Retrieved July 11, 2002, from http://sponsorship.pbs.org/secure/messages_credit.htm

Pearce, A. (1973). *The economics of prime time access.* Washington, DC: FCC.

Peterson, R. A., & Berger, D. G. (1975). Cycles in symbol production: The case of popular music. *American Sociological Review, 40*(2), 158–173.

Phipps, J. L. (2002, June 3). Editorial: Senators on the right track with Powell. *Electronic Media*, 9.

Pool, I. (1983). *Technologies of freedom.* Cambridge, MA: The Belknap Press.

President 'proud' to have Agnew in administration. (1969, October 31). *The New York Times*, pp. 1, 25.

The president's priorities. (1983, November 7). *The New York Times*, p. A22.

Producers, stations band together to protect PTAR-related rules. (1982, May 17). *Broadcasting*, 41–42.

Reagan upstages the networks on syndication. (1983, November 7). *Businessweek*, 51–52.

Red Lion Broadcasting Co. v. Federal Communications Commission, 395 U.S. 367 (1969).

Review of the syndication and financial interest rules, Sections 73.659–73.663 of the Commission's Rules, Report and Order, 10 FCCR 12, 165 (1995, Report and Order).

Revision of radio rules and policies, 7 F.C.C.R. 2775 (1992).

Roberts, J. L. (1998, October 19). TV turns vertical. *Newsweek*, 54–56.

Romano, A. (2002, June 24). P&G makes a discovery. *Broadcasting & Cable*, 17.

Schiesel, S. (2002, April 3). F.C.C. rules on ownership under review. *The New York Times*, p. C1.

Schlosser, J. (1998a, September 21). 'Seinfeld's' got plenty of nothing. *Broadcasting & Cable*, 74–75.

Schlosser, J. (1998b, November 2). Sewing up off-net plans. *Broadcasting & Cable*, 45–46.

Schlosser, J. (1999, July 12). Disney closes TV ranks. *Broadcasting & Cable*, 10.

Schurz Communications Inc. v. Federal Communications Commission, 982 F 2d 1043 (7th Circuit 1992).

Shooshan, H. M., III, & Sloan, C. R. (1982). FCC media ownership rules: The case for repeal. *Journal of Communication, 32*(4), 153–159.

Spear, J. C. (1984). *Presidents and the press: The Nixon legacy.* Cambridge, MA: MIT Press.

Spring, G. (1998, January 26). Networks drain thin talent pool. *Electronic Media*, 9.

Steele v. Federal Communications Commission, 770 F. 2d 1192 (D.C. Cir. 1985).

Steiner, G. A. (1963). *The people look at television: A study of audience attitudes*. New York: Knopf.

Steiner, P. O. (1952). Program patterns and preferences, and the workability of competition in radio broadcasting. *Quarterly Journal of Economics, 66,* 194–223.

Sterling, C. H., & Kittross, J. M. (1978). Stay tuned: A concise history of American broadcasting. Belmont, CA: Wadsworth.

Sterngold, J. (1997, October 7). Cries of 'foul' as networks buy into shows. *The New York Times*, pp. D1–D2.

Stroud, M. (1998, June 8). Muscling in on the money. *Broadcasting & Cable*, 26.

Syndication, financial-interest comments: High-stake rulemaking. (1983, January 31). *Broadcasting*, 28–32.

Television Bureau of Advertising. (2002). *TVB: Trends in Media—Nighttime TV costs and CPM trends.* Retrieved July 7, 2002, from www.tvb.org/tvfacts/index.html

Television Network Financial Interest and Syndication Rules: Committed to the Committee of the Whole House on the State of the Union and ordered to be printed. 98th Cong., 1st sess. (1983).

Text of President Nixon's address to nation on U.S. policy in the war in Vietnam. (1969, November 4). *The New York Times*, p. 16.

Tisch, L. (1989). Before the Subcommittee on Communication of the Senate Committee on Commerce, Science and Transportation. In M. H. Lauer & C. C. Murray (Eds.), *Motion Pictures and Television: The 1990's and Beyond* (pp. 309–336). Los Angeles, CA: The Regents of the University of California.

Transcript of address by Agnew criticizing television on its coverage of the news. (1969, November 14). *The New York Times*, p. 24.

Trigoboff, D. (2002, April 8). Less is more as Viacom retakes top spot. *Broadcasting and Cable*, 46.

Tunstall, J. (1986). *Communications Deregulation: The unleashing of America's communications industry.* Oxford: Basil Blackwell.

Tunstall, J. (1992). The United Kingdom. In B. S. Ostergaard (Ed.), *The media in Western Europe: The Euromedia handbook* (pp. 238–255). London: Sage.

Turner Broadcasting System, Inc. v. Federal Communications Commission [Turner I], 114 S. Ct. 2445 (1994).

Turner Broadcasting System, Inc. v. Federal Communications Commission [Turner II], 117 S. Ct. 1174 (1997).

Turow, J. (1991). A mass communication perspective on entertainment industries. In J. Curran & M. Gurevitch (Eds.), *Mass media and society* (pp. 82–117). London: Edward Arnold.

TV9, Inc. v. Federal Communications Commission, 495 F 2d 929 (D.C. Cir. 1973).

TV Season Preview (1999, August 31). *Variety*, A1–A42.

Valenti, J. (1989a). Come, networks, let us reason together. In M. H. Lauer & C. C. Murray (Eds.), *Motion Pictures and Television: The 1990's and Beyond* (pp. 273–286). Los Angeles, CA: The Regents of the University of California.

Valenti, J. (1989b). Keep your eye on the distant objective and not the one nearest you. In M. H. Lauer & C. C. Murray (Eds.), *Motion Pictures and Television: The 1990's and Beyond* (pp. 155–185). Los Angeles, CA: The Regents of the University of California.

Valenti, J. (1989c). Letters to The Honorable John D. Dingell. In M. H. Lauer & C. C. Murray (Eds.), *Motion Pictures and Television: The 1990's and Beyond* (pp. 127–135). Los Angeles, CA: The Regents of the University of California.

The Vietnam Speech: What to listen for tomorrow night. (1969, November 2). *The New York Times*, p. 2.

Vogel, H. L. (2001). *Entertainment industry economics: A guide for financial analysis* (5th ed.). Cambridge, MA: Cambridge University Press.

Webster, J. G. (1986). Audience behavior in the new media environment. *Journal of Communication, 36*(3), 77–91.

Webster, J. G., & Phalen, P. F. (1994). Victim, consumer of commodity? Audience models in communication policy. In J. S. Ettema & D. C. Whitney (Eds.), *Audiencemaking: How the media create the audience* (pp. 19–37). Thousand Oaks, CA: Sage.

Wild, D. (1999). *The showrunners: A season inside the billion-dollar, death-defying, madcap world of television's real stars*. New York: HarperCollins.

Wildman, S. S., & Robinson, K. S. (1995). Network programming and off-network syndication profits: Strategic links and implications for television policy. *The Journal of Media Economics, 8*(2), 27–48.

Wired. (1999, September 7). Viacom to Buy CBS. Retrieved July 9, 2002, from www.wired.com/news/business

The Wisdom Fund. (1997, July 25). Broadcasting fairness doctrine promised balanced coverage. Retrieved April 30, 2002, from http://www.twf.org/News/Y1997/Fairness.html

Wober, J. M. (1989). The U.K.: The constancy of audience behavior. In L. B. Becker & K. Schoenbach (Eds.), *Audience responses to media diversification: Coping with plenty* (pp. 91–108). Hillsdale, NJ: Lawrence Erlbaum Associates, Inc.

Wright, R. C. (1989a). Letter to The Honorable John D. Dingell. In M. H. Lauer & C. C. Murray (Eds.), *Motion Pictures and Television: The 1990's and Beyond* (pp. 121–126). Los Angeles, CA: The Regents of the University of California.

Wright, R. C. (1989b). Testimony of Robert C. Wright, President and Chief Executive officer National Broadcasting Company, Inc., Subcommittee on Communications, Commerce Committee, United States Senate. In M. H. Lauer & C. C. Murray (Eds.), *Motion Pictures and Television: The 1990's and Beyond* (pp. 337–366). Los Angeles, CA: The Regents of the University of California.

Youn, S. (1994). Program type preference and program choice in a multichannel situation. *Journal of Broadcasting & Electronic Media, 38,* 465–475.

Zap2it. (2002). TV Showlist. Retrieved July 11, 2002, from http://tv.zap2it.com/shows/showlist/

APPENDIX 1

Content of Prime-Time Network Television Programming 1966–1975 and 1989–2003 Coded Based on L. W. Lichty Program Hours by Quarter Hours per Week

	1966-1967		1967-1968		1968-1969		1969-1970		1970-1971	
Special/Varied	20	6.7%	20	6.7%	20	6.8%	12	4.0%	8	2.7%
Comedy	8	2.7%	12	4.0%	24	8.1%	19	6.4%	24	8.1%
Country and Western		0.0%		0.0%		0.0%		0.0%	4	1.3%
General/Talk		0.0%		0.0%		0.0%	4	1.3%		0.0%
Variety		**9.3%**		**10.7%**		**14.9%**		**11.7%**		**12.1%**
Musical Variety	16	5.3%	16	5.4%	12	4.1%	35	11.7%	28	9.4%
Light Music		0.0%		0.0%		0.0%		0.0%		0.0%
Music		**5.3%**		**5.4%**		**4.1%**		**11.7%**		**9.4%**
General	12	4.0%	4	1.3%	8	2.7%	22	7.4%	28	9.4%
Women's Serials	8	2.7%	4	1.3%	4	1.4%		0.0%		0.0%
Action/Adventure	74	24.7%	56	18.8%	24	8.1%	16	5.4%	12	4.0%
Crime/Detective	10	3.3%	22	7.4%	46	15.5%	32	10.7%	46	15.4%
Suspense		0.0%		0.0%		0.0%		0.0%	4	1.3%
Westerns	44	14.7%	54	18.1%	40	13.5%	26	8.7%	18	6.0%
Animated Cartoons		0.0%		0.0%		0.0%		0.0%		0.0%
Drama		**49.3%**		**47.0%**		**41.2%**		**32.2%**		**36.2%**
Motion Pictures	**40**	**13.3%**	**48**	**16.1%**	**56**	**18.9%**	**62**	**20.8%**	**54**	**18.1%**
Comedy/Situation	**52**	**17.3%**	**40**	**13.4%**	**46**	**15.5%**	**54**	**18.1%**	**50**	**16.8%**
Audience Participation	4	1.3%	4	1.3%	6	2.0%	6	2.0%	4	1.3%
Quiz and Panel		**1.3%**		**1.3%**		**2.0%**		**2.0%**		**1.3%**
Newscasts	2	0.7%	2	0.7%		0.0%		0.0%		0.0%
Forum/Interviews		0.0%	2	0.7%	4	1.4%	4	1.3%	4	1.3%
Documentary/Information	4	1.3%	4	1.3%		0.0%	2	0.7%	2	0.7%
News Information		**2.0%**		**2.7%**		**1.4%**		**2.0%**		**2.0%**
Children's Shows	4	1.3%	8	2.7%	6	2.0%	4	1.3%	4	1.3%
Sports		0.0%	2	0.7%		0.0%		0.0%	8	2.7%
Miscellaneous	2	0.7%		0.0%		0.0%		0.0%		0.0%
Other Types		**2.0%**		**3.4%**		**2.0%**		**1.3%**		**4.0%**
Total Quarter Hours	300	100%	298	100%	296	100%	298	100%	298	100%

Source: Sterling & Kittross

APPENDIX 1
(continued)

1971-1972		1972-1973		1973-1974		1974-1975		1989-1990		1990-1991	
	0.0%	4	1.6%	8	3.2%	4	1.6%		0.0%		0.0%
20	7.9%	16	6.3%	12	4.8%	4	1.6%		0.0%		0.0%
	0.0%		0.0%		0.0%		0.0%		0.0%		0.0%
	0.0%		0.0%		0.0%		0.0%		0.0%		0.0%
	7.9%		**7.9%**		**7.9%**		**3.2%**		**0.0%**		**0.0%**
8	3.2%	12	4.8%	4	1.6%		0.0%		0.0%		0.0%
	0.0%		0.0%		0.0%		0.0%		0.0%		0.0%
	3.2%		**4.8%**		**1.6%**		**0.0%**		**0.0%**		**0.0%**
20	7.9%	26	10.3%	20	7.9%	36	14.3%	40	15.2%	48	18.2%
	0.0%		0.0%		0.0%		0.0%	12	4.5%	8	3.0%
16	6.3%	12	4.8%		0.0%	20	7.9%	12	4.5%	16	6.1%
40	15.9%	42	16.7%	66	26.2%	66	26.2%	48	18.2%	28	10.6%
10	4.0%	18	7.1%	14	5.6%	12	4.8%			8	3.0%
16	6.3%	12	4.8%	8	3.2%	8	3.2%	8	3.0%	4	1.5%
	0.0%		0.0%		0.0%		0.0%		0.0%		0.0%
	40.5%		**43.7%**		**42.9%**		**56.3%**		**45.5%**		**42.4%**
66	**26.2%**	**58**	**23.0%**	**64**	**25.4%**	**58**	**23.0%**	**32**	**12.1%**	**40**	**15.2%**
44	**17.5%**	**36**	**14.3%**	**44**	**17.5%**	**32**	**12.7%**	**72**	**27.3%**	**76**	**28.8%**
	0.0%		0.0%		0.0%		0.0%		0.0%		0.0%
	0.0%		**0.0%**		**0.0%**		**0.0%**		**0.0%**		**0.0%**
	0.0%		0.0%		0.0%		0.0%		0.0%		0.0%
	0.0%		0.0%		0.0%		0.0%	20	7.6%	16	6.1%
	0.0%	4	1.6%		0.0%		0.0%	8	3.0%	8	3.0%
	0.0%		**1.6%**		**0.0%**		**0.0%**		**10.6%**		**9.1%**
4	1.6%	4	1.6%	4	1.6%	4	1.6%	4	1.5%		0.0%
8	3.2%	8	3.2%	8	3.2%	8	3.2%	8	3.0%	8	3.0%
	0.0%		0.0%		0.0%		0.0%		0.0%	4	1.5%
	4.8%		**4.8%**		**4.8%**		**4.8%**		**4.5%**		**4.5%**
252	100%	252	100%	252	100%	252	100%	264	100%	264	100%

APPENDIX 1
(continued)

	1991-1992		1992-1993		1993-1994		1994-1995		1995-1996	
Special/Varied		0.0%		0.0%		0.0%		0.0%		0.0%
Comedy	4	1.5%		0.0%	4	1.5%		0.0%		0.0%
Country and Western		0.0%		0.0%		0.0%		0.0%		0.0%
General/Talk		0.0%		0.0%		0.0%		0.0%		0.0%
Variety		**1.5%**		**0.0%**		**1.5%**		**0.0%**		**0.0%**
Musical Variety		0.0%		0.0%		0.0%		0.0%		0.0%
Light Music		0.0%		0.0%		0.0%		0.0%		0.0%
Music		**0.0%**		**0.0%**		**0.0%**		**0.0%**		**0.0%**
General	32	12.1%	40	15.2%	24	9.1%	36	13.6%	24	9.1%
Women's Serials	4	1.5%	8	3.0%	4	1.5%		0.0%	8	3.0%
Action/Adventure	16	6.1%	12	4.5%	8	3.0%	12	4.5%	8	3.0%
Crime/Detective	36	13.6%	36	13.6%	40	15.2%	40	15.2%	44	16.7%
Suspense		0.0%		0.0%		0.0%		0.0%	4	1.5%
Westerns		0.0%		0.0%	4	1.5%	4	1.5%	4	1.5%
Animated Cartoons		0.0%		0.0%		0.0%		0.0%		0.0%
Drama		**33.3%**		**36.4%**		**30.3%**		**34.8%**		**34.8%**
Motion Pictures	**48**	**18.2%**	**40**	**15.2%**	**48**	**18.2%**	**48**	**18.2%**	**48**	**18.2%**
Comedy/Situation	**82**	**31.1%**	**72**	**27.3%**	**76**	**28.8%**	**70**	**26.5%**	**80**	**30.3%**
Audience Participation		0.0%		0.0%		0.0%		0.0%		0.0%
Quiz and Panel		**0.0%**		**0.0%**		**0.0%**		**0.0%**		**0.0%**
Newscasts		0.0%		0.0%		0.0%		0.0%		0.0%
Forum/Interviews	20	7.6%	24	9.1%	32	12.1%	36	13.6%	28	10.6%
Documentary/Information	8	3.0%	12	4.5%	8	3.0%	8	3.0%	4	1.5%
News Information		**10.6%**		**13.6%**		**15.2%**		**16.7%**		**12.1%**
Children's Shows		0.0%		0.0%		0.0%		0.0%		0.0%
Sports	8	3.0%	8	3.0%	8	3.0%	8	3.0%	8	3.0%
Miscellaneous	6	2.3%	12	4.5%	8	3.0%	2	0.8%	4	1.5%
Other Types		**5.3%**		**7.6%**		**6.1%**		**3.8%**		**4.5%**
Total Quarter Hours	264	100%	264	100%	264	100%	264	100%	264	100%

Source: Sterling & Kittross

APPENDIX 1

(continued)

1996-1997		1997-1998		1998-1999		1999-2000		2000-2001		2001-2002		2002-2003	
	0.0%		0.0%		0.0%		0.0%		0.0%		0.0%		0.0%
	0.0%		0.0%		0.0%	2	0.8%	4	1.5%	4	1.5%	2	0.8%
	0.0%		0.0%		0.0%		0.0%		0.0%		0.0%		0.0%
	0.0%		0.0%		0.0%		0.0%		0.0%		0.0%		0.0%
	0.0%		**0.0%**		**0.0%**		**0.8%**		**1.5%**		**1.5%**		**0.8%**
			0.0%										
	0.0%		0.0%		0.0%		0.0%		0.0%		0.0%		0.0%
	0.0%		0.0%		0.0%		0.0%		0.0%		0.0%		0.0%
	0.0%		**0.0%**		**0.0%**		**0.0%**		**0.0%**		**0.0%**		**0.0%**
32	12.1%	24	9.1%	40	15.2%	52	19.7%	52	19.7%	60	22.7%	48	18.2%
	0.0%		0.0%		0.0%		0.0%	4	1.5%		0.0%		0.0%
12	4.5%	8	3.0%	12	4.5%	12	4.5%	4	1.5%	16	6.1%	16	6.1%
44	16.7%	64	24.2%	44	16.7%	36	13.6%	36	13.6%	34	12.9%	52	19.7%
	0.0%	4	1.5%		0.0%		0.0%		0.0%		0.0%		0.0%
4	1.5%	4	1.5%		0.0%		0.0%		0.0%		0.0%		0.0%
	0.0%		0.0%		0.0%		0.0%		0.0%		0.0%		0.0%
	34.8%		**39.4%**		**36.4%**		**37.9%**		**36.4%**		**41.7%**		**43.9%**
48	**18.2%**	**24**	**9.1%**	**32**	**12.1%**	**36**	**13.6%**	**48**	**18.2%**	**32**	**12.1%**	**32**	**12.1%**
76	**28.8%**	**80**	**30.3%**	**64**	**24.2%**	**60**	**22.7%**	**48**	**18.2%**	**42**	**15.9%**	**42**	**15.9%**
	0.0%		0.0%		0.0%		0.0%	16	6.1%	16	6.1%		0.0%
	0.0%		**0.0%**		**0.0%**		**0.0%**		**6.1%**		**6.1%**		**0.0%**
	0.0%		0.0%		0.0%		0.0%		0.0%		0.0%		0.0%
32	12.1%	40	15.2%	40	15.2%	48	18.2%	36	13.6%	32	12.1%	32	12.1%
4	1.5%		0.0%		0.0%		0.0%		0.0%		0.0%		0.0%
	13.6%		**15.2%**		**15.2%**		**18.2%**		**13.6%**		**12.1%**		**12.1%**
	0.0%	8	3.0%	8	3.0%	8	3.0%	8	3.0%	8	3.0%	8	3.0%
8	3.0%	8	3.0%	16	6.1%	8	3.0%	8	3.0%	8	3.0%	8	3.0%
4	1.5%		0.0%	8	3.0%	2	0.8%		0.0%	12	4.5%	24	9.1%
	4.5%		**6.1%**		**12.1%**		**6.8%**		**6.1%**		**10.6%**		**15.2%**
264	100%	264	100%	264	100%	264	100%	264	100%	264	100%	264	100%

APPENDIX 2

Content of Prime-Time Network Television Programming 1989–2003 Coded With 1990s Program Code Program Hours by Quarter Hours per Week

Comedy	1989-90		1990-1991		1991-1992		1992-1993		1993-1994
Situation comedy -- family	38	14.4%	38	14.4%	40	15.2%	32	12.1%	38
Situation comedy -- office	18	6.8%	20	7.6%	22	8.3%	22	8.3%	14
Standup or star comedian	2	0.8%	4	1.5%	6	2.3%	8	3.0%	20
situation comedy	14	5.3%	14	5.3%	14	5.3%	10	3.8%	4
TOTAL COMEDY	**72**	**27.3%**	**76**	**28.8%**	**82**	**31.1%**	**72**	**27.3%**	**76**
Animation		0.0%		0.0%		0.0%		0.0%	
Comedy - Variety		0.0%		0.0%	4	1.5%		0.0%	4
TOTAL VARIETY	**0**	**0.0%**	**0**	0.0%	**4**	**1.5%**	**0**	**0.0%**	**4**
Drama									
Light and medium drama	8	3.0%	4	1.5%	4	1.5%		0.0%	4
Heavy drama	20	7.6%	12	4.5%	8	3.0%	12	4.5%	
Personal, "real life" or family drama	8	3.0%	12	4.5%	16	6.1%	20	7.6%	16
Legal drama	12	4.5%	12	4.5%	8	3.0%	12	4.5%	8
Medical drama	4	1.5%	4	1.5%		0.0%	4	1.5%	
Action/adventure	20	7.6%	16	6.1%	12	4.5%	8	3.0%	4
Sci-Fi	4	1.5%	4	1.5%	4	1.5%	4	1.5%	4
Drama, stories -- other or general	4	1.5%	16	6.1%	4	1.5%	8	3.0%	8
Crime drama	16	6.1%	20	7.6%	12	4.5%	12	4.5%	8
Police, detective, private eye	24	9.1%	12	4.5%	12	4.5%	12	4.5%	28
TOTAL DRAMA	**120**	**45.5%**	**112**		**80**		**92**		**80**
Movies	32	12.1%	40	15.2%	48	18.2%	40	15.2%	48
TOTAL MOVIES	**32**	**12.1%**	**40**		**48**		**40**		**48**
Other									
Sports	8	3.0%	8	3.0%	8	3.0%	8	3.0%	8
Reality series	8	3.0%	8	3.0%	18	6.8%	24	9.1%	12
Newsmagazines	20	7.6%	16	6.1%	20	7.6%	24	9.1%	32
Children's Show	4	1.5%		0.0%		0.0%		0.0%	
Miscellaneous		0.0%	4	1.5%	4	1.5%	4	1.5%	4
Total 1/4 hours	264	100.0%	264	100.0%	264	100.0%	264	100.0%	264

APPENDIX 2

(continued)

	1994-1995		1995-1996		1996-1997		1997-1998		1998-1999
14.4%	34	12.9%	28	10.6%	20	7.6%	32	12.1%	26
5.3%	12	4.5%	22	8.3%	14	5.3%	20	7.6%	16
7.6%	20	7.6%	22	8.3%	32	12.1%	18	6.8%	12
1.5%	4	1.5%	8	3.0%	10	3.8%	10	3.8%	10
28.8%	**70**	**26.5%**	**80**	**30.3%**	**76**	**28.8%**	**80**	**30.3%**	**64**
0.0%		0.0%		0.0%		0.0%		0.0%	
1.5%		0.0%		0.0%		0.0%		0.0%	
1.5%	**0**	**0.0%**	**0**	**0.0%**	**0**	**0.0%**	**0**	**0.0%**	**0**
1.5%	4	1.5%	4	1.5%	8	3.0%	8	3.0%	16
0.0%		0.0%	8	3.0%	4	1.5%	4	1.5%	4
6.1%	20	7.6%	12	4.5%	12	4.5%	4	1.5%	4
3.0%	4	1.5%	16	6.1%	4	1.5%	12	4.5%	8
0.0%	8	3.0%	8	3.0%	8	3.0%	8	3.0%	12
1.5%	4	1.5%	4	1.5%	8	3.0%	4	1.5%	8
1.5%	8	3.0%	8	3.0%	8	3.0%	12	4.5%	4
3.0%	4	1.5%	4	1.5%		0.0%		0.0%	
3.0%	16	6.1%	8	3.0%	12	4.5%	12	4.5%	12
10.6%	24	9.1%	20	7.6%	28	10.6%	40	15.2%	24
	92		**92**		**92**		**104**		**92**
18.2%	48	18.2%	48	18.2%	48	18.2%	24	9.1%	32
	48		**48**		**48**		**24**		**32**
3.0%	8	3.0%	8	3.0%	8	3.0%	8	3.0%	16
4.5%	8	3.0%	4	1.5%	4	1.5%		0.0%	12
12.1%	36	13.6%	28	10.6%	32	12.1%	40	15.2%	40
0.0%		0.0%		0.0%		0.0%	8	3.0%	8
1.5%	2	0.8%	4	1.5%	4	1.5%		0.0%	
100.0%	264	100.0%	264	100.0%	264	100.0%	264	100.0%	264

APPENDIX 2
(continued)

Comedy		1999-2000		2000-2001		2001-2002		2002-2003	
Situation comedy -- family	9.8%	22	8.3%	16	6.1%	10	3.8%	16	6.1%
Situation comedy -- office	6.1%	16	6.1%	10	3.8%	10	3.8%	12	4.5%
Standup or star comedian	4.5%	12	4.5%	16	6.1%	14	5.3%	10	3.8%
situation comedy	3.8%	10	3.8%	6	2.3%	8	3.0%	4	1.5%
TOTAL COMEDY	**24.2%**	**60**	**22.7%**	**48**	**18.2%**		**15.9%**		**15.9%**
Animation	0.0%		0.0%		0.0%		0.0%		0.0%
Comedy - Variety	0.0%	2	0.8%	4	1.5%	4	1.5%	2	0.8%
TOTAL VARIETY	**0.0%**	**2**	**0.8%**	**4**	**1.5%**	**4**	**1.5%**		**0.0%**
Drama									
Light and medium drama	6.1%	8	3.0%	12	4.5%	8	3.0%	8	3.0%
Heavy drama	1.5%		0.0%	4	1.5%		0.0%		0.0%
Personal, "real life" or family drama	1.5%	12	4.5%	12	4.5%	20	7.6%	8	3.0%
Legal drama	3.0%	16	6.1%	16	6.1%	24	9.1%	16	6.1%
Medical drama	4.5%	12	4.5%	16	6.1%	12	4.5%	20	7.6%
Action/adventure	3.0%	8	3.0%	4	1.5%	12	4.5%	8	3.0%
Sci-Fi	1.5%	8	3.0%		0.0%	4	1.5%	8	3.0%
Drama, stories -- other or general	0.0%	8	3.0%	4	1.5%	4	1.5%	4	1.5%
Crime drama	4.5%	8	3.0%	8	3.0%	4	1.5%	12	4.5%
Police, detective, private eye	9.1%	20	7.6%	20	7.6%	22	8.3%	32	12.1%
TOTAL DRAMA		**100**		**96**		**102**			
Movies	12.1%	36	13.6%	48	18.2%	32	12.1%	32	12.1%
TOTAL MOVIES		**36**		**48**		**32**			0.0%
Other									
Sports	6.1%	8	3.0%	8	3.0%	8	3.0%	8	3.0%
Reality series	4.5%		0.0%		0.0%	12	4.5%	20	7.6%
Newsmagazines	15.2%	48	18.2%	36	13.6%	32	12.1%	32	12.1%
Children's Show	3.0%	8	3.0%	8	3.0%	8	3.0%	8	3.0%
Miscellaneous	0.0%	2	0.8%	16	6.1%	16	6.1%	4	1.5%
Total 1/4 hours	100.0%	264	100.0%	264	100.0%	264	100.0%	264	100.0%

Author Index

Subject Index

WITHDRAWN
FROM STOCK